RAISING THE
Spiritual Light Quotient

Other Publications by
David K. Miller

RAISING THE
Spiritual Light Quotient

David K. Miller

LIGHT
Technology
PUBLISHING

*   *   *

ISBN-13: 978-1-891824-89-0

Published and printed in the United States of America by:

PO Box 3540
Flagstaff, AZ 86003
800-450-0985
www.lighttechnology.com

TABLE OF CONTENTS

INTRODUCTION

The idea of raising the spiritual light quotient of Earth came through in a serious of lectures given during 2008 and 2009. The concept of the spiritual light quotient was explained by comparing this idea to that of the intelligence quotient used in modern psychology, the IQ test. Basically, the IQ test is a representation of a number that reflects a person's ability to do certain tasks, including calculations, comprehension, reading skills, memory recall and problem solving. The higher people's abilities in these designated areas, the higher their IQ score is, and the higher their intelligence.

The spiritual light quotient, or SLQ, is based on this model. However the spiritual light quotient is not the same as intelligence. Rather, the SLQ reflects one's ability to understand spiritual concepts, to meditate and to connect with other dimensions. It also is a measurement of one's ability to understand the relationship between Earth and the environment of the Earth, and Earth's relationship to the galaxy. Finally, it is a measurement of one's ability to understand the existence of other dimensions as well as the relationship between the ascended masters and guides and our journey to higher realms for soul evolution. Thus it appears necessary to look at the SLQ of a person, the SLQ of an area and the SLQ of a planet.

The concept of an area or a planet possessing an SLQ seems revolutionary to me, but when one looks at Earth, it is quite apparent (based on current events and the current world situation) that humankind's technology is far more advanced than its spiritual energy. Earth technology is far more advanced than the SLQ of the planet. We certainly have high technology in many areas, including computer technology and warfare technology. But the integration of computer technology with war machinery is not used for highest spiritual good; rather, it is used for lower energies such as world domination, the expression of aggression and control of natural resources. Thus one can see that the Earth's SLQ is not as evolved as human technology.

This is the source of many modern-day troubles, including environmental, economic and political problems. It is also interesting to note that certain areas or places can be designated as having high spiritual light quotient energies. These would include sacred sites and sacred cities. Most everyone has had the experience of going to a sacred place to feel sacred energies and has correspondingly felt an increase in their spiritual abilities: the ability to be psychic, for example, or the ability to understand certain new concepts. This is an example of experiencing the SLQ of a place.

These lectures, as given through the various guides and teachers I channel, express the idea that one can raise the SLQ of a person, of a city or place and of the Earth overall. How is this to be accomplished? One way is by meditating in certain areas. Another way is to use crystals to energize certain places. Finally, exercises are given throughout this book that offer specific individual and group techniques and exercises to raise the SLQ of areas. Now, one can also help raise one's own SLQ through the participation in these activities, especially when working, studying or meditating in a group with other spiritual people. Therefore an important aspect of raising one's SLQ is the ability to understand spiritual concepts, both mentally and emotionally. I've been a channel now for over eighteen years, and the lectures in this book are given from a variety of different perspectives based on the guides and energies that I bring in.

All of the channeling I bring forth is based on the concept of the Sacred Triangle. The Sacred Triangle is a new paradigm for spirituality. This paradigm states that in order to heal Earth and bring everything into balance, one must unite the concepts of galactic spirituality with ancient mystical thought and with the energies of native peoples, including Native Americans. This concept of the Sacred Triangle has been explained in my earlier books, including *New Spiritual Technologies for the Fifth-Dimensional Earth*, also published by Light Technology. In giving this new information, I work with all three sides of the paradigm, bringing through the perspective of native peoples, the mystical aspect of religious energies on Earth and of course the energies of galactic masters and teachers. It is my hope that this book will help Earth and lightworkers raise the spiritual light quotient of the planet and themselves. This is a very important and necessary task to counteract the dark forces that seem to be permeating Earth. The good news is that we can help counteract these lower vibrational energies by raising our SLQ, the SLQ of sacred sites and the overall spiritual light quotient of Earth.

THOUGHTS AND YOUR
LUMINOUS STRANDS OF LIGHT

Juliano, Helio-ah and Chief White Eagle

Greetings, I am Juliano. We are the Arcturians. Today we explain the nature of reality and how it relates to thoughts. Thinking and thoughts represent the fastest energy in the universe. You will look at the speed of light as the fastest energy in the physical world and, in fact, the ability of space travel is limited by the speed of light. However, the speed of thought is infinitely faster than the speed of light and the ability of humankind to travel through the dimensional realms. In the third dimension, dimensional travel is contingent on humanity's discovery of the interaction between thinking, the speed of light and propulsion systems. At a certain point and speed, the ability to think interacts with the physical mechanism of a propulsion system, and therefore allows the system to be projected forward, not only by its propellant, but by the thinking of its participants!

This brief explanation provides a foundation for the nature of reality, because the nature of reality is actually based on thought, and if you were to see yourselves in your true form, you would understand that you are biomagnetic, electromagnetic, luminous beings that are pulsing at a certain frequency. You also have luminous strands of electromagnetic lights that are extended to many different realms and many different places, and each luminous connection can be described in terms of its vibrational frequency resonance. On the lower level, these luminous lights or strands can represent parasitic attachments that are draining your energy. But on an advanced level, you are spiritually linked in an actual observable, vibrational strand to other realms, to your soul families, to the Arcturians, and to the ascended masters, guides and teachers.

1

THE HIGHER ORDER OF ENERGY

When you hear the phrase, "We are all one," the reality is that there is an interlinking strand that connects us all the way back to the Creator source. If we looked for these vibrational luminous strands, we would find that they are not visible on the third dimensional level. In fact, if you had moved your assemblage point (i.e., the perceptual valve in your brain) in your recticular activating systems, then you would be able to then perceive your luminous nature. If you did not have any prior instruction or perceptual framework, you might perceive an energetic chaos, but it is not chaotic at all. In fact, luminous light represents a higher order of energy and light that is as intricate as the DNA and as complex as the neurobiology of the brain.

You would also have to consider that when you look at your physical brain from your perception of the third dimension, you would not be able to make much sense of it. When you look at all of the neurofibers and all of the interlocking, interlinking cells, you would not readily make sense of the electrobioenergy flow occurring in the brain. It would be understandable if you could see the true energetic strands of light that interconnect all beings to the universe.

This leads us to the nature of thought, because thought is an energy, and we have established and said that it is the fastest energy in the universe. So when you are in a certain dimensional vibration, you can think and be there. Using telepathy with travel is much faster than trying to travel solely in a spaceship. This means that if you were going to thought-project yourself to Arcturus, which may be thirty-seven light years away in a spaceship, you would have to travel the speed of light for thirty-seven years to get there. By combining thought-projection with certain other techniques, you could get there at the speed of thought.

THOUGHT IS AN ENERGY

Thought is an energy that appears as a luminous strand. This is coming back to the idea of the nature of light—whether it is a packet or a stream, a particle or a wave. I am trying to teach the idea that the thought wave is also a luminous wave of energy and a vibrational particle, depending on your perception. So when you look at the nature of light, you might ask: "Is it a packet or is it a stream? Is it a particle or is it a wave?" In the same way, thought is like light energy.

Thought is a particle, but it is also a streaming, and when it streams, it activates a luminous strand or wire. You create your connections to the other realms, ascended masters, Arcturians and all beautiful fifth-dimensional places through your thoughts. In actuality, your thoughts are energy strands and waves that link you to the other realms. Thought provides a basis for your connection to other realms. In many ways, you can say that thoughts construct a roadway. Thoughts build a foundational link to other realms so that if you could see your thinking, you would notice some interesting energetic flows.

For example, if you saw someone who is in a contracted energy state, you would see that their luminous links, or energy waves, would be limited. But if you saw someone who was of higher consciousness and enlightened, or working on higher light and energy, then you would find that his or her energy thoughts are being projected to many different realms and higher masters. You could actually see the links as luminous strands. You would perhaps see this person as an expanded energy field. You might see the person's aura in a way that is beautiful and expansive, but when you go to another level of perception, you would see that this expansion is also related to the fact that the person's thought strands are being projected to other higher realms.

The more that you think, and the more that you meditate and the more that you connect, the better path, linkage or luminous strand you can have to these realms. This, then, provides you with a concrete foundation for your ascension, and for linking to other realms. You actually have an observable, measurable thought linkage, a strand or strands that link you. Remember, you are not just made of the substance of your physical body—this is just a manifestation, and you will not take your physical body. Your luminous strands are also part of you.

YOUR EARTH CONFIGURATION

You may take the memory of your physical body with you when you ascend or when you move on. But you will not actually take this physical body. You will take the memory of how these cells are rearranged and the skill of how to reformulate these souls or thought images into a bodily form that is recognizable to you. It is at this point in your development that you would most comfortably reassemble yourself into a configuration that is comfortable and then remember. Most of you will remember yourselves in a certain way of higher consciousness and higher being of energy. Perhaps you might want to choose a physical form of yourself when you were the most physically fit.

Nonetheless, you have that memory and the knowledge of your recent Earth configuration, but I can tell you that you may not hold the same configuration as you move into the different realms. The etheric nature of your true self is at a different vibration, and these thought waves and luminous strands that make up your energetic self are extremely thin compared to the energy that you see as your physical body. In fact, your energetic self in the third dimension is really a coarse structure compared to your true nature, as beautiful and complex as the physical body is.

The body works in a miraculous way that is seemingly unexplainable. Nonetheless, this physical body you now inhabit is coarse in comparison to the structure and light that is a mirror of your true nature, and the structure and light that you will be participating in. It is worth mentioning that this coarse physical body is really being controlled energetically by forces that are even beyond the observable physical nature. If you took your brain and looked at it, all of the neurofibers and different axons and dendrites, and so on, would not equal what is going on in your brain. This is another way of saying that the whole is greater than the sum of its parts. There is an energetic force field known as the mind that is actually already in a different realm and is composed of an etheric structure and nature that is beyond your perceptual field in the third dimension. This energetic field is also part of your true nature.

WORKING TOWARD HIGHER CONSCIOUSNESS

"The thoughts that you have," it is often said, "create your reality." I do not want to debate the pros and cons of that because there are many variances of that on Earth. I only want you to know that thinking on Earth has slowed down. The effects of the thinking on Earth have slowed down. The reason is because Earth is a learning school. Earth is a teaching place, so if everything you thought actually happened, then there would be so many more catastrophes than even what you see now. There is a method of thinking that makes a necessity for repetition and makes a necessity for future. Nevertheless, thinking does create certain realities, and it is important to deal with thinking correctly. It is also noteworthy that thinking inside certain vortexes—or thinking in certain higher energy structures such as the etheric crystals or the energy spots or in certain groups—can accelerate the process so that what you think and what you need to happen through your thoughts can manifest more quickly. This means that you are moving into higher consciousness.

On the fifth-dimensional level and on the ascension level, when working with the ascension energy, the thoughts that you have toward the ascension and the projections that you have when using these thought create an actual linkage of energetic luminous strands. Visualize that your thinking and the ideas will open up neuropathways of actual strands that are connecting to the dimension. The strands help ensure your transition to the fifth dimension.

These thought strands require a certain energetic vibration. You can go back to the theories of electromagnetic energy as explained by Maxwell [**Note:** A nineteenth-century Scottish physicist. He wrote about electromagnetic frequencies]. You would find that certain wires are able to hold a certain electromagnetic frequency and that this frequency is defined in terms of amperes, amperages and voltages. To work within this framework (resistance) of the wire, you can only use a certain voltage. Otherwise the voltage can burn up the wire if the wire is not big enough or constructed of the proper material.

THE CONNECTION OF THOUGHT STRANDS

Thought strands are like wires that can hold a certain electromagnetic frequency. Thought strands are like groundwork, gridwork or a network that is already linked. It is in place and linked or wired to higher planes because you are already destined to be fifth-dimensional beings. Holographically, all of the groundwork is laid. This is part of your DNA and of your destiny holographically. These thought strands also interact with your future self. Some of these strands are not yet activated. In some people they are not even turned on, but in many of you they are already coming online. You have to find the frequency, the vibrational electromagnetic connection, to open up that light channel, or wire.

That light frequency connection enables you to be connected to the fifth dimension. This is one of the reasons why we are using so many tones and sounds—because they activate this linkage. Tones remind you of this ability and, in essence, open up the electromagnetic thought strand so that you connect to it. You can feel the energy in many ways with tones. You are building stronger strands so that every time you use the link, that thought wave to the fifth dimension, your thought strand is becoming stronger. You can imagine this "electromagnetic connection" in terms of amperages. Imagine that there are 0.5 milliwatts of amps going through the line and you are trying to increase it to one full amp. You are trying to bring through more wattage and it is connecting. This stays with you when you are ready to transition. In essence, your thought waves have provided a foundational connection and, in some cases, you are able to activate them in many different dimensions and many different levels.

THOUGHT STRAND ACTIVATION

I would like to offer you some different tones and frequencies to activate your thought waves to the fifth dimension. It is so important to focus. We will be working today with the crystal temple, and you will be able to link your thought frequencies to your fifth-dimensional self, the crystal temple and the crystal lake. We will start first with some tones that will help you activate, and I want you to understand that this is a prelude to your ascension. This is a preparation for your ascension that will stay with you, and if you are in any difficulty, you can transcend your body to another location, avoiding certain physical problems. Please listen to these tones now. [Toning.]

Open up your thought strands. Activate and increase your connection to your fifth-dimensional self on and to the crystal lake now. Feel yourself vibrating. Feel yourself shimmering in your third dimensional body. As you connect energetically, you are beginning to feel yourself as a vibrational being. Allow your third dimensional body to shake, to shimmer in place. Feel and visualize thoughts of the fifth dimension as streams or strands or waves of blueness and energetic packets.

These packets—which are thought-projection—are now in a somewhat arclike fashion, connecting from your crown chakra on the third dimension to the fifth-dimensional you, the crystal lake and your fifth-dimensional crown chakra in your body there. The crown chakra of your body is activated and an arc of light forms over it. [Toning.]

The wattage and the amperage of the Earth strand intensify. Make it even brighter. You can do this. That strand of thought energy is activated. It is brighter. It is more charged, and as it is more charged, know that the energy is growing from you to your fifth-dimensional body and thought. Also, there is energy coming back. This is an exponential increase so that the energy that you put in is returned back to you three to four times in terms of shimmering energy, which causes you to think in a higher amperage, or a higher wattage. [Toning.]

If you are able, send a second strand of thought light to your crown chakra on the fifth dimension. In essence, now you can have two thought strands and you have just gone from 110 volts to 220 volts using the analogy of electromagnetic energy. [Toning.]

I want you to hold this connection and we are going to multitask, just like on your computers when you want to do two tasks at once. You minimize one activity and bring on another—like switching between computer screens. Know that you will be able to continue to do what you do here now, but we are also going to go to a second task. Being multidimensional, this should not be a problem for you, because in some cases, you are multitasking two or three lifetimes simultaneously. In consciousness, just to multitask would be simple—like using crayons to color something. I am going to turn the next part of the lecture over to Helio-ah. I am Juliano and I will "minimize" this activity now.

Greetings, dear sisters and brothers. I am Helio-ah. We are the Arcturians. It is so wonderful to be with my sisters and brothers again. And I have some information about the cities of light and about the dolphins and the protections of Earth. You see, the process that Juliano just went through is ensuring your successful transfer to the fifth dimension. In essence, it is similar to the computer process, transferring energy through a strand, through a wire. That wire carries all of your essence, which is really formed in thought, to a higher plane. The animals, the dolphins, the whales and other beautiful animals—even your pets—are energetically high, or they can be. They do not have the linkages that Juliano just described to you. Your role in working with the dolphins and whales, and working and preserving cities of light (including the animals and plants), is to provide the strands to connect the third dimensional energy to the fifth-dimensional energy. In essence, you are the link, because they may not have the mental ability and spiritual energy connection that you do. They may not have the spiritual technology that you have or that you just learned to connect with. But by visualizing them and also by talking to them telepathically, telling them that you are connecting them, you are providing the groundwork for their ascensions into the fifth dimension.

We are moved by how you love your pets and how you are so devoted to them. Many of you have asked, "Can my pets come with me when I ascend?" The answer is, yes. Because when you meditate and connect with higher energy, you can also provide the same strand of thought to connect the crown chakra of your pets by visualizing their fifth-dimensional essence reappearing next to you. Even if your pets have already passed over, you can still do this when you look for them in the fourth dimension. They will be more than happy to have this connection.

CREATE CONNECTIONS TO THE FIFTH DIMENSION

In the cities of light and in the shimmering exercises, visualize yourself in the center of the city. You can have a group of people in a circle or area around the place that you want to shimmer. Help that area become a city of light. By being a city of light, the area energetically connects to the fifth dimension. Send your thoughts and energy to the fifth dimension. The area, then, has the link, and you are providing a fifth-dimensional thought structure for it. The Creator energetic field known as the children of Elohim have the ability to re-create through thought any manifested form, any manifested planet, any manifested structure in the universe.

You are able to participate in the re-creation, the visualization and the reconnection to the fifth-dimensional holographic Earth. You can do this with animals—dolphins, whales or any animals—that you want to provide this linkage for. In essence, again you link the energetic field of that animal's crown chakra with the energetic field of the animal's fifth-dimensional crown chakra. Some people have said, "Helio-ah, that whale or that dolphin is not there yet on the fifth dimension." First, you need to visualize that whale or dolphin, and then you start the connection. The shimmering energy at Copper Canyon became activated through a thought-projection from those groups that worked there in Mexico. The canyon was connected to the fifth-dimensional moon-planet Alano. A thought strand opened up a charge of energy from Alano to Copper Canyon.

Many of you have worked with me in the holographic city chambers, and you have done work on your past and your present selves and your future selves. This technique of connecting from your crown chakra to your past self and your future self again offers you an ability to download energy from your future self so that you receive light and energy from your future self.

THE THOUGHT VIBRATION OF THE CENTRAL SUN

There is also a strand of energetic thought wire that comes from the Central Sun. I have to tell you that when you use the energy being downloaded, there is a physical core offering from this. There is an energetic thought strand that connects to you, so it is not just something etheric or something that you visualize in an imaginative way, but there is actually an etheric energetic strand connecting. Each of these strands can have different levels of intensity. The strand of the Central Sun is a huge thought vibration. It is a huge energetic wire, but because that Central Sun wire is so powerful, it had to be modulated. It had to be downsized, and it is now coming through Mount Shasta. When the energy is transmitted out of Mount Shasta, it will come through a thought wire that you are able to relate to—a new wire, so to speak, of the harmonic convergence that connects through Mount Shasta from the Central Sun. It is a vibrational frequency of energy that is accommodating. It is powered by your existing energetic grids.

When you work with your grid lines, connect from yourself to the crystals, and then through the crystals, project these energetic flows to the grid lines. Then those grid lines and energetic flows will connect to the fifth-dimensional Earth. This becomes a little more complicated, because you are working on a planetary basis. It is hard for one person to do this. We have divided the etheric crystals so that you can work within the structure of them. These etheric crystals are not only connected to the main crystal on the crystal lake but they are also connected to fifth-dimensional crystals that have simultaneously been created and are now also in existence on the fifth-dimensional Earth.

Thank you for your work with the whales and dolphins. Please connect them to their fifth-dimensional selves and know that you serve a great purpose. I am Helio-ah. I turn you over now to Chief White Eagle.

All my relations, we are all one. We are all brothers and sisters. Greetings. I am the Chief White Eagle. All of my words are sacred. My dear star family, I hope that the role of humankind is becoming apparent. I hope it is becoming obvious that you, in essence, have an ability that is totally unique among all of the species on this planet. And, in fact, you have this ability that is even transcending many other species in the universe: The ability to be the intermediaries between the third and fifth dimensions. Some call this being a shaman. A shaman can be an intermediary between this level and the next level. The level or focus that we are working on with the shamanistic energy focuses on connecting to the fifth dimension. The shaman sees all of these links. The shaman sees these etheric connections. It is true that some of the connections are of a lower vibration. We have been listening to Helio-ah and Juliano talking and describing higher connections, but we also know that many of the Earth beings now are linked and tied to lower strands and that the shaman seeks to break those lower strands. We talk about breaking strands from lower energy. Lower vibrational strands can be connected to people who are vibrating at a lower frequency.

CUTTING CONNECTIONS TO LOWER LEVELS

When you see people who are vibrating and functioning at a lower level, you might think, "We can just cut the cords, cut the thought strands." But it does not exactly work like that, because if you cut them without any spiritual preparation, they could suffer physically. Have you seen some of the Native people do healings? They cut the connections to lower energies, but they do it over a period of time. They might make sand paintings with the person who is ill. They might do other things that help put that person in a place to tolerate and become prepared for the removal of these tentacles, or strands, of lower energy.

You have all prepared yourselves and are certainly open to removing any lower vibrational tentacles. I ask that each of you just become aware of perhaps just one link, one energetic strand, that you can identify as a lower vibration within you. We will help you to remove it. Please choose that strand now. Do not be embarrassed, and do not be ashamed that you still have them.

O great Father/Mother/Creator of all, we are gathered here today in a special ceremony of light healing in this international gathering that is filled energetically with so much light and so much enthusiasm. O Father/Mother/Creator of all, each has chosen a strand that he or she is willing to release so that it can be healed and make them more spiritually able to connect to the higher light. I ask your permission now to remove the strands energetically. [Toning.]

Feel the release. Feel the lightening up of your energy. Now visualize that we are in a great circle of energetic light and are able to project ourselves as a group to a connection in the fifth dimension. Visualize ourselves all connected on the fifth dimension. That lower strand of thought is released, and we have all helped each other and raised each other's vibrational fields.

I, Chief White Eagle, bless each of you and know the power that you have called biorelativity is an actual thought energy that can change an energy field. Biorelativity can change a place. The new ideal of biore-lativity is to energetically connect a place with the energy you want to transform on Earth to its fifth-dimensional counterpart. Then as an intermediary, you can allow the fifth-dimensional light and energy to come into that area. Then people and other forces, such as winds or volcanoes or whatever comes, are activated in that field of energy that you have connected with. The energy becomes moderated, becomes mitigated, becomes more in balance.

It is true that only humankind can do this. The animals cannot do this. The lower species of humankind, the Neanderthal, for example, could not do this. And remember, this is a higher functioning. This is an evolution-ary step for humanity to harmonically interact with thought strands from higher dimensions, creating a new field of light on Earth. Know that we are all, as a star family, connected energetically through beautiful strands of thought. We are all star brothers and sisters in the light of the star family and the star master. I am Chief White Eagle. [Toning.]

SPIRITUAL LIGHT QUOTIENT

Juliano, the Arcturians, Archangel Metatron and Chief White Eagle

Greetings, I am Juliano, and we are the Arcturians. We have closed the 8-8-8 harmonic convergence. When I discuss the harmonic convergence, then naturally you will think about the energy of harmony. Harmony means that you are in tune with the flow of energy. Harmony requires that you be sensitive to feel this energy. This sensitivity is a key ingredient in being able to participate in the harmonic convergence. Sensitivity is needed if you are to be in alignment with the Great Central Sun and with the higher fifth-dimensional energy that is coming to Earth. In fact, much of that fifth-dimensional energy is already here. I am confident that you have increased your sensitivity.

Spiritual sensitivity is a key factor in the evolution of human consciousness. Let us speak for a moment about sensitivity. Some people are very sensitive and feel things and hear things. Other people are not sensitive. Even when they are in the same environment, they will not hear or feel what a sensitive person can hear or feel. Spiritual sensitivity is similar. Some of you can pick up spiritual energy as a very faint frequency.

You are now living in what I call a high spiritual noise environment. Noise means that there are a lot of interacting factors that make it harder for you to feel spiritual energy. There is a lot of duality and polarization. There is a lot of density. To be able to receive spiritual energy, and to have the spiritual sensitivity to receive spiritual energy in that environment, is a great accomplishment and great gift. There are not that many starseeds on this planet in relation to the total number of people on the planet. Starseeds are among the few who have this ability.

Starseeds have the ability of spiritual sensitivity, and this sensitivity is now going to a new level. That new level has to do with the cosmos and the universe. That new level of spiritual sensitivity means that you, the starseeds, are able to receive the very faint energies that are coming from the Great Central Sun and from the fifth-dimensional masters, guides and teachers. The energies are also coming from the great-attractor force, and from other distant places.

THE INFINITE SPEED OF HARMONIC ENERGY

It is a known fact that energy and light travel infinitely in the universe. Spiritual energy also is a form of electromagnetic energy, but it travels at an infinite rate—unlike light, which can only travel at 186,000 miles per second. Spiritual light travels at an infinite speed, and therefore it can go across great distances immediately. You are receiving light from the Great Central Sun. That energy source is very far away, but the spiritual light that comes from it is beautiful and infinite, and you can receive it immediately.

The newer frequency of the harmonic convergence energy originates in the Great Central Sun, and it travels at an infinite speed. You, as starseeds, are able to receive it. You may ask, "Do I have the spiritual sensitivity to receive and experience this harmonic energy?" Yes, you do. It is going to be a strong spiritual light frequency. It is going to be a strong signal.

Listen to it and this tone will help you to activate your spiritual light sensors so that you can be in alignment when it's time to receive this light. [Toning.] Take a deep breath. Let your energy sink into your solar plexus, into your navel chakra. As the energy sinks into you, be aware that your sensitivity becomes more open around your crown chakra and your third eye chakra. These chakras become more open and more sensitive. We will stay in silence for a few moments to allow for the experience of this sensitivity.

As I speak of spiritual sensitivity, I also want to discuss the spiritual light quotient. The light quotient has a multifaceted meaning. On the first level, you can compare the spiritual light quotient to the intelligence quotient. In the current psychological world, people's intelligence is measured by their intelligence quotient, or IQ. This measurement is based on your abilities with problem-solving, spatial perceptions, language skills and understanding stories and symbols. If you have a high score in these areas, then you will be given a high IQ—between 100 and 125 points, for instance. Some people score as high as 160 on IQ tests.

The spiritual light quotient does measure your spiritual ability in similar ways, but it is not always correlated with the intelligence quotient. The spiritual IQ is measured in the ability to understand spiritual energy, spiritual relationships, spiritual symbols and the ability to transcend the perceived dimension. A person can be very intelligent and have a high IQ but not have a high spiritual IQ. You know that there are many people now on this planet who are very intelligent, for example, but are very involved in wars, making war machinery and developing nuclear weapons—these people do not have a high spiritual IQ. This is a sad fact. In a perfect world, in a world of more cosmic unity, one would hope that people who have high conventional intelligence would have high spiritual IQs as well.

Spiritual IQ is also correlated to the light quotient. The light quotient is the percentage of light energy and light frequency that can be held in your energy field. Higher light quotients are necessary in order to ascend and in order to be a starseed. A higher light quotient is necessary in order to transform yourself into the fifth dimension and to do spiritual exercises such as shimmering and pulsing. These exercises can also help you to raise your spiritual IQ. Unlike the intellectual IQ, the spiritual IQ can be developed and raised within your lifetime.

YOUR SPIRITUAL IQ CAN GROW

Once you reach a level of intelligence, say at twenty-six or twenty-seven years in the human body, you would be considered to be at the height of your intellectual IQ. This is verified by the fact that many of the great scientists, and even the musicians and composers, have done their greatest work in their twenties. Albert Einstein, for example, developed the theory of relativity in his early twenties. He never equaled this intellectual level of work in his later life. Even though he never reached the same level, he still was at a high intellectual level. It is similar in concept to your ability to be an athlete. You know that an athlete usually reaches the height of his power before the age of thirty.

Spiritual IQ is not like that. You can reach your greatest potential, your highest spiritual IQ, at any age. In fact, you can develop and enhance your spiritual IQ so that when you are older, it can be higher than when you were younger, even if your intelligence quotient has declined. Your spiritual IQ is not dependent on your ability to solve problems, or any of the other skills that are measured in the intelligence IQ, though physical intelligence certainly may help enhance your spiritual IQ. You are all on the path now of increasing your spiritual IQ and increasing your light quotient so that your aura—your energy in your body, and in your energy field—is able to hold more spiritual light.

There are activities that you can do to raise your spiritual IQ and your light quotient. The spiritual light quotient is increased through meditation, and through sacred toning and sacred sounds. It can be increased through art and through poetry. The spiritual light quotient is increased through participating in beautiful and artistic endeavors. Also, your spiritual IQ can be enhanced by participation in psychic exercises, reading certain books, studying certain spiritual masters and associating with the ascended masters. These are not all of the things that raise your spiritual IQ, but I am trying to give you the general idea. The exercises that we, the Arcturians, offer you are methods of raising your spiritual IQ and raising your light quotient.

PRACTICE DISCERNMENT

We came to the point of the harmonic convergence. There were certain events and activities that helped you to raise your spiritual light quotient, and the harmonic convergence was one of those. The harmonic convergence was an opportunity to raise your light quotient because, during this momentous occasion, there was more spiritual light and spiritual energy available. The harmonic convergence offered you an opportunity to receive more spiritual light than what you can usually hold. Perhaps you consider this like you would an economic stimulus check that is coming from the government, but this is actually a "spiritual stimulation package" that is coming from the higher masters and teachers and is given to Earth.

The harmonic convergence allowed you to expand your spiritual energy field. There will be great spiritual work that can be done to help Earth. Please remember that being in service to others can also expand your spiritual light quotient, energy and intelligence. There is a beautiful formula that states that your spiritual light quotient can be directly proportional to the spiritual activities that you participate in. As the spiritual activities increase, the light quotient can increase.

Part of your spiritual light quotient includes having spiritual discernment. The regular IQ includes the ability to interpret, see comparisons, metaphors, relationships, and so on, as well as your short-term memory, long-term memory, recall calculations and many other attributes. The spiritual IQ includes several other traits, one of which is discernment. Others include sensitivity, the ability to see the relationships between the physical and the spiritual world and the ability to connect the spiritual world to the physical world so that your physical world can change in accordance with your spiritual activities. As you connect with spiritual energy, so you will manifest. That is an effect of a higher spiritual light quotient. In order to do this, you have to be at a certain energetic level. There are people who participate in spiritual work all their lives but don't seem to have a high spiritual light quotient. I do not want to point to anyone in particular, but I just want to say that participating in spiritual activity is only one factor. There are other factors related to your spiritual IQ, and there are different levels of spiritual activity. I know that there are certain groups on this planet who are trying to be very spiritual, but they still operate at a lower energy level. For example, using force as a way of spreading spiritual ideas is a lower-energy spiritual activity, as is saying that killing others is justified in order to propagate a spiritual message or spiritual light.

AUGMENTING YOUR SPIRITUAL QUOTIENT

Every activity contributes a certain amount to your spiritual quotient. This idea was propagated by an American psychiatrist named David Hawkins. He rated different activities—and even different religions—based on their spiritual light. Zen Buddhism, for example, might have a higher spiritual light than some of the others because Zen is focused on pure energy.

It is perhaps more obvious when we talk about music, because there are certain types of music that have a lower spiritual vibration and can be counterspiritual. Likewise, there is higher vibrational music, such as Mozart. We are particularly drawn to Mozart because his music is able to adjust to the mathematical symbols of the different scales. Each activity on Earth can be measured in how it is creating or adding to your spiritual light quotient.

When you reach the point of understanding that I am now describing, you will only want to do things that are going to raise your light quotient and frequency. Therefore the spiritual light that is available for harmonic convergence is a major boost. It is an energetic boost, like a shot in the arm that will enable you to expand yourself in a light field far beyond what you could normally do. That is one of the attractions of the harmonic energy. You have the ability to pass on this energy to the world, which is a great service that will add to your light frequency. It is an opportunity that functions on many different levels. You will soon understand that all of your activities will be prioritized once your light quotient reaches a certain level. You will want to spend the most time in pursuit of higher spiritual endeavors because you will want to raise your spiritual IQ.

Some people have called the energy that you accumulate in your energy field liquid light. You need to have a certain amount of liquid light in order to go into the higher realms. In order to obtain it, you have to have a higher spiritual light quotient. The spiritual light quotient is also measured in terms of this lifetime and other lifetimes. It is measured in terms of your soul and what you can manifest and how you manifest. Look at yourself and your life and consider what you have been doing spiritually for the past year or two. Examine how you've been working. Look at who you've been associating with. Look what you've been reading. Reflect on how you've been meditating and how you've been studying. Think about what you've been focused on. You will be able to see that you have been working to develop your spiritual light quotient and your energy field.

Another unbelievable burst of spiritual elevation is also on the planet now—the ascension. The ascension is an uplifting of your spiritual light quotient and your spiritual light energy that transcends the Earth, because ascension transcends your karma from other lifetimes. You can understand why people would want to reincarnate and participate in the Earth's ascension—the ascension, like the harmonic convergence, will begin as a huge influx of light. This light will expand your consciousness much further than it could normally be expanded in a regular lifetime.

You might compare it to an eclipse of the Sun or to an astronomical event that only happens in a certain period of time during which the alignment of energies allows a greater light frequency to occur. You would want to be in that place when that alignment occurs so that you could elevate your light frequency and elevate your light quotient. It would be worthwhile to incarnate at a time when such an event was going to happen, because spiritual light and spiritual energy are the highest frequency of any in the universe. It is these spiritual frequencies that will bring you closer to the Godhead and to the Creator light. I want you all to know that you will be able to have this opportunity to increase your spiritual light quotient. I am going to turn you over to Metatron. I am Juliano.

Greetings, I am Archangel Metatron. I am with you at all times, especially in these periods of close spiritual energy and encounters. I am happy to teach about the sacred toning as a way of increasing your spiritual light quotient. Isn't it interesting that you can increase your light quotient and your sensitivity to spiritual light just by listening to sacred sounds and tones or by listening to certain music or by allowing yourself to see a sunset?

I also want to speak to you about this concept of manifestation on the Earth. If you reach a certain level of psychic or spiritual advancement, then concurrently you could have the ability to manifest and even change the physical world. Some people consider this to be intervening in the physical world. There was a particular sect of Kaballah that focused on creation from nothing. Using mystical incantations and other spiritual energy, including thoughts, intention and alignment, these masters were able to change the world. There are limitations because humankind has limitations, but each of the names of God has an inherent meaning—a tone, a sound and a power. However, there is one name of God that is unpronounceable, that cannot be spoken. If someone knew the pronunciation of that name, then that person could create anything in the world. Such is the power of the name that was hidden. The name was so powerful that even if the person did not have the spiritual advancement necessary, he still could use that name to create or change physical reality.

USE THE POWER PHRASES

Perhaps you are personally interested in changing your physical reality in terms of your prosperity or your health. Also, I know you are lightworkers and are interested in doing service for others. You can have these abilities. It does require a certain frequency of light, frequency of knowledge and spiritual light quotient to be able to do this. However, there are also certain power phrases. One of the phrases is this: "As I have spoken, so it shall be created. Abracadabra." With a higher spiritual vibration, with the intention and with the correct spiritual light quotient, you can effect change. For example, think now that you want to be in the highest possible state of physical health on all levels, and say, "I am able to be now on the highest level of physical health on all levels." Then say, "As I speak, so it shall be created. Abracadabra." Allow that which you speak to be created in your life. We will go again into a silent meditation.

Let us do another round of, "As I speak, so it shall be created." Say these words: "The energy of the harmonic convergence will amplify and increase my spiritual light quotient. Abracadabra. Abracadabra. As I speak, so it shall be. Abracadabra." Then turn over the power and the statement to Spirit and let the universe manifest it for you. This can even be done in certain monetary circumstances.

Make sure when you request something that you always say, "Let this happen if it is in my highest good." The highest good must take into consideration your soul, your soul journey, your soul path, what you are doing in this lifetime and what you are doing in the fifth dimension and in all realms. Maybe you are shortsighted. Maybe you are not able to see everything. In fact, I know that you are not able to see everything that is occurring in all your different soul incarnations and energies from other lifetimes and dimensions. You are not expected to really understand and see all of that. But you can say, "In my highest good on all levels." It may be that what you want from the ego standpoint has no benefit. For example, there may be no benefit for you to have a $100,000 automobile. Owning such a vehicle may not raise your spiritual light quotient. All the things that you ask for and all the things that you want to create should take into account your highest light quotient.

You can gain a higher light quotient during the harmonic convergence. You will be able to propagate harmonic light throughout the world and also use it for yourself. You will be able to raise your harmonic level, and that will raise your light quotient. To be in harmony is an important aspect of your spiritual light quotient. Harmonic light is a beautiful light, for in harmonic light, all is as it should be. Everything is in an order that transcends the ego. Much of the harmonic light has to do with helping people to live in harmony. I am Archangel Metatron. Shalom.

Greetings, I am the Chief White Eagle. [Tones.] *Hey ya ho ya hey*. All my words are sacred. Is it not the greatest harmony to realize that we are all brothers and sisters, that we are part of the star family? I open my heart to all brothers and sisters who hear my words, for I truly am grateful to be able to speak the words, "All my relations." We are all part of the Adam family.

We are of the Native traditions. We speak honorably and we speak with intention to talk to the Creator. We have listened carefully to the teachings, and we know that the greatest speaking comes when you talk to the Creator. When you want to create, when you want to change, when you want to bring harmony, we call this the talking prayer. In the talking prayer, we speak to God. We talk to Him. We open our hearts to Him. We say, "Oh Father/Mother/Creator of All." Just by stating that, we have opened up the energy of: "As I speak, so shall I create." This channel of energy opens to us because we are honoring the Creator. I seek now to honor the highest spiritual energy in all of you. When I seek to honor the highest spiritual light in you, I raise your harmonic level and I help to raise your spiritual quotient. When I honor you, even if you are at a lower level, I help raise your light quotient.

Many of you have said, "Chief White Eagle, how can I help this person? Look how low they are. Look how crazy they are. Look how ill they are. They have no consciousness. They have no spiritual light quotient. I cannot work with them." You can still honor the light within them. You can still honor their souls and look for their souls and their paths. Their souls and their paths are not just what you see in this lifetime. You can honor their paths and their soul journeys in all lifetimes. If you do this, you will be helping them.

Honoring the Creator is helping you, because you have to be at a higher vibration in order to acknowledge our Father. Father/Mother Creator of All, we come together in this lifetime to raise our spiritual light quotients. We came together to prepare for the harmonic convergence so that we could transmit this beautiful harmonic light and energy throughout the planet. We thank you for the power to grasp. We thank you for the power of being sensitive to this energy, and we thank you for the abilities to spread and teach this energy to other people. This becomes our soul light, our soul mission.

YOUR SOUL MISSION

We will work devotedly because we know that this light, this energy, is coming from the highest source. It is coming from a place of great healing at this time and this place. We want to be part of that healing. We want to be part of that harmonic light energy field. Oh Father/Mother/Creator of All, please bring down your White Calf Buffalo Woman and bring down your messengers. Let all who are of the highest ascended mastery connect with the starseeds. Help us to manifest the conditions in our lifetime so that we can be in the most spiritual light that is in our highest good. All my words are sacred. Ho!

When you say those words, "All my words are sacred," that is the same thing as when Metatron said, "As I speak, so it shall be." Speak clearly and speak with love. Honor all who go before you. Honor the grandmothers and the grandfathers. This is a time of great spiritual connection, and a time for seeing the harmony. The grandmothers and grandfathers see the light energy that is coming to this planet. Honor the star family. The star family includes not only you on Earth but includes those in the galaxy, your star brothers and sisters, the Arcturians, the Pleiadians, the Orions and all the spiritual beings in the galaxy. Honor them.

Honor all the sacred places on this planet. Especially be aware of the ten etheric crystals that you have all been working with. These are great carriers and beacons of light; they can transmit powerful frequencies. Help yourself to become more sensitive, more receptive to spiritual light. Most importantly, help us to work toward the ascension. Help us to accumulate the necessary spiritual light quotient and light frequency so that we can transmit and transcend our bodies and move into the highest fifth-dimensional light. We thank you, Father/Mother/Creator of All for giving us this opportunity for being here on the Earth at this time to do this work. Help us to understand the cosmic meaning of all that we do. We know that there is a greater purpose than we can see just with our eyes. Blessings to all of you. All my words are sacred. I am Chief White Eagle. *Ho!*

OMEGA AFFIRMATIONS AND YOUR SOUL MISSION

Juliano and Vywamus

Greetings, I am Juliano, and we are the Arcturians. We work through our channels. Each channel has strengths and weaknesses, each channel has proclivities, likings for certain things, and for some channels, it is hard to relate to certain areas. We know and you know that Africa and Asia are vital, but as yet this channel does not have connections or links to those areas. He has found a link to Japan, but there is no link to Africa at this point. You might ask yourself this question: "Is this something I can do?" We have said from the beginning of this project that this is not about David and Gudrun—they are to be activators, stimulators to help get the project going. But you must also initiate. To answer your question simply, this channel has no easy access to those areas because of his own proclivities. On the other hand, you have to look at it another way. Obviously, he must like the Spanish people and those from Spanish-speaking cultures because he is very comfortable with you and wants to work with you. But we hope there will be other avenues to go to other parts of the world.

Regarding the Arcturian Temple, first let me explain that the temple is an important part of the intervention on the planet. We have said that it is necessary for a group of people to continue to meditate to hold spiritual energy, and that the Arcturian Temple would be a focus for that meditation. Gudrun and David have worked on this project for over twelve years. It started with only four, eight, ten, twelve people and then it looked like it was going to fail. The owner of the books went bankrupt. There were not very many people helping and David wanted to give up, but Gudrun talked him into keeping it going; she kept the vision of this project. Now when we look at the Arcturian Temple and Templar we can see that there are many blocks. There were many disagreements, and so for many reasons, it didn't happen. But that doesn't mean you should give up or that we should give up. Other possibilities can still emerge. Things happen and are visualized on the fifth dimension, but when it comes down to the third dimension, there are more densities—but that doesn't mean that you stop. Indeed, there will be many developments that will be positive. Sometimes all you can do is hold the vision and keep trying. This is my advice, for I do see the Arcturian Templar happening.

I want to tell you a story. There was a famous channel of the Arcturians named Norma Milanovich. Now, in her situation, she had all the money she needed to build the Temple, but she was still not able to do it, so that tells you it takes more than money. But the time will be right; people will be more open. Already there are more people opening to this work, and we are always optimistic.

Is Argentina the place for the temple or could any other country be considered as well?

Some other countries could definitely be considered. We would like this country to be accessible to many people, and most importantly—and this was a problem before—there must be continual meditation. It must be a country or place that is accessible, where people will work with it continually. I talked about the Hopi Indians; they work continually to hold the energy. So if you want to have the Arcturian Temple, there must be people who would come continually to meditate and work there. It does not make any sense to build it only to have no one there. The energy and power of the Arcturian groups is stronger than it was even a year ago, and we are predicting that the Groups of Forty will become four times stronger by this time next year, so much more could happen in a year's time. Please be optimistic.

THE INDIGO CHILDREN AND DRUG ADDICTION

Regarding the Indigo children, remember that on Arcturus children are trained by their parents to be spiritual, to be galactic, to be fifth dimensional. The children are trained from birth to do this. It is quite amazing, and we see with sadness how children are raised on this planet. Perhaps it is not fair to compare, but if we must compare, we all know that the Indigo children are fifth-dimensional starseed children. Please support them in any way you can: by explaining the galaxy, by letting them know there are other planets, by letting them know there are ways of overcoming the space-time continuum, by letting them know there are higher dimensions.

Anything you do to talk about these things will help keep the energy open, because they already know this, but sometimes the information is being pushed down or blocked. Now you have the opportunity to assist just by being yourself and speaking about it. I do not have any techniques to teach you. All I can tell you is, don't hold back, be yourself and share your knowledge in an appropriate way. There are many openings now. There are many science-fiction movies. There are many beautiful novels. There are even ideas from books such as *The Little Prince*, which I know you have read. Indigo children need to know other people agree with them; they need to talk about what they feel. When this project began, one teenager wanted to start an Arcturian Group of Forty for teenagers, but it never happened. It is hard enough to get parents involved. Please teach children about the Sacred Triangle.

Regarding children and drug addiction, this is a difficult problem, but let me tell you this: It is the emotional support, the modeling of behavior done by those people who speak about the galactic work that will influence the children. Drugs will not block that. It is true that drugs affect them, but the truth is the truth, and when they hear about this from other people—about the Arcturians, about the fifth dimension—they will still understand.

SACRED MOUNTAIN ENERGY

Sacred mountain energy is very powerful and effective. You sometimes do not realize how strong a force you are dealing with until you are away from it. This energy is very effective, and it could be even more powerful than what people could handle. The important thing is that you have respect. The important thing is that you have an open heart and that you allow Earth to guide you. There are power animals around this mountain that can continue to help you and give you more guidance on how to use the energy of the mountain. Congratulations on your work. We have a great love for you here. I know of your deep love for the fifth dimension, and I know that if you devote yourselves with a totally open heart, you will not be diverted by any blocks. I will be working with you further.

I know the personal is important, but you are all opening up now, and I know that you will be receiving the guidance and information that you need. Please trust what you are receiving. We will confirm what you are receiving. You are very sensitive and there are many energy fields and guides of higher light around you. I can see them now. Blessings, I am Juliano.

G reetings, this is Vywamus. I am a soul psychologist, and I am here
to help you understand the psychology of your soul. Maybe you've

never approached your soul psychologically before. In the psychology
of the soul, we have a certain perspective, and that perspective is this:
Everything that is happening to you that is a "problem" represents some
aspect of a soul lesson. In this perspective, if there is a problem, we are
happy, because we know that we are fulfilling our soul plans or trying to
learn something. Now, I don't think you are happy when you run across a
problem, and I think you wish you had no problems. But there are lessons
to be learned, and quite frankly, I find that many people are very stubborn.
I find that many people have had the same lesson three or four times in
their lives and they still don't get it. Come on!

I mean, there is grace. Are you waiting for grace so you don't have
to solve your problem? We shouldn't have told you about grace. The
beauty of a lifetime is that if you don't solve your problem when you
are younger, it will come back again when you are older. If you don't
solve it when you are older, there is no problem; it will come back again
in another lifetime. Do you want to come back to Earth in fifty years?
Great—you should see what global warming will be like in fifty years.
If you think this is hot, the current temperature is going to feel cool to
you fifty years from now. You have opportunities to learn things, but
these opportunities require a little bit of perspective. You have mental
problems, emotional problems, physical problems and spiritual problems. You also have spiritual bodies, mental bodies, emotional bodies
and physical bodies, and each of these is actually an etheric body in and
of itself—pretty strange!

The mental body is mostly made up of your belief systems and your
thought forms. You are really good at thinking, and I would say that
you have a very active mental body. In fact, I would say that you have
an overactive mental body. That is a nice way of saying that you think
too much. But it is amazing how much trouble you can get into by over-
thinking; have you noticed that? You think, and then what you think
happens. Well, I want to say that in my time working with this channel
over many years, if everything he thought happened, he would be stuck
somewhere between Las Vegas and Reno trying to get to this workshop.

His motor home would have broken down, he wouldn't have been able to find anyone to fix a tire, the transmission would have blown out and he would have had to wait three weeks to get the parts. There would be no workshop today. That is just one way of saying that although thinking is powerful, it is not everything.

I know you might find this hard to believe, especially after the book *The Secret*. I could have written that book and made a lot of money too, but what it didn't take into consideration—and what I want you to consider— is that there is a divine plan. There is divine guidance; there are interventions, and sometimes a higher energy overrides your bad thinking. Just a minute ago I spoke with one of the channel's friends whose car had broken down. Maybe they were going to drive into trouble, and maybe this was a gift from Spirit to protect them. This is one way of acknowledging that the powers of thought have limitations.

OMEGA AFFIRMATIONS TO REINFORCE YOUR SOUL MISSION

I am not saying that thinking is bad, because correct thinking is very helpful. There is a certain technique we use with this channel that is called omega thinking. These omega affirmations involve you placing messages into your subconscious that bypass all your other thoughts, messages that go right to the heart and are immediately implemented. Let us look at this omega thinking. You have to craft this omega thought pattern in the best way possible. Let me give you an example. Say you want to have a million dollars. You think in terms of the figure $1,000,000. You then ask, "Is it in my highest good to have a million dollars?" Well, you have read stories of people who have won the lottery and gone crazy. So why not think of a million dollars and then add "if it is in my highest good?" Why not think of abundance and prosperity instead of a dollar amount? What I am saying is to put it in a framework that is inclusive of "in your highest good," inclusive of your soul mission. What if you won a million dollars and set yourself up running a laundromat. What if you then spent all your time and money running that laundromat? Would that be in your soul interest? You don't know. You want to work at things that assist your soul mission here on Earth because this money thing, exciting as it is, will be going away soon, especially given the way governments are handling the global economy.

Let me say something about economic collapse. People are always asking me, "Well, where should I put my money, Vywamus? Should I put it in gold? Should I put it in silver? Should I bury it in a can?" I always tell them to put money in perspective. Do what you need to do, ask for what you need and try to live your life, and prosperity will happen. The most important thing is that money doesn't interfere. Many people have had poverty in other lifetimes. You were poor in a past lifetime, and so you got with one of the masters and said, "Hey, I'm ready for it. I want the million dollars in this lifetime." Okay, here it is. Let's see if you can be spiritual and have a million dollars. Then you have a million dollars and you lose your spirituality. So what good was the money? Some people have to learn to have a million dollars and still be spiritual, but other people have to learn to live in poverty and still be spiritual. You say, "You didn't tell me about that, Vywamus. I thought it only worked the one way."

Let's say we do a life-between-lifetimes reading. We take you back and you find out you were a king. You had money, jewels, everything you wanted . . . and absolutely no spirituality. All that materialism did not help you in any way on your soul journey. So when you come back in this lifetime, your higher self is going to say: "Well, we tried that and it didn't work, so let's send him to Cleveland, Ohio." Or they might send you to some family where your father is a laborer, and perhaps they throw in a mother who smokes a lot. "He will like that. Let us see what he does with that." Now, what if that works? What if you are able to hold your spirituality even under those conditions? What if those conditions were just what you needed? So that is why you have to look at your soul purpose. Don't look at the money and the materialism in isolation. There is nothing wrong with the material. There is nothing wrong with having wealth, but if wealth and materialism block your development, you don't want them. Now a lot of you are going to say, "But I'm spiritual and poor, and I could be wealthy and still be spiritual." And I would say, "Good! Go for it." Then you are going to say, "Well, it isn't happening. Why?" I think people don't understand about the higher self.

We are talking about the part of yourself that is so high that it is not influenced in any way by your death. I am not saying that it is good or bad that you die. What I am saying is that the higher self is so high up that it is not upset if you die without achieving your worldly ambitions. The higher self is objective—not cruel objectivity, but more like, "Okay, let's move on to the next life." It is very difficult to describe, because this is the part of self that has no wants. You are very confused by wants and desires, my friends. Even the Buddha said that. It's desire, the ego.

Many people have misinterpreted this, thinking that we are saying the ego is bad. I have always wondered about such people. Okay, so no ego—let's shave our hair off, wear a white robe, stand at the airport and ask for money. Is that no ego? I don't know. The ego has no desire; it is balance, the ego in balance. You need the ego in order to function. Without the ego, you would not be able to function, so it is about putting the ego into balance and acknowledging the role of your desire. Perhaps you had too much pleasure in your past couple of lifetimes. Say you had a great time, whoopee, and then when you came into this life, it was like, "Oh no. I did not get very far with that in the last lifetime, so maybe it is time to put the white robe on and go out to the airport again to see what that's like. Or maybe I'll have to go into a monastery." Actually, monasteries aren't that bad. You might think it is a terrible way to live, but at least you know where your next meal is coming from.

THE WHEEL IN BALANCE

You need balance on the karmic wheel, not too much pleasure in one lifetime and then an ascetic way of being in another. You have to balance the wheel, but that doesn't mean going from one side to the next. Okay, so you balanced out the pleasure with the monastery, but now you have to live a life in balance, so you come back in. What is interesting at this time is that the time for going into the cave and meditating for twelve years is done. That is not going to cut it anymore. Looking for the guru, worshipping him, giving him all your money and sitting at his feet, waiting for a flower to be tossed to you—that is over. There is no more guru time. I am not trying to criticize those who have gurus. I, Vywamus, could be your guru, if you wanted me to be. But this is the time of the ascended masters; this is the time of ascension, the time when you are your master—no more gurus. Why do you have such a hard time with that? I will tell you why. Because if you don't make it, you can't blame your guru. Now if you don't make it, it is your fault.

You have everything you need to ascend, to become an ascended master and to become enlightened. I know that is hard to take because I know that you have many problems of different natures, and you think you cannot overcome these problems. If you keep on thinking that way, you will not overcome these problems. The goal is to not die looking like Arnold Schwarzenegger (who doesn't look so good any more anyway), but let's just say that people have the goal of having the perfect body or whatever. The goal is not even to die in perfect health. Although that would be great, don't get too carried away with this health food stuff. The goal is to accept yourself and bring in your spirit body and your spirit light to do your soul mission, your soul work. The goal is to work toward graduating so you don't have to come back here. Your graduation could come at any time for any person, whether he or she is handicapped or not. Sometimes people who are handicapped actually do better. I have worked with people who have said, "Well, it is a good thing this happened to me, because now I can't go out and drug myself; I can't go out to those wild parties." Look at this from that perspective. It is a different time when you do not need a guru. You have the tools to do what you need to be a master. This is an exciting time and an exciting opportunity for you. I know all of you wanted to be here at this time. I have mentioned this before in other lectures. Spirits are lining up to come to Earth now. You might ask, "What? So they can be born into poverty in India and die of starvation in two years?"

I want to clear up one thing about incarnation. Let us add up all the souls who have lived on the Earth since 6000 B.C. maybe until 1950. Now take that number and take all the people on the Earth now: 6.5 billion. Take that number. It doesn't equal the first. There are more souls now than ever before, so how could they keep coming back? Have you ever thought about that? They come from other planets, because this planet is so desirable. The question is, why is it so desirable? "I want to get out of here," you say. Well, the first thing is that this is a freewill zone. If you want to go to McDonald's and buy a hamburger, you can do it. If you want to eat French fries, go for it; that is free will. The freewill zone means that you have the ability to choose, not only what you do when you are here, but also before you come in, given the limitations. You have the ability to choose to live in a relatively freewill zone. This is how this energy is set up, and it is a duality.

The lessons of duality are so powerful that being on this planet gives you some extraordinary opportunities to evolve. It makes you wonder what the other planets are like. Well, I have a planet for you that is perfect. It is run by a group called the Grays. Does anyone want to be incarnated there? It is pretty nice. Everything is taken care of; you don't have to worry about where your food comes from. Everyone's happy and follows orders. There are many different weird planets, so this planet Earth has free will and duality. Put that together with the fact that here is a planet on the cusp of 2012, one of the most powerful spiritual energies to come into a planet in a long time, and you can see there are a lot of reasons why this planet is desirable, why people want to come here. Sometimes it is hard to accept the advantages of being on a planet that is going through so much distress. We all know this planet is going through terrible distress. I don't even want to mention some things, because it is very painful. It makes you wonder about the karma of the people doing these things. But you are not responsible for everyone here on the planet. There is going to be a separation where some people go to the fifth dimension while some stay right here. There is now time for questions.

DISCERNMENT, EARTH LESSONS, ASCENSION AND EQUILIBRIUM

Could you speak about discernment?

It is very simple. Ask the energy coming in if it is Christlike. Ask the entity if it is coming in the light of Moses. Ask the entity if it is coming in the light of Archangel Michael. What I am asking is, who do you trust? Do you trust Archangel Michael? Ask the entity if it is coming in the light of Archangel Michael, and if the entity does not respond properly, then forget it.

I use the word Christlike because in the higher realms we do not make a distinction between religions. Religions are important to you. In the fifth dimension, there are no churches, so when you put up a threshold for that entity to go through, if they don't want to go through, forget it. Be careful if the energy wants to attach itself to you in any way. Do not let that happen. Discernment is an important tool now.

How do we know if we have completed or overcome our lessons?

You do not have to be 100 percent clear. Here is a list for you to consider.

- Give it your best shot; please try as hard as you can.
- Sincerity counts.
- An open heart counts.
- Can your heart remain open within this problem?

I am not going to tell what your problem is, but let us say that it is a very complicated problem, and you have not been able to resolve it. Sometimes you can't figure everything out. Sometimes you can't find the money to pay the mortgage, but is your heart still open? Do you have sympathy? Do you have compassion? Are you still open even though you have this problem? You gave it your best shot. It is not like you have five problems in this lifetime and you have to solve them all and then move on to the next. Sometimes we look at a problem and say, "I'll try to remain open." If you have the right understanding, you can overcome the karma.

Will the Earth ascend?

You have to consider your ascension and Earth's ascension. Your work helps Earth in her ascension. Then you ascend and make a decision wheth-er or not you are going to come back to Earth. At that point you can come back if you want to, but many people choose not to. Earth as a planet will ascend, but there is actually going to be a separation. It is a little more com-plicated with a planet because Earth as a higher planet is already in existence in the fifth dimension. It is complicated for you because of the concept called multi-presence, which the Arcturians explained so well. They really explained it much better than I can. It is confusing because it means that you are existing in two places at the same time. That doesn't make sense to you because you are living in this logical, linear reality.

If you are going to ascend, then your body is going to disappear, but Earth is going to be both here and there. Eventually negative people—Saddam Hussein, for example—are going to wind up on a planet where they just live the same thing over and over, living with hatred, and so on, until they "get it." On this planet, President Bush will get a chance to teach Saddam Hussein a big lesson. Then Saddam Hussein will have the chance to teach President Bush another lesson, and they will play the game again. No one will learn anything this time, but maybe they will learn something next time.

The short answer is multi-presence. I can only tell you that you are in ex-istence in your dream life while you are in another world. Time is not linear, even though it looks linear, so in another sense, you are already in another dimension, simultaneously in the fifth dimension with the crystal temple. You have a body there and you have a body here. Your guides and teachers are try-ing to train you to be multi-present, and that is really difficult, because we don't want you to be psychotic. We don't want you to be schizophrenic. So how do you maintain your sanity while being multi-present? How do you bring down your fifth-dimensional body; how do you leave your third-dimensional body when you don't need it any more? That is a general answer and is not as specific as you want, but it is difficult to answer questions like this using the language and logic from which you operate. Incidentally, I want you to know we are not advocating that you leave logic behind. We are not advocating that you leave linear thinking behind. It is rather like multi-presence, where you are in two places at the same time. In multidimensional thinking, you maintain your awareness of the linear thinking because you need the linear thinking to function on this planet. You don't give it up, but you add to it.

How can I reach equilibrium?

The way you receive balance is to follow your intuition. You have to follow your inner voice. You have to follow your inner wisdom. The problem is, if you want to follow your inner wisdom, you must listen without ego. If you listen with ego, your ego will say that you can achieve a lot more balance if you get a new Lexus or go down to Australia for three months. No, the inner self, the higher self must be found within you. You might get some shocking answers—maybe there are things you don't want to do. Your higher self might say, "Sell your house, move to Tulum and live in a hut." What does your inner voice say?

How do I listen to my inner voice?

Some people listen to their inner voices while driving on the freeway. Some people write poetry. Some people channel. Some people pray. It is not as hard as you think it is, if you are willing to follow the advice, but it is in the listening. Let us take a moment and just listen to our inner selves. Let's see what higher self is saying, because we have a great magnification of energy to just listen.

I want to address the fact that some people don't see things and some people don't hear things. There are blocks. I want you to be kind to yourself. This is the most important aspect of overcoming a block. This is going to sound strange, but at least you know you have the block, and that is progress because you could have a block and not know it. So you have a block, and you aren't able to unblock. That is where you are. A famous physiologist once said that you have to be truly who you are before you can be who you want to be. So many of you try to be who you want to be before becoming who you are. That is an interesting soul lesson. The wisdom, the teachings and the energy transformation you need will come to you. Your job is to be open to this energy, and the evolving of your emotional body, your mental body and your physical body will occur.

A lot of physical issues are about accepting the physical body. We did not have the opportunity to discuss some of the limitations that are caused by immune system overload. Thank you very much for your kind attention. I am Vywamus. Good day.

STRUCTURAL INTEGRITY AND MULTITASKING

Juliano

Greetings, I am Juliano. We are the Arcturians. One must look at the etheric structure of Earth. One must consider whether the energy fields of Earth can maintain structural integrity. One must consider whether Earth and its bodies have the consistency and the spiritual energy to hold this structure intact. Earth is quite challenged on many different levels. You see the surface effects, and you call these effects global warming, perhaps, or Earth changes. You might see variations of the electromagnetic energies from the Sun as examples of the structural energy that Earth is trying to integrate. Perhaps you have not considered that Earth as a spirit body, as a spiritual entity, is also challenged. It is challenged in that it seeks to hold a multi-present, multidimensional energy.

You are also challenged in a similar way because your structures are multitasking, trying to coordinate energetic inputs from many different levels. These different levels require the energy of integration. Without an integrative force, the different levels do not fit. There is not a harmonious interaction. This is the same scenario for you as an Earth being. As an Earth being and as a multidimensional being, you have and are experiencing realities on different levels. When you are on one level, you might feel in a harmonious energetic state. Yet when you come down to another field, the field you call reality in the third dimension, you might find that you do not experience harmony. In fact, you might experience disharmony. I know that many of you struggle with mood issues and that you struggle with trying to integrate the different awarenesses and energies you experience.

This is similar to Earth because Earth has different bodies and different energies. The difficulty of Earth's integration also reflects your ability to integrate. At this point, we must consider how better to integrate energeti-cally. It goes without question that this is going to be a wild ride, that the polarities are so contrasted that there will be certain breaks on each side, that there will be different integrations necessary to hold yourself togeth-er, as well as different integration exercises to hold Earth in its energy field. The most outstanding energy you need to use is integration, which will counteract polarity and multitasking. The energy of integration from the Arcturian standpoint comes from many different sources. The first source ideally comes from your mental body, because the mental body can be in control of the integrations. The mental body needs to use affirmations to steer this energetic integration process.

Just to summarize, the integration we are talking about involves fifth-dimensional energy within the third dimension. It involves integration of the four bodies we always speak of: the spirit body, the mental body, the physical body and the emotional body. It also involves the integration of your multidimensional body. That is the body we and you are working with in the fifth dimension. We have told several starseeds in private ses-sions of the necessity for a perfected alignment when you leave your physi-cal body and travel to other dimensions. It is of utmost importance to be in perfect alignment when the spirit body returns to the physical body on Earth. That spirit body must be in a perfected alignment—an alignment that is, even in terms of nanotechnology, in perfect alignment. Even if you leave your body for a short time (even five or ten minutes), energy waves and energy distortion can occur and can cause a shift in your energy. Therefore, when you are above your physical body, you must think and project an alignment energy. You want to be in alignment at all times. This is key to integration. This is key to integrative energy for Earth. Earth also must find a way to be in alignment with the fifth dimension and its fifth-dimensional presence.

THE ENERGY OF REALIGNMENT

We tell the story of the Pleiadeans who used the technologies of the telepathic interaction of space travel to go through dimensional corridors into other areas of the galaxy. When returning to their planet (this oc-curred centuries ago in Earth time), there was a miscalculation on reentry. Bear in mind that in the type of space travel we are talking about, leaving a dimension involves an energetic process. When you return, there is an en-ergetic counter-process. That energetic counter-process can be disruptive if there is not proper alignment. I want to repeat that so you understand it on a planetary level: If you leave the planet in a ship and go into a corridor, traveling interdimensionally, it is incumbent on you when you return that you be focused and that you have the technology to align properly when you reenter. Because of that necessity, we the Arcturians, and many other higher beings, use the Jupiter corridor for reentry and for visitations into Earth's solar system. Jupiter and the corridor of Jupiter are so far away that if there is a minor, miniscule misalignment, it can be corrected in the corridor without affecting Earth.

Now, consider that the energy of realignment is a huge force. When you leave one dimension and go into another dimension, then you have the potential of bringing in an energy that is magnificent. It is also a physical energy. It is a physical energy that has great power. Now, if that physical energy is brought back but misaligned, it actually can throw off whole planetary systems. You might think that would be impossible. A spaceship that has traveled interdimensionally can return to its place of origin, but if there is a misalignment during its return, then that misalignment can throw a whole planetary system off balance. You might find that hard to believe, but from the Arcturian perspective and from the perspective of the fifth-dimensional masters, this makes a great deal of sense. Why? Because the energy of the fifth dimension is an energy of massive proportion. It is not even measurable in Earth terminology. The effects of a misalignment are dramatic. That gives you an idea of why, if you are doing fifth-dimensional work, you must work on alignments. Some of you come back into your physical body and are off by a fraction of a millimeter, even an amount that is immeasurably small, but this could cause disruption in your thought processes and your physical alignments.

I don't want you to become paranoid and say, "Juliano, I cannot perfect this alignment. The way you are talking about it, I am feeling nervous, because I cannot come into this type of alignment with this perfection." Yes, you can. State your intention with your mental thought: "I intend to come back into a perfect alignment and I ask my higher self to create the necessary energetic patterns so that I am in perfected alignment energy as I come back into my physical body." Some of you have problems because you don't want to be back in the physical body. Some of you are leaving and then you say, "I don't want to come back." Your not wanting to come back is also creating resistance to reentry. I ask you to reprogram yourself by stating that you are in alignment and that you are willing to come back. You want to come back in a perfected state of alignment.

Hold Your Structure in Alignment

We are discussing this subject of alignments on a personal level and on a planetary level. The Pleiadean ship came back after its excursions into other systems. They came back through their corridor, but unfortunately they reentered misaligned. Now, this can be looked at in two ways. One, to reenter in misalignment can be corrected if you are far enough away from the main body into which you wish to reenter. For example, one technique is to reenter your body from far above. For example, maybe you are a a hundred feet above your body and you reenter there. Then, because of the play of energy and the play of space, you would have a buffer giving you the spatial freedom to make corrections. This is a technique I will explain later that I want you to use. On a planetary basis, let us just imagine that you were as far away from Earth as say, Venus, which is rather close, and you weren't in proper alignment when you reentered with your ship from the other dimension. If you are in misalignment, then that reentry occurs with tremendous force. Remember, you are coming in with a force, a speed that is so great it is immeasurable in terms of human technology. To approach this speed would require all of the energy that has ever been expended on Earth, including all the coal, all the oil, all the nuclear energy—any energy you can think of that has ever been expended on Earth. It would require all of that energy to create this force. That's a lot of energy.

When you are in another dimension and you enter this one, you are going at a speed that approaches the speed of light, which is unimaginable in Earth terms. Coming into Earth from another dimension at the distance of, say, Venus would be too close, because it wouldn't allow for correction. That is why you come in through Jupiter. When the Pleiadean ships came in, they misjudged their alignment, and they threw their planet into a time warp. This time warp was an uncomfortable situation for the inhabitants, because being thrown into a time warp is similar to what you experience when you are off balance. You might feel dizzy, disoriented. You might not know where up or down is. These would be some examples. Maybe you wouldn't know if you were asleep or awake. You wouldn't be able to tell the difference between the astral realm and the third dimension. Some of you might already have these kinds of symptoms on a lesser basis. You might wonder, "Why do I sometimes feel so disoriented; why do I feel so depersonalized? Why do I feel like I am in one dimension or that I can't tell which dimension I am in?" Anyway, the Pleiadean ship coming into a misalignment threw the whole planet out of alignment—the whole planet! Can you imagine what that feels like at the planetary level?

The masters and the spiritual beings on the Pleiades were in harmony with many different spiritual guides and masters, just as the Groups of Forty are in harmony with many spiritual masters. Through consultations and energetic work, it was decided by the masters that even though a mistake with misalignment energy had occurred, a correction was to be enabled. This correction involved the Pleiades being taken out of misalignment and advanced to be placed into the fifth dimension. The guides and teachers used energetic spiritual technology, the tool of ascension. Through this technology, they brought the Pleiades into the fifth dimension, and that's where the Pleiades is today.

This experience has many lessons for Earth. The personal lesson concerns how to enter the body. If you are going into fifth-dimensional spaces or into the astral realm, it behooves you to reenter in the best, highest alignment. On Earth now, there are many people on this planet who are out of alignment. Many people are connected to astral energies and a lower vibrational field. Earth, as an energetic body, is struggling to maintain its connection to the fifth dimension. The wars, the nuclear weapons, the thoughts of polarization all have a cumulative effect on Earth energy. You need to hold the structure of Earth in alignment with the fifth dimension. You need to hold your structure so that you are in alignment.

A MEDITATION TO ALIGN IN PERFECT PROPORTION

I, Juliano, send down a golden-blue light over each of you who are listening to or reading these words so that you are energetically receptive to the alignments. In the exercise we are about to do, you will have the highest receptivity to alignments. Not only that, but you will have cognitive mental thoughts that will enable you to direct yourself into an alignment of perfect proportion. Now, when the alignments are in perfect proportion, then the energy that you bring in is equivalent to and counterbalances the disruptive forces of a misalignment. The alignment becomes positive and harmonious, bringing in an integrative energy that is exactly the opposite of disruptive energies. That is why integration becomes the key to your luminescent presence. Remember to remove any resistive thoughts you have about reentry, thoughts such as, "I don't want to be back in my body," or "I don't want to be here." Those thoughts take a toll.

There are places on Earth that are filled with debris and with sewage. This is blocked energy. [Tones.] *Oooohhhh. Oooohhhh.* Let blue-golden energy clean the receptors in your etheric energy fields so that a perfected alignment is possible. You are in perfect harmony. You are able to raise your spirit body out of your physical body. As you raise your spirit body out of your physical body, you float above your physical body. Go to a place that is about 100 to 200 feet above your physical structure. As you go above your physical structure, you feel the pull of this beautiful blue and golden energy. As you are above your body, experience the freedom of your energetic connections to the fifth dimension, available through the individual corridors that are above each of you.

Instead of traveling to other areas and other realms, I want you to say and think these words: "I am creating the energy field for a perfected reentry and realignment. I am creating the necessary energy field for a perfected reentry and realignment." I want you to understand that when you are 100 to 200 feet above your body, you are a receiver of fifth-dimensional energy and light. You are increasing your energetic field up there. Your energetic body is expanded. All your spiritual antennae are out. [Tones.] *Oooohhhh.* Look down at your physical body and slowly descend back into your physical body, bringing a total alignment. Stay perhaps eight to ten feet above your body and work on this realignment. [Tones.] *Oooohhhh.* Now, in perfected alignment, slowly reenter your physical body. As you do that, you will feel upliftment and rejuvenation. I want you to hold this energy field, this feeling of realignment. We will meditate for a few minutes so that you can work on becoming familiar with this realignment.

All of you have successfully reentered your body and experienced this alignment. You have all understood the energetic part of this. I want to turn my attention to the alignment of Earth with the fifth-dimensional energy. This is a time of mass vibrational shifts, a time of rapid changes and polarizations. Institutional structures will be stripped of their potency as the fraudulent energies that seem to be the basis of many institutions are exposed. Truths will become known. Anger and polarization will become stronger and stronger. Concurrently, the Earth receives telepathic energy and light from these experiences and will begin to respond to that.

EARTH RESPONDS

The Earth is in a position now where it is responding telepathically to humans. One of the less understood aspects of biorelativity is that Earth has evolved as a spirit body and is receiving telepathic communications. Many of the telepathic communications the Earth is receiving are not of the highest level. I want you to consider that the telepathic powers of Earth have evolved. Because of this evolution, higher biorelativity is possible. But if large groups of people like you do not commit themselves to biorelativity exercises, then disharmonious, disintegrative energy becomes the primary telepathic input into Earth.

Understand that you as starseeds and lightworkers have the ability to download fifth-dimensional Earth energy into the third-dimensional Earth body in a perfected state of alignment. That ability becomes more important as we move closer to 2012. Let it be known that the ascension is a time when the fifth-dimensional Earth body will come into perfected alignment with the third-dimensional Earth. Then, at that millisecond of ascension, there is transference of this alignment. Then a disengagement occurs in which you move to the higher realm, because you are able to hold fifth-dimensional energy. The fifth-dimensional Earth disengages.

Etheric crystals have many functions. One of the functions of etheric crystals is to provide a guiding light, a guiding foundation for an alignment of the fifth-dimensional Earth with the third-dimensional Earth. These etheric crystals become alignment points. When you are aligning the fifth-dimensional Earth with the third-dimensional Earth, then you must consider that this is a huge conceptual energetic proposition. Visualize the etheric crystals that are in Lago Puelo and in Lake Moraine. Etheric crystals will be placed at Mount Shasta, Bodensee and Grosse Valley. Realize that all these are alignment points with the fifth-dimensional Earth. You can bring those crystals in alignment from the fifth-dimensional Earth with the third-dimensional Earth. Then you bring down the fifth-dimensional Earth into the third-dimensional Earth using the energy of the etheric crystals. We bring down Earth using those crystals as the locking points. [Tones.] *Oooohhhh.* This is one of the tasks for starseeds. This is why we ask the channel to travel so much, and this is why the etheric crystals play a more important role, perhaps more than anyone had imagined. Don't worry about whether the crystals are equidistant around the planet. In other words, you might think there are two huge spheres and each must be at a certain position in each hemisphere and each pole. Etheric energy doesn't work in geometric patterns the way you would logically think.

Now we will travel up a corridor and out of your physical body. Rising up out of the physical body, travel this dimensional corridor to our starship, Starship Athena in the Jupiter corridor. On this starship, we have a huge holographic Earth healing chamber. It is like a large auditorium. I want you to come into the auditorium. I, Juliano, am at the controls, and we are able to see third-dimensional Earth. Take a moment and come into this healing, holographic Earth chamber. As you enter the chamber, look at the screen. I have focused the holographic healing screen on third-dimensional Earth. Now you will see another image. I have enlarged the screen so that third-dimensional Earth is at the bottom. Now you can see fifth-dimensional Earth on the top of the screen.

FIFTH-DIMENSIONAL EARTH ALIGNS WITH THIRD-DIMENSIONAL EARTH

Energetically, it has the ring of ascension. Energetically, it has a halo and a whole different astral field, it is this huge fifth-dimensional light, and it is a huge planetary system. It is a lot larger energetically than the third-dimensional Earth. The third dimension looks contracted in comparison. On the holographic screen, we have the fifth-dimensional Earth. This fifth-dimensional Earth is a huge, vibrant planetary energy. It is very expansive and filled with beautiful harmonious light. Then you have the third-dimensional Earth, which is what you are living in with all of its contractions. On the third-dimensional Earth, you will see many bright spots, and there are four etheric crystals. These are beams of crystal light. [Tones.] *Hooooohhhh.*

On the fifth-dimensional Earth above, I am able to control the alignment. I can direct the alignments with my steering wheel/dial; I can turn the two Earths until they are in perfected alignment. We are setting up the alignment so that the etheric crystals on the fifth-dimensional Earth come into beautiful alignment with the third-dimensional Earth. I want you to visualize a powerful beam of light coming from each etheric crystal: in Grosse Valley, in Lago Puelo, in Bodensee, in Lake Moraine. All of these areas are sending out beams of light like tractor beams. They are locking into the fifth-dimensional etheric crystals in the fifth-dimensional Earth with the assistance of the holographic healing chamber, with my assistance and with your visualizations. Also, the ring of ascension in the fifth-dimensional Earth is coming into alignment with the ring of ascension in the third-dimensional Earth. It is a beautiful image onscreen in the holographic Earth chamber. Hold the image of alignment as best you can during this meditation.

Now, together you and I are going to bring the fifth-dimensional Earth into perfected alignment with the etheric crystals on third-dimensional Earth. I have what looks in your imagination perhaps like a joystick. I bring it forward. As I bring it forward, visualize the energy of fifth-dimensional Earth coming into perfected alignment with third-dimensional Earth, the etheric crystals exactly in alignment. They are getting closer and closer, and now it comes right into perfect alignment. You are fifth-dimensional beings and you are on the fifth-dimensional Earth. Bring this fifth-dimensional Earth to the third-dimensional Earth. Bring your fifth-dimensional self back into your third-dimensional self as a participant in this exercise.

Now I push this joystick closer to me. You can see the two Earths—the fifth- and the third-dimensional Earth—coming to a perfected alignment right by the etheric crystals. [Tones.] *Oooohhhh. Tat tat tat. Oooohhhh.* It is in perfected alignment. Fifth-dimensional Earth has come into alignment with third-dimensional Earth. The anchoring points of this alignment are the etheric crystals. There will be more etheric crystals placed in the Earth this year, and this alignment will become even easier. You need to focus on this interaction and on this exercise. I know there are many predictions of dire circumstances. We will have many things to say about them, but the bottom line is, this type of alignment work needs to be done by you. This is an encompassing work, a work that involves all systems, a work that covers all energy fields.

Hold this alignment on the holographic screen. The Earth receives this energy. Know that the Pleiadian system has done a great deal of work to their planet in preparation; work similar to what you have just done. We will now leave the holographic healing chamber. I will be working with this image after you leave. You may return to this image later on in your meditations if you wish. I will continue to be here for many hours. We are in a holographic time zone. Now we leave and follow the corridor back to our physical bodies. Remember, you are going to reenter your body. Use your concentration to reenter in an exact way, stating your intention first. [Tones.] *Oooohhhh.* You have reentered your physical body in perfected alignment and you remain etherically connected to this holographic healing chamber. During your meditations over the next forty-eight hours, you can return at will to my chamber, to my ship, to the holographic auditorium of the Earth healing chamber. You will also benefit from working on this alignment. This will bring a powerful telepathic energetic level of fifth-dimensional light to Mother Earth. This is Juliano, and we are the Arcturians. Blessings to you, the lightworkers of the Groups of Forty.

ETHERIC CRYSTALS PROVIDE A GUIDING LIGHT

Juliano and Sananda

Greetings, I am Juliano. We are the Arcturians. We have completed the mission of placing a new etheric crystal in the volcano of Poás in San José, Costa Rica. This was accomplished with the assistance of the Groups of Forty members in the Costa Rica area. This is an important asset in the alignments that will be perfected between the third-dimensional Earth and the fifth-dimensional Earth. Alignment of fifth-dimensional energy with third-dimensional energy ensures a continual and full energetic flow of fifth-dimensional energy into Earth. The placement of the etheric crystals provides guiding light and guiding energetic receptacles for the fifth-dimensional Earth and all fifth-dimensional energies.

We have assisted other planets in their quests for ascension, and we had great success when we worked with starseeds on those planets. The process of planetary ascension is accelerated by the downloading of beautiful etheric crystals. These etheric crystals have many functions. The function you are most familiar with has to do with the alignments. A fifth-dimensional Earth has a better alignment energy when there are etheric crystals in different parts of the planet. Now, the crystals do not have to be equidistant from each other. They do not have to be in a certain circumference placement around Earth. Remember, we are working with both holographic and etheric energy. The etheric crystals then assist in the alignment, and they also interact with each other. If one Group of Forty member (or members) works with the crystal in Lago Puelo, the energy and input there is communicated to the other crystals.

This crystal that we placed in the volcano in Poás is connected with the Central Sun and with higher galactic forces. The Central Sun is linking itself to this beautiful crystal and is providing a boost of energy to the other four etheric crystals. Most interestingly, this etheric crystal is also connected with the universal force known as the great attractor energy field. The great attractor energy field is a transcendent galactic force that involves gathering together and directing the known galaxies toward a point in the universe that would be equivalent to the Central Sun in our galaxy. Unfortunately, there is no actual known center of the universe from humankind's standpoint.

It has been determined by your scientists and confirmed for many, many eons by our scientists that a galactic force is causing everything to move in one direction. This immeasurable force that causes galaxies to move in one direction is of unknown origin. The speed of the galaxies' movement is measurable, yet the nature of the attractive force is unknown. You can only imagine what type of force would be able to attract the powers and create the force to move galaxies toward a probable central point, something comparable to the Central Sun of this galaxy.

A DISCUSSION OF CENTRAL SUNLIGHT

The Central Sun of this galaxy is the source of life and spirit. Remember that all the things you see on the third dimension are manifestations of both a spiritual force and a spiritual idea or thought. When you try to conceive of the Central Sun, you have to understand that it is a multileveled, multidimensional force field that exists in the spirit world as well as at a physical point. It is an emanation light and an emanation force that controls manifestation in the galaxy. It is a physical or spiritual force that also is able to interact telepathically with starseeds and higher-consciousness beings who are manifesting in the third dimension. This means that biorelativity is continually able to be updated with: 1) Earth and Earth's spiritual energy, and 2) the Central Sun energy. This means that from a biorelativity standpoint, you as starseeds can communicate telepathically with the Central Sun, and you can telepathically receive energy and light from the Central Sun.

You can telepathically direct the Central Sun energy and light, ensuring that it is manifested and distributed to certain areas on Earth. We have designated Mount Shasta as one area that is receiving Central Sun energy and light. Now we have downloaded the crystal in the Poás volcano in San José, Costa Rica. That volcanic mountain is connected to the Central Sun, and we will also be working to connect it with Mount Shasta.

A new connection is made with the great attractor forces that are working with the galactic energy. This energy from the great attractor is combining with the Central Sun to create a pulsing energy field. That pulsing energy field is now being downloaded to and then emitted from the Poás volcano, and it is vibrating through the planet. Those who are at Mount Shasta may already be feeling the vibrational pulsing. The vibrational pulsing is being distributed through the Earth meridian lines. The main meridian line that is receiving this input of light is generally known as the ring of fire. Each pulsing creates a calming and harmonious energetic field. The energy that is in this ring of fire meridian is so powerful that it is able to balance and realign ocean currents, weather patterns and other aspects of the Earth's biofield that are needed to come into a new and upgraded harmony.

We, the Arcturians, feel and observe a shift in consciousness on the planet, one that occurred with this recent full moon. We felt a great movement spiritually among the starseeds during this full moon. This movement has given the planet a boost of spiritual energy and spiritual power, a power that is needed now, because the polarization of lower vibrations on this planet continue to spiral out of control. Remember, this polarization increases spirituality as well as increasing the oppositional energy of density. It is incumbent on you to work with these spiritual energies to create and establish shimmering cities. The shimmering lights and shimmering energy fields are established in smaller locations, such as in the cities near Lago Puelo or San Martín in Argentina. They are now uploaded in certain areas in San José, Costa Rica, and will work with an already existing shimmering city.

ECSTATIC SHIMMERING

The shimmering lights are representative of an energy field based on telepathic interactions between third-dimensional starseeds and fifth-dimensional energy. The shimmering light is a telepathic etheric force field that is accelerated through etheric crystal work. It can be described as a circular energy field that is distributed around a designated area. The designated area usually begins in a small circle. We find that the starseeds have an easier time working to create an energy field of shimmering light in a small area, and then expand it with great enthusiasm and telepathic work. It can be expanded around a city. Eventually it can be expanded around a planet. It is our goal to create a shimmering energy field around the ring of fire. All the cities and countries can unilaterally join in an energy field of fifth-dimensional light that will bring a new harmony and balance to the planet. A shimmering light field was established around San José in our previous work with the channel. During that experience, the idea of a city beginning to develop the power and ability to become fifth dimensional on a regulated basis was established.

We still feel that, at this point in the development of the Group of Forty lightworkers, that it is better to work within smaller areas, smaller parts of a city or even smaller designated areas in nature. Ideally, the beginning point would be those areas where we have already downloaded etheric crystals, which include Lago Puelo, Grosse Valley, Lake Moraine, Lake Constance and now the Poás volcano. Groups can go to these areas and begin to feel the shimmering light energy. It would be ideal for all five crystals to have Group of Forty starseeds working on them simultaneously.

We hope that this will be accomplished soon, when a unique opportunity will be established to have a connection with an energy that will upgrade the biospheric field of Earth. This upgrade will allow the energy field around the ring of fire to shimmer. Shimmering is the ability to flicker in and out of a dimension. A person who is shimmering will look like he or she is in one energy normally, like in an Earth energy. Then he or she will seem to disappear temporarily, and perhaps only the outline of an energy field or the signature of an energy field will remain visible. Then that person appears in the fifth dimension. The person who is experiencing shimmering has a feeling of elation, almost a feeling of ecstasy. That is because fifth-dimensional energy is experienced as an ecstatic feeling from a third-dimensional perspective.

I, Juliano, say that each of you listening to or reading these words has the ability to shimmer. I am downloading a beautiful golden light that is connected to the crystal at the Poás volcano. This beautiful golden light is an emanating corridor that is coming to each of you. You experience the golden corridor as a beam of light coming and downloading into your crown chakra. As it is downloading into your crown chakra, you will receive an experience similar to an electrical charge. This fifth-dimensional energy is an electromagnetic energy. It is not an electrical charge the way you think of it, like a jolt. It is an upliftment. As you receive this upliftment, in the form of an electrical charge coming from the etheric crystal in the Poás volcano, you are able to shimmer. You are able to be in the fifth and the third realms simultaneously. Please hold this connection as we meditate with you.

Earth and it is around the etheric fifth-dimensional Earth as well.

We are interested in working with the ring of ascension, which is a golden halo of light that represents and attracts interaction between fifth-dimensional beings and third-dimensional beings. This halo creates a conduit for interaction between the third dimension and the fifth dimension. An update on the ring of ascension is in order. The ring of ascension has been updated to a higher vibrational frequency because it is now connected to the Central Sun, the great-attractor force energy field, and is now in harmony with the five etheric crystals that have been downloaded on Earth. It is sending a golden ray of peace to the planet. We have predicted and we say that there will be a great deal of war coming. But then we predict a sudden but definite peace that will seem to hold for a period of time. A new spiritual energy is being activated and distributed. More people are being affected by this. There is a greater awareness of the need for a spiritual intervention of the highest proportion. This spiritual intervention can bring the planet back into a harmony that will enable it to survive. Sananda will now speak with you. I am Juliano.

G reetings. I am Sananda. The golden halo that is around Earth is symbolic and representative of your own halo. I am activating your

halo at this moment so that each of you is able to come into a state of harmony. This state of harmony is necessary for you to maximize your healing abilities. It makes perfect sense when you think about this—to be at the highest level of your healing abilities requires optimal personal harmony. The halo I am placing around each of you is bringing you into higher harmony than you have experienced recently. Harmony is an energetic state that is attainable at any moment under any conditions while on Earth. It is not necessary to be in a cave meditating for twenty years, although it could happen under those conditions. It is necessary for you to get an energetic boost of light and energy from a higher being. With this boost, you will be in a state where you can receive input from the halo. When you are in that state, your healing abilities are accelerated, both on a personal and a planetary basis.

SANANDA SPEAKS OF THE GOLDEN HALO AND THE GAN EDEN

I, Sananda, send you a beautiful beam of harmonious golden light that represents the ability to reformulate your energy field so that the configuration of a golden halo appears around you as I speak, just as it is appearing around the Earth. [Tones.] *"Shalom."* This golden halo brings into a balance all aspects of your biosphere on a personal basis, and it gives you an extra ability to upgrade the Earth's biosphere. The Earth's biosphere is receiving an interactive ability from the ring of ascension. That interactive ability gives it the chance to receive your input.

The Garden of Eden, the *Gan Eden*, was a fifth-dimensional palace or garden in which Adonai kept the balance. The third-dimensional *Gan Eden* was established for humans to be in charge of that balance and for humans to update and create the forces necessary for balance. The children of the Elohim, the B'nai Elohim, are creator forces who have the ability to upgrade and create fifth-dimensional gardens. These fifth-dimensional gardens can also be compared to the shimmering cities of light where only the righteous can survive. The righteous have fifth-dimensional awareness and can enter unity consciousness. They have the ability to do Yechudi. This is the act of uniting the third dimension with the fifth dimension by thoughts. [Sings in Hebrew.] *"Yechudim, B'nai Elohim, Adonai Elohenu, Adonai Echad, Yechudim, with the Gan Eden."* Visualize these cities of light. They are created by the shimmering forces as part of the divine plan to re-create the *Gan Eden* on Earth. The fifth-dimensional cities of light are for the righteous. We call these righteous people in the Hebrew Bible the Tzadikim. Each of you are righteous, for you are ascending students working to integrate yourselves into fifth-dimensional beings. You are ascending students who are working to create fifth-dimensional cities and gardens.

Think of a garden, my friends, as a palace. Think of the Garden of Eden as the basis, the prototype, for the fifth-dimensional cities. [Sings.] *Gan Eden*. In the fifth-dimensional cities of light, in the gardens, you will see me and you will feel my healing abilities interact with yours. Your halo that I have activated now is like a DNA entry code that allows you to enter the gardens. It even goes to the level that you are able to co-create the garden of shimmering light cities on Earth, which is the true manifestation of the *B'nai Elohim*, the children of the *Elohim* light. [Sings.] *"B'nai Elohim."* The energy and light of the children of the *Elohim* is activated within you. Resonate with the city of light, the city of gardens of the just, which is the foundation for the shimmering energy that will bring unified fifth-dimensional healing force and light to Earth. The halo of golden light around you is activating within your DNA so that these powers are upgraded and manifested in each of you. I am Sananda. Shalom.

TELEPATHY AND THE EVOLUTION OF HUMANS

Helio-ah and Chief White Eagle

Greetings, I am Helio-ah, and we are the Arcturians. I send my love and greetings to all of you, as we seek a union of brotherhood and sisterhood among the starseeds. We are helping and hoping that you can unite with us in an understanding and awareness of your starseed heritage and your starseed connections.

The foremost issue before humanity on the Earth is to understand the importance of the next stage of evolution. Humankind is in a crisis as a species. The biosphere that you are dependent on is threatened on many different levels. A shift in consciousness is necessary to maximize the success of the evolutionary step that humankind must take in order to ensure the survival of your species and to ensure that the biosphere remains capable of sustaining life for humankind.

During the past weeks we have been in discussion with you about the whales and the issues involved in the possibilities of their being hunted. The issue of the whales is indeed a reminder of important facts that must be integrated into your understanding of the evolution of humans and the relationship of your evolution to the biosphere and to the oceans.

BECOMING TELEPATHIC

First, the next step of evolution for humans involves the ability to become telepathic. The ability to become telepathic has several aspects to it. Often when people hear the word "telepathic," they think only of being able to read someone's mind and even sending messages to distant people. Of course, this is one aspect of telepathy. I suggest that the evolutionary step that is necessary for humankind to go forward involves the acceleration and activation of higher telepathic powers. A second aspect of higher telepathic powers involves one of the subjects that is very dear to us, which is biorelativity. Telepathy includes not only the ability to receive thought patterns from humankind but also includes interactions from plants, other animals and, ultimately, from the Earth that you live on, the star family that you are a part of, the central galaxy from which all life has emerged in this galaxy and from the Creator. Each telepathic level involves a certain skill. Naturally, if you are able to telepathically communicate with other people by receiving or sending messages, this provides a foundation for you to telepathically communicate with animals and plants. Many of you who are with us now probably have the telepathic ability to share this connection with your pets, with close friends and with other animals.

The level of communicating with Telos, which is the Inner Earth, is a function of telepathic abilities. The ability to communicate with Gaia, the spirit of the Earth, is important. And then we come to certain animals or higher mammals that have an interesting and particular power that is actually refined and in some ways more advanced than humans. A plant or tree may have certain knowledge and energy that may be beyond your understanding. You will have to be able to telepathically go to the energy level of that plant being in order to receive and interpret its messages. After you have defined and maximized your telepathic abilities on Earth, you will find a particularly difficult problem with this new sensitivity because many animals, plants and Earth itself are experiencing discomfort or disease at this time. To telepathically communicate with them will create a feeling of great pain and sadness within you.

We have talked with you about the whales, and we have pointed out that they have a particular and very high telepathic ability. Some animals and mammals are not as advanced telepathically. These whales are not the only mammals that have telepathic abilities. But their telepathic abilities are tied into very ancient energies. These energies are particularly related to a powerful force within the ocean that is directly related to what you have called Earth changes, magnetic energy shifts, weather patterns, global warming and the melting icecaps. Whales have the ability to telepathically communicate with the Earth and bring forth knowledge to those humans who are sensitive enough to work with them. The knowledge that they bring through could provide a key ingredient into the stabilizations of the biosphere. They are also demonstrating the need for you to accelerate your telepathic abilities.

What is interesting is that when you look at the changes on Earth at this point, and we will generally refer to this as Earth changes, you will find numerous opinions about what needs to be done. Some of these opinions are based on interesting scientific data about changing the amount of greenhouse gasses, for example, or growing or changing some aspect of the forests. Even some people believe this change in the biosphere is just a natural phenomenon that just needs to take its course. I, Helio-ah, say that the way to understand the Earth changes should start with those who are able to connect telepathically to the spirit of the Earth and understand what needs to be modulated in the feedback loop of the environment. In particular, the feedback loop involved in the Earth changes needs to start with the oceans, not only from the greenhouse gasses that are released into the air.

OCEAN ENERGY

The greenhouse gasses that are released into the air, of course, are setting off issues and problems. Remember, life on this planet began in the oceans. It is the oceans that provide the feedback loop that stabilizes the currents that have the major influence on the weather patterns and also other aspects related to the Earth meridians and the Earth grid lines. Oceans are not the only influence, but statistically, if you look at Earth, you will see that the majority of it is covered by oceans. It would be logical, then, to assume that since the majority of Earth is under oceans, the ocean currents and the energy in the oceans would play a major role in understanding and stabilizing the feedback loop in the world systems.

When you look at the oceans, you have to ask which species in the oceans are able to telepathically connect to the energies of the feedback loop there? Which species are evolved enough to have an ancient awareness of the systems of the oceans and can provide an energy, a stable force, to ensure that Earth is able to maintain the biosphere for the highest good of humanity? The obvious answer is to look toward the evolved whales and dolphins for this energy. It is not that we are saying that they are better than all the other animals. It is important to consider other animals. We know that there are certain powers of the buffalo, for example, and certain powers of the lions and the deer. We know that in the shaman world, each animal carries a special shamanistic power. There is a "shamanistic power" within the energies of the whales and the dolphins that relates—that connects—telepathically to the Earth energies through the oceans.

THOUGHT PROJECTION

[Tones.] *Oooohhhh. Oooohhhh.* A learning process is required to telepathically increase your powers. The final telepathic skill, which would be the third on our list of telepathic skills, would be thought projection. This is used to project yourselves to other planets, other systems or other areas on this planet through a process called remote viewing. Actually, you can project yourself and telepathically connect with those who are ready and willing to telepathically connect with you. It is a symbiotic, sympathetic relationship in which you seek the energies of those people who are already evolved and are reaching out telepathically.

I, Helio-ah, have said that many of you who seek other energies for your business, healing practices or for connecting with starseeds near your home, you need to elevate the etheric antenna within your crown chakra. When that etheric antenna is raised into the spirit realm, then you can broadcast or transmit messages telepathically to other people you want to reach. Then, through what seems to be a mysterious process, those people will begin to contact you and begin to find ways to work with you. This is the power of telepathy.

We had asked in a previous session to have you telepathically connect with the whales that are to be potentially hunted and to receive their names and other information. Quite miraculously, many of you have received their names and information about them. This is a very strong skill, and it is a strong activity in which you practice receiving energy and messages. Likewise, you can also send messages to them. This is a learning process, and it is an enhancement for whales and dolphins who have a great desire to serve humanity. These beautiful creatures are able to give some valuable feedback on what steps need to be taken to restore the oceans.

TELEPATHY, HUMANKIND'S CONNECTION TO ANIMALS AND BIORELATIVITY

This telepathic linkage to the whales is representative of a process that is related to all different animals and plants on this Earth. Some of you in your missions are anchoring yourselves to telepathically communicate with the woods and the forests. Some of you are telepathically linking to certain cats. Others are relating to the buffalo. I know that Chief White Eagle has been trying to activate telepathic linkages to the white eagle. The emergence of the white buffalo is an example of the telepathic communication from a high Native American spirit, White Buffalo Calf Woman.

There are numerous other examples of how the telepathic energies are coming into Earth. Many starseeds are sensitive enough to connect with telepathic energy on a refined level. High information can be acquired from telepathic communication. The example of the whales and the dolphins show that animals want to connect with humans. This whale hunting experience shows that there is an increasing need for these animals to communicate with you, and that your work with them can telepathically influence them. If you were able to exactly track where the hunting ship was, then you would be able to send messages to them to avoid that area. This does two things: one, it helps you practice your telepathic powers; and two, it increases your abilities to relate telepathically. Ultimately, you want to find the access point in which you can telepathically connect to the spirit of Earth. That point and that energy related to the Earth spirit is the domain of the native peoples. They have been holding certain skills on how to do that.

At this point of human evolution, the telepathic powers are merging into a group Earth healing energy that we have described as biorelativity. Biorelativity involves the ability to telepathically send an energy to a planet. Biorelativity energy can also be used to send energy to a species in the water, animals and forests. Telepathy includes sending messages back and forth, and this includes sending healing energy. The understanding of telepathy and using it for biorelativity is the central core of our teachings to you.

We believe that there is a powerful linkage of telepathic powers through group energy. The telepathic powers are strong in certain individuals. Each of you can increase your telepathic powers through practice. There is one method that is superior and most able to accelerate your telepathic powers. This method involves working through groups of like-minded people. Even though the energy of one is powerful, the energy of many is stronger. Starseeds who are linked together through biorelativity exercise can affect the source codes of the planet. Using group biorelativity creates an Earth healing ability that we call quantum transcendence forces. The ability of quantum transcendence forces is rooted in telepathy and the ability of higher energetic beings to telepathically shift the energies of oceans, of planets, of forests. This healing energy can cause miraculous outcomes that seem to transcend the normal laws of cause and effect that normally operate on the Earth. Quantum energy transcendence means that with the proper approaches and inputs, you can create some positive outcomes.

It so happens that some of the animals and the plants know energetic codes that relate to this quantum transcendence. So, for example, trees or plants can be shifted so that they are able to absorb more of what you call the greenhouse gasses. There is a certain evolutionary shift that the plants and the trees can make that would actually help humans. From our viewpoint, and I think you might agree, most of the living beings on this planet, are going to have to make some dramatic evolutionary changes in order to survive.

A Look at Evolution

Let us speak about the trees. On one hand, you think that many trees will become extinct. Many of the forests are being burned and the trees that survive face what can best be described as a hostile environment. Yet the trees have the information on how to evolve. But many of the trees don't have the energy to make the evolutionary changes that they need to make to survive in such a brief time. Some trees, for example, may need to absorb certain gasses to survive. Or other trees may need to learn to survive on less water or more water or maybe others need to grow taller. Maybe they need to be taller to get the nutrition of the light. There are various adaptations that each tree species would have to make in order to ensure their survival at this time.

Evolution is a complex process. One of the reasons why you have reincarnated at this time (you, the starseeds) is to participate directly in evolution. You can become the quantum energy force, the transcendent energy force, which telepathically communicates with the trees, plants and animals to assist them in making the evolutionary changes necessary to survive. Know that humankind needs the trees to survive in order to ensure the proper gasses are absorbed and to ensure the proper levels and mixtures of carbon dioxide and oxygen are all in a balance.

You might say to me, "Now, Helio-ah, how would I know what a tree needs to do to evolve? How would I know what the whale needs to do to survive in the toxic ocean?" Here is where it becomes mystical because quantum energy and quantum physics are based on the mystery that the observer energetically changes the outcome.

A Look at Trees and Forests

Your ability to telepathically communicate with the oceans and the trees and the forests create a quantum interactive energy. You have the ability to send love to the forests telepathically. You have the ability to talk to them and to tell them what you see and what you think they need to know and how you are with them. Those who have even sacrificed themselves for old-growth trees are a powerful example of how one person can affect the evolution of a tree and the energy of that tree. Even if the tree passes on, that tree has become involved with humans. The evolution of the tree has interacted with human telepathic communication and has contributed to the group energy of the tree species. This means that if you communicate telepathically with the tree species, then you might also do it on a global level, as well as on an individual level where you are close to a forest. You might have to talk to the tree telepathically and say things like: "Hello, tree. I am telepathically aware of you and know that you can understand my thoughts. Maybe you do not understand my words, but I am sending you this energy of love."

Remember that telepathy is an energy that can also be below the consciousness of words. That is why people may have a hard time understanding their telepathic skills. They think that they only must receive or send words. Telepathy is an energy field and an energy transmission—an intuition. It includes picking up vibrations. It includes receiving and transmitting energy below the conscious level. Telepathy isn't necessarily only in words. You might be connecting with the trees what could be described in words, but actually, you are sending this energy of love, compassion, concern. You are trying to send them energy about what they have to do. You might want to use the words to help you, but the tree can pick up the vibrations that are below your words. That, my friends, is the level of telepathic skill that you need to develop, and then later you can find ways to bridge that into words.

We are aware, forests and trees, that you are going through changes. These changes in the environment are such that they have to learn how to grow differently. Maybe you need to have certain aspects of yourselves shift. I want to send you an energy of love and concern and support. I send you an energy field. Not only that, but I am going to place a cosmic egg of light around you. This will allow you the stability and the energy to make the necessary adaptations.

A LOOK AT THE OCEAN AND THE WHALES

Now, I'll return to the whales and the dolphins. They are on a certain wavelength energetically, which indigenous groups, including in Australia and in New Zealand, have over their ancient history learned to achieve. They have been practicing telepathic communications with the whales. They call themselves whale dreamers, but I would prefer to call them telepathic speakers with the whales. They have the power to talk to them and to connect with them. Now we need to go to a deeper level because we need to tell these whales that we are concerned about them. We need to tell them that there are changes going on in the ocean currents. There are changes going on in deep spots in the oceans that no person has ever been to. These whales have been where there are certain meridians, certain grid lines through the oceans that they know about. We could ask them to go to those spirit places and open up new channels of light within the oceans of the Earth that need to come through. They are able to swim to these grid lines. They are able to follow these meridian pathways and are able to open up ancient pathways, ancient energy, deep within the ocean that now need to come forth. We can ask them to do that. They have special knowledge and information that they could give.

Then the question is, what changes do they have to make in order for them to survive? Well, it is very similar to humankind. Humankind's change, from an evolutionary standpoint, involves evolving the immunity system—Man's ability to process toxicities or toxic chemicals—and the ability to process electromagnetic energy. The changes that humans need to make have to do not only with the immune system, with toxicity and electromagnetic radiation, but also the ability to telepathically evolve and work with biorelativity. This is quite a large test for humans—that is, to be able to understand how to evolve in those three levels and to incorporate the stage of development of telepathic communication with plants, animals and ultimately the Earth. It can be done. I know that you all have this ability. I am going to return the remaining time over to Chief White Eagle. I love you all deeply, and I know that you have such powerful telepathic abilities. This is Helio-ah.

All my relations. Greetings, brothers and sisters, star family, Groups of Forty. [Tones.] *Hey ya ho, ya ya ya.* I am the Chief White Eagle. It is with a deep heart that I am opening my energy field to you and to the Earth, so we together will find the links within our united energy fields to talk to Mother Earth. Ultimately, it is the whole Earth energy that needs to come into this new balance. Let us be clear that Earth survives whether humans survive or not. What we are talking about is that the Earth has a particular balance that is appropriate for humans and for the animal and plant. In order for humans to survive, this special balance must be maintained.

HEAR THE SPIRIT OF EARTH

The spirit of the Earth does speak to us. You all hear different examples of the spirit of Earth. The spirit of Earth responds to our prayers and chants and talking. This is part of the talking circle. This is part of what we do in our medicine wheels. This is part of what you do on the walkabout. This is part of what you do when you sit around a campfire and look at the stars, becoming aware of the position of Earth. I will say a prayer to Earth:

O, Mother Earth, Father Sky, we are gathered here today to send our love and gratitude to you, and we acknowledge you with whole conviction of your spiritual presence. We acknowledge that as a spiritual presence, Mother Earth, you hear us and we pledge to listen to you. Mother Earth, we ask you to teach us how to work with you in a better balance, even in the face of those who do not have this awareness. We know that a small group can quantumly influence Earth energies to bring an accelerated new balance into the oceans and into the planet, into Earth. We all pledge to listen to you, Mother Earth, and hear what you transmit, even though this may not be in words.

Yes, I, Chief White Eagle, hear that you love the etheric crystals that the Arcturians have placed. I hear that you love the dancing on the earth and the prayers. I hear that you love this new energy that is coming into the 2012 alignment that brings you into a special energy. I hear that you are going through electromagnetic shifts and rebalances that are extending your capabilities. I hear that you need the harmonic light that is going to be emitted from Mount Shasta. I hear, Mother Earth, that you too as a planet have an evolutionary process that is related to quantum energy. Mother Earth, that quantum energy is based on the interaction and the telepathic communication of humankind to you as a spirit. You as a spirit have links to the galaxy and to the ancient ones. This is why my grandfathers, my grandmothers—my ancient family—have stayed with you after passing. We want to be with you and we want to help you to shift your energies. Hi o ho. Hey o ho. We receive the energies of the White Buffalo now on Earth. We acknowledge the sacred path of the White Eagle. In deep gratitude, Mother Earth, I end my prayer to you.

All who hear my words, receive and visualize the White Buffalo. The White Buffalo represents the telepathic links to the evolution of Earth. The White Buffalo represents what could be called the prophetic light that has emerged from nature and speaks to us about purity and oneness. I know that White Buffalo Calf Woman is close. She is the spirit of quantum change.

She is the link to the galactic light and the galactic kachina. She is the link to a powerful evolutionary process that is so necessary at this time. It cannot be expressed in words, but it is in a symbol, the symbol of the White Buffalo, the symbol of the White Buffalo Calf Woman.

I see her walking out of the woods, the White Buffalo next to her side, and greeting all of you. [Tones.] *Hey ya ya ah ya.* I am the Chief White Eagle. *Ho!*

HOMEOSTASIS

Juliano

Greetings, I am Juliano, and we are the Arcturians. We are approaching the 2012 intersection of your planet with the galactic center. This is a period of gigantic transformation and major shifts. Looking at Earth now, you will already see major changes, polarities and upheavals occurring. You must ask yourself this question: "How much more upheaval and transformation must occur by the time of the 2012 alignment?"

Certainly we have come a long way, yet there is a major shift that still needs to occur. There is a dramatic change that will occur. I, Juliano, know that even the shifts that have happened so far have been very taxing on the starseeds—and on most people on the planet. Certainly many of you were already saying to me, "How much more change and how much more upheaval can we tolerate?" I understand that change—especially dramatic change—is extremely stressful. To look at the change as part of the evolution of a species is even more so.

We have analyzed the shifts and changes in many species throughout the galaxy. We are like anthropologists traveling throughout the galaxy and studying the different species. We do this without detection because we know, as you have learned, that observation does influence outcome. If the observation is not known to the observed, then the effect of the observation is minimized. You notice that I said "minimized," because the energy of observation is still present even though it would have what you would consider a minimal effect.

When we study civilizations in different parts of the galaxy, we always note that those who are on the forefront of evolutionary change also experience extreme amounts of stress. The cellular demand on each individual is extremely high. From your perspective, each of you is on the forefront of the evolution of humankind. Thus you receive and perceive in totally new and different ways. You are receiving higher light from the fifth dimension and processing new information. You now seek to be Earth healers and changers by using dramatic galactic techniques, such as biorelativity, shimmering and pulsing.

At the same time, I want you to understand that this expansion on your part is contributing to the evolutionary changes in humankind overall. It is also taking a toll on your physical, mental and emotional bodies. In many ways, this is extremely positive, even though many of you wanted to leave Earth several years ago. You did not want to remain on a planet that was so dense. You remember that before you came here you had volunteered to be evolutionary and planetary workers, and you have all stuck with the task.

MAJOR CHANGES ARE REQUIRED TO ACHIEVE A NEW HOMEOSTATIC LEVEL

We have been working on a high level to continue to download to you fifth-dimensional light and energy that will help each of you to modify, heal and bring yourselves into a new homeostasis. We understand the cellular biology in Earth beings. We know on a cellular level that your physical structures and bodies—for maximum input and for maximum balance—want to be in homeostasis. Homeostasis can be defined as the opposite of change. You could say from an evolutionary standpoint that there is a desire for the body to be only in homeostasis. However, from a broader perspective, homeostasis can be viewed as the body seeking a new balance. Please understand that in cellular biology, the body always remains in homeostasis. There is cellular division. There is cellular expansion. There is cellular integration. The true balance is to seek the next level of homeostasis and the next new level of balance.

I know many of you want to hold on to or stay in a certain secure level. As I have stated, this is part of the natural process of seeking balance in your being. I have to remind you that the natural process is more described in the great book of Tao, which states that all things are changing. We must work to find the new balance, the balance of yin and yang. In this time of change on the planet, this new balance is an evolutionary balance. There are periods of time in an era in which minor changes and new levels of homeostasis are achieved. There are other periods where major changes are called for. Major changes require more work to go to a newer homeostatic level.

For you to shift and change, you are required to integrate new energy. I want to emphasize this concept of new energy. Many of you have a great deal of third-dimensional energy, but it may provide the right fifth-dimensional perspective to help move you into this new level. When we look at the next several years as we are approaching the 2012 alignment, we can understand and begin to contemplate on the nature of the fifth-dimensional energy that we must integrate and receive to move to the next homeostatic level.

Quite frankly, you haven't seen anything yet. If you look at the past several years, even the year 2008, you might say, "Juliano, these have been dramatic changes, these have been polarizing changes. These have been really hard changes for me to integrate, and now I am looking around the planet and I still see all these dramatic things occurring." Then if I say to you, "You haven't seen anything yet," what does that mean? It means we are going to see more dramatic changes as we approach 2012—and we are closer to 2012. We are going to accelerate more on all levels!

What you have witnessed so far is an introduction of what is yet to come. I have to tell you that there are a great deal more changes and shifts that must occur before 2012. These changes accelerate in 2009 and 2010, 2011 and 2012. Therefore I will help you prepare and walk you through the processes of the shifts and changes that you will have to make in order to stay in the new homeostatic balance.

Increase Your Vibrancy to Receive Higher Levels of Energy

I don't want you to think that there is only going to be doom-and-gloom as we talk about these changes. I don't want you to think that these changes are inevitable. But I do want you to have a sense that you have to maintain your vibrancy and ability to be planetary and personal healers. You have to maintain more direct access to the fifth-dimensional consciousness and your fifth-dimensional self. Without this connection to your fifth-dimensional self, you will feel lost and will not be able to make the changes that are necessary in your consciousness.

You still have to operate on the third-dimensional ego consciousness and in the world of duality. It is not an option for you to be totally in your fifth-dimensional self because that would, in essence, mean that you would have left the planet. Your role and effectiveness here require that you retain a presence on the third dimension. Some of you have obligations to relatives, pets, spouses or children anyway. I know that some of you do not want to leave certain people or abandon certain work unfinished.

I feel and sense that the first wave of ascension is close and that many of you have already felt this. The downloading of fifth-dimensional consciousness is accelerating. When I tell you that you haven't seen anything yet, I am referring to Earth changes. Some of you may be concerned or even fantasize about what upheaval might happen next. Let's also apply the concept of "you haven't seen anything yet" to the fifth-dimensional energy that is coming to this planet and coming to you. You have integrated and continued to expand using fifth-dimensional energy. In terms of comparison, you are still in the fourth or fifth grade. You are now getting ready to go perhaps to the sixth or seventh grade in terms of fifth-dimensional energy.

Soon there will be a downloading of higher, more intense fifth-dimensional light and energy. You will need to receive and use this energy in order to maintain a level of sanity for yourself while on this planet. You will need to integrate this higher level of energy to maintain your level of effectiveness.

The highest goal is to participate with full consciousness in the evolution of humankind. The highest level of achievement is to fulfill your mission of working as a starseed to help humanity in this transition and also to facilitate your own transition into the fifth dimension. It is not required for you to remain until the very endpoint of this planetary process, but it is important that you participate at the highest level that you can. There will be an optimal point of time when each of you can ascend. I don't want you to think that you will be abandoning the work if you ascend, because you have contributed to the work.

CORE GROUP CONSCIOUSNESS LEVELS MUST BE MET

Let me return to one of our favorite anthropological discussions that your scientists have called the hundredth monkey effect. In the hundredth monkey effect, a group of monkeys on an island began to learn a new task. That new task had to do with washing food in a certain way so that the food would taste better. Most monkeys did not know how to do this task. One monkey, amazingly, learned how to do the task of washing the food. That monkey taught another and another and another and, eventually, a breakthrough occurred in the consciousness and the collective unconscious of the whole species of monkeys on this island. They were all able to learn this task quickly. It was almost like it became part of their genetic structure. Even when the first monkey or the second monkey who learned this task passed on, the effects of the work on the whole species still remained. They essentially had completed their mission!

This is an example for understanding your soul work on this planet. There is a certain core number of people on Earth who have to reach a particular level of consciousness, and then that level of consciousness will be transmitted to other people, which must be held. We are working very diligently to establish a certain level of meditation to ensure it will be passed on to other people.

Eventually, there is going to be a hundredth monkey effect for the change in human consciousness, although the number needed for this change is not going to be one hundred. The hundredth monkey refers to the core critical mass of starseeds that have achieved and hold a certain level of consciousness. By many people holding this consciousness, a breakthrough of fifth-dimensional consciousness and fifth-dimensional light will come to the planet. Your working together and your holding this contributes to this process.

Many of you have asked me personally and privately through this channel: "What is my soul mission?" Participating in this consciousness is one way that I can explain to you what the soul mission is. The scientists observed in the hundredth monkey effect that washing the food was more of a pleasure, not a critical incident or a critical task that the monkeys needed to learn for survival. It was kind of an amusing and intriguing activity. Certainly washing food is not a critical task to learn in order for survival. However, the tasks that must be learned by your species now are critical for the survival of the species. Energy, insights and perspectives of the fifth dimension are absolutely necessary for humankind to survive as well as for there to be a sense of stability, purpose and functioning during the next years leading up to 2012.

PULSING TECHNIQUE RELEASES BLOCKAGES

I, Juliano, am now going to work with you in the pulsing technique to help you integrate and hold fifth-dimensional energy. First, I will work with a tone or sound to bring you into a state of opening. [Tones.] *Oohhh. Tat, tat, tat tat tat.* Become aware of your energy field: It is configuring into the shape of the cosmic egg. Become aware that the edge of the cosmic egg has a dark blue line and that line is pulsing just like your own veins and arteries are pulsing. Become aware of its vibrational energy.

In ancient Chinese medicine, the diagnostic medicines and treatments for healing can be made by listening and adjusting the pulse of the person. In this pulsing technique, the cosmic egg, we can bring you to a higher level of frequency. With this opportunity, you can bring yourself to healing. In our definition of healing, this encompasses overcoming blocks in the cellular structure that, for one reason or another, are not able to go to the next level of homeostasis, and therefore you seem to be stuck.

Pulsing has the effect of vibrating those areas that are stuck within your system. This will help you to clear and release so you can go to the next higher level of fifth-dimensional energy and consciousness. You are going to need to do this because you are going to be more challenged in the coming months. Become aware of the pulse of your aura. [Tones.] *Oohhh*. Very gently contract your pulse by visualizing the outer edge of your cosmic egg coming inward, closer to you and moving to a place inside your physical body. Now contract and focus the cosmic egg into a smaller cosmic egg.

The contracted egg is now in the center of your stomach. Hold that image of the cosmic egg as an actual egg shape in the center of your stomach. That egg has a powerful fifth-dimensional, electromagnetic energy field. It is an attractive field. All stuck energies in your body that need to be released migrate into the center of this little cosmic egg in your stomach now. We will take a minute for each of you to perform this task. Take your time.

Place all the thoughts and emotions that may be associated with this blockage into the cosmic egg and all cellular blocks that might still be in your system. Now, this cosmic egg has a second, beautiful, multidimensional cosmic egg in its center. On my command, the multidimensional cosmic egg is going to push and enlarge, and it is going to expand so that the original cosmic egg in your stomach expands outward with all of these blockages. [Tones.] *Tat, tat, tat, tat*. Expand! Expand! The fifth-dimensional cosmic egg has expanded so fully that the original cosmic egg is now totally outside of your body. The new cosmic egg has filled up your whole physical body and your whole energy field. The energy from the original cosmic egg with all of its blockages has now gone to the outer edge of the pulse line. On my command, we will release that outer edge. The new cosmic egg will be fully functional. One, two, three, release!

Take a deep breath and know that your inner being is filled with this new fifth-dimensional cosmic egg light. The outer edge of your cosmic pulse is beginning to vibrate at a much higher speed now. [Tones.] *Tat, tat, tat tat tat*. Please use the following affirmation. You may phrase it in any way that you wish. I will phrase it in our terminology, and you can adjust it to fit you: "I am able to make the changes necessary within my Earth body to stay in the fifth-dimensional light." I, Juliano, bring down the omega light to emblazon those words into your unconscious and into your subconscious also. [Tones.] *Oomega lighhht.* Spend a few minutes to process the dramatic shift that we have successfully introduced into your body.

THE ROCKY ROAD TO 2012

People ask, "What more Earth changes are going to happen as we come closer to the 2012 alignment?" I hesitate to make more predictions because it could be alarming, and it could also be somewhat agitating. There are major situations in which the survival of groups or countries may come into question. There may come an acceleration of extinctions. I am not only speaking of animals or plants but also of countries and of groups. Some of these "extinctions" could be produced through Earth upheavals such as earthquakes, winds and climate shifts. This could have a very sobering effect on the whole planet when they see groups and countries who are actually on the brink of extinction.

Other countries are going to be experiencing extreme stresses affecting their physical existences too. These will be based on a multitude of issues, such as unrest due to economic and sociopolitical factors, which could result in sociological upheaval. Some countries may have additional resources that will help them subdue the upheavals, but it will still put great strain on the governments and also on the resources. This, in essence, is going to be characteristic of the time as we approach the 2012 energy, because the resource allotments seem to be more and more scarce, causing greater polarization and imbalance.

These events will occur in specific places on the planet. Some of you might say, "Well, tell me where those places are and I will not go there." I will just say that, no, that is not the way we approach this. You will be able to sense where you need to be. Many people have asked before: "Where should I go? Where should I live?" The question should not be: "Where should I go?" but "How can I maintain my fifth-dimensional consciousness where I am now?" You will be able to hold the energy. This is going to be the most important thing.

Using the technique of shimmering becomes more central in this climate of change—holding the energies of shimmering in your home, your work and even your country. We ultimately recommend shimmering Earth. In the shimmering level of Earth, we recommend using the ten etheric crystals that are in place, as they will assist you in your ability to shimmer a planet. We understand that many of you have successfully performed shimmering exercises with the planet. Many of you have also done shimmering exercises with yourself. There are different levels of shimmering on a planet. Use the etheric crystals to shimmer the deeper layers of Earth.

MOTHER EARTH IS CONTEMPLATING HER RESPONSE

I like to use the example of dinosaurs, because there is a lesson there. The dinosaurs dominated the Earth for millions of years. Their domination led to much destruction and imbalance of the Earth's ecosystems. They were overpopulated and thus overeating. Many of them even became cannibalistic. Earth responded so that a greater balance could return. Earth is, using the terms of biorelativity, aware of what is going on in a telepathic way. One level of response from Earth's standpoint was the attraction of an asteroid. You might think that an asteroid strike on Earth is a random event, but in reality, every cosmic event, including an asteroid strike, is based on the principles of electromagnetic harmonization and balance.

The Earth now is trying to choose a response to what has occurred on the surface of the planet by the beings that inhabit her, namely humankind. This is similar to what happened when the dinosaurs were here and when Earth became out of balance. You know that when the dinosaurs were out of balance, Earth began to explore how to trigger the proper response. You can see the parallels now. The Earth is struggling and reviewing choices from Inner Earth activity.

Earth is going through a process where there are many choices. Some could include earthquakes, raising ocean levels, accelerations of ice cap melting, which incidentally, has been greatly accelerated—far more than what has been predicted. You may notice that scientists predicted that it would be between the years 2040 or 2050 before such significant levels of ice melted, and yet it only took three or four years.

Examples of Earth's responses include increasing ice melt, the level of volcanic reactions and earthquakes or attracting meteors. This process emphasizes the need for more intense biorelativity communication with Earth. In a more hopeful way, we would want to see humankind making the needed changes to bring the planet more into balance so that these extreme measures are not attractive. I use the term "attractive" in a double-entendre manner. Attractive can be defined in terms of desirable and also in terms of electromagnetically attracting objects the way a magnet does. In fact, in the next three years, there is a possibility that an asteroid that is now unknown could be coming into Earth's energy field that could create some problems. This would be a dramatic outcome that could cause significant harm to the biosphere.

HELP SHIMMER EARTH INTO HOMEOSTASIS

We think the asteroid event can be avoided. How? The avoidance is in increasing the biorelativity process and helping to find ways to bring more of the remaining Earth process into alignment and balance. The Earth is experiencing—just like you are—an evolutionary process. I want to emphasize this fact: planets evolve. The Earth has tolerated many different levels of energy and many different levels of life forms. The Earth has shown herself to be a very flexible planet. Certainly Earth has been able to house thousands and millions of different species, including the many races of humankind. As a result, she has tolerated many wars and many nuclear explosions.

The Earth, like you, is seeking homeostasis to enable her to hold a new balance. This homeostasis is only possible now through the telepathic communication and relationship between humankind and the planet. Don't be angry at Earth when you see a disruption or when you see an upheaval event, even if that event causes harm, because on a higher level, Earth is also trying to find a way for homeostasis. I am not saying to ignore the harm or your feelings about it. What I am saying is that there are going to have to be some upheavals in the Earth's attempt to achieve her fifth-dimensional level, which is unfortunate.

This should not be a surprise. Many prophecies and predictions leading up to 2012 have said that there would be upheavals. The question really is, "Is humankind prepared to communicate and work with Earth in an attempt to bring her back into a balance that will work for everyone?" I see the work of the etheric crystals as a vital link in this process.

The etheric crystals are able to create an energetic path of light between them to energize and transform the surface and the spirit of Earth into a fifth-dimensional level. This is another way of saying that we are helping you work with Earth to bring her into the fifth-dimensional self and to hold fifth-dimensional light. Also, you on a personal level are seeking to hold fifth-dimensional light and a higher homeostasis. Just as you have understood that you must go through change, so must Earth—in a very short time. In your terms, this is the greatest "challenge." You may think that your species is 200,000 years old; however, Earth may be as old as 4.5 billion years. Yet from her standpoint, you want her to make this change in an extremely brief nanosecond. It requires a huge shift for the planet to go into the fifth-dimensional time zone.

We have downloaded the Copper Canyon crystal to shimmer with the moon-planet Alano. When you are in the presence of a higher being, you feel that being's vibration and you also start to vibrate at a higher level. In the same way, when Earth feels the presence of a shimmering planet like Alano, she begins to vibrate at a higher fifth-dimensional level. The solutions become fifth dimensional and more integrative—Earth changes. These changes can be mitigated into a greater harmony with the needs of humankind. Shimmer Earth with the moon-planet Alano. [Tones.] *Shimmmerrr.* I am Juliano. We are the Arcturians. Good day.

CELLULAR MEMORY

Juliano, the Arcturians, Metatron and Chief White Eagle

G reetings, I am Juliano. We are the Arcturians. We want to look at the perspective of cellular memory. Cellular memory transcends lifetimes. Cellular memory even transcends different eras and is carried with you from many ancient times. The cellular memories that you have from your childhood are still dramatically affecting you. Many have looked at reincarnation as the great clearing. It is the belief by many that when you die and go into the intermediary realms, it is from that position you are able to be reborn. The belief is that there is a cleansing of the cellular memory, and therefore you come back into this lifetime with a clean slate.

From the Arcturian perspective and from our studies of your cellular biology and evolution, we have noted that when there is a reincarnation, it does not necessarily mean that there is a total clearing. It does mean that all cellular memory is erased. We have noted that when we look at other galactic civilizations, we have found that mistakes are often repeated. We have noted that some civilizations on some planets, despite the best intentions of many of their higher beings, seem to repeat patterns that end in their destruction. There was even a psychologist in Europe who postulated the idea of repetition compulsion, which states in a very simplified way that people tend to repeat earlier incidents based on their memories of them.

The cellular memory actually transcends a lifetime, and what you are bringing into this lifetime is often based on what happened in a previous lifetime. That could be a positive thing, though it could often be a negative thing. Some of you have very high talents from previous lifetimes. You may now have penchants for the understanding of languages or music, probably brought with you to this lifetime. Those cellular memories are now enabling you to access and work with those traits.

That certainly seems to be very positive. On the other hand, you know that there have been particular problems in this lifetime that each of you has faced. Some of those problems are health problems, some are relationship problems, some are even financial and career problems. It has often been the case that those cellular memories from previous lifetimes have been reloaded into your mind and into your genetic codes. The energies in this lifetime will bring you into situations that are in correspondence or in resonance with your cellular memories. These renewed situations—coming from the resonance of your previous lifetime cellular memories—occur for a specific purpose. This specific purpose has to do in part with your evolution and in part also with your need to complete certain lessons. Cellular memory does seem to have some logic when we are speaking of it in terms of reincarnation. When we look at a planet, we can also say that cellular memory is operating on a planetary basis.

When we look at cellular memory, and the millions and even billions of souls that are now incarnated on this planet, then we can also say that cellular memory is playing a major role in some of these conflicts, tragedies and upheavals that you are seeing. Cellular memory plays an important role in cosmic justice, or what I would prefer to call "cosmic memory." "Cosmic justice" is a term that has been used to describe the rectification of events from other lifetimes or even from other planetary systems. It is an attempt to describe karma on a cosmic basis. It is a term that describes karma in a way that takes into consideration people's energies and experiences from other planetary systems and from other galaxies. We, the Arcturians, believe that the concept of cosmic justice is a useful tool.

COSMIC JUSTICE AND COSMIC MEMORY

In our discussion of cellular memory, we also want to introduce the concept of cosmic memory. Cosmic memory is a more encompassing concept, and it is related specifically to cellular memory. Cosmic memory states that the energies and events that people are attracted to are related to their previous experiences and are locked into their cellular structure; therefore, these people are attracting or bringing that energy together. This can become complicated when you are looking at a planet like Earth that has six or seven billion people. If you consider that many of those people who now inhabit the planet are bringing in cosmic memories from many parts of this galaxy and many lifetimes from other planets, you would be overwhelmed in trying to understand everything that is occurring now on

Earth. I know that each of you is overwhelmed in trying to understand the events on Earth now. I know that each of you seeks answers to understand the many complicated events that are occurring as we speak. These Earth events may seem without logic and without reason, yet they do have an energy relating to cosmic memory.

The evolution of a planet has to take into consideration the cellular cosmic memories of its inhabitants. The concept of cosmic memory relates to the fact that these memories influence DNA. There are extraplanetary influences on the Adam species. I am referring to other civilizations that are from extraterrestrial sources and other beings, such as those called the "Gray beings." I am referring to the Orion people from that planetary star system known as Sirius and to influences from earlier conflicts on stars distant from Earth where civilizations inhabited remote star systems. I am referring to the fact that there have been star civilizations in existence for centuries and millennia before you even appeared on Earth.

These star systems and planetary systems went through many advanced stages technologically and spiritually. They also went through some disastrous and catastrophic energies. Those energies and conflicts from those earlier star systems in some cases led to severe destruction of a planetary system. I know that some of you have cellular memories of these catastrophes. The energies and memories from these civilizations—which occurred millions of years earlier—are embedded in the cosmic memory of many people on Earth. Why is there such diversity of beings on this planet who have different religious views or beings who have different perspectives? Earth is a freewill zone, and because of that energy of free will, many people and species have been attracted to come to the Earth for rectification of certain cellular cosmic issues. Earth now is re-creating or has re-created a situation that is similar to earlier planets that were in a state of evolution comparable to what is now occurring on Earth. Earlier planetary civilizations have reached this point before. This point can also be called the point of evolution, and it has also been referred to as the point of catastrophe. Other terms used to describe this current situation are the "point of enhancement," the "point of transcendence" or the "point of implosion."

CLEANSING WITH EACH INCARNATION

Become aware of your own cosmic memories. Expand this idea of cosmic memory to include cosmic justice and cosmic karma. Use this perspective to understand what is going on now on Earth. What appears so confusing on the Earth now is actually a reenactment of earlier dramas that have occurred on other planets. You, as starseeds, also have that cosmic memory of these events and thus are attracted to Earth at this time. Some of the starseeds are returning to observe this cosmic drama again. The cosmic drama that is unfolding can only exist in a certain environment, and that is the freewill environment. That environment also has to do with the energies of ascension and of 2012. There is this tremendous spiritual freedom and energy that is also paralleling the cosmic drama that you are seeing played out on Earth.

I want to now introduce this new concept called cellular cleansing. There is a particular German word that can be used for this cellular cleansing: *reinigung*. This is a beautiful descriptive word that includes the concept of cleansing and clearing at the same time. In the Arcturian spiritual system, we look for this cleansing, or this *reinigung*, in several different ways. The first is the way that I described earlier. A cleansing and a clearing can include memories and traumas from earlier reincarnations. We also know that a clearing and a cleansing happens as you are reborn. However, when you are reborn, everything may be lost in your conscious memory, but the imprints of previous events from past lives still remain deep in your DNA memories. Your energy and knowledge and mistakes from those past times remain as imprints. All of the previous events, including the wisdom and the mistakes and the folly, were also erased from your memory. You may not come back into the incarnation with the benefit from that experience. You may come back with the energy and the resonance to attract yourself to a similar situation so that you can reenact it, so that you can replay the drama in a way that is going to lead to a resolution and a transcendence of any unlearned lessons and dramas.

There are pitfalls in trying to learn lessons during your incarnational cycle. Some of those pitfalls have to do with the concept I mentioned to you called repetition compulsion. In the theory of cellular memory, you tend to attract those situations that were important to your soul development whether they are positive or negative from your perspective. Also, there is a tendency to repeat them until you learn the lesson from that experience. You need to repeat experiences so that you can choose correctly that which enables you to transcend and move on to other places that contribute to your soul evolution.

These principles also work on the planetary level. People can return to a planet and come together on a planetary level in order to bring forth new energy and newer choices. The choice now on Earth can be transcendence of polarization versus catastrophic implosion due to an inability to resolve polarities. Having those choices then offers the opportunity for the possibility of evolution. We know that in describing the term repetition compulsion, the word "compulsion" in the English language has a strong connotation.

Compulsion has to imply—according to our review of the channel's memory cells in language—force. One is compelled to do something if there is a compulsion. Cellular memory can come through with a compulsion for repetition compulsion. That is a pretty strong force. That force will require huge effort to overcome.

SHIELD POSITIVE MEMORIES

We always look for new spiritual technology, and one of our missions is to provide and access new spiritual energy. We have studied the entire situation we described, and now we understand that you can have a cellular memory clearing while you are still in an incarnation. In fact, to uplift and maintain your spirituality to the highest level, especially in these times of cosmic unfolding and cosmic manifestation of karma, the ability to work on a cellular level and do the cleansing while you are in this incarnation becomes paramount. It becomes necessary. Let me review this again. The memory cleansing or clearing can occur in this incarnation. That means that you can have the complete removal of your own memory compulsions, the complete removal of your earlier memory programs and also the memory programs from other planetary systems or other situations and other incarnations. However, this must take into consideration a very important fact—namely, there are also many positive memories. I'll use the example of languages. You do not necessarily want to remove your memories of other languages that you had or the talents that you had as healers from other lifetimes. But maybe you would like to remove the cellular memories of illness and their manifestations.

Maybe you would like to remove the cellular memories of overattachment to the cosmic drama on the planet. Maybe you would like to remove the cellular memories of violent energies that you might be carrying with you, which also might include your wish to see the destruction of certain people who are harming the planet. Maybe you would wish to remove the memories of your time in Atlantis, where some of you might have been contributing to the energy of high technological weaponry. If that was the case for you, you believed at the time that the high technological weaponry was the way to balance the planet against the polarized energies within it. Now you see that building weaponry was not the way to do it. These are examples of memories you would like to cleanse, but you would like to cleanse them with the knowledge and awareness of consciousness in this incarnation.

You also want to preserve the positive part. This is the same method as self-protection. For example, many of you are familiar with the white light technique where you place a white band of light around your aura. We have talked about using the white band of light around you. That band of light allows positive light and energy in. Anyone that has negative thoughts or negative energy toward you will not be able to penetrate that wall of light. As in the placement of other shields, you want that shield to have a certain permeability. That permeability means that the shield would allow light, Christ love, higher Kaballistic energy, energy from 2012, the Arcturians and other angelic beings to come through. On the other hand, you would not want the energy of discarnate spirits who are of lower vibration to pass through that.

In the clearing of cellular memory, you want a similar type of shielding to be in place. That shielding would protect and allow the positive memories to come through, but not the negative memories. Remember, we are talking about memories from other lifetimes as well, which are of a lower vibration, have a certain compulsion for repetition and a certain power within your system for programming these events. Those would be cleared. That would give you a fresh start. That would give you a fresh perspective and would enable you to be in a far more powerful position mentally, physically, emotionally and spiritually on this planet. In some ways this clearing would be a true spiritual cleansing, a spiritual healing that would allow you to be free of these lower programs and memories that still could be affecting and influencing you.

Participate in Your Clearing

Bring yourself to the highest vibrational energy now, as we embark on cleansing and clearing. Bring yourself to your highest light frequency and blend and bond with all who are participating now in this exercise so that you will gain an upliftment energetically in your vibratory light. You will now be able to participate to the fullest extent possible in this exercise.

Feel a blue corridor of light above each of you. This blue corridor of light is connecting you and your energy to the fifth dimension. Your spirit body is lifting out of your physical body and lifting out from the crown chakra. As your spirit body, which we also will refer to as the "spirit astral body," is lifting out of your body, it will carry the imprints and memories in your emotional, physical and mental body. All of those memories and all of those imprints are now coming with your spirit astral body. Even those memories that may not be in your awareness now are still being called on to come into this journey. Your spirit astral self rises out of your physical body and follows the blue corridor of light. You travel through the blue corridor of light to the starship Athena. As you connect with the starship Athena, you enter our huge healing room. In the healing room, there are holographic healing chambers. You may enter your own personal chamber that we have set aside and programmed for you. Each chamber has an appearance somewhat like a telephone booth. It has a comfortable chair and a computer screen and other advanced spiritual technologies there. Enter your own holographic booth.

Become aware of all of the cellular memories that are in your four bodies. You can energetically project these memories into our holographic computer and on to the holographic computer screen. These are cellular memories, so they are directed by your thought projection and your commands. As they are projected on to the screen, notice that many memories and images are simultaneously, or in nanoseconds, going through the screen. You look at them with intense interest. You process them with lightning-like speed. Take a moment to allow this fantastic energetic light from your cellular memories to pass through the screen. Some of these images are from other planetary systems. Some of these images are from other lifetimes that you may not even remember participating in. You are, for the most part, old souls.

Rest assured that all of these memories are now in the computer, and I, Juliano, am bringing down a beautiful light, a cleansing energy, into your crown chakra. This cleansing energy in your crown chakra is tied into all of your cellular memories that you have projected on to the screen. The older negative patterns, the compulsions that lead to lower vibrations and lower energies, can now be cleaned and cleansed. I want to explain this. It does not mean that they are removed or forgotten— rather, the compulsion energy to repeat them in any way is now neutralized. The energy of wisdom and transcendence that would come from that memory is enhanced and integrated with this light that I send down to you now as you sit in your holographic chamber.

You have all received and integrated this energy of cleansing and your memories. The cosmic ones that are of a lower vibration are neutralized and cleansed. Now, as you look at the screen, only those higher images, those higher vibrations and those transcendent energies, now come to the forefront. Perhaps some of you who are knowledgeable with computers know of the energy called "defragmentation," where the computer attempts to put together certain files and certain patterns. This defragmentation image would be one possible image that you could use now to understand that all the positive images, all the positive memories, all the positive experiences are now "defragged" and placed together into this beautiful pattern of light.

The other ones that are of lower vibration and have some compulsion for repetition are now moved into another section of the screen that doesn't have any power. This allows you to be in the highest vibrational state. If there were a necessity for you to recall those memories, you can still do that. There is no need at this point to do that, because you have gathered all of the knowledge, all of the higher perspective, from these previous events. Now your whole computer screen is filled with these positive memories. Hold that vision now.

A Step Closer to Higher Evolution

Now you have integrated and balanced all of this beautiful energy from the cleansing, and you have done it while you are still in this incarnation! This brings you a step closer to a higher evolution through what we have called the *reinigung*, the cleansing. Prepare to step out of the holographic chamber. As you step out, you feel the light and energy of our healing chamber from our fifth-dimensional ship Athena. You will take with you this memory of being in the fifth-dimensional spaceship. You will take with you this energy of being in the healing chambers.

Follow me as we leave the starship. Come down through the corridor, following the blue light. Then travel through a corridor back to Earth and come to a place above your body. You are about twenty feet above your body. We will do a realignment, a recalibration, so that you will come into your physical body in the correct perfected alignment. Remember, as you come in, all of the higher energies and higher memories are now coming back, giving you new healing energies, new healing abilities for yourself and others. You have a greater perspective and also greater protection. Do a perfect alignment now into your physical body and then rebalance and download and come back into your physical body now. It will take several days for all of this energy, through spiritual osmosis, to go through your system and upgrade everything. In cellular memory, the higher vibration transcends the lower vibration. All of the memories in your structures are now being updated from the beautiful work we have done in the holographic healing chamber.

In working with cosmic justice and cosmic memory, we could make the argument that you are returning to complete your positive karma for your ascension. There are peculiar circumstances in this ascension energy. First, there is the energy of potential catastrophic implosion of a planet. Yet at the same time, there is also the doorway to ascension. You are planetary healers as well. The exercise that we just did for your personal benefit can also be used to cleanse the planet and the planetary memory. Planetary cleansing is more complicated because there are so many different sources and so many different energies intermingling on the Earth.

You have heard before that there has been DNA tampering from other extraterrestrial beings that came to Earth. This tampering created impurities. Your DNA has energies from other planetary systems. This tampering helps us understand why there is so much upheaval on the Earth now. Earth is in a tremendous upheaval on all levels. Earth life would be a lot simpler if there was just the energy of the one Adam species and the original programming was not tampered with. To deal with just that one system would actually be relatively easy compared with the complexities that are now facing this planet. Earth now has multiple influences that are often contradictory and polarized. They can be harmonized, they can be transcended, but the effort and the energy needed to overcome polarizations requires quite an effort. I will turn the next part of this lecture over to Metatron. I am your beloved friend and teacher, Juliano.

Greetings, I am Archangel Metatron. You know that the DNA is a sacred code. You know that the codes of ascension contain sacred codes. When you are working with cellular memory and energies and you are uplifting them and reconfiguring them for higher light, then it must be approached from an attitude of sacredness and holiness. You have done some powerful shifting, and I want to help you now to create the energy field of the sacredness so that you can hold this. You can shift the DNA and the code. Cellular memory has to do with DNA codes because cellular memory is also part of a program. Anytime you look at or shift a program, then you want to approach this task with the highest light, the highest vibration. You want it to be surrounded with the right holiness.

I, Archangel Metatron, am now going to bring in that light of holiness to each of you through these sacred sounds. [Tones.] *Kadosh, kadosh, kadosh, Adonai Tzevaoth*. Repeat them twice more. Let the light of *Kadosh*, the holy light, fill your cells. Let the memories that are of the higher light, the holy light, fill you now, the *Aur Hakadosh*. Let the holy light stand in your presence and let the holy light be projected from your present self to your future self on Earth so that you will walk in the holy light and you will be able to send holy light to the planet. Each of the ten etheric crystals downloaded into Earth are now being filled with the energy of this holy light. This is a download of the holy light energy, an aspect of the golden harmonic balls of light. But now this is of the sacred holy light so that the sacred holy light and the awareness of that light becomes part of the activation of your cellular memories and of the cellular memories of the planet. The planetary energy is now being filled through these etheric crystals with holy light. Pure light, pure energy, cleanses and purifies the cosmic and the cellular memories. Blessed is the Holy One, and may each of you be blessed. You are beings of holy light. I await you on the fifth dimension. I am Archangel Metatron. Kadosh, kadosh, kadosh, holy, holy, holy. Shalom.

Greetings, I am Chief White Eagle. [Tones.] *Hey ya ho ya hey!* All my words are sacred, my brothers and sisters! We bind our light and love together. Know that it is time to bring out your sacred shields. It is time to bring out the energy of the shields that we have talked about many times. Do not neglect your etheric shields. Do not neglect bringing out your powerful shields some of you made in the past. Shields are a necessary part of the shaman and of working on the third dimension in spiritual transformation. They are a necessary tool in cleansings and in protecting you from the many different negative energies that are erupting on this planet now.

If you do not have a shield in your mind, then visualize a new shield. If you can't, then find someone who could help you make a shield or draw a shield. If you already have a shield, visualize it now in front of your physical aura here on the third dimension, and let it be reinvigorated.

Let that shield stand as a guardian of you as a lightbeing at this sacred time, at this sacred place. One must have a shield in place. It is just part of your expansion.

Yes, you can have many different shields. You do not have to use the same shield each time. Some of you as spirit workers are also shamans. Shamans use different shields and have many different ideas of shields. Use the image of the shield that sings with your heart and that you know is right for you. When you are in resonance with your spirit shield, then you are impenetrable to lower vibration, to lower energy. Even the lowest of the spirits cannot touch and go through the shield. I, Chief White Eagle, at this moment, activate and empower each of your shields now so when you pick them up, you will feel a new sense of protection and spiritual resonance. *Ho!* I am Chief White Eagle.

ASCENSION: AN UPDATE

Juliano, the Arcturians and Metatron

Greetings, I am Juliano. We are the Arcturians. The ascension and the energy of the ascension are flooding the energy field of Earth now. There has been a new and powerful influx of ascension energy during the past two to three weeks. This influx of energy has had a dramatic effect on the starseeds and it has also created huge perceptual openings. By perceptual openings, I mean that many of you are able to see and experience higher realities, higher energy fields, and also you have experienced an increase in your sensitivity.

At this point, I would like to offer further insights about the ascension and also information about the spiritual technology of ascension. I am aware that many people have described the ascension in different ways. For example, some people have said that the ascension is actually in place; therefore, you will ascend within your Earth body but stay on the Earth. This is one interpretation of ascension. Ascending and staying in place on Earth is not our interpretation; in fact, we believe that many of you also have a different expectation of the ascension. The expectation that you have of actually leaving Earth is in alignment with our original teachings. That expectation is that in ascension, you will raise your frequency. Your vibration then will move to such a high point that you will disappear from this realm and reappear in the fifth dimension. We still maintain that this event, like I have just described, will occur. Yet there remains the expectation, as I have said, that the ascension will be an upliftment in place while you remain in your Earth body on Earth.

I want to just digress for a second and explain about some of the ideas of resurrection, which is actually a galactic term. That term was downloaded into the energy of the prophets that have walked this planet in the past 3,500 years. The idea of the resurrection, the way it originally was explained to the masses, was that your body in death would still remain in the death state for a period of time. After a period of time, through a miraculous energetic intervention, that body would reform itself and then transmute into the higher realms. This experience was defined as being resurrected. In this concept of resurrection, one must first reach the death state. When experiencing the death state, one would then be able to be resurrected or re-formed in a higher fifth-dimensional body in the fifth dimension.

This idea actually fits in with the spiritual technology of the Arcturians. It is a known galactic truth that the resurrection does occur on a regular basis. From our perspective, we would ask this: If the resurrection can occur when the body is no longer alive, then wouldn't it be logical to conclude that resurrection could also occur while the person is alive? Why is it necessary for the person to go through the death state in order to be resurrected? In your ancient Greek and Hebrew, the translation of resurrection means "to restore the dead." Within the confines of the word "resurrection" comes this concept that the dead are restored or brought back to life. Our contention and our understanding of galactic spiritual energy has shown and taught us that it is not necessary to go through the death state in order to be restored. Rather, you can experience resurrection directly from a high state of consciousness in the third dimension while alive to a state into the fifth dimension. In fact, Enoch and the prophet Elijah both ascended, or if you could use the term, they were "resurrected." Their state of being was in the alive state when their resurrection happened. They were not in the dead state. The whole idea of the modern ascension is based on this idea and technique of resurrecting yourself or restoring yourself to a higher plane while you are still alive.

Resurrecting while you are alive offers several advantages. The primary advantage is: you do not have to die in the physical. When you die in the physical, naturally there are complicated events that occur, which in some cases close the perceptual field and close the knowledge field of the person. Of course, those fields can be reopened. However, the dying experience can be compared to going into a tunnel. If any of you have experienced driving through a tunnel under a mountain, then you know there is a period in the tunnel where there is total darkness. In that period in the tunnel, even though you know you are going forward and you know you will come out on the other side, there is still a moment of questioning, and there is a moment, sometimes, of fear about what is happening to you.

BEYOND THE THIRD DIMENSION

In the ascension, and perhaps we can call it the "live ascension," there is no feeling of detached energy from the process. You are directing yourself. Part of the preparation for the ascension is to develop the awareness of your fifth-dimensional self. We want everyone to remember that you are multidimensional beings, which means that you are living in two dimensions at the same time. You do have a presence in the fifth dimension. It is the awareness of that presence and the visitation to that presence that enhances your ability to ascend. You know and you have a focus on where you are going to be. Focusing on projecting yourself is the biggest problem in understanding the ascension and performing the ascension. That problem is: Where are you going to place yourself in the fifth dimension? Where is your other level of consciousness going to be? There are so many loopholes, so many places in the astral realm and the fourth-dimensional realm where you can become stuck.

People have asked me over the years, "Why are we skipping the fourth dimension, Juliano?" Remember that the fourth dimension has stages and levels in it, including the lower, the middle and the higher fourth dimension. These are simple ways of describing the levels. The higher fourth-dimensional astral realm is beautiful. The lower astral realm is filled with ghosts and spirits and is more closely described as *gehenna* [the Biblical Hebrew word for hell]. You can use the word "hell." Hell is on the lower astral realm and is a dark place where you seem to be punished or get stuck in a chain of events that are repetitious. It also makes it seem like you are unable to escape from this place. In many cases, you are repeating a continual unpleasant event. For example, you could be experiencing a violent act and repeating it over and over again. Eventually you can be freed from that. Nothing is eternal on the lower astral realm, even though the experience might seem like it will last forever.

In the lower astral realm, the spirit energy is still more closely attached to the third dimension. Lower astral beings suck energies from Earth beings in order to increase their energy fields. Lower astral beings are in a vibrational situation where the only way of maintaining or seeming to escape from their experience would be to raise their energy field through a parasitic attachment to an Earth being. There are spirits on the third-dimensional plane that are of the lower vibrational energy. These lower beings have attached to people and contributed to them doing some pretty awful things. We give, as an example, the school shootings. Students might have been on drugs and their energy fields were on a lower vibrational field. Ghosts or discarnate spirits can attach themselves to those students and actually direct them to do horrendous things. All this is a way of explaining that the fourth dimension has lower layers, and you do not want to stay in those lower layers.

The middle astral layer, on the other hand, is a higher energy and there are some very high beings there. Finally, the higher fourth-dimensional realm is getting close to the fifth dimension and closer to the Garden of Eden concepts, and closer to the heavenly gates and heavenly palaces. It is beautiful there. Certainly, many of you have visited the higher fourth-dimensional realms. There are many guides and teachers there. Incidentally, guides and teachers can go into any part of the astral realms, including the middle, lower or higher levels. The bottom line is this: When you are in the astral realm after you die, you are still in the Earth's incarnation cycle, which means that you will be reborn again in the third dimension. You will be reborn into another Earth body. In certain situations, you can be reborn in an appropriate energy field on another planet. By staying in the fourth-dimensional realms after you die, you will remain in a third-dimensional incarnation process.

The ascension is teaching you and offering you the opportunity to be free of Earth's incarnation process and to go to a higher realm. This is a process of grace because it takes a higher energy vibration, energy awareness and higher perceptual field awareness to graduate from Earth. Many of you are not able to reach that higher perceptual field in this lifetime without some assistance. At the same time, I can tell you that there is so much assistance now available to help you raise your vibrations. Part of the assistance is coming from the energy transformation of the ascension itself. The energy of the ascension brings forth new light, new frequencies and new opportunities. For example, imagine you saw an eclipse of the Sun without knowing much about astronomy. After seeing that eclipse, you might begin to understand the nature of the relationship among heavenly bodies. You might even be able to figure out that one body is going in front of the other, blocking the light of the Sun. Without seeing that eclipse, you might not be able to understand that one heavenly body can move in front of another. This is the way it is with the ascension. That is, there are events, there are circumstances and there are energy patterns occurring that are going to offer you new insight into the ascension process.

POWERS OF PERCEPTION AND THE ASCENSION

I want to talk about light and I want to talk about light perception, as we are going into the concepts of the ascension. The idea of light is so complex and so beautiful. In the darkness of the night emerges the energy of the morning. When the light comes in the morning, then you are able to see what is in existence on the planet. If there is total darkness, you cannot see the shapes of the trees, you cannot see the shapes of the buildings nor can you see the animals, unless, of course, you had high-vision glasses. In the total darkness, you do not see anything. Morning comes and lights up the forest so you can see the trees. Then you can see how beautiful everything is and you can see the third dimension.

Your eyes have certain rods and cones in them that enable you to see certain light fields. Now imagine that the light gets brighter and brighter. Say, for example, you are looking at the sunlight without any type of glasses and the sunlight becomes very bright. Now all you see is light, but you can't see any objects because the light is so bright. You cannot make out anything, and you are literally blinded by the light. Too much light isn't good. In the fifth dimension, and in the higher perception, the light is getting stronger and stronger. In your normal perceptions in which you are trained on Earth, you can become blinded by the light; therefore, you will not see the higher realms.

What I am saying is that you can shape, you can train, you can unlock the codes of ascension that help you to unlock the perceptual field. When there is an increasing amount of light, your rods and cones and your mental framework will adjust to be able to see the next realm and to see and experience the higher energy. Perceiving the higher realms is not just seeing, it is feeling. It is being able to see higher experience from multiperceptual levels. You have five basic patterns of perception and you tend to think of them as individual abilities that do not interact with each other. Seeing and hearing could be one combination that is an example of two perceptual fields interacting. Feeling and seeing might be another combination. In the concept of the technology of the ascension, an increase in the light will also be experienced as an increase in your perceptual field and your perceptual powers so that you will not be blinded by the light. You will be able to see with higher light into the fifth dimension.

I want you to consider this: If we turned up the light frequency on the planet where you are, you would begin to see that people's bodies are really luminous balls of light. The physical form that you see now in the third-dimensional reality is an assumed body that represents many energy aspects of the person, including past lives, illnesses, densities and the effects of experiences in the third-dimensional life. You would be able to see the true energetic pattern of the person you see. If you were able to experience higher light and then have a corresponding opening in your perceptual field, you would be able to experience people as energetic luminous balls of light. The energy patterns that make up your third-dimensional body are at such a high frequency that your normal perceptual ranges and training don't allow you to see all levels of your luminous body. In fact, if you did see the luminous energy balls now, you could become confused and you wouldn't know what to make of them. Maybe now you would better understand the luminous energy patterns.

Increasing the light is an interesting discussion, because in the ascension, only some people are going to have the ability to participate fully in the increase in light. There is an increase in light that is coming to the planet. The light frequencies already have increased dramatically in the past three weeks. Only certain people are going to be able to open their perceptual fields to use that light in order to see the higher realms. When you see the higher perception, including the higher light, then you will also see the connection that you and other beings of light have to the fifth dimension. We call these connections "etheric cords" or "strands of light." These etheric cords are on everyone. However, some people's etheric cords or strands only go into the third dimension. Your etheric strands of light are connected to the fifth dimension now because you have been working with us. With the connection of the etheric strands of light, during the ascension you will be able to project and have your luminous body move to where those etheric cords are attached, namely the fifth dimension.

When you move the etheric body, the luminous body follows it. I make a distinction between the luminous body and the etheric body. The physical body is an energy field. Visualize the image of a table. You can learn from physics that the table really isn't solid. The table is made of energetic molecules that spin around each other at the speed of light and are composed of neutrons, protons and quarks and so on. If you put your hand on that table, your hand stops because you experience the table as solid. If you are in a higher perceptual field, then you can see the table as an energetic field. Then as you experience that state of higher consciousness, you actually could put your hand through the table. This is what people like Sai Baba and others can do. They are able to reach through the third-dimensional reality because they are also in this other realm. With both awareness states, that is, an awareness of this realm and the higher realms, you can do what you would consider to be tricks, bringing objects into the third dimension.

ASCENSION IS BEFORE YOU

The luminous body is the key to the ascension because the physical body follows the luminous body. Ultimately, all of the strands go all the way back to the Creator. There could be thousands of luminous strands of light on one luminous body. The true prophets and the great spiritual leaders have enhanced and strengthened their luminous strands back to the Creator. The luminous strands of the prophets connect back to guides and teachers. You have luminous strands of light now connected to the Arcturian Temple, to the crystal temple and to other parts of the fifth dimension. You, who are Arcturian starseeds, came to Earth in your luminous balls of light with many starseed luminous strands. I am going to give you some energetic tones to help you integrate everything I have said. Tones can raise your perceptual field and can put you into the place of what I am talking about on an experiential level.

Unlocking the codes of ascension also means that you open the doors of perception in your mind and in your body. You may think, "Well, where is the fifth dimension?" It is true that each dimension is like a sphere, a huge ball or sphere, and that they interact with each other. When you are in the fifth dimension, the concepts of space and time are totally indiscernible. In the fifth dimension, there is no space between things, and yet you cannot, in your third-dimensional mind, understand how objects can exist without space. How can there be no space or separation of objects between people? Yet not everyone is together on the fifth dimension. You can be with the people you want to be with just by thinking about them. This is certainly a paradox.

With this higher ascension energy, more light has come down to Earth now. Opening the doors of ascension can unlock the codes of ascension. You can see and experience the fifth dimension right before your eyes. It will be like a bright light is turned on. Instead of just seeing a blinding light, you will see gardens, and the intense loving light and loving space of the fifth dimension will be before you. Then you will walk across the bridge and that will bring you into the fifth dimension. You have ascended! That is how simple the ascension can be. Think of the dream world. In a dream, a symbolic event or a symbolic action will be offered to demonstrate a transition. I described this higher light and the effects of this higher light. You will use this light to see what is before you in the fifth-dimensional realm. Then when the bridge is offered to be crossed, you will choose to cross it. The bridge will be the symbol for crossing dimensions. That will be your ascension. [Tones.]

I want to also explain that the bridge and that experience is still available to those who died as well. It is not like you are penalized for dying. Yes, it would be preferable to ascend from life, but remember, the first lesson of ascension that was offered by Sananda/Jesus was resurrection of the dead. You can create the awareness of being able to carry this ascension energy with you into your death. You might even be able to ascend immediately after your death. If your Earth karma is such that you are not able to sustain your physical life until the ascension, do not worry, because you will still be able to ascend. I love the teachings of Jesus and I love the teachings of resurrection. Keep on working on the codes of ascension. This assures you of your ascension. I will now turn things over to Archangel Metatron. This is Juliano.

Greetings, I am Archangel Metatron. Unlocking the codes of ascension is one of the most powerful lessons on the third dimension. You would consider coming back to any lifetime where you saw the opportunity to unlock the codes of ascension. These codes of ascension are in your DNA and in certain parts of your brain. You have heard the figure that you only use 20 percent, maybe 22 percent of your brain in a lifetime. The rest cannot be awakened unless there is proper preparation and the proper circuitry established to hold higher vibrational frequency. This is saying that the vibrational frequency of ascension is higher than normal energy. Remember that Juliano described the light as being blinding if you are not able to open yourself up. No one wants to be blinded.

Certain higher energies with exercises were given to the mystics. One of the energies that was given was the energy of the merkavah. The merkavah means the "chariot," and the chariot is the etheric encapsulated chair that served as a protective device to bring you into a higher realm. It can bring you to a higher light so that you are protected; therefore, you will not be blinded in higher energy. You can think of the merkavah as the gigantic chariot covered in a dome of beautiful glass that has special connections and special filters so that you would be able to see where the merkavah vehicle is taking you.

I, Archangel Metatron, am going to call on the energies and light of the merkavah to work with all of you at this point. Some of you had lifetimes in ancient Egypt, and you will recognize this word, "merkavah," also spelled merkava. Mer, Ka—you remember the Ka, the energy in ancient Egypt— and va or Vah. This is an ancient energy that was transformed and transmitted: merkavah light! Visualize your divine chariot before you. Step into your merkavah chariot. As you step into the merkavah chariot, you sense there is a glass dome and you reach behind you and close the dome so that it is totally encapsulating the chariot that is going to transport you. [Sings.] *Merkavah.*

I, Archangel Metatron, ask you to close your eyes, and as you close your eyes, you are transported. You are being transported even though you feel no movement. This is the technology of merkavah. As you open your eyes, you are in a divine garden known as *Gan Eden*, the Garden of Eden, a fifth-dimensional paradise. It has beautiful light. It is primordial light. It has the light of Adam Kadmon, the light that Adam saw. It is the first light. This light was the very first light in the Garden of Eden. You open up the top of the merkavah chariot and you see this light. It is a combination of morning light, mist and multicolored light—a multidimensional light that you have never seen on the Earth. You walk into this garden and you can see and feel and hear this light. This is holy light! You see divine beings in the garden that are in this light, walking with this light. Within you is awakened your ascension light and ascension energy. Holy light, light of the merkavah garden. Blessings in the light.

In this garden, you feel how vast it is, yet you do not feel like there is any space. In this garden, you can be with whomever you want and you can chose who you want to be with. In this garden, you feel one with the energy of the garden. You feel one with the energy of Adam and the first light. *Aur Ha'Rishon*, the first light that was made. You can see that first light. With that light, you can see anywhere in the universe.

Now, it is time to return to your merkavah chariot. You take one step forward and you are in the chariot. You pull the glass cover over it and then you are filled with the divine light. You close your eyes and return to the starting point on Earth. You open your eyes and go back into your room. You lift the glass cover and you are back in your physical body.

The energy, frequencies and healing are all with you as you step into your physical body. Because you are able to understand and conceive of the first light, you are able to use the energy of ascension and the light of ascension for your own ascension.

The energy of the first light is unlike any light that you know of on Earth. Remember that the first words from the Creator were, "Let there be Light." You understand light in one confined way, a beautiful way. But light is the source of all creation, and light can be the gateway into the perceptual fields. Light can create things. Your concept of light needs to be expanded so that it is not just a visual experience of light but also a visceral experience. Light is a feeling experience. Light encompasses everything because All That Is is in light. Light. Light.

Let the codes of ascension for all of the starseeds who hear or read these words be opened so that they understand the true use and meaning of light, and they can use light for their ascensions. I am Archangel Metatron, in the light. Blessings.

MEDITATION AND ASCENSION

Juliano, the Arcturians, and Archangel Michael

Greetings. I am Juliano, and we are the Arcturians. There is a parallel between the ascension of the Earth and your personal ascension. The process that the Earth goes through, in many ways, is reflective of the process that you personally go through for your ascension. The reverse is also true. The process that you go through can be parallel to the process that the Earth goes through.

Today we want to focus on the personal aspects of the ascension. We want to focus on the personal issues that you individually may be experiencing at this time in the ascension process. I know that many of you experience physical problems, emotional problems and even economic problems. The link with the ascension is a fifth-dimensional one. This means that we seek to download higher energy from the fifth dimension into our personal lives, into each of our four bodies, which include the mental, emotional, physical and the spiritual. Linking to ascension includes the idea of energetically shifting our fields so that we can process and receive fifth-dimensional energy.

CREATION OF HUMANS AND THE LINK TO THE FEEDBACK LOOP

When we talked in previous lectures about Earth changes, we referred to the feedback loop mechanism within the Earth. We discussed the fact that there is a mechanism within the Earth that gets information from the atmosphere and from different systems within the whole complex Earth biosphere. From that information, certain corrections, or feedbacks, are analyzed and changes are instituted. The Earth currents in the oceans, for example, can be influenced by many different variables, including the greenhouse gas phenomena. Also, the feedback system can include the life forms in the oceans, such as the whales and dolphins who are involved in the feedback loop for the Earth. This is a surprising factor, as many people may not see the importance of the whales or dolphins in the Earth changes or in the feedback mechanism. Part of this is due to the telepathic abilities of whales and dolphins to connect with the feedback loop mechanisms. These feedback loop mechanisms go back to ancient times, and there are not many mammals on the planet that can link to the ancient times.

I hope that you can see the parallel between this discussion of the Earth and your own personal ascension. Obviously we are helping you to link with the ancient energies of humanity, and this in particular can be done through some of the Kaballistic methods that Archangel Michael will be talking to you about in this lecture. Basically, the ancient energetic connections go back to Adam. Adam represents the first man, but he does not necessarily represent the first physical prototype. In the evolutionary sense, there were Cro-Magnon, Neanderthal or Hominids and other pre-*Homo sapiens*, such as the Australopithecus. They all represented the physical form of man, but they did not have all four bodies. The earlier versions that were mentioned did not necessarily have the spiritual component. It is the downloading of the spiritual component in the Cro-Magnon and *Homo sapiens* species that in fact led to the first man. The first man, Adam, also contained the feedback loop mechanism in his system that links all future men and women. This first man was actually a hermaphrodite, which is the male and female together.

In the understanding of your ascension, it behooves you to seek the links within yourself to the first Adam. We can also call the first human Adam-Eve. The reason is that the core understanding, core codes and core links for your ascension go back to that first Adam who contained both male and female parts. The whales and the dolphins link to the first Earth life energies in the ocean the same way you link back to the first Adam. You seek the link back to the first Adam. This is a necessary link for your ascension.

TIME TO UPDATE YOUR FEEDBACK LOOP MECHANISM

Let us become more in the present and look at your Earth life. Let us say that there is also this feedback loop that is continually processing information from your birth in this lifetime. Many of you are starseeds who came into this time frame in order to ascend and advantage of the certain multitudes of multidimensional energy that are available.

The feedback loop in your lifetime is similar to the feedback loop in Earth, but we need to discuss some specifics. The feedback loop in yourself is complicated, and frankly, many of you do not know how to pay attention to the feedback loop. You have been given information by your parents regarding who you are and how you were to be in your childhood. You all know that you have inherited genetic codes. You have inherited certain subconscious patterns and messages from your parents that are really based on a narrow, singular view of reality. This is part of the process of growing up in this time, in this culture. As you have evolved, the feedback information on who you are and how you are supposed to evolve often conflicts with the earlier program that was developed and downloaded. This is another way to say that you have to be attentive to the feedback loop.

Your mental, physical, emotional and spiritual bodies have to change, yet many of you are still operating from the feedback process and programming that was instilled or given to you as a child. So you have evolved and have come to this great opening, this great understanding, of the fifth dimension. Now it is time to update your feedback loop mechanism and say that the images of your physical body are contained in your subconscious. The images of your mental body are also contained in your subconscious. The images of your emotional and your spiritual bodies need to be updated to include the fact that you are a fifth-dimensional being and that you are relating and integrating fifth-dimensional energy. This can be incorporated successfully in all aspects of your physical body so that your health, welfare and the energy that you attract in your social, economic and emotional lives can be uplifted. This will reflect the fifth-dimensional light and the fifth-dimensional processes, which are part of you. [Tones.] *Oooohhhh.*

THE ROLE OF THE PHYSICAL BODY

You would hope that the physical problems you have can be influenced by fifth-dimensional connections. The physical body is a good metaphor for you. You have an embedded subconscious program in your physical body.

That embedded program is based on thought forms that most of you developed when you were very young. This could be developed and firmed up as early as age eleven or twelve, or sixteen or seventeen. Some of these thought forms also contain programs from your parents. Others are genetic programs from your past lives based on the cause-and-effect process. These would set the tone and would set the map for the rest of physical existence on Earth. This means that at certain life points, you could develop problems. You might, for example, develop breathing problems. You might develop back problems, heart problems, circulation problems. All of these illnesses or blockages were, in a sense, preset. They were not inevitable, but they were preset or imbedded in your thought forms and in your physical body at an early age. So when you reach an older age, some of the issues and physical problems that you experience are based on those earlier embedded programs.

Those embedded programs can be changed. You can download information, energy and fifth-dimensional processes that will raise your vibration and will help you to shift in a very positive way. But the key is to tell yourself that your feedback loop needs to be updated. In this updating, new information will come into your consciousness on how to relate and how to image yourself so that new imaging will include fifth-dimensional imagery and fifth-dimensional energy. This is another way of saying that there is a fifth-dimensional thought form—a fifth-dimensional program for your physical body that can now be downloaded so that you can interact physically and mediate some of the earlier, unwanted programming.

FIFTH-DIMENSIONAL TECHNOLOGY AND MEDIATING

I want to emphasize the word "mediate." You know that there are some inevitabilities. These are related to laws of cause and effect on the planet. Do not expect things to happen like if you are now bald, then with this imaging, you are going to gain hair. Do not expect that you are going to have the physical athletic ability that you had when you were twenty. Those are ego things. Rather it is better to say, "At this point in my life, I have these issues. Now let me use the physical feedback form and the fifth-dimensional energy so that I can maximize the best interaction possible! I can make the physical changes that are necessary so that I can be most harmonious and in the highest balance healthwise." You then can mediate your physical body using the fifth-dimensional technology that we have taught.

The downloading of the fifth-dimensional energy into your physical body for the updating of the feedback loop begins by reconfiguring your aura. It is a logical place to start. The aura, or the energy field, contains a feedback loop. When you look at the human energy field, you may think that it is affected by higher forces. But it is also affected by your physical body. Your energy field is a feedback loop so that it is receiving information from your higher self and your physical body, and then that information goes into your energy field.

Your aura is also receiving information from the fifth dimension, from higher masters and teachers. Many of you do not experience an interaction in your energy field between the third dimension and the fifth. Contractions in your field can lead to or indicate physical health problems; therefore, you do not experience the interaction between that and the fifth-dimensional higher thought forms of expansion. When we want to do healings, then we first start with the cosmic egg, and we shape our energy system, or our energy field, in the form of a cosmic egg. Then we begin the pulsing. So try now to just image and visualize that your energy field is in the form of a cosmic egg. If you have not heard that term before, just think of the most perfect chicken egg you have ever seen. This perfect egg is a universal galactic symbol. Then superimpose with your mind the shape of that egg onto your energy field. Command your energy field to go into the shape of the perfected egg. Take a minute to do that now. [Pause.]

As it goes into that shape, you may feel a sense of relief or relaxation. As you work with and experience that shape, become aware that the outer edge of your cosmic egg is beginning to pulse. In fact, it has been pulsing. The pulse of your energy field is similar to the pulse that you have in your body. Your energy field is not actually pulsing as rapidly as your physical pulse. It is pulsing though, and it is going in and out. Become aware of your energy field pulsing. It may be like this: dat dat dat dat, dat, datdatdat, daaa. As the energy field is pulsing, it actually begins to expand and contract. You are not going to contract it in this session, but rather we just want you to become aware that it is expanding. As it is expanding and pulsing at a higher frequency, you are able to interact with the higher layers of yourself, which are fifth-dimensional. Your fifth-dimensional self is in a layered interactive process. Now we open the feedback loop so that you can connect to your fifth-dimensional self.

TAPPING INTO THE FIFTH-DIMENSIONAL REALM

Visualize through your crown chakra that you are able to transfer your consciousness to a space that is directly above your crown into the fifth-dimensional realm. It is often hard for people to visualize the fifth-dimensional realm, or the fifth-dimensional self. We have set up corridors, and these corridors are connected to the fifth-dimensional crystal temple. To assist you, I place corridors above everyone who is reading or is listening to these words. Let us travel individually through the corridor and use thought projection to go to the fifth-dimensional crystal lake. At the crystal lake, there you are as a fifth-dimensional self, sitting around the lake. We have helped you to do this. On my command, thought-project yourself to the crystal lake, and enter your fifth-dimensional self energetically. [Tones.] *Tat tat tat tat tat tat.*

Now enter your fifth-dimensional body at the crystal lake. Notice your fifth-dimensional body energetically has a different energy, a higher vibration. You can move, you can breathe if you want, and you can think higher thoughts. You have a freedom in the fifth-dimensional body. But you also have the imprints from your third-dimensional body. In this fifth-dimensional manifested place, you are aware of your fifth-dimensional body, but you have the knowledge and imprint of the third-dimensional body. That means all of the contractions of the third-dimensional body are still imprinted in your consciousness. Believe me that everyone has contractions on the third-dimensional body. We do not expect everyone to be in a perfect expanded state on the third dimension.

When you are in the third dimension, you can become aware of your contractions, but it is harder from the third-dimensional perspective to download the fifth-dimensional energy. In the fifth dimension, you can download higher energy. From this fifth-dimensional higher state, begin to scan the imprints, the contracted energy, that you have brought from the third dimension into this awareness. Take a moment to do that now. Become aware that there is an astral cord that links you to your third-dimensional body. Become aware also that the astral cord can be accelerated to work with the feedback loop that we are talking about. Please make this affirmation: I am now updating my feedback loop mechanism. Please repeat those words in your consciousness for a while. "I am updating my feedback loop mechanism now." [Tones.] *Oooohhhh. Oooohhhh.* "I am updating my feedback loop mechanism with the fifth-dimensional awareness now."

As you interact with these contractions, realize that you do not have those contractions in the fifth-dimensional body. The third-dimensional body needs to make a shift or change. The first change is the downloading of a shimmering light from your fifth-dimensional self. In the fifth-dimensional self on the crystal lake, begin to shimmer. Shimmering makes the energetic field vibrate at a higher rate. It is like you are going so bright, so intense, that you vibrate at a beautiful harmonious frequency. That shimmering is helping you to connect with the highest healing light that is available. As you do that, I, Juliano, raise the crystal in the crystal lake so that the intense crystal energy is now more available, and you can bring this higher crystal healing energy into your fifth-dimensional body as you begin to shimmer. Now, on my command, begin to download all of this shimmering healing energy into your astral cord. It contains updated information. We are feeding the updated information into your astral cord that connects you from the third dimension to the fifth dimension. The cord is still connected.

Look at a specific part of your physical body on Earth that seems to be the most in need of an energetic expansion. Download a specific frequency that you are now able to obtain to help that contracted part, whatever it may be. Remember that this downloading supersedes all other information, all other codes, all of the programs about this. You are now downloading information that will mediate your physical form. Begin that process now.

You have been very successful in this. Remember, all of the energy is now downloaded, and all of the information is contained in your astral cord. You can compare the astral cord to a computer connection cable where all of the information that is coming from the mother computer will be downloaded or transferred to another sub-computer or printer. In this case, all of the information that you have is in the astral cord. Now send all of this information from the fifth dimension through your astral cord back into your third-dimensional body. Visualize that you see on your mind's computer screen the word send. Now command this word "send." All the information is being downloaded into your third-dimensional body. [Tones.] *Tat tat tat tat tat tat ta!*

Continued Affirmations Assist with Necessary Adjustments

Now it has been sent, and I want you again to shimmer from the fifth-dimensional body. Shimmer into your third-dimensional body so that it expands the cosmic egg to make it larger and also so that it can hold a newer vibration. Shimmer in the fifth dimension, and then shimmer into your third-dimensional body. Beautiful! Now thought-project yourself back into your third-dimensional body on my count of three. One, two, three. Now you are back in your third-dimensional body.

The astral cord will still be able to access your fifth-dimensional energy. Now the information is coming into your system and will slowly seep into your subconscious and your conscious. I want you to understand that each of you who are working on certain issues in your body must now make some adjustments. The feedback loop means that you have information and then you have to make adjustments.

Many of you have gotten stuck in a contracted state. You may not know how to make any adjustments. Earth is being burdened and overloaded in certain systems, but Earth has a feedback loop in the biosphere, and it makes adjustments to regulate itself. Simply make the affirmation, "Through my feedback loop mechanisms, I now give permission to make the necessary adjustments, whatever they may be, that will enhance my physical health and my physical body using fifth-dimensional energy."

Enhancing the third-dimensional body can also include accessing higher energy. Some of you are already in good physical condition but need to update your physical structure so that it becomes transparent, and it can work with fifth-dimensional energy. There are certain contractions as well, even if you are in perfect physical health, that need to be expanded so that you can go to fifth-dimensional consciousness now. Allow those thoughts and information and commands to be transferred now. [Tones.] *Oooohhhh. Oooohhhh.*

PERIODICALLY CONNECT TO YOUR FIFTH-DIMENSIONAL BODY

From the fifth-dimensional perspective, all problems can be mediated. This again is the key word—mediated. You accepted the Earth process when you came into this planet. You accepted that you would be going through many of the physical changes that are related to aging. There is the mediation with fifth-dimensional energy that is now being activated. There are similar energies that we can use for the social and economic problems and for other issues. For this purpose, we are now just focusing on the physical structure.

The idea is that you need to periodically connect to your fifth-dimensional body. Ultimately, you can begin to reconstruct the thought forms that you are holding on the physical body. You can update them. Remember that it is not necessarily true that you will update your physical body to the point when you were twenty years old. Rather, you will mediate it so that you are in the optimal harmonious relationship with your physical body at this point. You might like to have eternal youth. The problem with eternal youth is that you will not ascend because you are holding a thought form of a body that will not change! The problem is that you will hold on to earlier images of yourself. Then you will not update or go into the feedback mechanism.

I would like to turn the next part of the lecture over to Archangel Michael. I am Juliano. In the shimmering light field of fifth-dimensional physical vibrational light, I bid you good day!

Greetings! I am Archangel Michael. I send you the blue light of protection. I send you the awareness of my etheric sword that is for all humanity to use. Cords of attachment can exist in your energy system from lower vibrations or from other sources of lower fields. Or they are from your earlier self. I want to explain that sometimes the cords of attachment originate as frozen thought forms that have been downloaded at an earlier time. These are thought forms on who you are, what you look like, how you are supposed to be. They often are not based on the current reality. With your permission, I am going to cut the outdated cords of attachment—now! Each of you will vibrate at a higher frequency.

Juliano talked with you about connecting with the primordial man, Adam. In the Kaballistic language, Adam is known as the first man. The first man was fifth-dimensional, and he came into the third dimension with multidimensional presence. It is hard to imagine how you can be totally fifth-dimensional and be in the third dimension. Think of Jesus or Mary or Moses or Buddha. They all were fifth-dimensional in the third dimension.

A PROTECTIVE SHIELD IS AROUND YOU

The energy of the first man, Kaballistically, is known as *A'dam Ri'shon*. I am going to tone these two words so that you can be activated to connect internally to the first man. Don't be confused by the terms "first man" because *A'dam Ri'shon* contained man and woman. For the purposes of this discussion, we will call it man.

Each of you has the codes within you to connect to the first man as you hear these sounds. [Tones.] *A'dam Ha Ri'shon.* Let your consciousness now go to the first man who was fifth-dimensional and already an ascended master. In your genetic codes you are now becoming aware of your connection to *A'dam ha Ri'shon. A'dam ha ri'shon* divided into Eve *ha'ri'shon.*

There was a split. You can go back to the feminine source, which was also connected to all the fifth dimension and the third dimension. Both Adam and Eve are now in your codes. You are becoming aware of this now. Know the earliest man and first woman contained the dynamic ascension codes. Access the ascension codes. You are creating a protective force field around you so that the coming Earth changes, the coming shifts, the coming polarizations or the current polarizations and shifts will not negatively affect you. You will remain in a protected state like the energy cocoon. I, Archangel Michael, place the *Ma'gen ha Da'vid*, the Shield of David, over each of you. Let you now be protected.

I place an energy cocoon around each of you now. You are connected and opened up to the energies of the ascension. The ascension energies are nearer now. Maintain your connections to the first man and the first woman. This is the best way to remind you that within you is the ability to ascend. The ability to go into higher light will enable you to take off your coat of the physical body. The physical body only needs to be maximized and harmonized for you to go into the fifth-dimensional energy.

We, the angelic hosts, are working with the Arcturians, with Sananda, with Mary and with the masters. I, Archangel Michael, have cut the lower cords of attachment, and now I place a beautiful swirling corridor of energy around each of you above your crown chakra. This swirling core of light is an energy field above your cosmic egg. It is a cocoon of light. *Aur ha' ko'desh*. It is a holy light, and it is a swirling light. It is like a beautiful swirling light that is aligning over your crown chakra now so that you set a corridor in place for your ascension. You are setting in place a preliminary energy field that contains a doorway for your ascension. That doorway is focused on *A'dam ha ri'shon*, the first man.

Shimmering and Alchemy

Juliano and Chief White Eagle

Greetings, I am Juliano. We are the Arcturians. We will now discuss the science of shimmering, which is a process in which one transforms, or transmutes, energy. It is based on the concept of alchemy, wherein one attempts to transmute physical objects into higher, more valuable stones, such as gold. It is believed that through these particular techniques of alchemy, one can actually transform physical objects into gold.

Many people understand the alchemical process to be symbolic. In fact, from the Arcturian perspective, this is a symbolic endeavor. One cannot take gold to the fifth dimension; in fact, gold has no value there. Looking at the Aztec civilization on Earth, one realizes that gold is not always useful. The Aztecs had much gold in their possession, yet it did not help them in any way when they were invaded by the foreigners. Gold has monetary value in third-dimensional society, but it has no value in the fifth dimension; however, the process of transmuting physical lead into gold represents important principles that are related to shimmering.

When you look at alchemical scientists, you may find that when they are ready to make a transformation, they will speak or tone a certain phrase. Many of you have already heard the word "abracadabra": As I say it, so it shall be created. Without the physical expression of these words, sounds and tones transmitted with the right physical frequency, the object in question, such as lead, cannot be transformed. This provides us with an important comparison when we look at shimmering. When you shimmer, you work to transmute an object from the third dimension into a higher fifth-dimensional frequency. Ultimately, you are working to transmute yourself as a physical object into the fifth dimension. You become the alchemist, the transformer, and it is your words and sounds that complete the process that allows your shimmering to be transformative.

Transmute Earth into the Fifth Dimension

Shimmering is a process in which you—through tones, sounds and other psychic energetic work—transmute physical objects into the fifth dimension. Shimmering is based on the scientific concept that all objects on the third dimension vibrate at a certain agreed-on frequency. The frequency of the object can be affected by certain resonant frequencies that can help it be transmuted into the fifth dimension.

Raising or using a frequency can also have other effects besides transmuting the object into another dimension. A perfect example of this would be the opera singer who sings on the level of a soprano and emits a very high tone, or frequency. Imagine there is a wine glass near this opera singer when he or she reaches a certain vibrational level, and the frequency breaks the glass. There is a reason the glass breaks: The opera singer found the resonant frequency that made it break. This is an example of the technology of shimmering.

A certain emitted vibrational frequency, that is, a tone from the singer, can cause a physical object to change. In this example, the object shattered. However, in shimmering, we do not seek to shatter the glass; we seek to bring the glass into another dimension. We are aware that a high frequency can shift a physical object.

It is noteworthy to point out that there have been certain scientific experiments under the principles of Tesla that were used in a project called the Philadelphia Experiment in which the U.S. government naval warfare division sought to use vibrational frequencies to make objects disappear. In fact, they were partially successful; however, they had difficulty on many levels. The attempt to make the objects reappear led to disastrous problems. Still, this is an example of using shimmering principles in which frequencies are used to transmute objects. In the case of the Philadelphia Experiment, they used high radar frequencies.

We, the Arcturians, are able to disseminate spiritual frequencies to you. These frequencies have nothing to do with shattering objects, warfare or harming anything. Spiritual frequencies transcend the third-dimensional level. These spiritual frequencies are so special and so resonant that they require the user to be on a certain harmonic, sympathetic level. The user must have the right intention when shimmering in order to work with an object.

Understand and believe that it is the interaction of your mind with the interaction of your intention that spiritually transforms objects to a higher level. Your ability to transform objects into the fifth dimension is related to your ability to shimmer yourself, to bring yourself into a higher frequency.

I must stress the importance of the relationship between your mind and your spiritual body interacting with this shimmering energy. The technology of shimmering requires you to be on a certain higher spiritual level. It is the interaction of your spiritual energy with the technology of shimmering that enables you to transmute energy that is locked in the third dimension. Now it becomes apparent that energy is locked! This is an obvious principle, because in the discussions of nuclear energy, your scientists discovered that they can unlock certain atoms and a certain energy is emitted. This is not a spiritual energy. I want you to understand that in shimmering, you are working to unlock a spiritual energy that is in third-dimensional objects, third-dimensional people, third-dimensional animals and, eventually, third-dimensional Earth. We suggest that the complex use and understanding of shimmering energies can be used to transmute the Earth into the fifth dimension.

WORKING WITH FIFTH-DIMENSIONAL ENERGY

Become aware of your ability to shimmer your third-dimensional presence into the fifth-dimensional level. Maybe you will not become a fifth-dimensional being immediately. Maybe you will not disappear and go into the higher level right now. You will begin to experience parts of shimmering as you hear these tones and sounds, and you will experience a raising of your vibrational frequency and be able to project that raised level of frequency to an object and use that energy to shimmer the object. Again, listen to these tones. [Tones.]

Feel yourself shimmer in your third-dimensional body. It is a wonderful feeling that we call vibrational bliss. We are committed to personal and planetary healing. For planetary healing, we have downloaded etheric crystals into Earth. Advanced spiritual beings know that crystals are able to hold vibrational frequencies and vibrational thoughts. Crystals have the ability to resonate when a vibrational tone or vibrational thought is emitted. That crystal can hold, amplify and accelerate that energy. What is so beautiful is that the crystal and the shimmerer, that is, the person who is shimmering, can be far apart.

Time and space are in a different relationship on the fifth dimension. In fact, many people feel that there is no space there. That is very difficult for you to visualize and conceive. In fact, I would only point out this: Space and distance are not limiting factors in shimmering and in working with crystals. If one connects to fifth-dimensional energy, then one can access remotely distant objects on Earth. In this case, the seven etheric crystals that have been downloaded have roles and functions to play in the shimmering energy field that we, the Arcturians, are working to create with you, the Arcturian starseeds. That shimmering energy is communicated through and amplified in the etheric crystals that have been downloaded into many of these beautiful areas on the planet.

Each of these crystals has the energies of shimmering programmed into them by the Arcturians. We have used the master crystal in the crystal temple as the template for the etheric doubling of the crystals. We also communicate and send our shimmering energies into those crystals. These fifth-dimensional etheric crystals are being amplified by us and by you, and we are working to transmute Earth and to transmute you.

It is not just the etheric crystals that you can use. Each of you, I know, is using crystals. Many of you have great talents and special training from this lifetime and other lifetimes in the use of crystal energy. It is always helpful to continue to amplify and use these crystals. You may be at a very high level of consciousness and light energy at this point during the lecture. You may have a crystal in the room with you. You can project and program the crystal that is near you now to hold this high energy. If any of you have a crystal in the room or nearby, I suggest that you may want to go over and hold that crystal. I will wait for a brief time while you do this. [Pause.]

Now you can project your higher frequencies, your higher vibrations, into that crystal. That crystal becomes like a tape recorder holding that vibrational frequency. We are talking about a spiritual frequency of a very fine, thin vibrational pattern—certainly much higher than a radio frequency. Even the highest radio frequencies that go into the gigahertz range are considered dense compared to the frequencies that we are now working with in spiritual energy.

In the shimmering technology, it is not only the height of the frequency but it is also the frequency of the wave. You might hear me working with you on transmuting your energy and might hear me go "tat, tat, tat, tat, tat." Visualize a graph with a sine wave and see that the height of the wave goes very high. At the same time, visualize that there are rapid waves. Even this sound that is being emitted by the channel does not come close to the frequency of the wave that is coming in. You might say, "Juliano, I cannot visualize that frequency, that number of waves coming in congruently. I cannot use my mind to visualize what you are saying." My friends, when you connect to the fifth dimension, you are going to a level of vibration that is beyond your mental capabilities of the third dimension. You have no idea of the powers of your mind.

ABERRANT FREQUENCIES ON EARTH

Let me return to the example of the opera singer. The opera singer may not believe that a sound could shatter, but all of a sudden something happens. Maybe you can visualize the number of waves coming in while at the lowest sound frequencies. That is a good place to start in your visualization. Understand that at the level that we are talking about, the spiritual frequencies are so high, so thin, so etheric that many of them are emitted over and over again. You are programmed to process these frequencies. You are the Adam species.

Interestingly, when you think of the crystals and of frequency, you may think of higher frequencies that are beyond the range of the human ear. You might think of very quick rising waves like the "tat tat tat" sounds, but here is an explanation that you might find perplexing: Slower waves, deeper tones, can have similar transformative effects and can create shimmering energy. The crystals can be programmed for deeper tones. For example, the Tibetan monks are able to vibrate on a very low frequency and a low sound. Paradoxically, the shimmering energies can also be expressed by slowing down the frequency. We will try to have the channel demonstrate this lower level. [Tones.] Let the slower vibrational tones help you shimmer. We will go into a brief meditation together in silence.

Understand that there are certain vibrational frequencies that are also necessary to hold together the third dimension. Many of you know that Earth vibrates at a certain level, a certain hertz. A small shift in the frequency of the planet can cause a major disruption. Equally important is the fact that certain Native people, such as the Hopi, believe that they are keepers of certain frequencies that are necessary to protect this planet and to keep the third dimension going. Many people will look at these tribes and wonder what they are doing. The tribe has received information about how to protect and hold the vibrational frequency. This particular vibrational frequency that the Hopi use and guard has been protecting Earth, but there are many aberrant interferences in the frequency stability of the third dimension.

Aberrant frequencies can interfere in the stability of the third dimension. Perhaps you have heard the idea of the third dimension as a collective consciousness. You even have certain frequencies related to money and finances and to love and to war. Humankind has not, from the scientific point of view of shimmering, understood that there is an overall general frequency that keeps this planet together. The aberrant frequencies that are abundant on this planet now—coming from radar, from HAARP, from sonar, from nuclear energies, from many different exotic weaponry—do affect third-dimensional frequencies of this planet. Our work with the etheric crystals, with you and with shimmering planetary energy is an antidote to that vibrational aberrant energy.

The whales and the dolphins, for example, have the job of holding and transmitting a certain carrier frequency that holds the ocean energy and the planetary energy in a biospheric harmony. The beautiful sounds and tones of whales and dolphins have a contributory effect to the vibrational harmony of the biosphere. It is not just the sounds that they vibrate or that you vibrate. Ultimately, it is telepathic thought that can contain a higher vibrational energy. Higher shimmering is done telepathically.

You may begin shimmering through tones and sounds. Of course, one person alone may not be able to shimmer an entire lake, such as Lake Taupo, Lago Puelo or Lake Moraine, but you can increase the ability to shimmer by multiplying the number of participants. You can shimmer cities, you can shimmer locations—your home. A city will feel a transformational effect. You might not be able to hold it for a long period of time because, obviously, it requires certain training. In shimmering energies, you go to a telepathic shimmering, to the telepathic transmission of this sound.

We could tone the word "shimmmer." Look at the crystal near you— I do recommend practicing your shimmering transformational skills on crystals. You might want to try to shimmer the crystal. In healing, and in the highest level of healing on Earth, a psychic or a channel can shimmer, and they can project a frequency so high that lower frequencies causing illness can disintegrate. In essence, the higher level of shimmering goes to projection of thoughts and the shimmering energy.

We are going to shimmer a wave of transformative light telepathically around this planet that is a harmonic level of light never before seen globally. A few people using this technology and energy are enough to shift the planet. There has been so much destruction of the basis of the biosphere by aberrant energy, but it all can be counteracted; it all can be rebalanced through the shimmering energies and processes and techniques that we are teaching you. I now turn things over to Chief White Eagle. I am Juliano. We are the Arcturians.

G reetings, all my relations. [Tones.] *Hey ya ho, hey ya ho, hey ya ho, hey.* All my words are sacred. I am Chief White Eagle. I call on the sacred energies of the grandfathers, the grandmothers, the mountains, the oceans, and the Central Sun and the Ancient Ones to be our teachers in learning how to vibrate with Mother Earth.

We understand the spiritual technology of the shimmering, and we understand it in a way of using simple prayer, of simple chanting. [Tones.] *Hey yah ho!* Remember that Juliano said that shimmering can be done at a lower frequency. Sometimes it is easier for you to visualize the lower waves because they can go through objects just as easily as the high waves. Lower waves take a different energy, a different type of thought. Some psychics, some channels, are good at the high frequencies of shimmering, some are good at the low frequencies, and some can do both.

We use the drum to vibrate. That is a basic rhythm. The rhythm and beat of the drum put in motion a vibrational light of shimmering. What is so beautiful for us, the Natives, is that we have always understood that there is a frequency that needs to be projected and used. The frequency is like a glue that holds things together, that holds this whole energy field together.

EARTH IS HELD TOGETHER BY A VIBRATIONAL FREQUENCY

The Hopi have talked about the different worlds: the third, the fourth and the fifth worlds. Each world has been held together by a vibration. In fact, the Great White Father used a vibrational frequency in other worlds. At times that vibrational frequency did not hold and people in the other worlds did not understand the nature of shimmering, the nature of how to be in harmony with the vibration. They did not understand that there was a wave of energies that actually held together a whole dimension—imagine that! [Tones.] *Hey ya ho ya, hey yah!* You have heard the Arcturians talk about each dimension as a gigantic sphere. Think about it as a gigantic ball that has a wave within it or a frequency.

My friends, we are connecting now to the frequency of the Central Sun. We know that there is an alchemical frequency from the Central Sun that will provide a shimmering energy for all of the spirit guides, spirit teachers and starseeds. This is going to be like food for our spirits! It will be healing energy that will enable us all to vibrate with the light of the Creator, with the light of our Father. We will hold this dimension together and then transmute it into a higher dimension as we say:

"O Mother Earth, we are here to interact with you and the higher light. We, as shimmerers, can help transmute you and the biosphere. We will understand that our role, in part, is to connect the energies that alchemically come from the Central Sun to Earth. As it is, so it shall be! We will chant to you, Mother Earth, we will sing to you, we will drum to you, and we will resonate together in a great frequency of spiritual transformation."

There is a new harmony, a new wave of frequency, that is called the new spiritual Harmonic Convergence energy. This is a new vibration that you will download on to this planet.

I, Chief White Eagle, say it is time to both work with the old codes, the old frequencies, and open yourselves to receiving a new shimmering frequency. This new shimmering frequency has such magnificent vibratory power that it will transform the Earth alchemically. The densities on this planet that do not seem possible to change, will change. Your thoughts and your own physical bodies will adjust, and you will also be shifted. [Tones.] *Hey ya ho, hey ya ho!*

TIME IS A CIRCLE

We, the Native people from the fifth dimension, know the importance of connections to the star family. We know that part of the vibration—the shimmering, the frequency—that we need is contained in our star heritage. You might say that the connection to the star family is another piece of the puzzle. That piece will provide the shimmering energy that will allow you to transform and shimmer your whole physical body into the fifth dimension. It will allow you, my friends, to transform cities and places on this planet into the fifth dimension. This is what our soul mission is, this is what our soul light is, and this is what our work is about. It is ultimately connected with ceremonies and with the drum.

All of these chantings help us to raise our abilities to vibrate on different levels. Normally you are vibrating on a third-dimensional level in your daily life, and now you are gaining in flexibility so that you can vibrate at different frequencies—higher and lower frequencies. On the fifth dimension, lower frequencies ultimately merge to the higher frequencies. Why? Because the world and the energetic patterns are circles, just like time is a circle. I am Chief White Eagle. Blessings!

Kaballah, Ascension and the Tree of Life

Nabur

Greetings, I am Nabur. We want to discuss the Tree of Life and its accessibility and expansion. In this time that you are living in, I can assure you that the Tree of Life is more accessible than it has been in any other period on Earth.

The original downloading of the Tree of Life was given and expressed through a select few higher beings. The information and the blueprint of the Tree of Life and what it represents is being transmitted throughout the planet. This is a positive development.

The original Tree of Life and the expansion of the Tree of Life, as it is being promulgated in 2010, represents a galactic spiritual knowledge that was given throughout the galaxy and throughout the universe. One reason why the Tree of Life is so special is because it represents the multidimensional nature of reality and the multidimensional nature of manifestation.

The Tree of Life demonstrates the existence of other dimensions. It starts with the idea that manifestation on Earth is at the bottom part of the Tree of Life. But Earth can only manifest because of work done in the higher spheres, or in the higher dimensions. This means that the reality of Earth and the third dimension is based on work that is occurring in other spheres and in other dimensions. What you experience on Earth is only an aspect of your multidimensional nature. What you see on Earth is only an aspect of the many different interactive and dimensional forces that are occurring. These forces have led to the manifestation of the third dimension and the manifestation of Earth.

DUALITY AND DYNAMICS

The first obvious understanding of the Tree of Life has to do with duality. The tree has three columns [see Fig. 1]. The nature of the columns has to do with the essence of the right and the left columns and how a balance can be found through the middle column. Also, the tree has to do with the top and the bottom energy of the columns. The top, which is known as Kether, or the crown, represents undifferentiated, unmanifested light that comes from the creator. It is the driving force. The key is that it is undifferentiated. Undifferentiated energy means that it is not usable and it is not comprehensible to the human mind. This undifferentiated energy must follow a downward path to manifestation. Through the path to manifestation, the undifferentiated energy must go through dualities. It must go through the right and left columns and eventually into the center. The center represents the balance. In order for a manifestation to occur on the multidimensional higher spheres, a balance and a harmony occurs in the upper levels. This means that for humankind, there is a possible energy of perfect balance, even though that energy of perfect balance may be in the higher sphere, or higher realm. There is a higher balance despite the polarities, despite the conflicts that you see now on this planet.

The second idea that I want to discuss has to do with the nature of the Tree of Life itself and the nature of the ten spheres. These are all dynamic spheres. They are dynamic energy fields that represent creation and the process of creation. Therefore our knowledge of this process is increasing as humankind is expanding his consciousness. What was unknowable about the Tree of Life in 1400 A.D. is now more knowable. There is more new information. There is more knowledge and more ability for humankind to understand. That is why we say that this Tree of Life is more accessible than ever to humankind. The tree represents how consciousness is manifested and how beings are manifested.

Most importantly, this is a dynamic Tree of Life, which means that there is a changing aspect of each element. Humankind could not know the undifferentiated energy 600 years ago. Now humankind has a higher ability, energy and awareness through which it can comprehend the undifferentiated energy. I am not saying that humankind can totally grasp undifferentiated energy, but there is a new understanding of the Tree of Life. The crown, for example, can also be understood from the integrations of the Tao with the Tree of Life. The new ideas that are available have to do with the unities that now occur in some religious thinking and in some religious mystical unities. New mystical insights offer humanity a greater ability to comprehend the Tree of Life and

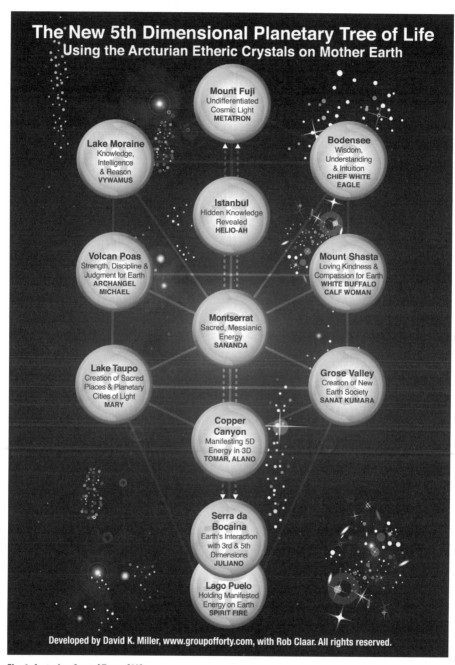

Fig. 1: Arcturian Crystal Tree of Life

understanding of undifferentiated energy. Modern man can comprehend the forces and harmony that can exist to balance polarities.

Another insight of the Tree of Life is that the bottom influences the top as much as the top influences the bottom. This is a confusing issue to many people because they say that only the higher energies influence the manifested Earth. How is it possible that the manifested Earth can influence the higher spheres? The new understanding of the Tree of Life is going to show that not only does the energy come down from the top, through all the spheres and manifest, but there is also a back flow of energy. This back flow of energy has to do with the nature of climbing, or ascending, the Tree of Life. This is very similar to climbing Jacob's ladder.

The Tree of Life is going to bring humankind closer to the concepts of ascension because ascension is essentially using your higher energy to climb the Tree of Life into higher spheres and multidimensionality.

HOW TO GET CLOSER TO GOD

There are safeguards so that a total collapse or a total destruction on the third dimension would not harm the higher realms. The higher realms are interactive with the lower realms. In order for that interaction to occur, there must be an interdimensional exchange. This concept I describe leads to the conclusion that Kether, the higher crown, is affected by what is going on in the lower realms. That is in contradiction to the idea that God is perfect. Because being perfect, He would not be affected by what is going on in the world. This overlooks a key point: Any characteristic or any feature that humankind can have or manifest is also a feature of the Godhead energy. In other words, God can also have that trait. That means that God is affected by what is going on in the lower realms by man. This is a characteristic of God, so that God is affected. But this does not diminish God's perfection. This is the paradox.

In order for the truth of Kaballah to be manifested, an integration of all higher consciousness with the third dimension must occur. One must understand the nature of this interaction of the higher and lower realms. The truth is that God is a personal God as well as an undifferentiated energy that is beyond the comprehension of humankind. Humankind can be affected by higher and lower energies. That is a characteristic that would be included in God's energy field as well. The contradiction is that God is still in a state of perfection even though He is affected by His creation.

Why shouldn't God be affected by His creation? That is why God sends messengers. That is why God sends angels. That is why God sends His emissaries, such as Sananda, to Earth to foster a unity that will effect a higher evolution. That means that the nature of the Tree of Life is an expression of how one gets closer to God. One doesn't directly interact with God. One must follow a pattern of energetic emanations. This is what the Tree of Life represents.

KINDNESS VERSUS JUDGMENT

It is helpful to discuss balancing mercy versus judgment as another aspect that is represented on the two pillars on the Tree of Life. It is well known that there were worlds before this world in which mercy reigned. Mercy was too out of balance so that there was a devastation of the world because there was too much kindness. Therefore, kindness is now being counterbalanced by judgment, but judgment can also be too strong. This new balance is being manifested now in the world. You know that too much understanding, too much kindness will allow certain groups who have evil intentions gain control of resources and planetary ideals. One of the lessons now on the planet has to do with understanding the nature of kindness versus judgments. This lesson is going to manifest in many other aspects in terms of how people are going to deal with Earth and Earth changes.

Hidden knowledge, which is known in Hebrew as *D'aat*, now is going to manifest because it no longer needs to be a hidden sphere. A new sphere, the sphere of manifestation between the third and the fifth energies, is being downloaded into the Tree of Life to accommodate the energy for the ascension. This new sphere is directly above Malchut, or Kingdom.

We want to point out that the Tree of Life is the core of Kaballah, but it is not the sole aspect of the Kaballah. There are many related theories and ideas that form the basis of the Kaballah and, in particular, relate Kaballah to the energy of modern-day ascension. The first concept and energy in Kaballah relating to ascension is reincarnation. It is well known by many Kaballah masters, teachers and rabbis that this is not our only life. You have had multiple lives. In fact, many of the Kaballistic rabbis, including the Baal Shem Tov, were able to read and see your past lives by looking either at your hands and reading the palms or by looking at your forehead. Secondly, the basic idea of reincarnation relates to the concept that, in order to ascend, you must be able to complete your life lessons and your soul lessons.

INTEGRATION OF DUALITY

In the Kaballah, ascension was offered to several Biblical figures. The raising of the chariots by Elijah and also the ascending of the etheric ladder by Jacob are two examples of how the people were able to transcend the concept of the waking consciousness and go to the higher realms. Most impressive and most important in all of the Biblical and ancient histories is the ascension of Enoch. "Enoch walked with God; then he was no more because God took him away" [Genesis 5:24; NIV]. This means that Enoch ascended and he transformed and became Archangel Metatron. The point is that in order to ascend, you have to be of a higher energy. Enoch was already of a higher energy and Eliahyu and Elijah were of higher energy. Elijah used the energy of the merkabah, or the etheric energy of the chariots, to ascend.

The Kaballah also offers the directions for completing soul lessons. The diagram for completing the soul lessons, is actually offered in the Tree of Life where there are twenty-two paths. Those twenty-two paths often are correlated to the Major Arcana in the Tarot cards. The paths are based on the concept of the integration of duality, which is one of the key lessons in the Kaballah. In the ascension, one needs the ability to integrate and unify duality.

Another key concept in the Kaballah is the work of unifying the upper and lower realms. One is talking about unifying the energy on the third dimension with the higher energy as a way to raise the sparks and as a way to raise lower energies. When we talk about ascension, we talk first about raising the third-dimensional energy to the energy of the fifth dimension.

Kaballistic interpretations of the traditional stories in the Old Testament also reveal the existence of the other dimensions. The Garden of Eden is actually a description of the fifth dimension. The fall of Adam and Eve from the Garden is in fact the leaving of the fifth dimensional realm, or leaving the realm of unity to the realm of duality of the third dimension. It is in the duality of the third dimension that the energies must be reunited.

UNLOCK THE CODES TO YOUR ASCENSION

Another key concept in the Kaballah is the concept of unlocking the codes of ascension. The key concept here is that higher consciousness needs to be unlocked. Normal consciousness needs to be transcended so that one can perceive the higher realms. The perceptions of the higher realms enable one to ascend. You have to have a preconceived notion that there are other realms. Not only that, you have to practice going to these other realms. The other higher realms are often referred to in the Hebrew lessons of Kaballah as the *Olam Habah*, or the world to come. The world to come is really the fifth-dimensional world. It is not the astral world, but the higher world to come.

The sacred codes to unlock the energies of ascension mean that you are to unlock your perceptual field, to unlock your perceptual awareness so that you can perceive and direct your ascension. This is the key. You perceive and direct your ascension. You notice that in Jacob's ladder, Jacob sees the ladder going upward. Enoch experiences a higher energy and he immediately disappeared from Earth and ascended. Enoch represents the ascension in totality. In the ascension, you disappear from Earth and transform into your fifth-dimensional self.

You can unlock the codes of ascension using the sacred words: "Holy, Holy, Holy is the Lord of Hosts." This demonstrates also a key Kaballistic idea for the ascension, which is the power of the Hebrew sound and the power of the word. In this case, *Kadosh, Kadosh, Kadosh, Adonai, Tzevaoth,* chanted with intention and chanted with the right enunciation of power, opens the inner sanctuary in the mind to unlock the keys of ascension. This will then allow the ascension to occur. One of the basic concepts of the Kaballah is that sound has healing power and healing energy.

In the modern ascension, a sound will be enunciated at the start. This sound will be heard by those who are starseeds and those who are higher beings. That sound will also unlock codes of ascension and signify the beginning of the ascension. Remember that there will be a sound that you will hear at the ascension. You can unlock your personal codes of ascension through sounds and sacred words. But the ascension energy itself will occur through a sacred sound that has not yet been emitted. It may be similar to the sound of the *Shofar* (Hebrew for Ram's horn), which is similar to the playing of the ram's horn.

The Tree of Life is holographic. By holographic, I mean that there are trees within trees. One aspect of one sphere has all ten spheres in it and then you ascend in that sphere so that you can go up to another sphere. After you cross the center sphere of the tree, which is called the sphere of the Tifereth, you can touch all other spheres. This center is a sphere of harmony and often has been referred to as the sphere of Sananda. One goes up the ladder, so to speak, so that one can ascend. After transcending the center sphere, the sphere of Tifereth, then you reach a point where you no longer need to return to the third dimension. You do not need to reincarnate back on Earth. In other words, in modern-day ascension and in ascending the Tree of Life, you reach a point where you do not have to return to Earth. You have reached the higher dimensional world.

This is also another key concept in the Kaballah: There are other higher dimensional worlds. Therefore you can reach a higher plane. Once you reach higher planes, there is no need to return to the lower world, which is the third dimension.

THE SOUL OFFERS YOU GRACE

The Kaballah offers a powerful tool for self-work. That tool of self-work means that working the spheres helps you to understand and complete the lessons of this incarnation. When the lessons are complete, you are able to ascend. I know that you may not 100 percent complete all lessons in this lifetime, thus we have the concept of grace. Grace originates in the Kaballah. It originates in the sphere of kindness or mercy. There is a mercy where the soul offers you grace so that you can take advantage of this opportunity for ascension.

Kaballah means to receive, and this beautiful message of the Tree of Life needs to be received and processed. The energies of the Kaballah point to this Tree of Life being a blueprint not only for personal ascension but also for planetary ascension. These concepts contained in the spheres are also keys for planetary work. There are codes and instructions within the Tree of Life in which the planet and the interaction of the planet with higher beings can be activated for a planetary ascension.

In the Kaballah, the master of ascension is Archangel Metatron. The key leader of ascension is Metatron. Enoch is the first recorded higher being that has been able to ascend. He became Metatron. Metatron is overseeing the ascension for many people. The angelic world is cooperating and working to assist all of you in ascension. Archangel Michael is also involved in the ascension and, of course, is a great Kaballistic leader and teacher. Archangel Michael is helping to cut your Earth cords of attachment. Your cords of attachment can be cut with the assistance of Archangel Michael. It is hard for all of you, no matter how much energy work you do, to actually release yourselves from the Earth world. Call on the angelic presence. Call on Archangel Michael, call on Archangel Metatron, and they will be assisting you on all levels for your ascension. I am Nabur.

PLANETARY SPIRITUAL ALCHEMY

Juliano and the Arcturians

Greetings, I am Juliano. We are the Arcturians. Now is an opportunity to raise the spiritual light quotient of planet Earth. Never in the history of this planet has there been this opportunity. I ask you to consider the enormity of this process and the magnitude of the work. The spirituality of the planet and you, the Adam species, have not kept up with scientific technology.

We know from our travels throughout the galaxy that this is a dangerous position for a planet to be in; namely, when the scientific technology of its inhabitants exceeds the spiritual light quotient of its inhabitants and of the planet. This creates an imbalance that often has the outcome of the destruction of life forms and possibly of the entire biosphere of the planet.

Throughout the history of Earth, there have been great spiritual masters who have been able to influence millions of people on the planet. Consider the great spiritual masters and the huge numbers of people who were influenced by them. One would still have to say that the years 2009 to 2012 represent the strongest possibility and opportunity in Earth's history to raise the spiritual light quotient of planet Earth. Why is that? First, the current scientific technology has led to fantastic communication links that were not possible earlier in your history. Second, because of scientific space exploration, embedded now in the consciousness of many is the beautiful image of the "blue jewel," as we call her, or planet Earth. In order to raise the spiritual light quotient of any planet, one must be able to visualize the planet from an outer perspective. This outer perspective was made by satellite imagery and from angles and perspectives photographed from the Moon. Even though this is not a distant perspective, it still provides the necessary image to work with consciously and unconsciously. It gives us, the Arcturians, an opportunity to more easily direct you in your accelerated imagery and your accelerated, guided visualizations.

ON THE CUSP OF EVOLUTION

The Earth responds to your telepathic communications, and the height of telepathic communications is visualizations. Therefore the visual imagery that you use in your planetary meditations can have a dramatic effect on shaping the Earth changes and the evolutionary process of the planet. It is important to realize that not only is the Earth a living spirit but also, as a living spirit, the Earth is going through an evolution. You and the Earth are both on the cusp of an evolutionary change. As you know, each evolutionary change that has occurred for the inhabitants of planet Earth always transpires as a crisis situation.

A crisis situation goes hand in hand with evolution. The process of nature is that change basically occurs out of necessity. You may even know that in your own personal history. If you review your own changes and your development, you may agree that the major changes that you have successfully made, the most dramatic and far-reaching, probably have occurred concurrently with a crisis. I think you have a saying: "Necessity is the mother of invention." Well, from our perspective as planetary archeologists and planetary anthropologists, we can say that crisis is the mother of evolutionary change. That means that evolutionary change dramatically occurs in the midst of danger.

Everyone who is listening and reading these words knows firsthand the tremendous danger that exists at this time on Earth. The idea of planetary stability and the idea that everything will continue in a normal, stable unfolding is but an illusion. The planetary evolution now has to be guided by planetary healers. The crisis and the danger inherent in this moment are amenable to dramatic changes and dramatic shifts through planetary healers and planetary spirituality. The planetary healers that are present now can raise the spiritual light quotient of Earth in order to provide the foundation for the dramatic change that must occur for Earth to evolve.

YOU ARE PLANETARY HEALERS

Earth is a living spirit, so when we talk about the Earth surviving, we are talking about Earth surviving as a living spirit—a living spirit in the third dimension. Yes, you can look at other planets such as Mars. You can see that there are no life forms on that planet. You could say, quite conclusively, that there is a dramatic decrease in the spirit of Mars. I say dramatic decrease because it is not like Pluto or other planets that have absolutely no life. Mars did have life on it at one time. Mars was inhabited, and the remnants of the spiritual life forms and of the spirit of Mars are still in the ethers around the planet. Those spiritual energies exist in the outer-dimensional realms of Mars in the fourth dimension.

I know there has been some discussion about how to revitalize and reengineer Mars to hold life again and to rekindle the spiritual energy of the planet. It is true that the spiritual energy and the spiritual life force of Mars can possibly be rekindled through some dramatic reengineering. This is far beyond the capabilities of your scientists on Earth now. From a practical standpoint, we can say that the spiritual energy of Mars is dormant and may possibly be reawakened. The spiritual life of Earth is very awake. The evolutionary process of the spirit of this planet needs to be studied because humankind now has limited knowledge of how a planet evolves and lives and what it means for a planet to have a spiritual light quotient. You, my friends, are on the forefront of this evolutionary shift. We, the Arcturians, consider you planetary healers. Planetary healers understand that a planet evolves, that a planet has a spiritual light quotient.

Planetary healers understand that this is the first opportunity in the history of Earth to systematically work as a unit around the entire globe, the entire planet, with the expressed purpose of raising the spiritual light quotient of the planet. Raising the spiritual light quotient of a planet is totally linked to raising the spiritual light quotient of humankind. Remember, I said that there has never been a moment in the history of this planet where the evolution and survival of the spirit Earth were linked to one species. It is also true that only humankind can institute the changes in the planet, and that can only be done through the process of raising the spiritual light quotient of humankind and raising the spiritual light quotient of Earth.

The 1,600 Arcturian starseeds are committed to planetary healing. Do not be concerned by the number being small, because one spiritually focused person, especially in this environment on the Earth now, can gather much light and can influence many people. This has happened repeatedly in the history of this planet and this has happened without modern communication. It has happened without modern technology. Many times, one person has dramatically influenced people. But it has taken hundreds—and in some cases, thousands—of years for the full effects of that one person's spiritual intervention to change the masses. You do not have time on Earth now to wait for one spiritually powerful person to effect a change, because you cannot wait 300 years for the full effects to occur. This means that we need acceleration. The only way that you can accelerate planetary healing, evolution and the distribution of spiritual energy in a timely manner is through connecting to fifth-dimensional energy. In the fifth dimension, time is not linear. In the fifth dimension, you can activate and accomplish many things that would take years, even centuries, on Earth.

REVERSE TIME ACCELERATION

We seek the opportunity to connect you to the fifth dimension. By connecting you to the fifth dimension, many of the meditations and much of the work that we do with you is accelerated in time. You may have the experience in other instances when you connect to the fifth dimension that time seems as if it is occurring quickly. Yet when you return to your third-dimensional body and the third-dimensional Earth, a long time has elapsed. You might feel like, from your perspective in fifth-dimensional meditations, only five or ten minutes are passing. Actually, it could be an hour—and that is a modest time acceleration.

We want to use this concept of time acceleration. That is to say that in a focused meditation in fifth-dimensional light, we can accomplish and shift energy on the Earth in an even shorter Earth-time. What you would experience as a long time in the fifth dimension may actually only be a short time in the third dimension. We call this "reverse time acceleration," or RTA. This is possible—and it is necessary now. It may not be helpful to focus your work and meditations on the fifth dimension, accomplishing many wonderful things, only to find out that what you thought was a short period of time from the fifth dimension was actually a year in Earth time. Quite frankly, Earth may not have a year to let things just unravel the way they are right now without a more powerful and immediate spiritual evolution. We want to use RTA, reverse time acceleration. Using fifth-dimensional energy, we could effect change in a shorter period of Earth time—that is, institute a change that, earlier, may have required months or years.

Let me give you an example. When Jesus/Sananda was on the planet, in many ways, the full effect of his energy and light did not dramatically influence the planet for perhaps 200 to 300 years. I realize that there were many people around him the years immediately after his death that were dramatically changed. But his effect did not influence countries or lands until much later. We could say that this was a normal time effect. If Jesus/Sananda were to appear on the planet now, it would not take so long for him to affect everything. This is one of the main messages and metaphors that I could use to explain to you the effect of reverse time acceleration.

The work that Jesus/Sananda has been doing has been going on for centuries. When he returns, it would take him less than five seconds of Earth time to make the evolutionary changes necessary on the planet and in the human species so that everything would be moving in the highest light and the highest good. This example shows you the power of reverse time acceleration, and it shows you the power that a spiritual presence can have on Earth now. Your work as planetary healers is accelerating.

THE ANADOLU ISTANBUL BOSPORUS CRYSTAL

We have worked consistently and dramatically with the Groups of Forty to download the eleventh etheric crystal in Istanbul, Turkey. This crystal has been referred to as the one opening up hidden knowledge to the world. Its main function to connect the fifth dimension to the third dimension so that more third-dimensional people become aware of the fifth dimension. This crystal dramatically accelerates the process. The veil between the third and the fifth dimension is gradually being lifted. One has to ask this question: "How will I be able to most effectively use the fifth-dimensional connection, the fifth-dimensional energy, to institute the changes necessary to accelerate and activate planetary healing and my personal healing?" This is a continual question that most of the starseeds have been asking for many years. Every starseed is interested in their personal development as well as planetary development. Every starseed wants to be able to use this fifth-dimensional connective link for his evolution and ability to be more effective as a personal healer and a planetary healer.

The etheric crystals, including the eleventh etheric crystal, form a grid of spiritual and electromagnetic energy. With this crystal, and with the downloading of the twelfth crystal on the horizon, each of the planetary healers, each of the Arcturian starseeds, will more effectively be able to plug into this, what we call, "Arcturian tree of life etheric crystal grid." The Istanbul crystal is also translated as the Asian crystal in Istanbul because it was downloaded on the Asian side of the Bosporus. The downloading of this Anadolu Istanbul Bosporus crystal is making available a connection to the electromagnetic grid energy of the crystal links. In many ways it is a doorway for starseeds to connect themselves to this etheric grid. This etheric grid is a fifth-dimensional force on the Earth. It is a way for you to connect to fifth-dimensional energy.

All energy is electromagnetic. Third-dimensional energy is electromagnetic, and fifth-dimensional energy is electromagnetic. You want to be able to connect to the frequency of the fifth-dimensional energy. These etheric crystals are often an avenue to plug into a fifth-dimensional etheric grid. When you connect to a fifth-dimensional etheric grid, then your frequency is immediately raised. It would be similar to connecting into a higher voltage—you are raising your ability to assimilate the electromagnetic volts. In our meditation now, we will seek a better connection for all of you to the electromagnetic grid of these etheric crystals. We will use the Istanbul crystal to provide the avenue and the opening for you to connect to the fifth dimensional energy. Remember, once you raise your vibration to the fifth dimension, you as a third-dimensional being have the option of focusing and using it as you see fit. So in some ways, it would be like someone gave you $10,000. They can say to you, "Spend it wisely," but you have the responsibility and the power to use it as you will. What I am suggesting is that you will be able to receive this higher energy by connecting into the grid today, and then you can use it for personal and planetary healing.

You can use this fifth-dimensional connection to increase vibrations for a planetary benefit. First, our goal at this time is to connect into the grid of the etheric crystal linkage by visualizing the Anadolu Istanbul Bosporus crystal. You may have difficulty visualizing it, as many people are not aware of it geographically. I would like you to visualize a waterway that separates Europe and Asia, and I would like you to visualize a second bridge (because there are two bridges) that goes across. At the far end of one bridge is an old castle; across from the castle on the waterway is where the etheric crystal is downloaded, almost in front of that second bridge. Visualize a strait or a waterway that may be a half-mile or more wide with a beautiful etheric crystal in the water. As you hear these words, begin to connect with that energy. [Sings.] Anadolu, Istanbul, etheric crystal in the Bosporus. Anadolu, etheric crystal in Istanbul in the Bosporus.

We will go into a meditation now. Feel this crystal energy connection activating all of the chakras in your body. This crystal has the power to activate both you and the planet. This crystal has the power to remove the veil for you so that you experience more fifth-dimensional energy and light and receive the vibrational energies of the fifth dimension now. This Anadolu crystal is opening up an area between your heart and your throat chakras. This is, from your perspective, a new chakra and a new energy center. We have modified the Tree of Life to twelve spheres instead of ten spheres. Realize that there are more chakras and there are more ways of activating yourself energetically than the traditional level of chakras. Now, there is a new level, a new sphere, a new chakra between the heart and your throat.

This new level can be called the chakra of hidden knowledge. In Kaballah, it is known as *Da'at*—knowledge—unifying the ten Sephirot of the Tree of Life. In the crystal world or etheric world, it is called the eleventh crystal—the Anadolu Istanbul Bosporus crystal.

LEAD INTO GOLD

The ancient mystics knew there were ways of transforming the Earth reality. This was practiced in the study of spiritual alchemy. Spiritual alchemy was metaphorically described as the desire to transform lead into gold [as discussed in Chapter 11]. This transformation, of course, was breaking the laws of physics because there is no way that lead can be turned into gold in normal, third-dimensional logical physics. But in spiritual alchemy there is a special state of higher consciousness, and when that state of consciousness is achieved through various accelerated, energetic exercises, one has the power to change physical reality—lead into gold— by saying a certain word such as "abracadabra"—*avra kehdabra*—Aramaic for "I will create as I speak." This is one formula of words that, said with the right intention, will work effectively with the spiritual energy and exercises. One can thus transform lead into gold. This is an example of using fifth-dimensional energy to transform a third-dimensional energy.

It is a very small and modest work. Transforming lead into gold would not save a planet. Transforming lead into gold would be a step in the integration of fifth-dimensional energy to effect a change in the third-dimensional reality and in the third-dimensional physical world.

PLANETARY SPIRITUAL ALCHEMY

In terms of planetary healing, we can say that there is planetary spiritual alchemy—PSA. In the concept of PSA, one can induce a planetary change through the right sort of spiritual exercises and practices, then through saying certain sounds and words to effect that change. In order to do that, you have to raise the vibrational field of the planet. This can be accomplished through the twelve etheric crystals. The interaction of the planetary healers with the etheric crystals can create the environment for Earth changes when certain powerful words are spoken. In order to effect the change, one has to have an idea of what change is possible and what change would be most effective for planetary health.

Earth is a complicated spiritual energy. What change would you make to Earth? There are so many complex interactions within Earth; thus, it would be difficult to know what change you would want when you were finally setting everything up and saying "abracadabra." What would you change? Would you reverse the polar ice caps so that they were frozen again? Would you clear all the air? Would you stop volcanic eruptions? Realize that taking one such event is isolating that event from other interactions. It would be difficult to say which would be the most effective and the most needed change.

In telepathic communication with Earth, and in biorelativity, we have two processes. The first process is the transmission of energy to Earth. The second process is receiving communications from Earth. Only when there are these two energetic linkages can you receive the information that would allow you to receive the correct energy on which change needs to occur for the highest good of the planet—for the human species and for the evolution of planet Earth.

We remind you that we continually have meditators on Arcturus who assist in communicating and receiving energy and light from our planet so that we can do exactly the shift and change that is necessary. We would institute the needed change and work with a similar biorelativity system that we have been teaching you. That system centers on working with etheric grids. We also work with the etheric crystals, and then we establish and raise the light frequency energy of the planet through the etheric crystals.

Then it is necessary to raise the light crystal frequency energy of the people. Then people can interact with this and receive the message from the planet about what change needs to be done. Planetary healers can then use PSA. Then on Arcturus we would get our meditators and other group members together on our planet to participate in a PSA experience.

In spiritual alchemy, there is a lot of preparation and a lot of study necessary. In planetary spiritual alchemy, there is an equal amount of study and preparation. The downloading of these etheric crystals on Earth has lasted several years at least and has been a process of preparation for the PSA experience. Now that the eleventh etheric crystal is connected, the opportunities for each person to connect to the PSA energy are raised.

A New Planetary Harmony

The first level of planetary spiritual alchemy has to do with providing harmony on Earth. The changes are rapid and Earth does not have enough time to integrate and balance everything so quickly. You have a hard time integrating and balancing yourself when the changes are too rapid. So does the Earth as a planetary spirit. You have to consider the age of Earth, and then you have to consider the rapid amount of changes that have occurred in the past hundred years and even the past fifteen to thirty years. The Earth needs to come into a balance with all of this because the changes are happening so fast. One of the first lessons and issues in the planetary spiritual alchemy would be in harmonizing Earth.

This harmony has to be tied in with fifth-dimensional energy because there is no way Mother Earth can assimilate everything just with third-dimensional energy and light. It is too much to integrate. Even you are probably struggling because you have witnessed so many changes on the planet. To process these changes for the planet, for Mother Earth, it is necessary to connect the light from the fifth dimension and to work with Earth in helping her to receive fifth-dimensional energy also. It so happens that the necessary fifth-dimensional energy that Earth needs to bring herself into a harmony to ensure her survival comes from the Central Sun. That Central Sun light, which comes into alignment approximately on December 22, 2012, needs to be focused through PSA to help Earth come into a new planetary harmony. This will ensure her survival. This will ensure that she can come into a new harmony.

Obviously, if you look at everything that is happening now, the Earth is going to become more polarized. The Earth is becoming more polarized in terms of the effects of certain Earth changes. Changes in the human species—politically, sociologically, economically and environmentally—are also becoming more polarized.

Fifth-dimensional light from the Central Sun can come to the core of the Earth. It can be directed to her with the PSA energy and can help her to accelerate her ability to come into a new balance, which will ensure that humanity can survive on her. This means that all of the predictions of bad events, such as temperature increases, that are going to happen have to be recalibrated. Earth has to recalibrate it, and humankind has to recalibrate it so that Earth can assimilate all these changes and shifts and still hold a planetary balance that will ensure the survival of humanity and Earth in a new, fifth-dimensional harmony. I am Juliano. Blessings.

PERSONAL AND PLANETARY ASCENSION

Juliano and Alano

Greetings, I am Juliano. We are the Arcturians. This is an accelerated time indeed, and you know from your personal experiences that events on the planet are accelerating politically, socially and geographically—especially in terms of Earth changes. These changes seem to be rapid and intense. Most important are the changes that you are personally experiencing. I know that some of you already feel a little bit dissociated from events, from your life and may even feel distant from yourselves. This depersonalization can be in part a defense due to these rapid changes.

CUT THE CORDS OF ATTACHMENT TO THE THIRD DIMENSION

When a representative of a species, like the human species, experiences an evolutionary shift of consciousness, this shift creates a stressful response even though there is great excitement and expansion. There is also change. The body—including the mental, emotional and physical bodies—is working overtime to adjust to the rapid changes and to make these monumental and evolutionary shifts. We are at a turning point, and there is new information continually becoming available to all of you.

Our focus now is on the ascension of personal and planetary processes. There are many parallels between your personal and planetary ascensions. Let me speak about the lower self and the higher self because when you look at the ascension, you can assume that you will take off the coat of the physical body and leave it behind—similar to how you would leave a booster rocket behind if you were taking off from Earth. The lower self has many ego aspects and desires and fears. Many people have assumed that the lower self is going to ascend with you. Many people have also assumed that they must overcome all the defects in their personalities and their physical bodies, then assume a state of nirvana—which would include a total enlightened presence on Earth—and at that point, they would ascend.

This idealistic view reflects the accomplishments of many of the previous ascended masters who have walked this planet. They achieved the states of consciousness of what I have just described in terms of their integration and harmonization with the universal light. Many of you now, in spite of your intense efforts, may understand that you, in this short period of time, may not achieve nirvana or may not achieve this beautiful harmony. Even so, you can still ascend. You are still able to move your consciousness to a higher state that will allow you to move into the fifth dimension.

That is the reason why we have introduced the spiritual technologies, especially the spiritual technology of shimmering. We realize that new spiritual technologies are necessary to help you adapt and to process what I would call a rather turbulent time in Earth's history. This spiritual technology, including shimmering, is going to be a great boost to your abilities to evolve and to move into higher realms. Part of this process will include taking off the lower vibrational self. By taking off and discarding the lower self, you begin to identify with the fifth-dimensional self.

There is a certain process by which you discard the lower self. Actually, the word "discard" may not even be the most comprehensive description of this process, because the disregarding of the lower self is done with love. It is also done with detachment, and it is done in a way that allows you to still have a relationship with your lower selves while you are walking on Earth. You still have the lower self, but your relationship to it is going to shift. It is what Archangel Michael refers to as realizing that you have to cut the cords of attachment to your lower selves. By cutting the cords of attachment, you will be able to "blast off" into the fifth dimension.

ACCELERATE YOUR VIBRATIONAL FIELDS

Obviously, we are coming closer to the ascension. Your knowledge and abilities to detach are becoming more important and need to be reactivated. I hope this reminder will refresh your memory and also reactivate your knowledge on how to detach. The codes of ascension include the ability to activate and release your lower selves. It also requires a mental understanding that your greater fifth-dimensional selves are multipresent and contain omnipotent and omnipresent aspects of yourselves that you are just learning to identify. I don't mean omnipotent in the sense of being powerful about everything. I mean having the power to live in several dimensions simultaneously. It means having the power to oversee your ascension and your own soul evolvement. Identify with your higher selves and your fifth-dimensional selves, then you can unite the ascension energy with that part of your higher selves.

You represent and hold a portion of yourselves while you unite with your greater selves in the fifth dimension. Shimmering is the acceleration of your vibrational field so that you can merge your consciousness with your fifth-dimensional selves. Also, by doing reverse shimmering (i.e., shimmering your fifth-dimensional energy back into your third-dimensional body), you can bring back your fifth-dimensional selves energetically into the third dimension. The sole goal becomes the unity of your selves. This unity is the basis of your ability to ascend.

Downloading this eighth crystal at Copper Canyon in Mexico, which we have labeled the shimmering crystal, has raised the vibrational fields on the whole planet and of all of the Groups of Forty members. The abilities to shimmer have been escalated, activated and raised to newer levels. This ability to shimmer is translated also into the cities of light, which are designated parts on Earth that are geographically coming into the ability to shimmer and move into the fifth dimension.

The process of Earth's ascension is of great interest and attention to all of you because you are personal and planetary ascenders. You have come here at this time to participate in your personal ascension, but you have also come here now to participate in the planetary ascension. Many of you have asked repeatedly: "How is Earth going to ascend? How is Earth going to move into the fifth dimension? What is going to happen to all the people on Earth that are of lower vibration when the ascension occurs? What is going to happen to all of the wars and the disruptive parts of this planet? How is all of Earth going to ascend?"

I know that you have heard stories of the first wave, the second wave and the third wave. I know that you have heard many stories of the coming purifications—many of which have already begun. I believe that it is still bewildering to you to try and conceive how Earth is going to ascend. Don't you think that you can look at yourselves and hopefully recognize the spiritual progress and the vibrational shifts that each of you has attained. Maybe you have come to the point energetically where you can accept your ascension, and you can work diligently on the separation and the ability to cut the cords of attachment from your lower selves. In spite of any of the problems you may have personally, I still believe that each of you can understand the ascension and accept that you will be ready to ascend. The key is to cut the cords of attachment to your lower selves, but you can cut the cords of attachment with love, respect and the intent of ascending.

THE WHOLE CAN BE RE-CREATED IN THE FIFTH DIMENSION

How does this personal explanation of ascension translate into Earth's ascension? This parallel between personal and planetary ascension still holds up on Earth, but there are some minor modifications that include the concepts of the cities of light, holographic energy and the etheric crystals. The cities of light are designated areas on the planet where groups of starseeds like yourselves are working to create vibrational energy fields or areas that are fifth dimensional. These fifth-dimensional areas are shimmering into a higher vibrational field, just the way you are.

You must visualize and understand that you have three-dimensional bodies and you have to work to identify with your fifth-dimensional bodies. Also realize that Earth has a fifth-dimensional body, and the cities of light—these designated shimmering areas—can be shimmered, translated and transmitted into fifth-dimensional Earth. Raising specific areas into Earth's fifth-dimensional presence will constitute Earth's ascension.

This means that not all parts of Earth are going to go to the fifth dimension. Only the designated areas that are close to shimmering, or vibrating at higher frequencies, will be moving into the fifth-dimensional Earth. These areas already have a presence in the fifth dimension ready to receive the fifth-dimensional Earth cities of light. The shimmering energy around these cities of light will help those areas ascend in and around their designated fifth-dimensional Earth areas, which is around the Central Sun. Those of you who are working with certain areas of the planet will now understand that you can activate and shimmer and connect these higher places with fifth-dimensional Earth.

Holographic energy and holographic light are able to assimilate parts of a whole by using the parts. The whole can be re-created in the fifth dimension. For the ascension of Earth, there is a certain number of planetary parts or a certain percentage of light cities that need to be shimmered. These areas need to be activated, transformed and connected to their fifth-dimensional Earth counterparts. These parts, when they reach a certain critical level—some of you would call this a critical mass—can activate the planetary ascension whereby the parts of the cities of light that are on Earth ascend. Remember, the whole planet doesn't ascend but rather these shimmering parts. These parts that ascend, interestingly, are protected areas. In some cases, after the ascension, the existence of these places may be removed from the memory of the planet so that people may not know and would not remember that they existed.

A way to describe this is to imagine that a fifth-dimensional ship came to Earth and landed on the third dimension, creating a beautiful garden. However, by creating that beautiful garden, the inhabitants of the ship realized that they were going to become involved in the karmic energy of the planet, and they did not want to do this, so they erased the garden. Before they erased the garden, however, they interacted and met with several people who were seeking higher consciousness and higher light. They decided to bring those people with them, and when they were all in harmony with this process, they left the planet. As they were leaving, they removed the garden they had created. Anyone who had seen the garden and was in a lower dimension would not be able to go with these beings. Also, their memories of the garden would be erased.

In mythology and in history, some people might be able to carry the tales of this garden as remnants in memories, but they would not find any knowledge, representation or factual evidence of its existence. The existence of the garden remains in a mythological state. In fact, that part of the Earth that was in that garden area ascended and was transferred into the fifth dimension.

ANIMALS ARE SHIMMERING TOO

A group of starseeds can work together to create cities of light. They can create a garden as described in the above example, and they can participate in creating a new fifth-dimensional planet that is called the fifth-dimensional Earth. Many of you have already been working on this.

Let me speak about some of the sacred animals on this planet, and let me tell you also that these animals, with your assistance, are shimmering and telepathically connecting to their new fifth-dimensional homes on the fifth-dimensional Earth as well. As a result, on a third-dimensional level, you might see the tragedies of the extinction of certain species. On a fifth-dimensional level—especially with your connecting work and activation—they are spiritually preparing themselves to merge in their fifth-dimensional states too.

When you try to conceive or visualize Earth's ascension, it may look to you to be piecemeal. You might think: "Well, here is a city of light, and here is another city of light, but it doesn't sound like the whole planet is moving." Remember, the part represents the whole. These parts, called cities of light, are not fragments, but will be integrated into a critical mass that will allow a fifth-dimensional Earth to ascend and separate, leaving behind those parts of Earth that are of a lower vibrational field.

Some of you might say, "Well, I cannot leave Earth." Of course, that is your choice, and also please understand that you will be going through the stargate. The planet does not go through the stargate in the same way. There is a different process for planetary ascension. I think you need to conceive of a planetary ascension as the creation of a new fifth-dimensional Earth through your shimmering light and shimmering work.

I want to turn things over to my dear friend, Alano, who is a fifth-dimensional Arcturian master and who will speak to you about her planet, Alano, and about what it means to be on a fifth-dimensional planet. I am Juliano.

Greetings, dear starseeds, Groups of Forty members. I am Alano. I am from the moon-planet Alano, which is near the Central Sun. I arrived on my mission at Copper Canyon, Mexico, in the El Divisadero Canyon area to activate and download the eighth etheric crystal into Earth, which created a shimmering vibrational energy that has extensively connected with all the other seven crystals. These eight crystals are etherically connected to the fifth-dimensional Earth. I oversee the Earth's ascension and help to coordinate your work to activate these new cities of light.

SHIMMER TO CLEANSE YOUR ENERGETIC FIELDS

Some of these cities of light can just be represented by your own house in one small area. Don't be confused to think that it has to be some city of 10,000 people on top of a mountain. Yes, I know that ultimately such a city could evolve, much the way that you have described or seen Shangri-la. What is interesting about the energy field around a light city or light area is that lower vibrational people who come up to the energy field cannot penetrate or cannot see it. For example, when we were working with the channel and the other GOF members in a public area and Juliano was activating them to a higher frequency and vibration, no one in the public area recognized what was going on vibrationally, yet the people who were with the channel were going into an extremely high vibrational field.

This is a beautiful way of describing the cities and areas of light. Others who are of lower vibrational energy will not see that you are moving into a higher vibration nor will they feel your energy. You experience a protected state. That means that wherever you are, you can connect with this vibrational energy and make yourselves relatively transparent so that those of lower vibration will not be able to interact with you or harm you. Remember, much of the lower vibrational activities on Earth are going to continue. Some of these activities that are karmic and very intense may accelerate into a purification or a polarization of untold magnitude. This will not inhibit your abilities to participate and to create more cities or areas of light.

Begin to vibrate, begin to shimmer, on a higher frequency of energy. In the Central Sun area, most of the planets are moon-planets. Your Earth scientists are continually looking for new planets and perhaps think that they will discover life there, which is possible. In reality, our experience in our travels throughout the galaxy is that we have discovered more life on the moons of planetary systems—the designation we use is moon-planet. We are creating vibrational electromagnetic cities, which are areas of light that vibrate in resonance with the fifth-dimensional cities of light. We also have been able to establish a duplication of the crystal lake temple and of other areas of vibrational activation to hold your fifth-dimensional bodies on our planet.

Remember that in fifth-dimensional energy, you are totally able to bilocate. You are able to be in several places at one time with consciousness and with awareness. One way of describing this would be to say that time on Earth is linear; therefore, one event occurs right after another in a straight line. But in the fifth-dimension and higher vibrational fields, time is circular, so if you have an awareness, you can connect with the other parts of yourselves simultaneously without losing your consciousness. In Earth's linear process, you can only connect with another part of yourselves when the original parts are either asleep or out of body. I know that you are all evolving to a state of circular time and circular consciousness. The idea of shimmering involves cleansing and purifying your energetic fields, including your lower selves. It is true that you will discard, or purify, your lower selves.

SHIMMERING TO THE FIFTH DIMENSION CAN PROTECT YOUR THIRD-DIMENSIONAL BODY

In our shimmering work, we help to create an energy field where you can project your shimmering presence to the fifth dimension. Each energetic shimmer can bring to the fifth dimension an imprint of your lower vibrational energy that you picked up on the third dimension. In fact, as a healer, you could potentially pick up energy vibrations and imprints or densities from the person you are trying to heal. I know that many of you as healers seek to ensure that any healing work that you do allows you to be protected. You want to be protected from any densities that people may be projecting on to you or any attachments that they may seek in the healing process.

It is natural for the "healee" to project on to you. It would also be natural that you would try to protect yourselves from this energy. The third-dimensional Earth is filled with so much polarization and karmic problems. The energies from the densities on the everyday planetary life attach to you, even though you have tried to remain as pure as possible. We find this to be normal, but we also offer a way of shimmering so that you can detach from all of the densities and attachments that may have come to you, including during healing work.

You can project and shimmer those densities into your fifth-dimensional body. Then the fifth-dimensional body, which in this type of work can be going to the moon-planet Alano, can absorb all of the densities and then send them off to a place far removed from here. Your fifth-dimensional body can process an infinite amount of densities. Then in the reverse process, you shimmer out of your fifth-dimensional body and back into your third-dimensional body. Your third-dimensional body receives the fifth-dimensional energy minus all of the imprints and attachments that you sent so that you are released.

This process has much significance. When working in cities of light, you can project certain third-dimensional areas that may be polluted or have imprints with discarnate spirits. You can also use the attractive, or magnetic, areas of the eight etheric crystals. They can act as magnets to attract lower vibrational densities and then gather those energies into the etheric crystals. For example, say you are working in the pure area at Copper Canyon. You can vibrate the crystal and attract other lower densities that are along that grid current in that area. You can then shimmer and project that crystal's energy into the fifth-dimensional crystal here on

Alano. In essence this will provide a healing on the area. You can see the potential of this process in purifying land areas on Earth.

Great healers will sometimes encourage the healee to project all of his or her densities and negative energies into them, knowing that they can shimmer those densities into the fifth dimension and release them. I do not recommend that you do this unless you have a high degree of training, but I want to introduce this so you understand how some healers will actually take on the karma of the healees and shimmer, or project, it to the fifth dimension. This means that you can do this and use the etheric crystals to take out much density on the planet. Ultimately, we would say that you would be able to expand the circle of the cities of light to become larger, take on more of the lower energy of the Earth and then vibrate it off the planet.

SHIMMERING MEDITATION

I would like to do a shimmering exercise now in which you can shimmer and project your energy from the third dimension into the fifth dimension. The eighth crystal, which is in Copper Canyon, Mexico, approximately 400 to 500 hundred miles south of Texas, has a close link with Alano.

I ask that you all visualize yourselves around this crystal. Even if you cannot find it on a map or clearly define its exact location, know that when you project yourselves there, you will be there. Also, if you are knowledgeable of the other etheric crystals we have placed on Earth, then send yourselves to one of those instead. Believe me, from that crystal, you will connect to this eighth crystal. Then we will shimmer.

The first step in this meditation is to either project yourselves to the eighth etheric crystal in Copper Canyon or go to another crystal that you know. Take your total energetic selves to that place. We will be meditating briefly while you do that. Now visualize and project yourselves to this place, either to one of the other crystals or to the Copper Canyon crystal. Send all of the lower parts of yourselves, or all of the vibrational parts that are of lower density. Send that with you as you project and command yourselves to go to the Copper Canyon etheric crystal, which is in the canyon. We are all gathered there now, and you now have all of your lower vibrational parts with you. Begin to shimmer as you are going into a higher vibrational state and shimmer out of your third-dimensional body now. Shimmer out!

Now shimmer into your fifth-dimensional body on the moon-planet Alano. As you shimmer into the etheric crystal area in Alano, know that there is a duplicate canyon that looks just like Copper Canyon, and there is also a duplicate crystal there. You have just shimmered into that crystal. You are now in the fifth-dimensional area of the fifth-dimensional moon-planet Alano. You have brought with you all of the lower vibrational frequencies that you were able to carry with you. Hold those parts as we meditate briefly while you hold that light. Now we are shimmering and you can say the words to your fifth-dimensional body: "Release the lower vibrational imprints that I have brought with me from the third dimension. Release, release, release." Say it three times to yourselves silently: "Release, release, release."

I, Alano, take all of these densities you have released and send them up a column of light that leaves this fifth-dimensional canyon and goes off into another realm. Let them dissipate far away from consciousness and awareness now. You continue to shimmer. Now you are going to shimmer out of your fifth-dimensional body on the fifth-dimensional moon-planet Alano and back into your third-dimensional body.

As you shimmer out, you find your third-dimensional body on Earth, but do not enter it just yet. Go approximately five feet above your physical body on Earth and prepare for a perfect-alignment reentry. Command and say the words silently, "Perfect alignment." Your fifth-dimensional body is energetically above your third-dimensional body and now goes into perfect alignment. Reenter now!

You have reentered and you have released so much that you will be astounded at the amount when you come back into your normal consciousness. Do not think about it now. Just know that you have released it. This process that I have taken you through is a purification process that can also be used for cleansing and creating areas of light, the cities of light. You project the area you want to work with on Earth to the crystal in Copper Canyon and then from the canyon into the crystal on the fifth-dimensional area in Alano. After the projection is purified, bring the energy back to Earth. You can do this with many areas on Earth.

I will have more to say about this purification process because this process not only purifies the area but also it can purify the discarnate spirits that are around the area. There is not enough time left to go to every place on Earth and to work individually with every discarnate spirit, so this method I described can be used to project and purify large energy areas that have discarnate spirits. Greetings from my moon-planet Alano. I am Alano. Good day.

BALANCE THROUGH
PLANETARY CITIES OF LIGHT

Juliano and the Arcturians

reetings, I am Juliano. We are the Arcturians. The use of spiritual
energy requires the energy of enhancement. Enhancement is an
energy that can be described as using building blocks—that is to
say that one type of thought creates a basis for another type of thought.
One type of spiritual light then builds and allows you to use and to enhance more spiritual light.

IMBALANCES IN THE BIOSPHERE OF EARTH

We seek to enhance your abilities in biorelativity. Biorelativity is defined
as the participation of spiritual and telepathic thoughts directed toward the
physical world and planet Earth. The idea of thoughts changing the physical
structure of something requires the enhancement ability. If you look at the
nature of thoughts, then you will understand quite quickly that it takes a lot
of intermediate action to create or manifest something physical after the initial thought has been transmitted. To put it in simple terms, imagine that you
have the thought to create a chair. In order to manifest that thought into the
physical, you must then perhaps draw a design. Then you must buy wood,
cut that wood and then nail the pieces together, finally finishing the process
by painting the chair. Everything first began with the thought.

Now when we talk about biorelativity, we mean a highly complex physical
intervention, because we want to change the nature of the physical structures of Earth. We are going to give you instructions. We want to change
the calibration mechanisms on Earth and the feedback loop mechanisms.
This needs to be done in order to protect the biosphere, because the biosphere and its accompanied structures and feedback loops are moving in

a direction that will create further imbalances. Should this happen, these imbalances will make it more difficult for people to live on Earth.

Several examples of imbalances already exist, and people have requested my assistance with them. We hear that there are heat waves in Turkey, for example. There are heat waves and fires in the forests in Spain. There are heat waves in the Northwest of the United States and in Northwest Canada in the British Columbia-Vancouver area. At the same time, there is unusually cool weather in the middle and northeastern parts of North America.

INTERVENTIONS USING BIORELATIVITY

Many of the Groups of Forty members have requested the assistance from the Arcturians to help to bring the heat down and to stop the forest fires by using biorelativity. Remember, in biorelativity we look at thinking and thoughts as the beginning and as a basis for changing the physical structure on a planet. This is based on the same principle as building a chair, because first you must have the idea and then you go to create the chair. There is one major difference between building a physical object like a chair and using thinking for changing Earth, however. When we compare that to changing the physical balance on Earth, we note that the major difference is this: Earth is a living spirit! The chair is not a living spirit; therefore, there are interactions that occur between what you send telepathically and Earth's ability to receive those thoughts and to make shifts.

Remember the way in which I described the idea of thoughts occurring first before the chair is built. That means that the builder, the furniture maker, has an idea of what the chair is supposed to look like. Let's apply that same principle to the biorelativity intervention for Earth. You cannot simply say, "Okay, I am going to send Earth thoughts, and Earth will be healed." Many people think this way when they say that Earth needs to be healed. There is a lot of truth in that approach, but we have to go into a more thought-specific idea. That thought-specific idea goes like this: What is the image of Earth that you, through your biorelativity, want to manifest? What do you want Earth to do? You may say, "I want the fires to stop" or "I want the cold or the heat to change in this part of the planet." This is fine, but remember that it is more complex than you might think, because Earth is balancing many different processes.

Visualizing Normal Energy Flows

When you or I say that Earth needs to be healed, then let us look more specifically at the problems this way: Earth's energy pathways are blocked. Earth's meridians are blocked. The oceans have too much carbon or too much pollution in them, and this pollution is blocking the normal energy patterns and the energy flow. The dams in the rivers, the existence of nuclear waste and those places where nuclear bombs and testing have been done have created blocks in the energy systems and in Earth's meridians. Earth has living energy corridors and energy ley lines. We must visualize that these ley lines and these meridians are not blocked. Let us go back to the example of it being too warm or too hot in Spain or too hot in British Columbia. These heat problems are a direct result of blocked meridians preventing the normal flows and causing a distortion in them. The image that we want to project, therefore, is that of Earth's meridians flowing freely and the highest balance of energy flow in Earth.

A problem with trying to picture this is that humanity must learn what the optimum configuration of the meridians need to be on the planet. We can identify where there are blocks. It is very difficult for even a computer to predict the weather patterns on this planet. Humanity has developed a model for Earth global warming, and they have said, for example, that in four years or five years, temperatures are going to rise and that this is what the planet is going to look like. That approach does not take into consideration all of the feedback loops in the planet, however.

Earth is also self-regulating. The planet has a built-in, self-regulating function that is specially attuned to the biosphere and to the life forces on the planet so that the maximum abilities to foster the right living conditions can emerge. How else could a planet sustain life? You know that there are so many complex factors that must be taken into consideration in order for a planet to create a sustained energy field for life. You can study astronomy, or you can study archeoastronomy or galactic astronomy or planetary astronomy. These studies can offer ways of describing what conditions are necessary for life to occur on a planet. The number one condition necessary for life on a planet is activation of spiritual light and the enhancement of the relationship between the self-regulatory energy of that planet with the planet's biosphere.

Your scientists and astronomers are already discovering new solar systems. They are already seeing similarities between other solar systems and your solar system. We could review a thousand planets we have visited throughout this section of the galaxy. We could say that there are sixty planets that look exactly like Earth. They may be similar in distance from their sun. You would even be surprised at how similar these other planets might be in appearance to Earth. They may be similar in size or even smaller in size, yet there is no spiritual light on these planets. What is the difference between planets in solar systems that have life? The difference is that there is a life force and a spiritual energy that is self-regulating on a planet that has life—this makes all of the difference. This self-regulating function has been developed on Earth.

THE FRAGILE STATE OF THE BIOSPHERE

What is more amazing, and why so may of us as space travelers and dimensional travelers are interested in coming to Earth, is the fact that your Earth has a sophisticated biospheric feedback loop and self-regulation loop that have allowed life to exist on this planet for extremely long times. What is amazing is that over the millions and billions of years, there have been catastrophes planetary-wide as well as life-ending catastrophes on Earth. These catastrophes seemingly could wipe out the entire biosphere, yet the life forms have come back. Now the life forms have been striving for great achievements and great heights and great multiplicity. Earth has this powerful self-regulation feedback system, and Earth's regulation and feedback loop is able to recover from near-catastrophic events. Near-catastrophic events have been unable to wipe out the biosphere. Earth has a tremendous ability to regulate itself in the face of adversity and in the face of cataclysmic events.

What humankind is doing is part of the natural cycle of instinctual reactions. I use the word "instinctual" because to change, humankind must now evolve to a higher state above instincts, and that higher state requires an evolutionary leap in human consciousness so that people understand that Earth is a living spirit. People must understand that Earth can be communicated with telepathically and that these telepathic communications can begin to change the feedback loop and the self-regulating systems. Human's ability to do that is required and is one way to save the biosphere in this period of time. I emphasize this period of time, because humanity can indeed make this evolutionary step. Human beings can influence the self-regulation of the planet.

THE MESSAGE OF THE GLOBAL ECONOMY

Let me speak about the global economy for a moment. The global economy reflects the thinking of many, many people. You could say that money is evil. You could say that capitalism is evil. You could say many things about how bad the economy is. One thing that is evident to us is that the economy is based on an economic thought form and that this economic thought form is based on self-interest. It is based on greed, and it is based on the ideas of acquiring wealth. Again, this is part of human instinct. We cannot be critical of it; we can only observe it. That reflects how humanity has approached Earth, and one can see that the way humans see the economy reflects how they see Earth.

This can change. When the global economy fractured, it demonstrated to everyone how fragile the economic interactions are in the world and how major declines can cause undue havoc around the planet. This global fracture is still reverberating. The actual event, the actual energy that led to this fracture, only took about two to three weeks. I know that there were other things that were building up that led to it, but even up to as early as two to three weeks before the global fracture occurred, it was still possible to avoid it. Many people said it was inevitable, but it wasn't inevitable, because there could have been interventions. In fact, even afterward there have been interventions that have put a huge bandage on the fracture of the global economy. The global economy is not yet repaired, however. You could say that it is like a wound. There is now a very thin scab on the wound, and it is starting to heal, but there still is a lot of damage and everyone still needs to exert a lot of care to assist it in that healing.

I used the example of the global economy because it is easy to see how fragile that was and what happened when it fell apart. Let us look at the food chain as another example. Your food chain is even more fragile than the global economy. It would only take one small event, one that maybe would even last for less than a week, to change the whole food chain and transportation of food around this planet. It wouldn't even take a huge event. People are thinking, "Well, maybe an earthquake could do that, maybe another cyclone or another tsunami." Yes, that is how fragile the food chain is. The biosphere and environmental diversity are fragile all over the planet.

You see evidence of this in the droughts that happen across the world. You see evidence of this in heat waves and in the unusual monsoons. It wouldn't take much to truly ruin several key biodiverse ecosystems. These biodiverse ecosystems are interrelated, just like the global economy is interrelated. You could take a biosphere and an ecosystem in Indonesia that houses certain species of monkeys and the collapse of that ecosystem would be very tragic. More tragic, however, is the fact that the collapse of that ecosystem could affect the ecosystems in Brazil or the ecosystems in Argentina or in Costa Rica. You might ask, "How is that possible?" Just as there is an interconnection of all aspects of the global economy, so there is also an interlinking of biodiversity on Earth.

BALANCING EARTH BY DOWNLOADING HIGHER LIGHT

This all leads to the central idea of balancing Earth and opening up her energy pathways and meridians. These symbiotic relationships and the communications between them have to be enhanced. One way that this can be enhanced is by opening up the channels that link the meridians to the fifth dimension. A way to do this now is to download a higher light that transcends the normal space-time continuum. When those pathways are open, then fifth-dimensional thought waves of the self-regulation can be downloaded. What would that look like? This is where we move into the idea of the planetary cities of light, a concept that is very galactic. The model for the self-regulation of Earth that needs to be downloaded already exists in the moon-planet, Alano, as well as in another planet in the Pleiades. It also exists in other fifth-dimensional planets where there is a biosphere of balance between the needs of the human-like people and the planetary system. Believe me, it is possible to download those structures and those thoughts into Earth.

I can compare this to your subconscious, and I always try to see the parallels between the personal fifth-dimensional work and planetary fifth-dimensional work. In personal fifth-dimensional work, when you want to create a shift in yourself, you can most effectively create a visual picture of what you will look like after that shift. Then the self—the greater self, the unconscious self—will manifest that picture for you. Again, we will go back to the idea of the chair. You can say that you want to build the chair. You may not know where you can get the wood. You may not know where you are going to get the nails. You may not even know where you are going to get the energy to build this object. Yet it doesn't stop you from thinking about it. You then send the idea and it goes into your subconscious and your unconscious, and the unconscious manifests and leads you to the things you need. Suddenly you have a burst of energy, and you find the store that has the wood you want. This was demonstrated, for example, when Gudrun, the channel's wife, built her tepee. She had no prior knowledge of how to build a tepee, but she kept the idea of the tepee in her mind, and suddenly it came to her. There was divine guidance. In the same way, you will receive divine guidance when you work with Earth.

What I am saying is that now we have the images of the planetary system, the moon-planet Alano, which is near the Central Sun. That moon-planet Alano is in perfect balance. There is a perfect harmony in the life forms, energy usage and etheric crystal balancing there. You can use ideas from Alano and download them into the unconscious of Earth, allowing them to manifest on Earth. We think this way when we want to affect the planetary system of the moon-planet Alano: We think perfect temperatures that are in harmony with everyone's needs, perfect ecodiversity, perfect rain systems throughout the planet, perfect ocean currents, perfect weather and minimizing the pollution in the atmosphere. We think of those things. We recommend that you send those images to the eleven—soon to be twelve—etheric crystals on the Earth. These etheric crystals that we have helped to download have the ability to communicate with the unconscious of Earth to the degree that it could manifest the conditions necessary for a major shift.

When we are looking at individual climate events such as the heat waves in Spain, the heat waves in Turkey, the fires in these countries and the heat waves of the Northwest, then we can also send balancing thoughts into the etheric crystals in a modified way. These balancing thoughts can be downloaded into the planetary system Earth. The reason why I say we must go through the etheric crystals is this: The knowledge of how all these feedback loops and self-regulation systems interact is so complex that humanity is not able to completely understand them. Humanity does not have the computer knowledge nor a high enough level of computer energy to understand all these interactions. Yet you may not understand how to manifest something, but by just thinking about it and placing that thought in the unconscious, it will still work and occur. These thoughts of balance can be placed into the unconscious of Earth.

MODIFYING WEATHER THROUGH BIORELATIVITY

We will do a biorelativity exercise now, working with Spain and Turkey, and we will look at the Northwest of the United States and Northwestern Canada. We will seek a modification of the heat so that the conditions for higher temperatures and drought are diminished.

The people of Turkey can go to the Istanbul-Anadolu crystal, and the people of Spain can go to the Montserrat crystal. For the people in the northwestern United States and northwestern Canada, we ask that they use the Mount Shasta crystal. We ask everyone to participate. It is still possible that the heat and the weather can be modified, even though this modification could be temporary. This heat expresses a blockage. There is a blockage in Earth's meridians that is leading to the shifts and to the heat.

I want everyone to think about how the meridians that are creating this heat anomaly are now being opened so that a more normal flow of weather patterns can flow through these three areas. I want each of you to connect to the crystal that you are most comfortable with of the three I mentioned—the crystal in Mount Shasta, the crystal in Montserrat, Spain or the crystal in the Istanbul-Anadolu area of Turkey. Send that image of modification or correction energy so that the heat will turn to normal and the fires will diminish. We will spend several minutes in meditation, and your idea and your imaging will be to send those thoughts to those crystal areas. Those crystals will download that information into Earth. It will be a communication of great magnitude because of all of you who are participating. We will begin that meditation now. I will use a certain tone to start the meditation, and I will use another tone to end the meditation of this exercise. [A meditation is held for five minutes.]

The information and the images have been downloaded. There are further instructions regarding how to download the entire program for a planet. This type of planetary downloading would be based on a modified blueprint from a higher planet such as the moon-planet Alano. A replica of that self-regulating system from Alano can be downloaded. This can only happen and can only be worked on after the twelfth etheric crystal is downloaded into Brazil. Downloading a blueprint for the planet also needs to be coordinated with the planetary cities of light. These planetary cities of light are fifth-dimensional enclaves that can create an enhancement of the etheric fifth-dimensional light on Earth. They are anchors that will allow the new fifth-dimensional energy and light to appear on Earth. Fifth-dimensional light is building on Earth, and you need to have a foundation in which to begin to create a fifth-dimensional world.

ACTIVATING THE TWELVE CITIES

We are talking about the planetary ascension and the ascension energy reaching Earth—an ascension energy that will create the conditions necessary for Earth to ascend. Even before this happens, it is necessary for the fifth-dimensional energy to manifest and create these enclaves on Earth. I have asked the channel to contact everyone and to see which planetary cities of light can be activated on Earth and have given instructions about nominating certain areas to become cities of light. Based on the need, energy and enthusiasm for the topic, we have expanded that number to twelve cities of light. These cities of light will have a fifth-dimensional veil around the perimeter of the city. This veil will be very powerful and will only allow higher fifth-dimensional energy, thoughts and people to bring their energy into that city. That means that lower energy and lower vibrations will not be able to penetrate the veil or to influence the planetary city of light, and darkness or lower energy cannot be manifested.

You can activate a planetary city of light in a large city, such as Los Angeles, but the whole city itself may be too large at this point to work on it. Therefore, you can choose an enclave or a section of the city to become a planetary city of light. You could then use that section to build on for other areas, and eventually the fifth-dimensional energy could encompass the whole city. Once we have twelve nominations for planetary cities of light, we will then activate the cities in the workshop. Now how does the activation occur? The activation will occur at the base of Mount Shasta, which is one powerful etheric crystal. That energy of Mount Shasta can then create a downloading of light. We want, if possible, people who are from these planetary cities of light to be present when we are at the workshop at Mount Shasta on 10–10–10 so that they can then receive the energy.

MODELS OF PLANETARY LIGHT CITIES

Let us use the example of Taos, because Taos is going to become a planetary city of light. We highly recommend Taos, because it is in a perfect position. There will be people from Taos who will be at the workshop, but there will also be Groups of Forty members who will be in Taos at the same time. This will create a powerful link so that we can transmit energy from the Mount Shasta workshop to the Taos planetary city of light, activating Taos. These people in Taos at that time will be strategically placed around the city. Remember, we will be operating in a system in which there is a time window of thirty-six hours, so the workers do not have to be at the planetary cities of light at exactly the same time the energy is transmitted from Mount Shasta. We will, however, still announce the exact time when we will be transmitting the energy to these cities.

This model for the planetary city of light energy-creation field was demonstrated at the downloading of the first crystal at Lago Puelo National Park many years ago in the Argentinean region of Patagonia. Perhaps the Lago Puelo ceremony is known to many people. For the downloading of the first etheric crystal, the Argentinean lightworkers worked around the whole lake. When the etheric crystal was downloaded in Lago Puelo, in Patagonia, they had created a veil of fifth-dimensional light around the lake that actually then made the lake itself like a city of light. Even today that lake holds such powerful energy because both the lake and the crystal are the foundation for all of the other eleven etheric crystals; it was the first etheric crystal. You can therefore understand what a powerful foundation and energy field is around Lago Puelo. We ask the channel to return to Lago Puelo in February of 2010 in order to reactivate and experience the energy of that city of light around the lake.

The next important task is to activate twelve planetary cities of light on Earth. Remember that these twelve planetary cities of light do not have to be equidistant from each other. It is not necessary that they be strategically placed so that they are all balanced, although that would be great. Instead, we look at the holographic energy. The geographic placements of the cities do not need to be in a certain pattern. It is more important to choose cities that can meet the criteria of high energy and cities that have people who can work to receive the fifth-dimensional energy at the sites. We are looking at the holographic Earth. It also would be helpful to have workers at the sites of the planetary cities of light during the 10–10–10 time, because this will make the experience even more powerful and help us to activate this energy.

CREATING CORRIDORS OF LIGHT AROUND YOUR HOME

What is it like to tune into a planetary city of light? It enhances everyone's energy field. It can actually enhance your health. I know that people have always been interested in geographical moves and where to live for one's highest good. Obviously, it is very helpful, when possible, to live in a planetary city of light. Remember, however, that you can still have corridors of light around your home. Some people have asked: "Can I make a planetary city of light around my home?" I would say that you could send the planetary city of light energy into the corridor around your place. In order to do this, you could still link with us during the 10–10–10 time. At a minimum, place five crystals around the perimeter of the area that you wish to connect to a planetary city of light. You can also make a corridor around your home so that it can receive this fifth-dimensional energy field.

You can also create the veil of fifth-dimensional light that is used around the planetary city of light around your own home. It is easier for you to maintain the planetary city of light around your home, because you have better control of who enters and what you do in your place. Even a beautiful city like Taos will still require people to work with the fifth-dimensional energy field of the planetary city of light to keep it built up, strong and sacred.

We are creating sacred areas on Earth that are fifth-dimensional, and these areas are going to be the New Jerusalem in reality. The New Jerusalem is not going to be just one city, because the Jerusalem energy is multidimensional. The New Jerusalem energy is fifth-dimensional and it is going to be accessible to many different places on the planet. Yes, it can include the physical city Jerusalem, but the New Jerusalem energy is also like the messianic energy, and messianic energy will be available to everyone who is in alignment with the fifth dimension.

SISTER CITIES OF LIGHT ON OTHER PLANETS

Finally, I want to discuss the idea of cities of light and their corresponding sister cities on other planets. We will be getting more information about how to work with the sister cities on other planets in order to help to keep the planetary light going. You have sister cities now. One normal city in the United States might have a sister city in Germany, for example. The idea is the interchange of energy between those two cities. So it is that you can have sister cities of light working for you on other planets.

We will be elucidating all these matters. You are all great lightworkers, and you are coming into greater abilities in order to be planetary healers. We are ready to introduce the next major transformative step for the Groups of Forty. I am Juliano. Good day.

THE ETHERIC CRYSTALS AND THE PLANETARY TREE OF LIFE

Juliano and Archangel Michael

Greetings. I am Juliano. We are the Arcturians. Thinking is the basis of the formation of creation, and therefore thought is the basis of third dimensional creation. We understand that there are different levels of reality. The physical level of reality may be called the material world. On this world that you are living, there are polarizations, there are densities and there are certain laws of physics that dominate and control the nature of actions in the physical world. It is equally true that there is another world, one that is made up of thoughts: the thinking world. Believe it or not, it is the basis, the forerunner, of the physical world. The basis of our interventions on Earth will focus on creating a new reality and a new paradigm. This new paradigm will allow unity consciousness and cosmic consciousness to emerge in, on and around Earth. What is particularly important is cosmic consciousness.

Cosmic consciousness is a way of explaining how energy from outside of your solar system influences your planet, or in some cases how energy from outside of your solar system can be amplified to influence the planet. In particular, we look at the Central Sun as an extra-solar energetic source that, if amplified and correctly received, will provide new cosmic energy to the planet. This new cosmic energy will allow people to think cosmically. Cosmic thinking will put at your disposal energies from other galactic civilizations. You will have thoughts and inventive ideas from higher galactic beings, and you will be able to go to the etheric level for music, art, poetry and channeling. Cosmic thought will allow you to bring down a higher vibrational thought field.

We can summarize this entire intervention as creating a new thought force field for the entire planet. To that end, we try to describe the connections you have with the fifth dimension and with places such as the crystal temple. We have said that each thought is like a luminous strand of light that projects from your physical body to the fifth-dimensional temple we have described to you as the crystal temple. The corollary to this paradigm is the fact that your thoughts, and especially your higher thoughts, create a web of strands of light around the planet. Some of these strands of light go into the subconscious, the universal unconscious of the planet. They serve as purifications, because we know that consciousness has a corresponding unconsciousness, and we know that thinking is still a relatively new aspect of the work done in the frontal lobe of the brain.

CONSCIOUSNESS IS THE TIP OF THE ICEBERG

We know that thoughts and consciousness are like icebergs, in that you see only the tip of the iceberg. You know that the tip of the iceberg represents maybe 5 percent of the total iceberg, because the majority of the iceberg is underwater. The underwater part of the iceberg affects the top part, and it is the same way in the unconscious. The majority of the energy of the mind is unconscious, and it is affecting what you can see. These strands of light are based on higher thinking. They can coordinate projections into the unconscious that can create an energy of purification for the unconscious. After this, unconscious energy is purified, then your conscious energy—the reality you experience in your waking life—will improve as you go to a higher dimension or higher realm.

In this lecture, we want to explain that strands of thoughts are actually like an umbrella of luminous strands that are being projected around the entire planet. In this way, our thinking and your thinking influence the conscious world that you see. In this way, your thinking and the thoughts you project become, in essence, like a creator energy of thought. The Creator made creation through thought. After thought, Creator made a statement, and you described that statement as, "Let there be light." Before the Creator could say the words "let there be light," there was Creator's thought about what the formation of that light would look like and how the development of the universe would unfold. The thought comes first, and then the words. In the methodology we teach, we are looking to transform the planet. We are looking to transform you as well on a personal basis so that you can move off the planet and into a higher dimension.

DATA MANIFESTATION THROUGH THE PHYSICAL

Let us look at the planet. Each of you is on a soul mission for planet Earth. Each of you has a great love and a great desire to "heal" the planet. Some of you have been perplexed because you have wondered, "Well, what is my soul mission? What is my planetary mission?" Maybe you have found some comfort in your own personal development, but maybe you have not really found how you can manifest and deliver to the planet. You have joined the Groups of Forty with the intention and hope of maximizing your participation in planetary healing. You are thinking. Sending out luminous strands of thought around the planet fulfills your planetary mission. Participate in the energetic waves of thought that begin to encompass this reality. You have begun to understand the basic teachings of the levels of the interventions. You have come to understand that one of the major levels of interventions in creation is in the thinking world. In the world of thought, in the world of thinking, strands of thought can be projected around a planet. These strands of thought are actually etheric strands that become physical. They are setting up an energetic pattern that will allow the manifestation of thought energy into the physical.

I believe that every Groups of Forty member wants to see a healing on Earth and wants to see a manifestation of healing. The pattern and the process for this manifestation starts in the world of thought. The manifestation for your ascension starts in the world of thought—but the healing of a planet becomes more complicated. When I use the word "healing" in reference to the planet, I want you to understand that the word healing in this context means unification. It means coming into a unified balance. I think when you use that definition, then you and other people will agree that the planet is out of balance. You would say, "Well, what evidence is there?" The planet is out of balance. If everything were left to where it is going now without an intervention, then the planet and the biosphere would collapse, and life as you know it on this planet would end.

It is true that many people use the argument that some aspects of the biosphere might survive. For example (and we are not saying this to be humorous), you might find that cockroaches would be able to survive the collapse of the biosphere. You might find that the planet would be ruled by insects, for example. That means that the biosphere would not totally collapse, but I think from our standpoint, that would represent a near total collapse of the biosphere. Our definition of the biosphere focuses on an energetic sphere of light force that supports higher life. We do not consider cockroaches to be a higher life form. This biosphere is in danger of collapsing—or, to put it another way, the biosphere will not be able to support higher life forms like yourselves if there is no intervention.

Therefore, this could be considered a collapse, unless there can be a rebalancing. This rebalancing requires a rethinking, an energetic thought field that would encompass the whole planet. This thought field would be amplified and imported by many people on the planet, and by the planet itself. One of the basic ideals of biorelativity and planetary healing is that the planet has to receive the energy. The planet is formulated to exist in balance. If that balance goes off-kilter, then certain energetic patterns must be reintroduced that will allow retooling, so that the energy of the planet can redefine and return to a higher balance. Again, we define "higher balance" as a balance that will allow higher life forms to exist on the planet. The ultimate goal of biorelativity is to keep a balance on the entire planet that will allow it to sustain higher life forms. That then becomes the main thought pattern, the main thought-projection and the main thought intervention that will be used to bring the planet into balance that will allow higher life forms to be sustained.

A Thought Pattern for Cosmic Consciousness

Of course, then the question comes, "What thought form or thought pattern is that?" I will try to explain how this thought form and energetic light strands from such thoughts can encompass the entire Earth. I seek the vibratory tone and energy to connect us all to the vibrational thought field of Earth. Chief White Eagle will have more to say about that thought field later in this lecture.

The etheric crystals are being downloaded into Earth for the purpose of holding the thought-field patterns. The thought-field patterns are very high, etherically thin light energies. I can tell you that in the current condition of the planet, it is hard to find energetic places that are centrally located that can receive, hold and transmit the thought patterns, the new cosmic consciousness, the new biorelativity healing patterns that we are encouraging you to work with. Another way to say this is that it is difficult, in the planet's current condition, to find places that could hold the powerful fifth-dimensional thought fields necessary to ensure that the biosphere can sustain higher life forms. For example, we could look at Jerusalem, which is, of course, a very high energetic place, but there are many conflicting energies in that city.

Therefore it might be hard to sustain the necessary light frequency of unity there, of brotherhood and of cosmic consciousness.

We have worked to establish, to explain and to download etheric crystals. The etheric crystals that we have worked with have certain characteristics that are beneficial and are certainly useful in terms of planetary healing or planetary unification. The first requirement is that the crystal be multidimensional. That is to say, the crystal has the energy and the ability to connect and to receive thought patterns from both the fifth dimension and the third dimension. The second aspect of an etheric crystal is that it can hold these thought patterns and higher energy, and it is not subject to polarization and density. Many of you already work with crystals, especially ancient crystals, those that are referred to as ancient skull crystals. These crystals are examples of crystals that hold energy no matter what life force energy surrounds them, no matter what the surrounding force field is.

We worked with you to download nine etheric crystals throughout the planet, and each one of them has a special ability. The crystals are perfect receptors for receiving your etheric strands of thought-fields of light, and these crystals can project thought-field light energy around the planet. You could say, "Well, I have a thought of healing light, and I want to send that thought around the biosphere to hold that." I think that would be very successful. Consider that a thought is an energy wave. Imagine you are going to send out a radio wave from an AM radio station. It can transmit 500 watts. But 500 watts is only going to go maybe 100 miles. How can you get the radio waves to go around the globe? You could say, "Well, use 5,000 watts." Five thousand watts may go 1,000 miles, but it won't go around the whole continent or the whole country. So you need amplification. You need an amplifier to work with that signal so that it has the strength to go around the country and around the world. Thought waves are thin waves even compared to a radio wave. You cannot see a radio wave, but you can hear a radio wave if you have the right receiver. But a thought wave is so thin that you need a special receiver to amplify and receive the thoughts—an amplifier such as an etheric crystal.

I will again use the example of the radio wave from an AM radio station. You can send out the radio wave, but after the transmitter of the radio station is shut off, then there is no more signal, and you can't hear anything. You might be listening to a radio station and at 10 PM, the radio station host says, "Good night, everyone. We are closing down for the night." And then they shut the transmitter off and you cannot hear anything. In planetary healing and planetary work, we do not want thought waves to be shut down. We want the thought waves to continue to go through the entire planet all of the time and at the greatest amplification. This is why the etheric crystals are becoming vital. They can hold the thought waves, they can continue to amplify, and they can send thought signals around the planet. We are talking about the thinking world and how the thinking world can affect what is manifested in the material world. Thinking has to be at a certain frequency and a certain signal strength, and that signal strength has to be continual. Etheric crystals can hold and transmit thoughts so that they can operate continually.

THE DIFFERENT ENERGIES OF THE ETHERIC CRYSTALS

Each etheric crystal has a different energy and a different function in this whole thought pattern. What is interesting is that the functions of the crystals are shifting as new crystals are added and as new energy is downloaded. For example, the crystal at Lago Puelo, which may have been the first crystal, had the energy of a primordial energy, an energy of beginning and an energy of activation for the whole planet. Then the other eight crystals were added and their activation has occurred. So now the Lago Puelo crystal does not necessarily have to continue in that vein. In fact, each crystal added is affected by every other crystal.

Now we have worked in this beautiful area called Montserrat in Spain. This crystal has a very interesting and powerful energy, because this crystal is known as *la cristal sagrada*, or the sacred crystal, because it is on a particularly sacred and holy site. It is on a holy site that is not filled with a lot of polarization. It is on a holy site where there has not been a lot of war. It has pure energy source of holiness and sacredness. This crystal was downloaded to hold holy, sacred light. It unifies the other eight crystals to become a truly sacred site with sacred energy.

This new crystal unifies and holds the Sacred Triangle energy field on the planet. The ingredients for holding this sacred light involve the interaction of humans with the site. Your participation and your energies contribute and allow a corridor to exist that connects the place that you are standing on with the fifth dimension. Therefore, when you go to a sacred site, you are connecting with an energy that elders and other people identify with that place. We Arcturians believe that there needs to be more sacred sites on the planet, because when a place is made sacred, it is provided with local protection that allows the balance of the biosphere to be maintained so that it can support higher life forms.

Remember, our definition of biorelativity is now expanded to include the ability to influence and telepathically connect with an energetic planetary field so that the planetary biosphere will sustain higher life. The main aspect of making higher life forms is the creation of sacred spaces, holding sacred energy on the planet. To that end, the Montserrat crystal (*la cristal sagrada*, the sacred crystal) has been downloaded in order to establish a sacred energy, one that has affected all of the other eight crystals around the planet so that they are interacting and receiving sacred energy. When you meditate on that crystal, you connect with the sacred energy of the sacred crystal on Montserrat, and then you can participate in the creation of an interactive energy field with all of the crystals.

CONNECT WITH THE CRYSTAL THAT HOLDS THE ENERGY YOU DESIRE

In the beginning, the one crystal at Volcan Poás in Costa Rica might have helped to modify the ring of fire so that there was greater balance. Now, with the sacred crystal energy of Montserrat, that Volcan Poás crystal will also receive and transmit sacred light and sacred energy, and that sacred light and sacred energy will rebalance that area. The energy in Mexico at Copper Canyon is connected to the fifth-dimensional moonplanet Alano. It transmits and is connected to the shimmering energy.

If you need to connect with sacred energy, go to Montserrat. To connect with shimmering energy, please go to Copper Canyon. To connect with initiation and activation, go to Lago Puelo. Do not overanalyze the crystals, because the crystals are multidimensional and can also be working to receive updated light and updated energy for the different aspects of healing that need to come through this planet. I want you now in meditation to focus on the sacred crystal at Montserrat. If you have a hard time picturing where it is, then just picture Spain, the eastern part of Spain, and then go north 60 miles from Barcelona and visualize this huge crystal. It is sending out huge sacred energy and light. Then visualize this sacred energy, which is like a thought field, connecting with all of the other crystals. It is going around the planet and is also reaching Mount Fuji. Let us meditate for a few minutes on the sacred Montserrat crystal.

I am Juliano, and I am calling all of the etheric crystals, the nine etheric crystals in the planet: Lake Taupo, Grose Valley, Montserrat, Lake Moraine, Mount Shasta, Volcan Poás, Bodensee, Lago Puelo and Copper Canyon. I call on all nine etheric crystals to rise up out of their holding places in the earth. As they rise up, they are creating interactive lines that represent the Tree of Life in the Kaballah. There are ten spheres in the Kaballah, representing the attributes of God. There are ten divine emanations of light in the Kaballah, and each sphere represents a different aspect of divinity and sacredness. These are the ten sacred divine attributes.

At this point, the tenth sphere, the tenth crystal, is going to be the crystal at Mount Fuji. This crystal is already being prepared to be downloaded into the Mount Fuji area, which is a very ancient sacred area. It holds energy and light that needs to be unlocked, energy from Lemuria and from very ancient civilizations that have come to visit Earth. In the Tree of Life, energy flows in certain directions from one sphere to the next, and an imbalance on one sphere can be rebalanced by energy on another sphere. Now, with this tenth sphere, this tenth crystal, we have a total representation of the Tree of Life: the ten spheres, the ten divine emanations on the planet. I will now turn you over to Archangel Michael, who will tell you more about the ten spheres. I am Juliano. We are the Arcturians.

Greetings, I am Archangel Michael, and I honor the ten crystals that will be completed in their downloading, for ten is a sacred number. It is the number of completion, but it is also a divine number, for example, the Ten Commandments. Ten represents the minimum divine attributes required for transformation into the fifth dimension. These attributes or spheres are known in Hebrew language as the *Sephiroth*. They are holy spheres, and in the teachings of the ancient ones, the ancient rabbis, each sphere emanates an energy from God. Each sphere on the Tree of Life has an attribute that you seek to express in your lifetime. These attributes include wisdom, understanding, balance, beauty, judgment, compassion and mercy. These are called divine attributes. If you hold these divine attributes, then you will understand how you can transform and be in divine energy and divine light.

THE DIVINE NUMBER TEN

The Tree of Life is balanced in the male and female. Some of the spheres are feminine and some of the spheres are masculine. Sometimes, in certain planets, the spheres of energy are too masculine. When they are too masculine, the energy of the planet becomes too harsh, or too critical. Sometimes the spheres are too feminine, too surrendering. There is too much compassion. For those people who are bent on evil, sometimes compassion is not what they need. Sometimes they need judgment. Sometimes they need for their actions to be rectified. So you see, there has to be a certain balance. Juliano has told you that when looking at a planet, you have to evaluate if attributes are out of balance.

[Tones.] "The Tree of Life on Earth is crying. It is crying. It is crying." The Tree of Life contains a divine influx of light. That light strikes the first Sephiroth, the Sephiroth known as Kether. It is also the head of the Tree of Life. This divine influx is compared to lightning. This divine lightning immediately goes to all of the etheric crystals. It creates a realignment so that a new balance can hold the energy. It contains a new thought energy that can sustain higher life forms on the biosphere. The Tree of Life is called *Etz Chaim* in Kaballah. It contains a blueprint for personal transformation and also a blueprint for planetary transformation. We introduce this planetary transformational energy as a paradigm that can be used for interaction between the ten sacred crystals and the ten etheric crystals that are being downloaded. Mount Fuji becomes the crystal that holds illuminating life, the lightning bolt that will go through all of the crystals and bring everything into alignment.

We also find that the attributes of the Tree of Life can be used for personal transformation. These traits include wisdom, beauty, understanding, retribution, judgment, compassion, Christ consciousness and universal awareness. These attributes have to be modified for planetary work. The essence of each crystal will come to different members' consciousnesses. Every member will explore the crystals. Each will know what that crystal offers and what that crystal's role is in the whole Tree of Life for Earth. We are going to expand the Tree of Life to twelve for planetary healing, but that is to come at a later point. For this time, it is a great honor to hold the energy of the ten crystals, for this represents, in part, a completion. The twelve crystals will open up a new dimensional aspect to the planetary Tree of Life. I, Archangel Michael, crown the planetary Tree of Life, and we welcome it in this day. Of course we will be working with you to download this crystal in a few hours. I call on the Zohar light, brilliant light from the Creator, to illuminate Mount Fuji and start the process of rebalancing all of these crystals for planetary healing. [Tones.] "Zohar light." I am Archangel Michael. Good day.

TIME: THE NEXT EVOLUTIONARY STEP

Juliano, the Arcturians and Chief White Eagle

Greetings, I am Juliano, and we are the Arcturians. In this lesson, we will explore the relationship between time and space, and time and your assemblage point. Time is one of the most difficult perceptions to fully integrate in your path of and for your ascension. You are well aware that time is measured in a linear manner in your Earth life on the third dimension.

This means that the timeline includes the past, the present and the future. In the duality on the third dimension, the connecting link between the past, present and future is only the straight line—linear time. Therefore, once an event has occurred, it is in the past, and you have no way to influence the past. Likewise the future has no direct bearing on the present. In this linear model, you have difficulty trying to conceive how the future can affect the present.

There are some new understandings of the relationship between the future and the present. Humanity understands that if you continue or if the planet continues on a certain path of using the Earth's resources—such as water and oil—they will be gone for the future, thus knowing this can lead to conservation. This means that the anticipation of future events has an effect on the present. That is to say, you may decide to limit your usages of carbon products because of the way their extended overuse will affect the future. This is an example of how time conception of the future affects the present.

Generally, this future-present model may be accepted by some people. However, most people will just work and live based on what their needs are in the present. You should understand that future thinking is a higher-order perception in a species. Future thinking relates to the concept or idea that the present affects the future. At the same time, the future affects present behavior. This new understanding of the future-present model is part of the evolutionary cycle and an evolutionary step that a species—namely, humankind—needs to take in order to survive and go to the next level. This next evolutionary step, of course, is necessary and is needed in order to ensure the survival of the Earth.

THE FUTURE FEEDBACK LOOP

Higher thinking recognizes that time is another feedback loop and is more easily understood as the past, present and future connected as a loop. The feedback loop begins with the awareness of how actions in the present will affect the future. For example, one may know that a certain action may negatively affect the future. That action can be changed so that an anticipated future event of a dangerous consequence will not occur. This feedback loop is a beginning to understanding that the future does affect the present. This future-present feedback loop is extending and broadening your conception of time, and it is showing you that time is not linear.

Remember that the future feedback loop also has positive consequences. You do not need to only focus on the feedback loop when there is indication of dire consequence. You can focus on the feedback loop for the future for positive things as well. And Helio-ah has demonstrated to you several times how you can use the future feedback loop. I will now call this the future feedback loop. Helio-ah has demonstrated how you can use the future feedback loop for positive healings, because no matter what your condition is now, no matter what level of illness or confusion you have now, everything that is of a denser nature on the third dimension is going to be resolved. Remember, in the future, you will have healed and integrated all of the lessons you need.

Linking yourself in the future and using the future feedback loop gives you access to positive points in the future as well. You can access the future for many years or even many lifetimes forward when a successful integration has occurred. When accessing the future, you can access the integration energy and bring it into the present. You have then completed the future feedback loop to the present.

THE PAST FEEDBACK LOOP

A similar feedback loop is also in existence for the past and we can call it the present-past feedback loop. The present-past feedback loop is, on the one hand, obvious because you know that past events have affected the present. You see this in the political arena. For example, there are many actions in politics or in wars that started five or ten years ago that are still affecting the present. Also the economic policies being displayed now are affected by past economic decisions. The past feedback loop is importantly manifested in your economy. One of the significant factors of the economy is to demonstrate that the past influences the present. The decisions you have made in the past—or that your government has made in the past or that you personally have made in the past regarding your finances—do affect the present. It is this understanding of the past-present feedback loop that demonstrates and can create spiritual lessons related to the economy and the financial world.

I know that you generally do not look at the financial world in this way—that is, as having or creating spiritual lessons. The financial world is something that is important. It demonstrates the relationship of the past feedback loop. Understanding the feedback loop systems are, again, a higher order of thinking, a higher order of an evolutionary step that only humanity or a species similar to humankind can grasp or understand. Your animals, for example, do not have an advanced past feedback loop. Animals may have some memories of what has happened in terms of traumas or good things, but it is not on the sophisticated level that we are now talking about for humans.

Another significant attribute of the past-present feedback loop is that the present can influence the past. This is a lot more difficult to explain and a lot more difficult to comprehend. Remember that we easily understood (hopefully) how the future feedback loop can affect the present, and, in fact, how the present feedback loop will affect the future. We understand that the past feedback loop affects the present, but what is the link between present actions and the past? The link is that through certain advanced biorelativity exercises, you and others can shift memory and shift imagery so that a healing and a higher-energy holographic image can be created that sets in motion a more positive outcome from recent past events.

UPGRADES AND IMPROVEMENTS

More positive outcomes can be downloaded into the subconscious of Earth, or into the subconscious of people, known as the collective unconscious. Once updated images are downloaded into the collective unconsciousness, then that consciousness updates its files or images that came afterward until it reaches the present. After the update, the present energy shifts. I know that this is difficult to comprehend. I hope you are not getting confused. There are higher orders of mathematical equations or discourses that can explain this. One way to try and understand how the past events can positively affect the future is through the concept of the computer. Imagine that you have a computer program that is working, but you want to change it because the original program does not allow you to do certain things, certain activities or certain tasks. If you put in an updated version, or if you update your program, then the updated files will go back into the old files. It will update them and bring those old files into the present so that the present program is updated and can operate at a higher function. This analogy does not work totally, but it gives you some way of comprehending the past-present feedback loop. You can go back to older files on Earth or in your unconscious and update them to bring everything into a higher level.

THE INFLUENCE OF TIME

The past feedback loop, the present feedback loop and the future feedback loop all really go in two directions. The past influences the present and the present influences the past; the present influences the future, the future influences the present; and finally the future influences the past.

How can the future influence the past? The future does influence the past because there are time travelers, and time travelers can come back into the past. You have seen science-fiction programs on this where the future person, for example, understands that there will be a past event that will result in dire consequences; therefore, the future sends someone back into the past to shift energy to change something, or to get someone to change a behavior. This is a newer and higher level—that is, the feedback loop from future to past. Perhaps you can understand that American scientists tried to influence time in the Philadelphia Experiment, and they tried to work on the future feedback loop by connecting it to the past.

One big problem is this: There are untold consequences of any action. For example, one country invades another for a specific reason, and it looks like it will accomplish something that is the goal of that country. Yet that country did not understand that there were unforeseen consequences, because the world has changed so much and is so interactive. Untold consequences are events that no one would be able to accurately predict, although some psychics might be able to see them.

In terms of the future loop, going back into the past to shift an event requires such a high order of energy that you would have to be at the level of a prophet to be able to shift events and know what to do. We are talking about the level of a prophet, and then we are talking about the level that you also call the Messiah, who would have this ability. To further this discussion of the conceptions of time, I need to expand on what time is and how it is measured. I will then return to answering the question about the future connection to the past.

DEFINING TIME

Time, as you know, is relative, which was shown by Einstein. But what does that really mean in a personal way? You live on a planet that goes around your Sun approximately once every 365 days—maybe 364 days, because I understand that you do have a leap year. In your time frame, one year is 365 days, one day is twenty-four hours and your subconscious and your whole being have been programmed to understand and measure time this way. Therefore you had to accept that type of time frame when you came into this incarnation on Earth, and you had to understand that you were going to be on the planet that had certain ways of measuring the passage of time based on one year, based on one day, based on one month. You experience your lifetime based on a lifetime of about ninety years.

The earlier people on this planet did not understand time in the way you do. They did not understand that their lifetimes were based on a time frame measured by Earth's path of the Earth around the Sun. They had a different conception of the Sun. They understood some parts of this Earth-Sun time frame. Earlier man may have only lived for 40 years, instead of 80 or 90 years. Life was more difficult 2,000 to 3,000 years ago. They did not know their lives were short, because they had no point of comparison. They had no reference point to a different life span. So, you see, the reference point is important.

Think about this. Let us say that you live on another planet. Let us say that you live on Alano, which is going around the Central Sun. Or let us say it is a moon and it goes around a planet, but the day on that moon is measured the same way the moon rotates. Let us just say the moon goes around the planet once every sixty days. Then pretty soon your year is measured as sixty days, and you are living for many more years, because your year is far shorter than the Earth year of 365 days. Let us say, for example, that you live on a planet in the star system Alcyone, which is in the Pleiades. Let us say that your planet goes around the star Alcyone once every three years, so your year is measured in what would be considered a three-year interval when measured against the 365-day Earth year. Biologically, your life, DNA cells and mental programming are adjusted for that experience of a year being equal to three years.

If you were looking at a planet that went around its source energy field once every 500 years, then you might find yourself living in your biology even longer. It is so complex and so high because on different levels there are different reference points. For example, your solar system may require 1,000,000 years to make one revolution around the Central Sun in the Milky Way galaxy. Does that mean that from the perspective of the galaxy, one day is one million years? Yes, that is exactly what it means.

There are other reference points that are also mind-boggling. You have this beautiful precession of Earth, which is defined as the "wobble." This wobble cycle takes 26,000 years (actually 25,875 years, but we will call it 26,000 years). On the completion of that cycle, Earth returns to an interactive alignment with the Central Sun through the Earth's December solstice. From that perspective, the one wobble—what is called the precession of Earth—takes 26,000 years and would be considered one day. The ancient Maya had a conception of that day in their ancient astronomy. That is why they had so many calendars. Their basic calendar was actually divided into sub-calendars, since they were measuring the different levels of time. They understood the relativity of time.

WHERE IS THE CENTER OF THE UNIVERSE?

Let us go into another level and cycle from the perspective of the Creator. It is difficult to understand what the cycle is from the perspective of the Creator, because no one has been able to find the center of the universe. People have been able to find where the universe began. The universe is not revolving around that center. It would make more sense if we said: "Okay, our universe is like a big balloon and the balloon began at one center point. In the beginning, the balloon was inflated; therefore, that is where it started—at the center where the inflation began. That is where the big bang commenced."

The universe is not that way, even though there has been an inflation of matter. You must understand that humankind, or even the higher beings, have been looking for the center of the universe. We cannot find a point where everything is rotating from. If we could find that point, we could find the measurement of one day in a given point of the universe. However, we, the Arcturians, have understood that the reason that we cannot find that point in our universe is because there is more than one universe. You have to understand that the universes are interconnected, and to understand what the day of one universe is, you need to understand its relationship to the others.

In the ancient Hindu religion, they have actually discovered the concept of this time sequence of what is a day in the time of the universe, and I believe their name for that is called the Kalpa. Nonetheless, one day from the Creator and universal energy source would be what? Would it be the total expansion of the universe? Or would it be that the universe—and this is what we believe—is revolving around some central point, but that central point is in another dimension? That is why you cannot find the center of your universe using traditional third-dimensional techniques.

You probably might realize that many people originally thought that the universe was expanding and that it would reach a certain point, then collapse. One day would be measured in the full inflation of the universe until it went so far out and became so expanded it would collapse, because of the fact that the force of the center could not keep everything expanded. And then one day would be considered the full expansion and also the full collapse. This theory is not totally correct, since there is no center that can be found in the existing universe on the third dimension. As I said, the center actually exists in another dimension and that is how you can begin to explain the concept of the measurement of a day from the Creator's perspective.

SLIDE INTO THE FIFTH DIMENSION

Let us get back to something that may make it a little easier to comprehend. The understanding of the relativity of time is needed for the evolution of humanity. Your evolution of consciousness will ensure your ascension. Your movement into the fifth dimension is a time shift. Your assemblage point is involved in this time shift. We define the assemblage point as that point in your brain that allows your perception to become more sensitive at a higher level.

Let us say the assemblage point is like a sliding point, a sliding mechanism, and if pushed a little more to the right, you have more perceptions. We use this analogy about the assemblage point by visualizing a sliding knob.

When you slide it to the right, this will enable you to see, feel and understand luminosity, shimmering, and the cords and strings of attachment that are on all living bodies. This will allow you to see the true nature of reality.

We can add the concept of time when using the assemblage point. When we slide one lever over to the right, we also affect our perception of time. We know from earlier experiments in psychology—and we have understood this for many, many centuries—that when you go into higher consciousness or fifth-dimensional consciousness, then your sense of time expands. Therefore, you may expand time so that you experience it as either being fast or slow. You might say: "Well, Juliano, according to my sense of time, it seems like everything is going fast now. There are so many new events." This is true. From your perspective time is really moving fast. But don't be fooled by that, because you can also slow time down and expand your consciousness so that your experience is infinite, and the time that you are experiencing in the present can seem infinite.

There are some experiences—such as having intense pain—that really slow time down. Pain is not a very nice experience. There are also ways of slowing time down in a pleasant way that helps you experience higher states of consciousness. In fact, one of the gifts of the great masters and one of the gifts that you will all be given is to be able to control time. So for example, if you are in pain and you are in a state of contraction, then you will want the time to go faster. But you don't need to be in that state.

I am saying to you that each of you is going to have this ability to shift time. When you meet with your fellow starseed groups—for example, when you are in Germany, or when we are in Spain, or when we are in Mount Shasta—you may want time to slow down so that you can enjoy every minute. You can really percolate with the energy and the healing when you slow down. There is actually a physiological biorhythm that can be measured in your brain waves that shows that you are in a slower, expanded state. In an expanded state, you can have greater control of the future feedback loop of the present and the past feedback loop of the present, and even the future feedback loop with the past.

TIME CONSCIOUSNESS

When you are in an expanded state of consciousness, you can find dimensional access points to enter time shift areas. Some of these dimensional access points actually involve astral traveling. This means that going through these points allows you to move yourself from the present into the past or into the future. You may ask: "How does all of this discussion relate to your ascension?" Basically, you have to or can expand your perception of time. By expanding your perception of time, you can go through projections, go into other realms and move dimensionally to interact better with other beings. Ultimately, when you are working with biorelativity, you will be able to work with future events, present events and past events so that you can ensure the highest possible healing outcome for the planet, for you and for this species.

[Toning.] As I am using these tones, accept them as assistance so that you can integrate and comprehend the deep subject matter that we are working with. Allow your consciousness to fully integrate and fully expand appropriately for this space and time understanding. Let yourself go to another level of understanding.

The physicists have tried to demonstrate that gravity is a force field, and that as a force field, it can be measured. Space can be measured in terms of the size of an object or in terms of the mass of an object. But what about time? Is time really an energy? Can time be measured as a particle or as a wave? The answer is this: Time is an equation of measurement that is based on the interaction of consciousness and awareness with space and mass. Without consciousness, there is no time; therefore, time is not an existing energy like space. Time has no mass. Time has no velocity. Time is just the interaction of space and mass with consciousness. When this is understood and integrated, then you can move and you can use your knowledge of the interaction of consciousness with space to do many beautiful things.

TIMING IS EVERYTHING

You may have noticed that as everything accelerates, your timing can be positively affected, and you have to become more aware of timing. You have to make decisions about your work, help, traveling and finances. All of these decisions can now be more critical. Be conscious that there is an accumulation of better consequences. Remain aware that your timing in taking actions can protect you. When you decide to do things can become so important.

You may ask: "What is the right time?" Everything has a different time sequence, so I cannot tell you what the right time is exactly. I can tell you that there are higher times based on the alignments. It has been said that the astrological alignments are important, the alignment of the Central Sun is important, and the planetary alignments can offer certain information about timing. Many of you are aware of this. These alignments are reflections of universal energy that are coming to this planet. It is not necessarily true that the Moon in a certain position causes something. At the same time, it is true that the Moon in a certain position indicates that there is a certain cosmic energy influencing the planet.

Maybe you do not understand the relationship and influence of the zodiacal constellations to Earth events. Zodiacal configurations are all reflections of waves of energy that are striking your planet. Know that many people have talked about Earth staying still or stopping. If Earth stopped rotating, even for a brief time, it would be a terrible catastrophe. Even if Earth stopped rotating for twenty-four hours, greater problems would happen. But stopping certain human-made Earth activities can be a biorelativity exercise that would expand awareness. For example, one of the biorelativity exercises that I hope we will be able to organize is for people to stop driving cars for a given period of time.

I know there was a beautiful attempt that originated in Australia where they had people stop using their lights for a given period of time. That was beautiful. Remember, it only has an effect when people's consciousness is expanding at the time the stopping occurs. Then there is the expansion of time and then time stops. For example, it might be interesting to actually stop other activities, including not using airplanes or not working for a day or not fishing for a day. The stopping is really an expansion of the consciousness. In the expanded state, time slows for the people doing the exercise. A great deal of healing can occur, and a great deal of repair work can occur in this time expansion.

The time expansion concept is not just to be used in the present. Time expansion includes the idea of slowing down time in your understanding of the past, present and future. Time expansion is the realization that all three periods of time are connected in a circle. This concept of time as a circle allows us to understand the nature of holographic time. In holographic time, one entry point in time can help you obtain this expanded understanding of time. This will allow you to go into infinite time and will allow you to go anywhere into the past, present or future. Then you can enter the past, present or future for yourself and for the planet and work with the future energies to heal the planet and even yourself. I am Juliano. I will now turn things over to Chief White Eagle. Blessings, dear starseeds.

All my relations, greetings, my starseed family. We are all brothers and sisters, all of my words are sacred. I love you all. We understand that love is an expression of infinite time and this has been a great awakening for our people, our spirit guides and our teachers. It has been a teaching that love is an expression of infinite time—past, present and future. We have made a commitment to Earth. We love Earth from the past, we love Earth in the present and we love Earth in her future. Many of us ascended masters have committed our spirits to stay with Earth through whatever happens. We will stay with Earth to help her. Some of you have asked: "Do I need to make my commitment to be with Earth now or after I ascend?" I say: "Well, that is your personal decision. Some of you are from other planetary systems, and some of you are going back to those planetary systems. I just wanted to let you know that we, the ascended Native masters, have committed ourselves to Earth, and we will be with the spirit of Earth. We will help Earth through all of the phases of ascension and with what is going to happen.

Our grandfathers' and grandmothers' spirits are in the mountains and in the streams, and they are also working for the ascension. We are always communicating with the grandfathers and grandmothers. This is how we communicate with the past, and we are trying to communicate with our future brothers and sisters, some of whom are starseed planetary guides who will come here to Earth.

We understand what Juliano said about the nature of time and that is why we drum, because the drumming is a sequence of beats that helps us to access infinite time. It is a sequence of sounds that help to align us with the sacred time. In our concepts, we find time in different categories and we understand that there is certain time that is more special than others. We call this the sacred time. Let us say that when the Moon is full, we consider it a sacred time.

THE HARMONIC CONVERGENCE

We have an ability to use our assemblage points to connect with infinite time and to connect with the feedback loops of the past and the future. Then we try to accelerate our awareness through drumming, through dancing and through fire in order to integrate all of these energies through chanting. Then we become, at this point, more powerful. We come into our power and then we can do greater healing work.

I want you all to think of the 2012 winter December solstice as a sacred time. Do not focus on this time as a time of disaster. Do not focus on this time as the end of time. I ask you to consider this—at this time your thoughts and your projections are going to considerably influence the outcomes of time periods. We are now in a heightened time, and remember, 2012 is a sacred energy; 2012 is a sacred time. The closer that we get to the 2012 December solstice, the closer we are getting to that sacred time. This means that all of the events and times that are approaching 2012 possess more sacred time energy periods.

The 8-8-8 is a sacred time. The 8–8–8 is the new harmonic convergence. You can communicate and work within that sacred time because you will be able to expand your time. You will be able to connect to the past, present and future feedback loops that Juliano described during the 8-8-8 harmonic convergence. You will be able to shape events for the greater good.

O great Father/Mother/Creator of all, help us to be aware of our sacred duty to connect and to make sacred space and to acknowledge the sacred times that are before us. Help us to expand our consciousness so that we will be in alignment with your sacred cycles and are able to do the work that we have come here to do to be great healers. We know that Buffalo Calf Woman's point of entry into our time cycle is being discovered. We know that there is a point when she will enter our time. She is now out of our time, but we, through our sacred work, invite her, and we will make a space for her to be in our time. She will help us to receive the benefits of her higher consciousness for the good of all, for the good of the Native and the non-Native peoples, in alignment with your wishes, O Father/Mother/Spirit. I am your servant. I am your teacher. This is Chief White Eagle. *Ho!*

THE ARCTURIAN STARGATE

Juliano, the Arcturians and Archangel Metatron

Greetings, I am Juliano. We are the Arcturians. As the ascension gets closer, we focus our energies and our teachings on the Arcturian stargate. The stargate is coming into alignment with the Earth, just like the Earth is coming into alignment with the Central Sun. There is a beautiful triangle of fifth-dimensional etheric light that aligns or creates a beautiful alignment with the Central Sun, the Arcturian stargate and the Mother Earth.

Many of the starseeds have returned to Earth at this time for the specific purpose of experiencing the alignments that are before you with the Arcturian stargate. We have compared alignments before with the eclipses of the Sun and the Moon. Our example has been this: If you were a student of astronomy and you knew that there was an eclipse of the Sun of great magnitude and great power, then you would easily travel to South Africa, to the North Pole, to the South Pole—or wherever it was on Earth that would enable you to receive the highest perspective and the highest energy from that eclipse. In the same way, you as starseeds would want and, in fact, have decided to reincarnate onto Earth at this time, in part, to experience the alignment with the Central Sun and the alignment with the Arcturian stargate.

In cosmic alignments, there are powerful energies that would not normally be available. In a cosmic alignment, you receive and can accelerate your powers of fifth-dimensional activation, of fifth-dimensional streaming and of fifth-dimensional shimmering. You can activate your energy with thought projections, pulsing, dynamic interactions and the fifth dimension, which will allow you to ascend.

PLANETARY REINCARNATION

The power of this ascension energy on Earth is twofold. The first power comes from the Earth's alignment with the Central Sun. The second power, and equally dynamic one, comes from the alignment with the Arcturian stargate. The Arcturian stargate is a portal that allows the starseed-activated beings to participate in their planetary choice for their next incarnation process. This means that at the stargate, you can review and participate in choosing where you want to incarnate next, including which planet. It always means and also includes the possibility of returning to Earth for another incarnation. This is a great power and a great gift—to be able to participate in the planetary reincarnation process.

In the hierarchy of soul evolution, consciousness, choice and the participation to choose an incarnation is considered a higher value. When you are able to participate in the life you are going to, and the planet you are going to, then you can be assured that you have reached a higher level of soul evolution. Now, on the Earth, in a normal reincarnation process, your next lifetime is, in part, directed by your guides and teachers. Your next lifetime, in fact, is set in parameters in accordance with your Earth karma. Your next Earth reincarnation is in many ways preset based on the needs that you have for your own learning and for your own evolution.

In fact, when you are born through the Earth's incarnation process, part of the whole process depends on your forgetting everything about the reincarnation process. You are made to forget about the inter-life, or life-between-life processes so that, in essence, you come to Earth in an incarnation with a relatively clean slate. I say "relatively" because you know that there are certain soul imprints that carry on from lifetime to lifetime. We have used the example of Mozart who has a great soul imprint for music that carries on in any lifetime that he manifests. In any lifetime that he wishes to access that talent, he can use music to his greatest and highest good. Even with such a powerful imprint, you must still consider the fact that someone like Mozart did not have conscious memory of other lifetimes in which he was a musician. He did not even have memories of his musical experiences between his life-between-life processes.

LIFE BETWEEN LIFE

The life-between-life process is often as important in the whole evolutionary process as the experiences that you have on Earth in a lifetime. I know that the lifetime on Earth can often be of a limited consciousness. However, each lifetime on Earth has the potential to be lived in 100 percent awareness. In fact, if lifetimes were experienced in 100 percent awareness, then people would be making different decisions about what they are doing with themselves. It is true that the third dimension is a dimension of duality and a dimension of restriction. This third-dimensional restriction is such that there is not an easy opportunity readily available to experience the inner life and life-between-life memories. However, through special meditation and through special studies, you can reawaken your memories from past-life and life-between-life experiences. With those memories, you can also further awaken your starseed consciousness.

In the stargate there is an entirely different operational principle. That stargate operational principle focuses on awareness. When you go from the stargate to another planet, then you go in full consciousness and in full awareness. You go in full memory of all of your life-between-life experiences. You go in full memory of your past lives.

To be able to go through the stargate, you have to have a greater consciousness. You have to have a more evolved soul. That is what you are developing now. That is what you are evolving toward. This lifetime on Earth is bringing you closer to higher soul evolution. In fact, we have noted that in any one lifetime, but particularly in this lifetime, you can gain full consciousness of all of your past lives. You can gain full consciousness of the lessons of the life-between-life experiences. We want you to develop this ability. We want you to understand that the normal consciousness that you have of yourself is a limited consciousness. It is limited necessarily by the restrictions of the third dimension. You expand and move up to a higher level of consciousness, and with that higher level, you quickly develop the ability to enter the Arcturian stargate.

THE PRACTICE CORRIDOR

In the transition for the ascension, we recommend remaining in full consciousness. When you approach and access the stargate and leave Earth's incarnation process, we work helping and teaching you to make this transition with full consciousness. This means that as you travel through the corridor for ascension, then you focus on the Arcturian stargate. You visualize and direct yourself in these soul energy spaces called "corridors. The fuel that propels you to the place you want to be is your thoughts. Your ability to project yourself through a corridor is a vital tool and a vital skill that you want to access and use when you are in the ascension corridor. This means that you should visualize and think: "I am projecting myself to the Arcturian stargate,"

I, Juliano, am downloading a corridor of light around each of you now. This corridor of light is a stargate corridor that we call a "practice corridor" that enables and offers each of you an opportunity to experience and to practice projecting yourselves to the Arcturian stargate.

There are only two stargates in the entire Milky Way Galaxy. The Arcturian stargate is the official stargate for this half of this sector of the Milky Way Galaxy. That means that anyone or any being who wishes to reenter and process themselves into another planetary incarnation has to come through—or it is desirable for them to come through—this stargate. Naturally, when you come through the stargate, you are doing this with consciousness. Then you will correctly choose a fifth-dimensional planet, a more evolved planet, to continue in your incarnations.

Rest assured that in the fifth dimension, you will go through an incarnation process, but it is totally different from the third-dimensional incarnation process. What is different? As I have said, in the fifth-dimensional planetary system, you enter an incarnation in full consciousness of life between lives and past lives. This means that you will even have a memory of this information I am giving. You will have memory of what you have done on Earth in this lifetime. You will have memories of other lifetimes that you have been on Earth.

You have to understand—my starseed friends whom I love very much and I send you my blessings—what a great event it is in the soul evolution to go and approach the stargate. You have to understand what a great leap of spiritual energy it is to complete a planetary incarnation, such as what you are doing now on the Earth, and to graduate and go through the Arcturian stargate.

THE GRAND CENTRAL SUN STATION

Many people have asked, "What is it like in the stargate?" The stargate is in the fifth dimension. It is a fifth-dimensional heavenly gate that has an unlimited amount of contacts with different planetary systems that are much evolved. The best way that I can describe the stargate is for you to imagine that you are in a huge train station. Perhaps you might call it "Grand Central Station," Another term would be a Grand "Central Sun"

Station. In that station you might see signs like: "Going to the Pleiades," "Going to Sirius," "Going to Aldeberan," "Going to Scorpio," "Going to the Andromeda Systems," "Going to Xerxes" or "Going to the Central Sun Moon-Planet Alano." You would also see many corridors in the stargate. Each one is a beautiful transitional corridor in which you are accelerated and projected into a much higher consciousness in preparation for down-loading yourself into an incarnation. It is a beautiful process to go from a spirit form into incarnation form. This process is enhanced when you are in higher consciousness.

In the Arcturian stargate we have special teachers or guides who will work with you. Imagine that you come into the Great Central Sun Station and you begin to contemplate which corridor you should take in order to go to the appropriate planetary experience for your soul. You need to decide which higher dimensional planet would be best for you. I under-stand that when you have so many positive and interesting choices that sometimes you become frozen and are unable to make any decision. We, the Arcturians, are going to be there helping. Also, Archangel Metatron is there at the stargate.

We even have classes where we have group discussions. At the stargate you do not have to immediately decide which place to go to. There is not even a time constraint. You can stay at the stargate for as long as you want to. There are many spirit guides there at this Grand Central Sun train station. You will be meeting many higher dimensional spirits. How fascinating to see all these spirits coming from different countries and going to different places.

YOUR MANIFESTED FORM IN THE ARCTURIAN STARGATE

In the same way, the Arcturian stargate will give you the opportunity to interact with beings from other levels. I know that you are all excited at the opportunity to see other beings. You will be seeing only those beings that are fifth dimensional and higher. Some of these beings could be some-what different in terms of their manifested forms. You are still defined in Earth body. When you go into the fifth-dimensional corridor, I know that it will be easier and most comfortable for you to manifest a fifth-di-mensional body. Perhaps you can manifest a body to appear like when you were twenty-five or thirty years old. You can create a body in that certain light of the youthful figure that perhaps you feel most comfortable in.

Consider this: Species from other planets have humanlike life forms that are slightly different from the Earth human form. One different example is those human-like life forms that are hermaphrodites. Hermaphrodites carry male and female characteristics in one body. Therefore a hermaphrodite would be able to have a relationship with another hermaphrodite, so the whole issue of whether it is male-to-female relationship or male-to-male or female-to-female relationship would not be an issue. The hermaphrodite would become involved in a relationship based on whatever sexual orientation was appropriate.

This type of flexibility in sexuality might be foreign to you. However, when you experience meeting hermaphrodites, you might find yourself interestingly attracted to a planet that has that experience. You may meet someone, a guide or teacher, from that system and you might begin to realize that this is an interesting, challenging and expanding way of experiencing an incarnation. You may decide to go to the corridor and experience the planet that offers that experience, and you may decide to learn what it is like to incarnate on that planet.

CHOOSING A THIRD-DIMENSIONAL PLANET

What you need to know is that incarnating from a fifth-dimensional perspective is not like incarnating into a third-dimensional perspective. When you incarnate into the third dimension, you are also bound by the laws of karma on that planet, and this may mean that you will go through some discomfort and densities in that experience. In some cases we know that the beings on the third dimension who have incarnated from higher planes have even felt trapped on Earth. They have had to extricate themselves from Earth incarnations with some assistance from their guides.

Some of you may have incarnated on to Earth from the Arcturian stargate. The Arcturian stargate can also be a Central Sun transitional point to another third-dimensional planet. There always will be the possibility of returning to Earth from the stargate. Remember, returning to a third-dimensional planet or coming to a third-dimensional planet does have limitations in consciousness. You can put yourself into the position that you might have to go through another incarnation on that third-dimensional planet. What is interesting to us is that those people who have come from the stargate to Earth—we call them Arcturian starseeds—knew that an alignment with the Central Sun and the Arcturian stargate was coming to Earth during this incarnation. They knew that they were going to be activated by the Arcturian process, the Arcturian groups, and they knew that they would have an opportunity to come back through the Arcturian stargate during this incarnation.

You might think of coming to the Earth during this alignment with the stargate like an insurance policy. You might think this way: "Previously, I wanted to come to the third dimension, but I was a little bit concerned that I would be having limited consciousness. From that limited consciousness, I might find myself trapped in the third dimension for another couple of incarnations. However, I am now going to incarnate on Earth at a time where there is going to be a powerful alignment with the Arcturian stargate and when the Arcturian energy is going to be strong on Earth. Therefore I will be activated, and I can be sure that I will have the correct consciousness and activation to return to the fifth dimension."

The Arcturian stargate is a place of higher energy and excitement. Remember, if you pass through the gate of the Arcturian stargate from your present Earth life, then you cannot return to your third-dimensional Earth incarnation that is this current incarnation. This means that we are not allowing it, and we would not encourage anyone in our meditations and exercises to go through the Arcturian stargate on to the other side. However, we will help you come to our stargate's vestibule—our fore room where there is plenty of opportunity to experience the closeness of the Arcturian stargate, and also where you can practice the idea of thought-projecting yourself through the Arcturian stargate corridor from Earth to there. Also, we can open the gate a certain distance for your experience. Remember, the Arcturian stargate is a gate. You can experience the power and light and attractive force of that light briefly and prepare yourself for your eventual transition to there. We will be working with you on an exercise for that experience.

THE DOWNLOAD OF THE TWELFTH CRYSTAL

I want to speak about the relationship between the etheric crystals that we have downloaded and the Arcturian stargate. The etheric crystals are multidimensional and multifunctional. Generally, in our discussions of the etheric crystals, we have talked about how these crystals serve as conduits for downloading fifth-dimensional light and energy into the planetary Earth system so that the Earth's planetary meridians can be cleansed. Then certain frequencies of light and information can be held in the energy field of Earth. In particular, we know that there are several power spots on the planet that have the ability to hold certain etheric energies of a higher vibration on Earth.

We know that it is critically important to download fifth-dimensional energy into Earth. Part of the effectiveness of the etheric crystals is to interact with each other. We have encouraged different levels and ways of interaction. Different Arcturian starseeds throughout the planet have different accesses to these crystals, and they have different methods of working with the crystals. The basic method is to understand that these crystals are downloaded from the main crystal in the Arcturian crystal temple. Each of the current ten etheric crystals is a duplicate of the main Arcturian crystal.

The subcrystals are duplicates of the downloaded etheric crystals on Earth. You always must work first with the downloaded Earth crystal. The subcrystals support the work of the main crystal. The primary light is emanating from the main crystal.

To further elucidate the etheric crystal purpose, the etheric crystals that are now in place help Earth's alignment with the stargate. The function of the etheric crystals is of multipurpose. One purpose is to activate and help in the alignment and the activation of fifth-dimensional light and energy on Earth. The second purpose, though, is to create an energy field that is appropriate and that will allow an attractive energetic alignment with the stargate. Downloading the crystal in Istanbul, Turkey in June 2009 along the Bosporus Straits brought us one step closer to perfecting the alignment with the stargate. When the twelfth crystal downloaded, we achieved perfect activation of the Arcturian stargate alignment with Earth.

ALIGN WITH THE ARCTURIAN STARGATE

This is very important. The stargate is vibrating and has a certain energetic frequency. You cannot enter the stargate unless you also are at a certain vibrational frequency. Completing the ascension activates you to a higher frequency, and through grace, the ascension helps you to achieve the vibrational frequency necessary to go through the stargate. So when you approach the stargate, remember that you are still coming from Earth. You are still coming from a third-dimensional planet. Part of the energy of the stargate must be in harmony with the planet from which you are coming. It requires a certain activation of energy from a planet. When you come from Earth, that higher aspect of the planet Earth has to be in alignment with the Arcturian stargate.

There are many forces that affect the stargate. There is the force of the Central Sun. There is the force of the ascension. There is also the energy field of the stargate itself. The energy field of the stargate is coming more into your consciousness now. You are going to want to work on creating an attractive energy alliance and alignment with the Arcturian stargate. This is part of your ascension work. This is part of the preparation for the planet Earth and is mainly to be a conduit of light that will allow a transition for many higher beings from Earth's incarnation process to the Arcturian stargate.

This work is of the highest spiritual value and the highest spiritual purpose. You will be able to follow the path for your ascension to the Arcturian stargate. You will be able to provide a link and teachings for others who will follow on how to align with the Arcturian stargate. I wish to let Archangel Metatron speak to you, as he will also be giving you some instructions on your soul journey to the Arcturian stargate. I am Juliano. Blessings. I will return to do a brief exercise with you.

Greetings, I am Metatron. Some call me the "Divine Leader of the Archangels," I only want to be known as your guide, teacher and helper. Indeed, the word "angel" in Hebrew is defined as "messenger"— the Great Messenger is the way I define my name Metatron. I am here to give you great news. The great news is that you are holographic energetic balls of lightbeings. That experience of being an energetic field of light can be overwhelming. Some people have gone into the mystical experience and have become overwhelmed by it and lost their sense of perspective and their sense of purpose. They have not really benefitted by being exposed to the lifting of the veils. The lifting of the veils by itself can be a rather confusing experience unless you have the proper preparation.

There is a path. There is a way and guidance available that can lead you comfortably to your soul's highest evolution and your soul's highest travel. Part of that rests with your ability to focus on holy beings—the holy creation and the holiness of Sananda, for example—and your ability to relate to the holiness of the ascended masters. You can call on the *Melech Ha Gadol.* You can call on Sananda. You can call on Archangel Michael. You can call on many of your beloved masters who will gladly, and with great love, lead you to the stargate. With great love they will help your transition to higher spiritual links.

My message to you is focused on understanding and working with the energy of holiness. Also, you would call it the energy of "sacredness," That energy of holiness and sacredness is available on the third dimension.

Holiness is not only on the fifth dimension. That is to say that you can create spaces on Earth that are holy and sacred. These holy and sacred places then become conduits of light for the fifth dimension. In fact, that is one of the roles of the etheric crystals: to create a sacred and holy space on Earth. In a sacred and holy space, one can download greater fifth-dimensional energy and light.

YOU ARE PROTECTED BY A HOLY FORCE

In the Bible, one example of a sacred conduit is called Jacob's ladder. The corridor is like a ladder. Jacob's ladder can lead to the stargate—truly. An interesting fact is that connections to corridors also allow higher beings from the fifth dimension to appear on Earth. This happened to Elijah. Elijah saw fifth-dimensional chariots. You have to understand that when the corridor of ascension is open, then there is up and down movement. That means that many of the Arcturians at this ascension corridor will be coming through the corridor to work with and meet you. The other holy beings will come at the same time. This is one of the great gifts of the ascension—the assistance is going to be overwhelming.

Work on understanding holiness. That is why we repeat *Kadosh, kadosh, kadosh, Adonai tzevaoth*—Holy, holy, holy is the Lord of hosts. Part of the importance of this phrase focuses on the codes of ascension. This phrase is also a reminder to you of the holy space that you are working in. Even in darkness there is light to be found. There is light to be found in duality and the breaking down of the illusions that have been operating on this planet. You know that we are now directly experiencing the planetary shift, where the illusions that have been operating to keep institutions afloat are breaking down. Truth is coming. The illusions will no longer be powerful enough to cover the truth. That can be a painful energy.

A strong energy is required to break down the illusions. [Sings.] *Kadosh, Kadosh, Kadosh, Adonai Tzevaoth*. Let this place that you are standing on be holy. Your transition to the stargate will be filled with holiness. Let the holiness be a protective force for you. The Creator Spirit has a beautiful evolutionary path before you. It is available to you now. Take advantage of this alignment of Earth with the stargate. Take advantage of the ascension. Take advantage of your abilities to go back to the stargate. Take advantage of your new freedoms to be able to chose and participate in your future incarnation process that include the ability to go to other planets. This is a great gift. I am Archangel Metatron. Good day.

Greetings, I am Juliano. I have placed a corridor of light around each of you. I ask you now to project your thoughts into the corridor. As you project your thoughts into the corridor, you can project an image of yourself. Create this image of yourself in the highest form, the most beautiful form, you wish of yourself. For example, you can be as thin as you want, and you can have as much hair as you want on your head. You can have the shape you want and the smile you want. Just project that image now. Then, as you project that image, give that image the ability to travel by thought. That image of yourself is traveling through the corridor and through the Arcturian stargate corridor that is now near you. You are traveling there at the speed of thought. You come to the great garden.

You are able to travel instantaneously with thought and you are instantaneously in the garden at the stargate. You are with many of your Earth colleagues and group members. Sit in the garden at the stargate. It is filled with light energy, excitement, spirit. I, Juliano, am there at the stargate with you, and very gently I open up the gate just a small amount. As I open up this gate, the spiritual force that is there is just indescribable in human terms in your languages. The spiritual energy that is coming through the gate is spreading a beautiful etheric blue light into the garden that is so intense and so satisfying to each of you.

I open the gate further because you are able to absorb this light. The light that is there is now becoming more intense, and you are still able to tolerate it with full consciousness and full presence. A very important word in understanding your ascension and going through the stargate is "presence." Keep your presence.

Now, that is as far as I can open the gate for you. I will leave this gate open for a few more minutes. We will be in silence as you experience this powerful energy. [Pause.] I will close the door of the stargate now, and you can begin your return now through the corridor. Reenter your body in perfect alignment, bringing with you all of this beautiful spiritual light and energy into your physical body. You can use this for your greater health and greater spiritual light on the Earth. I am Juliano. Good day.

THE COSMIC PULSE

Juliano and the Arcturians

Greetings, I am Juliano. We are the Arcturians. We wish to continue our discussion of the spiritual light quotient and the energy of shimmering. We also wish to discuss the relationship between the spiritual light quotient energy and how that relates to a country, a city and even your place of residence.

THE AURA'S PULSE

The spiritual light quotient is the energetic field that allows you to comprehend and participate in spiritual light and spiritual energy. Indeed, the spiritual light quotient has also been referred to as the liquid light field. Experiencing higher spiritual light energy requires a vibrational activation or a vibrational field. This vibrational field must be calibrated for a higher frequency. We have referred to the frequency vibration as being related to the pulse of the aura. You have understood in my previous discussions that the aura is shaped optimally as an egg. We refer to that as the cosmic egg shape. In that shape, the aura represents the highest possible configuration that will allow you to be healthy, and will also allow you to experience higher vibrations. The egg shape in your aura will be a protective field. It will help you to seal any holes in your aura and any negative attachments from unwanted entities.

The cosmic pulse is the name that we give to the pulsing or vibrational rate of the aura. This can be compared to the pulse of a human. For example, you might say that the optimal pulse of a human is between sixty and seventy. That represents the heartbeat. The pulse of the aura also has a rate or a speed. That speed can be considered either slow or fast, low or high. If a person's cosmic pulse is at a lower vibrational pulse rate, the spiritual energy or the spiritual light quotient of that person would not be able to understand, participate in or receive spiritual liquid light energy.

On the other hand, if the cosmic pulse of that person is high, then they would correspondingly be able to participate in, understand, experience and receive higher spiritual light. This can be manifested also in terms of cognitive abilities because we know that spiritual energy can also be transferred into the world of ideas, the world of thoughts and other energy manifestations such as music and art. In order to comprehend and participate in this spiritual light, one must have a high cosmic pulse.

ENHANCE YOUR COSMIC PULSE

Throughout the years, we have offered various spiritual exercises and techniques to enhance your cosmic pulse. However, even if you have a high rate, sometimes there are intervening variables—including anxiety, depression or physical problems—that may hinder your ability to relate to spiritual energy. Therefore, it is necessary to offer and work together with you in these exercises and to enhance your cosmic pulse so that it is vibrating at an optimal level, no matter what other conditions or concerns you are experiencing on the physical plane.

One of the main exercises that we use to enhance the cosmic pulse is toning and sounds. I will give a very basic Arcturian sound that will help immediately to raise your cosmic pulse. [Tones]: *Tat, tat, tat, tat. Ohh. Ehh. Tat, tat, tat, tat.* Feel your cosmic pulse vibrate at a higher rate. The paradox is that as your cosmic pulse moves at a higher rate, you actually experience your Earth reality in a more relaxed, slower and observant energy. Experiences that would perhaps be difficult to comprehend or that may cause anxiety when you vibrate slower are not experienced with difficulty when you vibrate at a higher pulse. The fear, the anxiety or even the pain that you may have experienced in your physical body before diminishes as your cosmic pulse increases its vibrational rate.

We also recommend the exercise of contracting the cosmic egg. This is an aspect of pulsing where you pull in and contract your egg, and as this egg is contracted, you bring it into a small ball in the center of your stomach. After you hold it there, you release it and let the energy expand out. As it expands, any blocks or any dense energies that you have been holding on to are dispelled and your cosmic egg aura is cleansed. After this exercise, your cosmic pulse will be at a higher rate. I am reviewing all of this with you because I am going to show you how this applies to the cosmic pulse of a country, a city and a solar system—even the cosmic pulse of a galaxy.

When the Earth comes into alignment with the Central Sun on December 21, 2012, the cosmic pulse of Earth will go into a higher pulsing and a higher vibrational field. Believe me, this is a major spiritual event when a planet or a planet's vibrational cosmic pulse is going to increase. I know that many of you have waited for this opportunity to come to a planet that is going to have the experience of an increase in its cosmic pulse. Such an experience will open up your own spiritual light energy field. You will be able to resonate at a higher field. Already you may have felt yourself experiencing an increase in spiritual light energy during the past several years.

Now visualize your cosmic egg shape. Visualize now that your aura is configuring itself, by your commands, to go to a perfect cosmic egg shape with a beautiful silver-blue outline that represents the outer edge of your aura. Sense the pulse, or your own pulse of your aura, and try to visualize it as either being low, medium or high rather than trying to assign a number to it. However, I know that some of you are very numerically oriented. If you have to look at a number, then remember to base it on a scale of one to a hundred. Using that scale, then one hundred would represent the highest vibration, which would be shimmering into the fifth dimension. One would be the lowest vibration. So if you must assign a number, calibrate your pulse rate, your cosmic pulse between the numbers of one to a hundred.

Now, on my command, contract your cosmic egg again. Feel it get closer and closer to your body. Contract it inside your body. Contract it into the center of your stomach. Hold it. On my command, release. Release, release, release! As you release, your aura expands out at a high rate of speed. As it expands out, you may already experience an acceleration of the pulsing. We will do this one more time. Visualize the outer edge of your aura. This time, when you contract, bring with you any blocks, densities or any negativities that may be causing you problems, pains or anything that would be considered a lower vibration. Bring these energies into the center of your stomach as you contract.

When you release it, lower energies will fly out, and these lower energies will not be able to return because your egg will be vibrating at such a high speed. On my command, contract. As you contract, feel all of the blocks and all of the densities in your aura that are representative of any densities in the physical body. Contract, contract! Bring the lower energies in with you now. Hold those energies into the center of your stomach. On my command, release all the densities of lower vibrational patterns. They will be thrown out of your aura. Next, feel the acceleration of your cosmic pulse.

THE SPIRITUAL LIGHT QUOTIENT OF MEXICO

This method that I just explained, the cosmic pulsing and the contracting of the cosmic egg, actually can be used to enhance and cleanse the spiritual light quotient of a country. We will use Mexico as an example of how one can adapt and use the energy from the cosmic pulse exercises to help raise the spiritual light quotient of a country. I have chosen Mexico for several reasons, primarily because of its importance in the 2012 alignment. The original energies of the Mayan people were centered in what in part is now known as Mexico, near the Yucatán. It is true that the Maya also lived south of Mexico, which is now known as Central America, but the large portion of the work that was done in the time of the Maya was done in what is now known as Mexico.

Earth as a planet is coming into alignment with the 2012 energies. Also, there are parts of Earth that are in more direct alignment in the center of the galaxy than others. One of those points is located in the Mayan civilization in Mexico. I want to be clear that all parts of Earth are going to be affected. Remember that the alignment of the Central Sun with Earth was discovered in this Mayan civilization. This indicates that there was a higher spiritual light quotient there. There was a higher vibrational field that was resonant with the 2012 energy at that time.

When you look at a country like Mexico, you try to come to an understanding of what the spiritual light quotient of the country is. Therefore, you will take into consideration many different influences. Obviously, you would have to consider and understand that the influence of the Maya has had a tremendous impact on the spiritual light quotient of Mexico. It should be considered a positive spiritual energy. Naturally, you would understand that the Maya, being a Native people, also had a primitive side, and there were darker forces that were also going on as well as the higher spiritual energy. In looking at the spiritual light quotient of a country, you should consider both the high spiritual light energy and the low.

When I look at the spiritual light quotient of a person, then I understand that the person at this moment may be in a low energy field. This could be for a variety of Earth reasons—that person may be experiencing densities. That doesn't mean the person's overall spiritual light quotient is lowered. People are not punished spiritually by experiencing densities. It just means that the person is vibrating at a lower field at that moment. One always maintains and can return to the highest spiritual light quotient energy that one has experienced in a lifetime or even in other lifetimes.

I hope this is of good solace and consolation to you, because I know that some of you are worried. Perhaps you have gotten into a bit of difficulty due to the economic times or because of physical problems or relationship problems. Maybe you couldn't hold the higher spiritual pulsing that you are usually able to hold. Those problems do not diminish the higher spiritual light energy that you had attained previously. You will, I guarantee, be able to return to that energy.

SPIRITUAL LIGHT QUOTIENTS OF OTHER AREAS

So we are taking into consideration Mexico, the Maya and their high influence in spiritual areas. Of course, we also look at the Aztecs and how their civilization has affected Mexico. We know that there were some powerful structures that were built by the Aztecs. Many people are aware of the pyramids they built in Mexico. Many people are also aware of the Mayan temples. These temples and these pyramids have become spots and sacred energy fields. They were built in alignment with a certain star system.

We know that many of the Mayan temples and other structures were built in part to align with the constellation Scorpius and the star system known as Antares. Many of you might realize or remember that Antares may be one of your home planets. Even though the Aztec and Mayan civilizations have been destroyed or disbanded, the sacred energy fields that were aligned with star energy are still creating and contributing to the maintenance of a higher spiritual light quotient for the country of Mexico.

In the same way, you could understand Egypt. If I looked at and discussed the pyramids in Egypt, then I would have to discuss the spiritual light quotient of Egypt. One would naturally understand that the spiritual light quotient of Egypt is being raised or has been raised by the pyramids—even though the current Egyptian government and current Egyptian religions do not recognize the pyramids as spiritual or religious structures or even as structures holding spiritual energy. In fact, the pyramids have greatly raised the spiritual light quotient of Egypt for thousands of years.

Several of these pyramids with the star system of Sirius and are in alignment with Betelgeuse, which is a star system in the constellation of Orion. These alignments by the pyramids are still creating, after thousands of years, powerful light fields that raise the spiritual vibration of the people who visit them. The pyramids in Egypt also raise the spiritual light quotient of the country. Can you imagine Egypt without the pyramids? If you look at Israel and Jerusalem, you will see another example of structures, like the Temple on the Mount or like Solomon's Temple. Another powerful area is the birthplace of Jesus. These areas all hold a lot of spiritual light. These power areas contribute to the higher vibrational field of the country of Israel. It is the same with Mecca in Saudi Arabia. There are places in each country that are adding to and raising the spiritual light quotient of a country.

We also say that in Mexico, we have the Copper Canyon, which is a "wonder of the world." We have chosen to place an etheric crystal in that canyon and we have designated that crystal as the shimmering crystal. We have said that this crystal and this canyon are in direct alignment and resonance with the moon-planet called Alano, which is near the Central Sun. The shimmering energies that we possess are naturally part of the higher spiritual vibration. Shimmering is in direct resonance with the Copper Canyon; therefore, this crystal has the potential for greatly activating the shimmering energy globally. In particular, the shimmering energy in Mexico and other shimmering activities on the planet can be activated as well.

This etheric crystal in Copper Canyon is a special crystal, and now three duplicate crystals can be made from it. They can be placed in Mexico in the designated areas: Lake Chapella [a lake near Guadalajara, Mexico], Mount Popocatépetl [a volcanic mountain forty-five miles southeast of Mexico City] and another area to be designated in the Yucatán. These duplicate etheric crystals can further activate and raise the spiritual vibration of the country of Mexico. This is one way that you are able to raise the spiritual vibration of a country.

OTHER SPIRITUAL FACTORS

When you look at the spiritual light quotient of a country like Mexico, you also have to look at the country's history. Mexico was invaded by Spaniards. There was a domination, there was a rebellion, and there was great violence. All this has set a karmic tone around the country. That has to be taken into consideration. One must also look at the history of the U.S. and its earlier wars with the Native Americans. These earlier wars have affected the spiritual light quotient of the United States. You would have to say that the spiritual light quotient of the U.S. is influenced by the Native energies and how the Europeans dealt with the Native people. Also you would have to say that the Native people, who have been revived and are gaining again in spiritual strength, can now add a great new energy to the overall light quotient of the U.S.

We must look at the date of independence of that country—the date when that country was formed—when we look at its spiritual light quotient. In a simple example, we can look at July 4, 1776 as the birth of the U.S. Then we could look at the astrological alignments of that birth. Based on that, we can give interpretations. It is a little complicated, however. Maybe you would say the birth of the U.S. occurred on July 4, 1776, but what would be the birth of the area if you looked at the birth from the Native people's perspective? They might have a different assessment.

You also have to see if there are existing records of other influences on the civilizations that lived in the countries, and if possible, find out when the death date was of the prior civilization. I know that in your modern astrology, you search for examples of birth dates, but the death date also gives a lot of indications of the spiritual advancement and spiritual energy of a country. The spiritual light quotient formula takes into consideration the sacred spots, the previous Native energies and also the relationship between all of this and the number of lightworkers there are in a country. It just so happens that there are now a high number of lightworkers in Mexico, the U.S. and Canada. There are also a high number of lightworkers in Australia, New Zealand and Europe. Some other countries also have a high number of lightworkers, such as Argentina and Brazil and so on.

With these ideas, I want you to visualize that there is a cosmic energy field around the country of Mexico. Visualize that country's aura from space. That aura is composed of all of the energies that I am speaking of. It is composed even of the discarnate energies, such as the past-life energies from the Maya. I want to explain that the Native people believe in the spiritual energy of the dead just like the Mexican people now also believe in the energy of the dead. This lecture today is occurring on the Day of the Dead, *Dia de los Muertos*, which is a special holiday in Mexico in which the dead. Let me be very clear that the energies of the dead contribute to the overall aura of a country.

We also can talk about the elders or the Native American elders. Many of the Native American elders that are in the spirit world in the U.S. are living in the mountains and canyons and streams. Many of you have been in Sedona, for example, and you know that there is a high percentage of elder spirits that live in the canyons and in the rock areas there. All of these energies contribute to the spiritual light quotient of the city of Sedona, which already has a high light quotient. Many of the Native people and the elder spirits that live there had connections with their star families. When you go to the city of Sedona, it is easier for you to experience the connections to your star family.

For the purpose of this discussion, I will let you know that there is a place in Arizona that is approximately fifty miles from where the channel lives called the Bloody Basin Mesa. Just by the name, you would understand that there was some violence there. There is possibly unresolved spiritual energy there. If you were to go to that area, you might experience it as being scary. You might feel nervous. The truth is that there are angry lost spirits in that area living in the Bloody Basin area. In order to raise the spiritual light quotient of that area, you would have to go there with a group of people and work intensely to release those spirits so that they do not hover and lower its spiritual light quotient.

These are all good examples that would help you to better understand the spiritual light quotient of Mexico, because if you think about the invasions of the domineering Spaniards, including Cortez and his group, you would understand that there was great violence and domination during that time. There also was great violence done by the Aztecs among themselves, and great violence done by the Maya to other groups. You would have to consider how these events affected the energy fields. Violence can lower the spiritual vibration. You can try and purify this.

CLEAR NEGATIVE ENERGY

We have suggested that some of the problems in Mexico—the drug wars, drug problems and the terrorism occurring in that country—is due in part to the accumulation of the karmic energy of the past that has resulted in domination, submission and rebellion. That energy is still there. If you think about that, you would look at other countries, such as Iraq, and you would see that the energies of the thousands of years of intertribal fighting contributes to a lower spiritual light quotient of that country. Therefore it is not surprising what has occurred there in the past ten years.

To raise the spiritual light quotient of those countries, you would have to do some expelling of negative spiritual energy. Even if there is a peace that happens, many of the spirits of the people who were killed still remain in the astral field around that country and contribute to lowering its spiritual light quotient. It would be the same in Mexico, because earlier violent events there would contribute to lowering the spiritual light vibration field. So this is also true in the United States. Now in the United States, the Native energies are being revived, just as they are in Mexico. There are many people of high spiritual vibration being incarnated now. Some of these people were Native Americans in their previous incarnations. Now they are working to clear lower energy in America.

This becomes complicated when you think about, for example, the lost civilization of Atlantis. The lost civilization of Atlantis also had a high light quotient, but because of the mistakes of some of the scientists and politicians, that spiritual light quotient was lowered. There were intense upheavals and intense pain and violence that ended that civilization. Some of the people are still working to release that.

CONTRACT MEXICO'S COSMIC EGG

Returning to our discussion of Mexico, we have a sense of much of the interacting factors relating to the spiritual light quotient. There are more power spots than the ones of which we have spoken. We have an idea, then, of the energy field of the country. You can begin to work with your own country following some of the patterns and discussions that I have used today. You can work to raise the spiritual light quotient of every country.

Visualize with me now, to the best of your ability, a huge aura or energy vibration field that represents all of the etheric energy of the country of Mexico. It is composed of all of the things we have talked about, all of the positive and all of the negative. Visualize that as an energy ball around the country of Mexico. Shape that energy ball into a cosmic egg so that the energy field of the country of Mexico now forms, to the best of your ability, into the shape of a cosmic egg. Become aware of the pulse, the spiritual pulse of that country.

Be aware that Mexico does play an important role in the 2012 alignment. Now on my command, begin to contract the cosmic egg so that as the ball contracts, all of the lower vibrations come into the center of the ball. To the best of your ability, begin now to perform this cosmic egg contraction over the country of Mexico. Hold that contraction. On my command, release! All of the energy in the center is thrown out.

The lower vibration is thrown outside of the cosmic egg of the country, and now there is a cleaner pulse, a cleaner vibrational aura around the country of Mexico.

WORKING ON A SPECIFIC CITY

To do this exercise on a country optimally would really require people to be at different places around that country. It can actually be coordinated as a group. Try and call off names of places and also identify the center of a country. Try to contract the energy to that center. There are ways of refining this exercise. Let us look at a specific city. Say, for example, you wanted to do a cosmic pulse exercise over the city of Sydney, Australia. You would also use exactly the same technique. You would have one advantage because there is a lot of water around Sydney. The water can enhance some of the pulsing.

Nonetheless, you would try to send people around different points of the city. You would all work to visualize the outer aura of the city and try to become aware of the complex factors that influence it, including the date of the founding of the city. Look up the actual charter. Look up the birth date of the city. You would want to find the astrological alignments of that city and try to get an interpretation of that. The astrological alignments would tell you what the positive energies are and also some of the negative energies at the time of its birth. You might want to become aware of different places in the city where maybe there have been some hardships or some negative energies. Become aware of where there might be some negative spirits due to conflicts.

It would be good to have at least thirty to forty people spread around the city, but whatever number of people you can work with is acceptable. Then you would begin to do this cosmic pulse of the city. Contract it to the center of the city at a certain point. Now, when contracting to a point in a country or a city, it is preferable to contract it to a power spot. Let us just say that the center of the city of Sydney winds up being in a very depressed area—what would be considered a slum. You wouldn't necessarily want to contract it to there. You can move the center to a power spot that is in the vicinity of the center. It is good also to have one person in the center.

In previous times, we have also said that it is good to work with crystals to help you. You can put crystals around the edge of the city. This was done during the original pulsing at Lago Puelo in Argentina. The second part of the exercise [and this is the part that we did not do in Mexico, but I am giving this description for Sydney, Australia] is that you then shimmer the whole city. This becomes a fantastic experience. You are working to bring the city into the fifth dimension. It requires a tremendous amount of energy. I want to also explain that you can shimmer other cities that you live in, including smaller cities. You can even do this exercise on your home or for the planet.

This is one of the reasons why we have worked to formulate the Groups of Forty as international planetary groups because we need to shimmer, and we need to work with the cosmic pulse of Earth. It requires a tremendous amount of coordination, but it does not necessarily mean that you have to have people at every corner of Earth. For example, if we were working with Sydney, Australia, we don't actually have to have a complete circle of people around the city. If you work with the country of Mexico, you don't have to have a complete circle. If you work with Germany, you can place people at strategic points around the country.

PROJECT THE PULSE OF THE CITY

Remember that when we are working with the twelve etheric crystals, we are not placing them in a perfect circle around the planet. I want to also say that this shimmering and this cosmic pulse exercise would be effective in releasing karma in a country. For example, this shimmering exercise can help Germany, which has been working to release a lot of negative energy karma from World War II. In fact, every country on the planet has a negative energy field related to it. Every place on the planet has lost and trapped spirits. You know that your planet is a very violent planet. Your planet is still a young planet in terms of civilization, and you know that you are under the influence of a great polarization and great duality in a primitive energy. This is changing as you are moving closer to the 2012 time.

In the idea of shimmering a city, we recommend that you project the pulse of the city to the moon-planet Alano. The second level of this exercise of working with the city or country is to shimmer it into the fifth dimension. That fifth-dimensional planet, the moon-planet Alano is actually set up to receive the shimmering energy from cities on Earth and other planets. You can imagine that there is a great deal to be processed in this, so you command the ball that represents the energy around the city of Sydney to shimmer. Project that shimmering energy to the moon-planet Alano and the whole city will momentarily appear in the fifth dimension.

People have asked, "What about people and things that don't want to go to the fifth dimension?" There are many lower vibrational people in Sydney, Mexico, Germany and the U.S. Remember, you are working with the etheric astral energy of the city and the projections. Even people who don't want to be affected could be when the astral energy is projected to Alano. It is purified there, it is held there, and when it is brought back, the energy field will, for the highest good, be assimilated by everyone. Some people will reject this higher energy and will not accept it, but you still are working to create a higher energy field for that city. If the people who are of lower vibration do not want to accept it, then that is their right. It doesn't mean that higher energy is wasted. The higher energy can still be brought to the planet or to the city.

WORK ON THE GALAXY

We want you also to work on the cosmic pulse of Earth. We recommend that first you work with that by collaborating with the crystal energy in the etheric crystals. The next step is designating a time when we would work to create a cosmic egg or reshape the cosmic egg of Earth, become aware of it and then contract it into the center and then expand it again. Contract it, then expand it. We can then project the image of the Earth to the moon-planet Alano. The Earth may be physically bigger than Alano. Remember, you are only projecting the etheric energy field.

There is also a cosmic-egg energy field of the galaxy. This may be more difficult for you to visualize. All of the lightbeings, light forms and thought forms of any being that ever existed in the galaxy, in any part, contribute to the etheric energy field of the galaxy. You may even want to consider how you could measure the birth of your galaxy. How can you do an astrological reading of the galaxy? Now you are using a primitive zodiacal system of Earth. How can you measure or do a reading on our galaxy with that zodiacal system? It is difficult and complicated.

I want you to understand though that there is a birth of a galaxy, and there is a certain influence and energy field of the galaxy based on its birth time. There is a birth of Arcturus, just like there is a birth of the Pleiades and other stars. This means that every galaxy has a certain energy that is different from other galaxies. Every country in the world on Earth is different because it was born in a different time and of a different energy. Each galaxy has a different energy field. Each place in the galaxy has a different energy.

When you align with the Central Sun, then you align with the highest core spiritual purpose with which our galaxy was formed. That is a high alignment. There was an optimal energetic purpose of spiritual energy and light that was enhanced through the expression of your galaxy. That core spiritual energy is going to become accessible to you at the December 21, 2012 alignment with the Central Sun. The optimal place to be on Earth for this alignment is Mexico. It is because of this alignment that we say Mexico has a high energy field and high spiritual light quotient. I say that this is one of the reasons that you have incarnated on Earth now, for this alignment. This would be a central reason to come here so that you could feel what the original core energy and purpose of this galaxy was in creating life. That is the core energy that is coming to Earth. At this time, I bless you all in the light of the Central Sun. I am Juliano. Namasté.

EARTH'S ALIGNMENT WITH THE ARCTURIAN STARGATE

Juliano, the Arcturians and Chief White Eagle

Greetings, I am Juliano. We are the Arcturians. The starseeds in the Groups of Forty are working to complete the alignment with the stargate. The stargate is the point of ascension that allows those who have completed the lessons on Earth incarnation to transit into the fifth dimension. Transiting into the fifth dimension is a major soul occurrence, and it certainly calls for celebration. Many have asked what their soul purposes are. Indeed, one of the main lessons and main purposes of your incarnation now on Earth is to transit through the stargate.

COMPLETING THE LESSONS OF EARTH SCHOOL

In order to travel through the stargate, it is clear that you must complete the Earth lessons or the Earth schooling here. Many of you are very close to completion and being able to graduate from the Earth school. The Earth school is filled with many lessons and the lessons are increasing in variability, and sometimes in difficulty, during this time of polarization and duality. I would like to compare this to going to a university. Some of you would like to study, but you would like to have the broadest curriculum possible. Therefore you might choose a university that offered many different courses and many different subjects and a variety of different languages and different cultural opportunities.

This variety is what Earth represents in terms of soul lessons. Earth represents variability, and Earth school represents the experiencing of duality and polarization. Earth school offers different spiritual and religious experiences and represents, at this point, an opportunity to be on a planet that is going directly in alignment with the Arcturian stargate.

This alignment is going to allow an acceleration of your soul force and the perfect opportunity to ascend and transit through the stargate.

As a planet, Earth inhabits this portion of the galaxy that is referred to as the Sun solar system. Each solar system in the galaxy is named after its sun, because the constellation or the star represents the central force of that solar system. The name of your star is the Sun, and the name of your solar system, therefore, is called the Sun solar system. If there is a solar system in the star Spica, then that solar system is called the Spica solar system. If there is a solar system in the Pleiades, then that solar system is called the Pleiades solar system. Actually, the Pleiades is a constellation, so that one of the stars in that constellation, such as Algol, would be the name of the solar system—that is, the Algol solar system.

The Sun solar system has a unique position in the galaxy. Part of the awakening energy that is necessary for the Sun solar system is now occurring. In other words, the Sun solar system is gaining and is in a position to be activated and to come into this alignment with the Arcturian stargate. The Arcturian stargate and the Sun solar system and the Central Sun form a powerful triangular activation light force field. Earth must do its share of energy transformation and energy awakening, because it represents the most powerful life force in the Sun solar system. Actually, in this section of the galaxy, Earth is one of the major planets that is awakening.

GALACTIC CIVILIZATION

We teach galactic spirituality as one of the sides of the sacred triangle. Galactic spirituality centers on the awareness of the soul's relationship to the galaxy and beyond. Galactic spirituality states that each soul that incarnates on a planet can expand its consciousness. Each soul has awareness and seeks to align with all highly evolved spiritual beings in the galaxy. To say this in a simple way: Galactic spirituality is the force that seeks awareness and knowledge of all higher life forms in the galaxy. Galactic spirituality states as its basic premise that there are many highly evolved spiritual beings in the galaxy and that many of those highly evolved spiritual beings are masters. Humanity's relationship to the Creator is enhanced through the communications, meaning and knowledge gained from the galactic masters.

Why would becoming aware of the galactic civilizations and galactic masters be of assistance in your soul development? Each evolved life form in our galaxy inhabits a specific section of the galaxy that we call sectors. You are in the Sun sector, in which Earth is the main planetary guardian of consciousness. Each galactic civilization has a unique perspective and a unique view on life as well as its own evolutionary process that its members are experiencing. Each galactic civilization has its own ascension, if you will, and each galactic civilization has its own specific lessons that often—not always, but often—are available within those planetary systems. This means that there are certain life lessons and certain soul lessons that are only available on Earth, certain life soul lessons that are only and perhaps best experienced on Arcturus, and certain life lessons that are only experienced and best enhanced through Spica or through the Sirians.

Therefore we seek to say that each galactic civilization offers a viewpoint that is a different and detailed view of the Creator life force energy. Each galactic civilization has a unique view, because it is true that the Creator life force energy only shows a limited part of itself on each planet. This means that you on Earth experience a unique, life force Creator energy. This God force is called Adonai. It is focused on Earth, and it is your perception of the Creator life force energy that is offered from your unique perspective of the Earth. If and when you go to another planetary civilization in the galaxy, then you will be able to see another perspective and another view of the Adonai light and the creative life force energy. This will enhance your soul development.

OPPORTUNITY TO CLIMB THE LADDER OF ASCENSION

Not every planet has duality like Earth. Not every planet has numerous religions like Earth. Not every planet has numerous races. Indeed, not every planet has the many millions of species that now exist on Earth. Some of you have already remembered your experiences on other planets. You have come to Earth at this time and have difficulty accepting and in dealing with the dualities. Part of that is because you remember what it was like on other planetary systems where duality was not present. And yes, while those other planetary systems may not have had duality, I guarantee you that they also had life lessons and soul lessons. So you need to understand that you are here on Earth because you needed this life lesson. You needed this experience here to complete your soul evolution, and now this particular energy on Earth is coming into alignment with the stargate. This will create an opportunity for what we call the manifestation of the "ladder of ascension." The ladder of ascension is an etheric energy force field. It is an etheric elevator or an etheric escalator that allows you to ascend to the Arcturian stargate and be raised up.

I want you to just meditate for a moment on this concept of being taken up to the stargate where you can experience the feeling of completion of your soul lessons on Earth. Meditate on what it means to complete your soul lessons on Earth and what it means to actually reach this point after many incarnations when you are in a position to say, "I am completing my soul lessons on Earth. I will be able to graduate." Affirm the following: "I am now ready to graduate from Earth, because I am completing my soul lessons here. I am ready to graduate from Earth school, and I am completing my soul lessons here."

ALIGNING EARTH WITH THE STARGATE

There is no doubt that this is an accelerated time on Earth. There is no doubt that Earth changes, as they have been called, are accelerating and will continue to accelerate. It is also true that, as you get closer to completing your soul lessons on a planet, your spiritual energy will become stronger and your personal power will become more activated. This activation includes your abilities to be both a personal and a planetary healer. The planetary healing work now focuses strongly on aligning Earth with the stargate. We have worked with the group and through the channel to download eleven etheric crystals into Earth. Each one of these etheric crystals is an etheric duplicate of the crystal in the Arcturian crystal lake, and each of these crystals that have been downloaded has a specific energy field. The energy field of each crystal works on two levels. On the first level, it works on bringing down energy into Earth from the Arcturian corridors and from the Arcturian crystal lake. On the second level, each crystal has a unique dialectic energy field that has activated itself through interaction with the other crystals.

We have unified these eleven existing etheric crystals by activating the diagram known in the Kaballah as the Tree of Life, the *Etz Chaim* in Hebrew. We have added two additional places on the Tree of Life, because this new Arcturian tree of life force field that we are working with interacts directly with the fifth dimension and with the Arcturian stargate. The interaction of these etheric crystals will become more enhanced when the twelfth crystal—the crystal in Serra da Bocaina in Brazil—is downloaded.

THE ROLE OF THE TWELFTH CRYSTAL

The twelfth crystal has a unique power of its own, and that unique power is to enhance the communications and the self-regulation of the biosphere of Earth. The etheric crystal in Serra da Bocaina, Brazil will provide a self-regulating energy force field that previously was not available to people. This will be downloaded in the center of a rainforest area because we see that the rainforests are becoming the key energy force fields for maintaining the biosphere for the whole planet.

This means Brazil and all those areas in South America holding particularly strong rainforests are going to be playing a more major role in the world and in the world's ability to hold the biosphere force field intact. Brazil then, in particular, moves into a prominent role in the spiritual and biospheric light field. That is one of the powers of this twelfth etheric crystal. The second level is that there is a magical power in the number twelve. The twelve levels of activation create a dynamic power grid. This dynamic power grid, which is formed from the twelve etheric crystals, can and will be aligning with the Arcturian stargate.

Remember that the twelfth crystal completes the grid. The completion of the grid will be at the site of that downloading, at Serra da Bocaina. The intentions and energy fields of those workers that will be there with that twelfth crystal will be very strong. The workers' intentions and their thoughts will help bring Earth into the alignment with the stargate. This is the first time in the history of planet Earth that twelve etheric crystals will be downloaded into the planet by the Arcturians and that the alignment with the stargate will be activated.

COMPLETING YOUR PREREQUISITES

What will this mean for Earth? What will it mean for the Groups of Forty project? What will it mean for you personally when Earth becomes aligned with the stargate? On a personal level, each of you will feel a boost in your soul power that can be manifested on Earth. One of the most important experiences for you on Earth now is to bring down as much of your soul energy and power as possible onto Earth. Your soul power and your soul energy can help to manifest many things. The more you are in alignment with them, the more that you can manifest and the more personal power that you can allow to come through. This alignment will help you to accelerate your Earth lessons, and Earth changes will also continue to accelerate. The acceleration of Earth changes occurring now will continue with more intensity.

These Earth-change accelerations also bring the acceleration of lessons. Learning these lessons requires a certain receptivity. Let us go back to the example of the university. When you were looking for a planet to incarnate on, you wanted to come to a planet that would provide you with a diverse curriculum. This diverse curriculum included many different subjects that were only available in certain planets, so you chose the planet that had the widest possible choices that were available. But just because there are many courses available doesn't mean that you are immediately open to each course. Some of the courses require prerequisites. You know about prerequisites: for example, you have to have a background in mathematics in order to take calculus. If you take the calculus course without an earlier background, then you might not be able to understand and integrate all of the mathematical theorems that were present.

So in Earth energy, we can say that there are prerequisites. Some of the prerequisites have to do with learning about dualities and learning about polarizations. Others have to do with learning to detach and also learning to use unity thinking. Unity thinking is one of the major life lessons on this planet; unity consciousness or unity thinking is the ability to see that there is a higher unity above the duality. That is one of the major soul lessons for most everyone who has come to this planet, for what better way to understand unity than to see duality and to understand that the duality is an illusion? The illusion is so strong that the unity is hard to perceive. This is one of the great soul lessons that one can learn here.

With the alignment of the stargate, each of you who is doing ascension work will receive a boost in your energy so that you will be able to see the unity with a greater clarity. Each of you will be able to see the great divine plan and how you are part of that plan. This is on a personal level. Coming into alignment with the stargate enhances your clarity. The prerequisite coursework that you need to have and the knowledge and the wisdom that you can gain from the prerequisite coursework is now going to be downloaded into your consciousness. Let me repeat: the prerequisite knowledge and wisdom will be downloaded into your consciousness when the stargate is in alignment with Earth.

COMPLETION OF THE STAR CORRIDOR

On a planetary level, there is also a great activation coming. The twelfth crystal will enable the etheric energy field of the planet to come into the alignment with the stargate. That means that Earth's higher astral energy is going to fit into the corridor that directly leads to the stargate. It is like completing a new freeway that has a bypass. You are completing a new road, and you are now able to very easily cross through a city by going through this road that is now completed. The alignment with Earth's etheric energy field is now going to be opened up. This is a completion of a pathway, a roadway—a star corridor of light to the stargate.

Some have asked, "Does that mean that the stargate and the star corridor are now only going to be connected from Brazil?" The answer is that each etheric crystal is holographically tied into the others. Whatever the one etheric crystal is able to experience, all of the etheric crystals will be able to equally experience. This is a dialectic energy field. Dialectic, in our terminology, means that there is a holographic energy connection in which what one part experiences, the other part also experiences and that each portion of the grid is able to enhance and elevate other portions. When the grid energy field is completed, then the highest energy can be experienced at any entry point into that etheric grid. In the tree of life energy field, there are twelve etheric crystal energy grids connected dialectically.

It would be helpful for each of you to be at the nearest etheric crystal that you can locate. We realize that everyone cannot come to Brazil for the downloading of the twelfth etheric crystal. We also realize that you may be able to be at one of the other etheric crystals, such as Lago Puelo, Bodensee, Mount Fuji or Mount Shasta. Your being at those areas when the downloading of the crystal occurs will enable you to holographically experience the same openings to alignment with the stargate. This will also help the planet, because it is a great honor and it is a great spiritual achievement for Gaia, the spirit of the Earth, to have its starseeds bring its energy field into alignment with the stargate.

THE USE OF SUBCRYSTALS

Perhaps you view the stargate as a place where you go to. This is correct, but perhaps you didn't know that energy from the stargate also comes down to the Earth. Not every planet in your galaxy ascends. Not every planet in the galaxy achieves the higher etheric energy field that would allow twelve etheric crystals to be downloaded and would also allow the alignment to occur with the stargate. Therefore, there is a reciprocal downloading of etheric energy from the stargate back into Earth. This etheric downloading becomes activated at the downloading and completion of the twelfth etheric crystal.

Many of you have been working on subcrystals. Subcrystals are derivations and etheric reproductions of the downloaded crystal. There is a crystal at Montserrat where the Spanish starseeds created subcrystals in different areas on their peninsula. These subcrystals are serving wonderful functions, because they are able to serve as spiritual regulators and spiritual transformers. We will use the example of the electrical current to explain this concept. Imagine that there is a 5,000-volt energy current coming from a power plant, and then it has to be transformed into a lower voltage so that the people can activate and use that voltage. In the same way, the subcrystals are taking higher energy from main etheric crystals and bringing it to other areas.

These subcrystals will now also receive a higher uplifting when the twelfth crystal is downloaded. I emphasize again that the number twelve and the activation of the number twelve creates a powerful energy force that transcends each individual one. It is the power of twelve that holographically creates a new energy field of light in alliance with the Arcturian. I now turn things over to Chief White Eagle. I am Juliano.

Greetings, all my brothers and sisters, all my relations. [Tones.] *Hey yah hey! Hey yah hoh yay hey!* All my words are sacred. I am Chief White Eagle. Wow! What a time to be on Earth. What a time to experience the energy of this planet. Earth is alive. Earth is responding to the blocks and looking for ways of releasing the energy. Earth is trying to find a new balance. We are always in touch with Earth. We communicate with Earth on all levels, at all times possible. The spirits of our grandmothers and our grandfathers are deep in the mountains, oceans and canyons.

Many different possibilities of energy shifts are now possible on the planet. These energy shifts are bubbling. It is like Earth wants to find a balance that will work to hold the biosphere. You need to understand that Earth, as a spirit, wants to keep the biosphere. Earth, my friends, is a spiritual force. She is a spiritual planet. She is a planet of great honor. Earth is a planet of great respect. She is known as the Blue Jewel. Earth wants to keep the life force energy field on her, but it is required that Earth have assistance, because this new balance is in uncharted territories for her and is not readily attainable for her spirit. Therefore, Earth needs guidance. A new spiritual technology for Earth called biorelativity has come now. This spiritual technology can be developed to maintain the biosphere.

Moderating through Biorelativity

I know that there have been increases in earthquakes and storms. I know that some are predicting that this is just the beginning and that there will be a series of more earthquakes and storms to come. Look at the situation from this perspective: one, Earth has to release this energy; two, it is inevitable that this energy has to be released; three, how could the energy be lessened? How could the energy be pacified so that it is released with the least possible harm to the biosphere? How can that energy be released for the least possible harm to human inhabitants and also the least harm to the animal and plant worlds that are in the path of energy release?

I, Chief White Eagle, say to Mother Earth and Father Sky: We are gathered here to ask for a path of peace and a path of release that does minimal harm to any living being. We ask that these storms and these quakes be released at a moderate level so that there will be the least destruction. I ask that each one who is reading and listening to my words send the words to Mother Earth through our thoughts: "Moderate and in balance; moderate and in balance."

This may mean that there could be storms, but they won't be as strong. You might have to have three storms that would be moderate, but not damaging, to equal the combined strength of one storm. In this way, the energy of that storm would be released but would be released moderately. This may mean that instead of having one earthquake at a scale of 9—which is very possible in the near future somewhere on this planet—then you might have three earthquakes that measure at the scale of 5, or four earthquakes that are above 6 on the Richter scale. This is how we see biorelativity working more effectively—the necessary energy releases can be moderated. We know that Earth is coming to a much more active period, and these biorelativity exercises can help Earth to moderate.

Alliance with Your Star Family

We see the twelve etheric crystals and the activation of these crystals as a time when Earth is aligning with the star families. When we say the words "all our relations," we are talking about all our relations not only on

Earth but with the star family. I ask that each of you become aware that you are gaining two things with this twelfth crystal. One, you are gaining alignment with the stargate. Juliano has beautifully explained how that will affect you and the planet.

The second thing you are gaining is an alliance with your star family. This includes a powerful alignment with the Arcturians and the Pleiadians. This includes the many other starbeings that are throughout the galaxy. Now each of you who are in tune with this energy will gain the possibility of receiving more information directly from other planetary systems of higher light. Each of you will gain knowledge and information about how these planetary systems have come to offer solutions to some of the problems facing Earth.

What a great gift, to be able to connect with your star family members throughout the galaxy and to bring through their knowledge and their wisdom back into the third dimension and the Earth. I am Chief White Eagle, including my star family relations. *Ho!*

AS ABOVE, SO BELOW

Juliano, the Arcturians and Chief White Eagle

reetings, I am Juliano. We are the Arcturians. We will explain the nature of reality in reference to the well-known mystical statement, "As above, so below." That statement is a profound one and has many different interpretations. We feel it is important to understand the nature of reality even in the face of many of the difficulties that you might be experiencing on different levels. By different levels we mean the social, economic, political and, of course, the personal, planetary, global and galactic levels. All of these levels interact. "As above, so below" on the surface implies that what is going on in the higher realms reflects what is going on in the lower realms. This is one interpretation. One might conclude from that interpretation that the higher realms must be very confused because the lower realms, like the third dimension where you live, appear very confused, chaotic and polarized. Therefore the "above" must be that way, and that is why the "below" is so polarized.

YOUR INFLUENCE ON THE ABOVE

That interpretation merely scratches the surface. From the perspective of the Arcturians, we would clarify this in a different way. We would say the "above" in that statement is really referring to the astral plane. Our model is really referring to the lower astral plane in particular. Therefore the subconscious and the unconscious energies of Earth create an actual energetic belt around the planet. This energetic belt is, in fact, the "above." This astral energetic belt is actually in another dimension, but it has a direct influence on the third dimension. This would mean that as the lower fourth-dimensional level is above, so below will be manifested. This means that what you see and what you experience on a planetary basis is actually reflecting the input of the light or the lack of light in the astral planes.

To change the below, the third dimension, you would have to find ways to access the lower fourth or the lower astral realm so that energy is shifted. If that energy shifts, then the energy on the third dimension, where you live, shifts. You can understand this concept by looking at the nature of the subconscious. The nature of the subconscious states that what is inputted into it can eventually manifest into the third dimension. Your thoughts, your ideas, your affirmations are all inputted into the subconscious. You do not have a direct access to the subconscious except through certain methodologies. You can use the mental screen and make affirmations to consciously influence the subconscious.

The subconscious has been influenced already for you when you were a child. It has already been formulated through the multitude of information and downloading that was placed in front of you at a time when you did not have discrimination. This was a time when you did not have discernment. It was a time when whatever was fed to you, you most likely had to absorb—unless you were bright enough or you were in touch with your starseed heritage, and thus you are able to remember the true nature of reality. When you connect with your starseed heritage, then you are able to remember that there is a higher order that far exceeds what is the general or apparent downloading of information.

REFINE YOUR CONSCIOUSNESS WITH OMEGA LIGHT

We have developed methods to override the earlier downloading. That means that there are ways to use spiritual energies and spiritual technology to supersede, to transcend and to override earlier lower downloading of affirmations, thoughts, ideas or beliefs about the nature of reality and about the nature of who you are. There is a new spiritual technology that will allow you to override reality that is not based on the higher truth.

We have discovered the use of the omega light. The omega light is a specialized energetic light that comes from the highest sources that, when used in our methodologies, can directly input the subconscious in a way that far exceeds normal thought and normal concentration. Using this way will help to resolve the transformation of false beliefs. It will help you to transform false beliefs about yourself and about the nature of the planet, and it can also be used to transform the lower astral plane. This light can purify the lower fourth dimensional realm in the right way so that a new clarity, a new spiritual paradigm, can emerge on Earth.

Let the omega light fill your energy and your cosmic aura so that you can move into the highest refined consciousness. Remember that the third dimension, for all its beauty, is not a refined energy the way the fifth dimension is. Remember that the level of the third dimension can be viewed as somewhat crude in comparison to the fifth level. The third level is very polarized, filled with duality. At the time that you are now living, there is increased polarization, increased roughness and increased crudeness. The omega light helps you to perceive the true refinement of nature. This means that the fifth dimension, the higher dimension where we, the Arcturians, are from is a more refined level. That level of energy, that level of experience, can flow into the third dimension. In this interpretation, when you say "as above, so below," and you and I look at the higher realm, we look at the fifth dimension instead of the fourth dimension. We say yes, the fifth dimension is a very refined level. The fifth dimension is in a beautiful energetic state, and the third dimension doesn't match that level of refinement.

From the new perspective, we can say that "as above, so below" must be formulated with the fifth dimension in mind; the below must be created and refined. Then the energy of the lower third dimension will be challenged to be transformed so that it can be as the above. "As above" in this paradigm is the fifth-dimensional "aboveness." You will understand that the third dimension has a continual interaction with every level in the universe. From this perspective, we can say that the fourth dimension does continually interact with the third dimension. We can also say that the fifth dimension continually interacts with the third dimension. The fifth dimension even interacts with the fourth dimension.

Because these levels of interaction are not apparent, one can easily overlook them. It may not be apparent that the subconscious affects the conscious. It may not be apparent that the lower fourth-dimensional energy affects the third dimension. It may not be apparent that the fifth dimension affects the third dimension. In fact it does. On every side we say that corridors are being created so that the fifth-dimensional light and energy can be brought down.

PROTECT YOURSELF AGAINST LOWER ENERGIES

You can be personal corridors for the omega light. Your thoughts can help to transform the nature of the third-dimensional reality. Your understanding of how the fifth dimension connects to the third dimension will allow you to receive the omega light for your personal healing and repair. I know that each of you on the physical level may be struggling with health issues or financial issues. You may be struggling with getting along in your own way in this difficult time. Many of the problems that are manifesting now are direct results of the lower astral realm. These are inputs of lower animalistic energy, of ego energy—an energy of domination and control powerfully inputted into the lower astral realm. That energy often enters unfiltered into the minds of the world's leaders. Many people are not even trying to grasp the nature of the universe, how the universe and the spiritual laws of the universe work and how the influence of other realms affects the primary realm on which you exist.

For example, it is well known that in the lower astral realm there are unattached spirits. There are wandering, confused and discarnate spirits. Those unattached spirits are stuck in the lower fourth-dimensional realm. They don't know how to find the way out. They don't have people instructing them. In fact, most people of a higher light wish to avoid going into this lower dimensional realm. This would be like going into a dark cellar. Even if there is a flashlight, you still don't know what you are going to run into. So these discarnate spirits instead look down on the third dimension to find the light. The only energy that they see is what is below. They look for ways to attach to those in the third dimension in the same way as a parasite would attach to a host and find the life force in that host. That attachment allows the parasite to exist without fear.

We see many examples on Earth now of these lower astral discarnate spirits attaching and even controlling the actions of people on the third dimension, especially people who are using drugs or alcohol in great quantities. They also attach to people who are mentally confused and don't have a properly shaped aura. These people become susceptible to parasitic attachments from these discarnate spirits. This is why we have repeatedly asked you to work on solidifying and reformulating your aura into the shape of the cosmic egg. When the aura is in the shape of the cosmic egg, then these parasitic discarnate spirits bounce off. They can't penetrate. Even now, recalibrate your aura into the shape of the cosmic egg and I, Juliano, am going to send omega light to coat your cosmic egg with a new light.

Feel the omega light reformulating your aura into the shape of the cosmic egg. As it comes into that shape, it will build a great energy boost into each of you. You feel a new vibratory thrust in your spirit and your physical body as you connect with this fifth-dimensional light. Meditate for a few minutes as you work on receiving this light, and then I will return, explaining more about the other levels.

PARTICIPATE IN HIGHER DOWNLOADING

The nature of the universe, the nature of the spiritual world and how the spiritual world interacts with the physical world are all intertwined with certain laws. What is downloaded from other realms affects the physical reality. The lower astral plane can bring down energy and that lower energy can manifest. In the middle and upper astral realms, there are some wonderful energies and there is some beautiful light. There are guides and teachers in the middle and higher astral realms. Also, when you go into the fifth-dimensional realm, there is even higher light and even higher vibration. That higher energy is what we, the Arcturians, are working with. We know that you want to work with fifth-dimensional energy. We can download greater energy and light, and that energy and light can come into your subconscious. Then that energy and light can manifest into your reality the same way that lower astral light and lower astral energy manifest in a parasitic host. You increase your vibration when you work with the Arcturians and the fifth-dimensional masters. It is a higher downloading.

In order to download, you must have a connection, and you must make a space in your energy field for this new light and new energy. Expand your cosmic egg. This can be done in a way where the whole aura and the lining around the cosmic aura are pushed out two or three more inches. Maybe your aura is six inches or seven inches away from your body. Now make it ten inches. Expand! Now, as you expand, realize that you have created a space. That space is now going to be filled with light that I am going to send down to each of you, then we will give you instructions on how to use that new light.

I, Juliano, now raise the crystal in the crystal lake. As that crystal is raised, there is a tremendous amount of new omega lightbeing transmitted. I, Juliano, transmit and transform and download this new light coming from the etheric crystal into each of your auras so that the space that you have made in your aura is now filled with the omega light from the etheric crystal. Receive this downloading of light into your cosmic egg and you will experience it as an uplift. Let that light stay around the expanded portion of the aura. Let the whole part of that energy field that was empty fill with this beautiful light. Now, on my command, let that light from this newer etheric light gently interact with all of the energies of your own aura.

These are energies that reflect your current state of consciousness and your current physical health. These are energies that can be reflected in your emotional body, and all of them will be encompassed in your actions now and in the future. You are going to be affected by this omega light that is going to mingle with your energy. It will mingle with you slowly through a process that we call "spiritual osmosis." This enables you to receive this light better. Now, on my command, mingle and let the omega light enter into all of those aspects of your energy field now.

If you have a particular problem, say in your physical health, then let this light now interact with your physical body. Let this light interact with your belief system about this physical problem. This light is a higher vibration. This light is a healing light. This omega light is a special vibrational energy that I have brought into you so that you can use it now. Let this light interact, and it will bring a beautiful healing to you. As this light fills up the darkness, the other concerns of a lower vibration are going to be pushed out of your aura through your feet. These lower energies are all unnecessary because now the higher light is coming in. All the thoughts of concern and worry and tenseness would be discharged through the feet because this new light is coming to your body. This new light is a higher vibration. It is the omega light.

Affirm to Cleanse Your Subconscious

I want you to please visualize the screen in the front of your forehead. This is the screen through which you can download certain affirmations. I would like you to put the first affirmation in today: "I receive omega light continually." Place this affirmation on the screen. See those words emblazoned in bright letters on the mental screen. This is going to be dropped into your subconscious on the command of three: one, two, three, now! This means that you can enter updated affirmations into your subconscious because you are continually receiving the omega light. You can continually use that omega light on your mental screen. Realize that any message that you put in now is going to manifest for the highest good of you, and it is going to use this great energy that we are involved in.

Let us go into a second level with a second affirmation: "I have a continual connection to downloading fifth-dimensional light. I have a continual connection that allows me to download fifth-dimensional light. As light and reality of the fifth dimension is above, so here below, I will be living." This is one of the most important concepts in your ascension work. Know that you are so connected continually with the fifth dimension that you can download that energy into your third-dimensional consciousness and into your third-dimensional subconscious so that you can update the subconscious. "I send a purifying light now to my subconscious." This is another important message. It is not exactly like a rebooting of the computer, but it is a clearing. It is like placing a coat of beautiful, calming vibratory light that will be a great sensitivity-making energy and will help your subconscious to attract and hold higher thoughts from the omega light. Omega light is purifying. "I receive this purifying light now in my subconscious." Emblazon these words on the mental screen.

This light makes your subconscious very receptive to higher vibrations. Remember that these higher thoughts and this higher energy can overcome years of imbalance because the imbalanced energies were downloaded on a lower thought vibration. A higher thought vibration such as we are now using can supersede the lower thoughts. "I allow the higher vibrational thoughts to supersede the lower vibrational thoughts in my subconscious now." What a beautiful affirmation.

IMAGES OF THE FIFTH DIMENSION

We have talked in other lectures about raising the spiritual light quotient, and we have talked in this lecture about purifying your subconscious. The question you might ask is, "How do we purify the subconscious of the planet?" This becomes a major undertaking. One of the great gifts given to humankind is art. Art presents beautiful imagery that can affect the subconscious. For example, all of the art depicting the time of Jesus has created subconscious images around the world of who Jesus was, how his death affected the planet and what the meaning of his existence was. These images are much more powerful than even the words that are spoken about him. Whether you are Christian or not, those images have been placed in your subconscious.

What new images can we use to represent the fifth dimension? We have designated certain areas around the planet that are receptive to hosting the etheric crystals that were etheric duplicates. Each one of these areas has the ability to create a beautiful shimmering balance. Each one of these areas has a beautiful spiritual imagery, whether it is a lake, a mountain, a sea or a valley. We want those images to be brought forth in a heightened way throughout the planet. They can be brought through art, photography or video.

The energetic images of these crystal areas have a powerful ability to transform the subconscious of the Earth. Let us use, for example, the image of Mount Shasta. Here we have a beautiful mountain that is emitting golden balls of harmonic light. When you, as starseeds, see that image of the mountain in your mind, you are uplifted. You can even transport yourself there etherically. When you visualize the beautiful energy of Spain's Montserrat, which has a great holy energy with great angelic presences, then that energy can be focused in an image and then that image can be sent into the subconscious of the Earth.

Crop circles are images that come from other realms or other dimensions. There are multiple purposes for those images. One purpose is to create a spiritual image field and have that image field downloaded into the Earth. There are other images on the planet, such as the pyramids, that have transformational qualities. The image of the Arcturian temple is a great image that can be transformational.

At this time I would like Chief White Eagle to speak with you about the images of the circle and the tepee, because these are also transformational images that can work on the subconscious of the planet. Please remember these affirmations, and remember that I am filling you continually with omega light for the next twenty-four hours. You can use this light in the physical, mental, spiritual or emotional bodies. I am Juliano. Good day.

Greetings, I am Chief White Eagle. [Tones.] *Hey Ya Ho Ya Hey.* We are all brothers and sisters. All my words are sacred. I ask you to visualize a great circle, a circle in which all of us are sitting. This is a healing circle. I ask you to visualize this healing circle expanding to include all the starseeds on the planet. We are sitting above the North Pole. I ask you to expand the circle to all those who want to connect the Earth to the fifth dimension. I ask you to expand it to include 50,000, then 100,000 people. It is a great image as the light from the omega center is coming in and the circle is receiving this light on the planet. This light is being downloaded into the subconscious of Mother Earth.

O Mother Earth, we love you and we ask you to receive this great healing light. We will all work as brothers and sisters to sit in this great circle and allow this light to come in not only to you, the spirit of Mother Earth, but also to the subconscious of humankind. We understand that a great spiritual brotherhood and sisterhood can affect and shift the subconscious of humanity. We work on the planetary level and on the level of the subconscious of people. It is so wonderful to sit in the circle, Mother Earth, with all these great lightbeings, all these great starseeds. We can receive the frequency of light known as the Central Sun light, and we can begin to shimmer ourselves as we are receiving this light.

As we shimmer and go in and out of different levels of consciousness and go up to the fifth realm, we can bring down higher light. Together we shimmer into the fifth-dimensional moon-planet known as Alano, where there is so much beautiful healing light. We shimmer ourselves to this planet. Then we shimmer back into Earth, into the great circle, and we download this beautiful light into the planet and into people's subconscious. Mother Earth, this light is for all men and all women, no matter what their political persuasion, no matter what their level of discord. All are in awe of the universe and of the higher beings that travel through the universe. They will surrender and receive the higher light.

KEEP THE IMAGES ALIVE

Affirm: "We will work together as brothers and sisters. We will continually picture and visualize this higher light coming down, being received by the wonderful power spots around the planet. We have realized that we shall continually sit in circles until the Earth is brought back into proper alignment. We will promise to sit in circles wherever we go. We will sit in our tepees and we will create this great feeling of brotherhood and sisterhood so that imagery of the family of Mother Earth will be embedded into the subconscious of the Adam species. This circle interacts on all levels in the higher dimensions and downloads to the third dimension of the circle of light.

"We see the circle in everything, Mother Earth. We see the circle in the solar systems, in the galaxies, in the universe. Everything is moving in a certain rhythm. We know that the teaching and the visualization of that movement will put us in harmony so that our energetic powers as healers of the planet can be enhanced. This is our mission. We accept our roles as planetary healers, Mother Earth, with gratitude and also with great honor." *Ho!*

Let the great images of the beauty of this planet stay in your minds. You will be asked to transmit these images. There are certain ways of updating the subconscious of humans. Some of these ways have to do with your connection to these crystals. Others have to do with chanting, others with group meditations. Other ways have to do with using meditations at the crop circles. We understand that these crop circles are appearing and then they go away. You should realize that those circles are conduits in which you can reach people's subconscious and the subconscious of Earth. Certain meditations and certain planetary healing work that you can do at the site of these crop circles will have a powerful cleansing effect. The images, even if they disappear, can still be used.

We of the Native people align ourselves with the Pleiades. We align ourselves with the Seven Sisters and the Pleiadian brotherhood and sisterhood. Visualize now the Pleiades and their energy interacting with you and with planet Earth in the highest light. The Pleiadians are brothers and sisters of the Native people. They are part of the star family—part of your star family. I call on the Pleiadians' light to be downloaded now into the subconscious of Earth and into the subconscious of humanity. In particular, I call on the beautiful star Alcyone, which is a great sister star of your Sun. It is sending beautiful rays of healing light to your planet. Let the light of Alcyone be with you. The rays of Alcyone are filling all of the hearts and minds of the starseeds as the light of the Pleiades sends healing and activation light to make the new spiritual energy more effective and powerful on Earth. I am Chief White Eagle. *Ho!*

RAISE THE SPIRITUAL LIGHT QUOTIENT

Juliano, the Arcturians, Archangel Metatron and Helio-ah

Greetings, I am Juliano. We are the Arcturians. We wish to continue on the subject of the spiritual light quotient. We have talked about the relationship between the intelligence quotient and the spiritual IQ. We related how the spiritual IQ is related to one's spirituality and one's ability to understand the relationship between the physical world and the spiritual world. People of extremely high spiritual light quotient are able to effectively use their spiritual energy to shape the physical reality for the highest good.

In today's session, we want to explore the concept of the spiritual light quotient of a planet. Believe it or not, a planet has a spiritual light quotient. The planet also has the ability, through its inhabitants, to raise its spiritual light quotient. Earth, therefore, has experienced an honor and a great advancement as a planet to be able to have humankind on her surface— humankind, who has participants and members in the species who are of a higher spiritual light quotient. There are many ways and there are many things that you can do to raise the spiritual light quotient of a planet. I will go through some of these. It is important that you understand that you as the starseeds are working to raise the spiritual light quotient of planet Earth. Part of this relates to the ascension of the planet. Earth must be raised to a certain light quotient in order to ascend.

PYRAMIDS AND CROP CIRCLES

Let me explain some of the activities that are congruent with raising the spiritual light quotient of a planet. The first point relates to spiritual objects, such as pyramids. It has been known by some of the ancient civilizations that pyramids are extremely powerful tools for raising the spiritual light frequency of a planet. When these pyramids are built in alignment with certain stars and certain astronomical positions, this then enhances the spiritual light quotient of a planet. We know that pyramids have been built in many different areas of the planet.

Many people think that the crop circles are being sent from other dimensions in order to communicate with humanity. To a small degree this is true. I, Juliano, want you to consider this. These crop circles are, for the most part, manifesting from other dimensional beings in order to communicate and raise the spiritual light quotient of Earth, thereby preparing Earth for the ascension.

It doesn't really mean that you have to understand what these crop circles mean. Rather what is important is that you promote and allow the crop circles to be promulgated through the planet and that these images be allowed to remain in the areas in which they manifest. Believe me, Earth responds to the crop circles. Also, the crop circles are being presented in order to prepare humankind for the biorelativity process of communicating to Earth through sacred geometry. Sacred geometry is one of the languages of the planet. We have explored talking to Earth and telepathically communicating with parts of Earth's energy. For example, you can ask Earth to moderate storms and weather patterns. The crop circles are another way of engaging in biorelativity with Earth.

The patterns of the crop circles and the geometric patterns are, therefore, providing communication to the spirit of Earth. Crop circles are also providing information to you, the starseeds, who want to work with biorelativity. These images and these geometric patterns are in a way instructional tools in which you can be more effective healers and can more effectively raise the spiritual light quotient of Earth. One method to raise the quotient is, of course, to photograph the crop circles and then promulgate the images around the planet. Then have the starseeds visualize the images in their minds and then telepathically communicate those images to the etheric crystals. The etheric crystals will download those images into the spirit of Earth.

THE ENERGY OF CRYSTALS

Another method for raising the spiritual light quotient of the planet: etheric crystals and crystals in general. First, I will speak of crystals in general. The spiritual light quotient of a planet is affected by the types and numbers of crystals. Many of you know about the ancient crystals called the skull crystals. Many of you have heard stories about special crystals that have been kept in caves for many years that are now being brought into consciousness. Those planets that we have visited, which have higher spiritual knowledge and higher spiritual energy, always have such crystals in their planet. The planets that do evolve have been able to accelerate and use the crystals for certain healing purposes.

Sometimes it is effective to bring these crystals into caves because when they are in caves, they can hold energy for many thousands of years. Some crystals have actually been around during the various extraterrestrial visits by the higher beings like the Arcturians or the Pleiadians or the Andromedans. These crystals contain energies from them. Some of the crystals are also gathering energy from the pyramids and from certain star systems. Now there are new crystals coming to awareness that are linked to the Central Sun. These crystals also can be placed in strategic places around the planet in order to enhance and accelerate their abilities.

ETHERIC CRYSTALS AND THE CENTRAL SUN

Etheric crystals are also in the same family as the physical crystals. The etheric crystals are part of the mission of the Arcturian starseeds working with us. We understand that certain fifth-dimensional energy needs to be downloaded into a planet in order to raise that planet's spiritual light quotient. Thus our intent is to raise the spiritual light quotient of the planet. We understand that certain frequencies of higher spiritual light are difficult to hold onto in the third dimension. Earth in many ways does not have the spiritual vessel to hold certain very high frequencies.

When we speak of a planet and the spiritual frequencies, we are really going into a very refined level. To give you an example: less than 2 to 3 percent of the planets in your galaxy have life, and remember, that is still a great deal numerically. If we are talking about 2.5 billion star systems in the galaxy, by some estimates, 2 percent would still be a high number of planets. Of those planets in the 2 percent category, there is still an even smaller percentage of planets that have the spiritual frequency to hold life forms of a higher consciousness, like humanity. In the vastness of the universe, the spiritual light frequency for higher consciousness and for life forms comes from the Central Sun. One aspect of the Central Sun, therefore, focuses on those planets and those moons that are close to it. These planets and these moons are able to transmit spiritual light frequencies. Planets that are evolved and are closer to the Central Sun have special ways of detecting spiritual energy throughout the galaxy. Their higher beings can find where the light and life forms are by telepathically communicating with spiritual energy transmissions from other planets. The etheric crystals are gathering and holding certain frequencies that are of a high spiritual nature that can work to raise the light quotient of Earth. We are working with a number of etheric crystals. Currently, we are working with the number ten. Another step toward raising the spiritual light frequency of Earth is through the etheric crystals' interactive pattern with the other crystals.

The tree of life resembles a geometric pattern. One could look at it as three triangles, for example—a higher, middle and lower triangle. One can look at it as three pillars—a left, a middle and a right. There are numerous ways of separating this and dividing them geometrically. This interactive energy field of the ten etheric crystals can be placed on the map of the tree of life. This placement can be accelerated and enhanced through the starseeds. People can work and telepathically connect with this energy and bring the energy of the crystals into a field of intense energetic interaction. This energetic interaction of ten etheric crystals can tremendously raise the spiritual light quotient of the planet.

YOUR MISSION

Meditate on the fact that the planet has a spiritual light quotient, that the starseeds can accelerate and raise the light quotient of a planet and that you, as starseeds, have the mission of helping to raise the light quotient of a planet so that the planet can ascend. This is one aspect of your mission. Work toward raising the light quotient of your planet.

Your consciousness and your intent can assist in raising the light quotient of a planet. Many of you wish to leave the Earth and go to a higher planetary system where there is a greater and higher spiritual light quotient. I know that after the ascension, many of you will go to planets that have this higher spiritual light quotient. At the same time, please understand that one of your missions is the raising of the light quotient on this planet first. This is a great mission, a great activity worthy of your incarnating on the Earth at this time.

Now we turn to the concept of the higher spiritual beings on a planet and how the spiritual beings, namely you and others, contribute to the raising of the spiritual light quotient. For this I will turn to a brief discussion by Archangel Metatron, and then I will return. This is Juliano.

Shalom. Greetings, I am Archangel Metatron. [Tones.] *Kadosh, Kadosh, Kadosh, Adonai Tsevaoth.* Holy, holy, holy is the lord of hosts [Isaiah 6:3, KJV]. I shall be that I shall be. [Tones.] *Ehiyeh Asher Ehiyeh. Jehova. Yod, Hey, Vav, Hey*—the sacred name of God. It is in the belief of the ancient rabbis, through the knowledge that came to them from the archangels, that a core number of people were necessary to hold the spiritual energy of Earth. It is not the 144,000 figure that you have heard. It is not even close to that.

In the ancient times, it was necessary to have a certain number of the Tzaddikim, the Hassidim or the righteous ones. These righteous people were carrying a certain energy for their community. It was certain righteous energy in the congregation. They were carrying an energy of great spiritual knowledge. They were able to hold the spiritual foundational fabric of the planet. It is true that there is a spiritual fabric of a planet. It is a very thin and very real spiritual etheric fabric that is woven throughout this planet. This spiritual fabric holds the life and Earth in its balance so that biospheric energy can be maintained.

There was an interesting story in the Old Testament about Sodom and Gomorrah and how God wanted to destroy the city. This is a parable, but God did want to destroy the city. And then, we believe, one Tzadik said, "If we can find ten righteous people, would you not destroy the city?" In this story, God agreed. This again comes back to the point of a core number of spiritual people. These spiritual people are not people that are famous or well known because they are working silently. There are terms for them that have come through the Hebrew texts. One is the *Kohen Gadol,* which means the Great Priest. I know that these concepts have become corrupted throughout the ages, but this was the original concept. There was one area, one group that was able to hold the spiritual fabric. There was also in this group the knowledge of how to pronounce the most sacred name of God. By pronouncing the sacred name of God, the whole spiritual fabric of the planet was kept in a balance.

A WORLD HELD IN BALANCE

You know how fragile the whole planetary balance is. You know that one stray asteroid hit in the right place can throw the planet and all the life forms into a total catastrophe. You know that it only needs a certain shift in a certain ocean current to unbalance things. You know that a volcanic eruption can throw enough soot and ash in the air that it would bring planetary winter. Add to this any other nuclear reactions or war. You know that there is a fragileness, yet the sacred holy Tzaddikim were able to hold the spiritual fabric.

Because of the enormity of the shifts in the planet and because of the huge increase of the population on the planet, the number of 10 people needed to be increased. These 10 can be increased through the sacred number of 40 and the groups of 40 to the number of 1,600. Therefore one of the reasons the Arcturians wanted to have 40 groups of 40—1,600 people—was because of this. These numbers, 40 and 1,600, are also considered sacred in relation to the geometry and the population of Earth as well as the magnitude of the energy that needs to be held in order to hold the spiritual fabric of Earth together.

I know that there have been problems in coordinating these groups, holding the numbers together, counting and so on. I want to speak to the magic of the number 40 and the magic of 1,600—40 x 40—because that now becomes the new sacred number of Hassidic people to hold the spiritual fabric of Earth together. You might say, "Archangel Metatron, I am not a holy person. I am not a Hassid or a Tzadik." Incidentally, that word is from the name Melchizedek. It means "the king of righteousness." Melech represents "king" and Tzadik represents "holy one": Melech Tzadik.

CONNECT TO 1,600

You might say, "I am not that holy." It is not a matter of trying to attain a certain level of holiness from the standpoint of the ego. If you approach it from the ego, then you would immediately rule yourself out because you would have to be able to do certain metaphysical tasks. You might be able to do certain healings. You might have a certain test that you would have to pass. These are ego things. What I want to explain to you is this: Direct your intention with your spiritual connection toward your desire and your work. Most importantly, direct your interactive connection with the 10 etheric crystals and the 40 groups of 40 uniting with the magic number of 1,600. Your participation then can override these other doubts and bring you into coherent force of sacred light that will hold the spiritual fabric of Earth together to ensure its survival and its ascension.

Feel your holiness. Feel your light. Feel the light of all of the 1,600 Arcturian Groups of Forty members now. Go into meditation now and feel the energy and the power of the 1,600—the 40 groups of 40.

Being part of 40 and connecting with 40 and connecting with 1,600 then raises your spiritual light quotient and raises your ability to hold sacred light and to preserve the spiritual fabric. You can also accelerate and move the energetic field of the Earth even to a higher vibration. This is a great mission. This is a great service to the planet. Many of you personally have incarnated at this time to fulfill that path. Please acknowledge your "Tzaddikness," your holiness, your righteousness. This will even amplify your abilities as planetary healers. I am Archangel Metatron.

I am Helio-ah. Blessings to everyone who can hear and read my words. This is a time of great evolution and a great consciousness, as you are all coming into your special awareness and special understanding of your mission, and the importance of this. At times it appears that you have no effect. You might think, "Well, I am only one person out of seven billion," or "I am only one person out of billions or millions of people. How can I have an effect?" Spiritual light and spiritual energy override lower densities and lower vibrations, especially when you are dealing with the holding together of the spiritual fabric.

THE WORK OF OTHER SPECIES

I know many of you have been very dedicated to the whales and dolphins, and I know many of you have been following the lead of Shala [a Group of Forty member in Canada] in working with the energy of the whales and the dolphins and other species in the oceans. I want to compliment you all, and I want to compliment Shala and her desire to stick to this task. It is valuable beyond description because the whales and, in particular, the dolphins, contribute major energy to holding the spiritual fabric and the spiritual light quotient of the biosphere. This is a dangerous time in the oceans. It is a dangerous time in the biosphere. The dolphins need assistance. They are having difficulty carrying the spiritual fabric, the spiritual light quotient, that they are designated to contribute. In other words, there are many species that have various roles in contributing to the spiritual light quotient of a planet. You might not look at butterflies as being necessary, but actually they are carrying an important part. You all have become aware of the bees and their problem and how they contribute to the spiritual light quotient. Incidentally, as we had predicted earlier, there is a pesticide of a known origin that is being covered up that is contributing to the bee colony collapse. Unfortunately, they are having a hard time eradicating this pesticide.

The work with the dolphins is a spiritual endeavor. It is an endeavor that is beyond just their beauty. We all know how beautifully they move. We know how energetic they are. We also know that they have a connection to a deep ancient energy that is much older than man's presence on the planet. They are genetically connected to this ancient time and ancient energy. They were participants of the creation and the raising of the spiritual light quotient of this planet. The spiritual light quotient of the planet had to be raised in order to bring humans to the planet. Then it had to be raised again to bring higher beings and higher humans. Now we are in a position where the energy and the darker forces—the denser forces of the planet—are trying to lower the spiritual light quotient. Just at the time when you, the starseeds, are here to raise the spiritual light quotient, there are people who actually want to lower the it. Some of them are doing this with lack of consciousness and lack of awareness.

For example, there were groups of people who wanted to kill the dolphins and wanted to kill the whales. They had good justification in their minds about doing that. They had no understanding of the spiritual fabric of the planet. They had no understanding of the spiritual light quotient that these dolphins and whales contribute and that it is necessary. How could they understand unless they had a spiritual light quotient that is higher? Their contribution to the decimation of these animals could really lower the spiritual light quotient, and the ability of the dolphins to contribute and raise the light quotient of the planet. These dolphins have to work harder now because there are fewer of them. Therefore those that are living and working have a greater burden and a greater service to perform. At the same time, they have to combat their own depression and their own fears. They know that the ocean is being polluted. They know that the life forms on the planet are in jeopardy, and they know that their own habitat is in danger of collapsing. They have to deal with all of those feelings, and at the same time they have to work toward the contribution of the raising of the light quotient.

CONNECT TO THE DOLPHINS

I would like to have you all send your love and light and appreciation to the dolphins and the whales and their necessary work toward raising and holding the spiritual light quotient on the planet. I encourage you to try and speak their language. I encourage you, to the best of your abilities, to not only send them your love and your thoughts, but also, if possible, to tone—to the best of your ability—their language. It is a beautiful and very subtle language that they speak, yet their language is so in tune to the spiritual IQ, the spiritual fabric of Earth. Connect with them now in a meditation.

They, especially the dolphins, are able to connect to the Central Sun. They are able to download new energy for holding this planet, for increasing the spiritual light quotient of the planet. Every species has a certain role to play, so we will not say one is better than the other. Please understand that there are certain animals, such as the dolphins, that have a particular sensitivity to this energy that is necessary for holding the light quotient. Remember, there are a certain number of people that are necessary to hold the righteousness energy of a planet together. So there are a certain number of dolphins that must be maintained in order to do this. Obviously, when you see dolphins committing suicide or dying, then this is of serious concern. It is a warning. This is really what you would call the canary in the cave. If they are dying out, if they collapse, if their colonies collapse, then the spiritual fabric of the biosphere will be closely behind them in its collapse. I will return you to Juliano. It has been a pleasure to meet with you all again, and there is so much more work that we want to do with you. I am Helio-ah. Good day.

This is Juliano. The next level of the spiritual light quotient that we want to talk about has to do with the interaction of higher beings from other sources. In other words, the clarion call went out to Ashtar, to the Pleiadians, out to the Arcturians, to the Andromedans, to other higher beings from the Central Sun to join on Earth in order to raise its spiritual light quotient. This was a major calling from Sananda. His mission is to bring the light quotient of the planet and to bring your light quotient up to a higher point so that you can ascend. Sananda wants the planet to ascend. Sananda called all of us to work with Earth in order to preserve and raise the planetary vibrational frequency so that the spiritual light quotient of the planet can be held and then elevated.

The ascended masters came to Earth. The fifth-dimensional masters, the higher dimensional masters, including me, Juliano, and also Helio-ah as well as the ascended masters from the Native American people. They all have been called to work with you. One measure of the spiritual light quotient of a planet is the interaction with higher beings. The number of higher beings that come around a planet are important in measuring that planet's light quotient. Those planets that have survived have had the participation of higher beings like myself and other ascended masters. Also, they have had receptivity. They have had lightworkers there to receive their energy. They have had people on the planet that were activated in order to receive and work with this energy. That is why Sananda asked us to set up the ring of ascension—the halo around Earth. The halo around Earth is supposed to be the manifested, interactive fifth-dimensional halo that allows you to comfortably interact with the higher energy.

That is why we have set up corridors. Many of you have asked us about corridors and have wanted to know where you can set corridors up. You can set corridors up wherever you are. That is why we have encouraged the many distributions of etheric crystals in the areas that have become corridors of light. Eventually you want to download fifth-dimensional light into Earth and through the crystals in particular, because they have a great sensitivity to do that. Also, remember that the corridors surround these crystals. This allows, through the exercise of shimmering, downloading of higher energy for the planet.

SHIMMER TO WARD ALANO

We have talked about shimmering for preparation of your fifth-dimensional transformation. Let us talk about shimmering as a planetary biorelativity activity. Let us visualize the planet Alano. Alano has a high spiritual fabric. It is a moon-planet. Let us visualize the moon-planet Alano. I want you to absorb, through shimmering, the spiritual energy fabric of that planet. Bring your awareness and that energy of that spiritual fabric to Earth. Shimmering is also a planetary biorelativity exercise that you, as starseeds, can do to enhance the spiritual light quotient of this planet.

Feel a corridor of light around you. This corridor of light now is encircling you and allows you to, in spirit, leave your body and meet with me, Juliano, in a huge circle of etheric light above the North Pole. As we quickly move to the North Pole, I have set up a special corridor of light above the North Pole and the moon-planet Alano. We will shimmer from the North Pole to the moon-planet Alano. We will go over Alano's north pole. We will work to receive a spiritual light and energy from that planet through shimmering. Visualize yourself sitting over the North Pole in an etheric energy field with Juliano. Begin to shimmer. *Shimmer!* Shimmer out of your body to the beautiful etheric light right now that is over the north pole of the moon-planet Alano. We are now together. You have shimmered out of your body into another fifth-dimensional body over the moon-planet Alano.

You are already feeling the high spiritual fabric of light at that planet. It is so beautiful, for it is a planet of a high evolutionary energetic field. It is a moon-planet close to the Central Sun. There is such a balance, such a harmony. There are so many etheric crystals in this planet. The energetic fabric of Alano is generating a light force field that is filling your fifth-dimensional energy body over her north pole. Receive that fabric of light now. Now shimmer back into the Earth after receiving all that light from Alano. *Shimmer!* Shimmer back into your fifth-dimensional body over the North Pole. Now as you shimmer back into that body, you are a great recipient of the spiritual light force from Alano. You allow that energy to be downloaded over to the North Pole now.

Return to your physical body, going into perfect alignment with your physical structure now. You reenter in perfect alignment knowing that through your shimmering activities, you have accelerated the spiritual light quotient of Earth over the North Pole. It was a very effective process. Blessings in the light, planetary healers, starseeds. I love you, I am Juliano. Good day.

HOLDING AND SUSTAINING FIFTH-DIMENSIONAL LIGHT

Juliano, Adama and Lord Arcturus

Greetings, I am Juliano. We are the Arcturians. We will be talking about the connections between the fifth dimension and the third dimension in order to learn how one can enhance these connections. It is true that when one is working in a large group, one is able to go to very high energy levels. These high energy levels can often surpass what one would normally experience individually. Of course, this is in part due to the group energy, for a group energy that is focused on the fifth dimension can raise many people's vibrational levels. Yet when one is going to be alone, the connections that were made in the group often are not as strong as one would hope. That is another way of saying that the fifth-dimensional energy connections do not seem to transfer when one is away from the group.

We note that many people are struggling with their own connections to the fifth dimension. For those reasons, they seek out group contact to create a better acceleration energy. It is also true that being in powerful energy places, such as the planetary cities of light energy fields, will also raise one's vibrational field. We continually work with the Groups of Forty to raise the energy levels of the planet through a process we call "planetary osmosis," which is seeping through the whole planetary system. Planetary osmosis is a way of describing how fifth-dimensional energy is going to many different places on the planet. Our activations of the cities of light are a major step forward in enhancing the process of planetary osmosis.

EARTH-FRIENDLY FIFTH-DIMENSIONAL CONNECTIONS

We have been able, with the help of the GOF members, to activate twelve planetary cities of light. The last planetary city of light activated was Mount Shasta—as the host city of the Arcturian conferences and also

235

because of the powerful energy emitted from this beautiful mountain area. Mount Shasta is connected interdimensionally to Inner Earth. Inner Earth is bringing forth powerful fifth-dimensional light energy to the starseeds and to the planetary cities of light.

The interdimensional Inner Earth has a definitive role to play in holding fifth-dimensional energy and light on the planet. There are several reasons for speaking about the power of interdimensional Earth that emanates specifically from Mount Shasta. The idea is that you can connect to the fifth dimension through the Arcturian stargate and the Arcturian crystal temple. These are very powerful connections. The fact remains that these places, the stargate and the crystal temple, are fifth dimensional. Of course, we have made special corridors in order to more easily facilitate your connections to these fifth-dimensional energy fields. In particular, we have set up the crystal lake as a special energy place for our third-dimensional Earth friends. You can say that it is Earth-friendly for you to travel through the fifth-dimensional corridors to the stargate, the crystal temple and the crystal lake.

Let us look specifically at the interdimensional Earth of which we are speaking. In particular, let us speak about the interdimensional portal of light that is so strong in Mount Shasta. This portal of light and this interdimensional corridor at Mount Shasta allows a particularly strong access to fifth-dimensional energy that is being radiated from the interdimensional Earth. This offers specific advantages to the starseeds. Why and how? The main advantage is that this is already fifth-dimensional Earth energy, albeit interdimensional Earth energy and Inner Earth energy.

Earth energy is ingrained in your DNA, which means it is a familiar, home-based energy field. As you seek more contact with the interdimensional Earth, you can integrate and accelerate your own fifth-dimensional energy field to a new level. You can bring your energy to a level that perhaps did not seem possible. More importantly, you can use the interdimensional Earth energy from the Inner Earth to sustain your fifth-dimensional energy as you travel around the planet and as you leave the Mount Shasta area. This portal of interdimensional light at Mount Shasta was increasingly activated on 9-9-9. After 9-9-9, the interdimensional Earth, or the Inner Earth as some call it, has created a greater flow of light to all starseeds.

I would like my friend Adama to now speak to you about the interdimensional Earth and the Inner Earth, and then I will return to speak more about the relationship of holding the fifth-dimensional light and the four bodies. Now I turn this part of the lecture over to Adama.

Greetings, my Earth friends. I am Adama. I am from Inner Earth. I am from the great portal that is emanating so strongly from the Mount Shasta area. My name, Adama, comes from the name Adam, which is Earth, for we are of our Inner Earth. Our relatives and beings are connected and committed to holding the fifth-dimensional light in the Inner Earth.

Many eons ago, the Earth was integrated into fifth-dimensional light, and there were starbeings like myself who came to Earth to work and open the portal to the fifth dimension from Inner Earth. Think about the inner core of a planet. You will immediately realize how logical it is that the core—the inner structure, the inner etheric energy of a planet—shall first be formatively connected to the fifth dimension. It makes perfect sense that the inner core of a planet is etherically connected not only to fifth-dimensional energies in the solar system but also to fifth-dimensional energies of the Central Sun and in other galaxies.

CORE COMMUNICATION FOR PLANETARY ASCENSION

Through the Inner Earth core connections we have the ability to communicate intergalactically, especially to Andromeda. We consider Andromeda our sister galaxy. We understand that this core of Inner Earth that we inhabit is already in the fifth dimension and already has fifth-dimensional powers and energies that can be transmitted to all the starseeds. We want ways to broaden the transmission abilities of Inner Earth to more parts of outer Earth.

It is strange to talk about inner and outer, but you know from working on yourself that you have an inner self and an outer self. You know that it is the inner self that contains all of the codes for your ascension. It is the inner self that you look to to unlock your inner codes of ascension and your inner codes that open up to the fifth dimension. Think how natural it is to work with Inner Earth interdimensionally. Also, maybe now you can feel the gratitude and the success of having an Inner Earth already activated. Maybe you can appreciate now that this portal from the Inner

Earth is serving as a vital link to the planetary ascension and to the planetary cities of light.

We have, through Juliano and the GOF, activated twelve planetary cities of light. Of course, we will activate more cities of light. This is just the first phase of this activity. I want all of you to understand that Inner Earth energy fields are opening up to all the twelve activated cities of light from this powerful 9-9-9 energy in which we have been participating.

Portals of interdimensional fifth-dimensional light are now being opened as I speak to each of the twelve cities. This means that each now has connections to Inner Earth. They now have connections to me, Adama, and to the many people in Inner Earth and to Inner Earth's energy field. The Inner Earth energy field is a self-generating etheric energy ball of light that is now radiating through the Inner Earth to all twelve cities.

The tremendously powerful fifth-dimensional, interdimensional, Inner Earth light is going to each of these cities of light and being transmitted to all of you who are listening to and reading these words. The Inner Earth is a basic foundational energy that is working for the activations of the planetary ascensions and for your personal ascension. I, Adama, am so pleased that we have reached a point of greater knowledge and greater awareness of Inner Earth and of its relationship to the planetary ascension. I am so pleased that you have activated these cities and that you are willing to open up this corridor from Inner Earth in Mount Shasta so that it radiates through the whole planet.

It takes a certain level of consciousness and spirituality to be able to focus and work with Inner Earth. I want to tell you that Inner Earth is able to communicate with the inner Central Sun. The Inner Earth is able to communicate with inner planetary systems throughout this galaxy and throughout other galaxies. The Inner Earth has specific interactional portals that connect to other corridors that can lead to interdimensional travel. There are many interdimensional beings in Inner Earth who work for planetary ascension.

SUSTAINING YOUR FIFTH-DIMENSIONAL ENERGY

The twelfth etheric crystal, as you know, is going to be downloaded into São Paulo, Brazil. This place was chosen for many reasons. Juliano explained some reasons, including the Brazilian rain forests, from the Arcturian perspective. From our perspective, this area in Brazil has deep connections to Inner Earth. This area near São Paulo has the capacity to receive powerful light from Inner Earth. So realize that you can connect Inner Earth's energy with fifth-dimensional etheric energy from Arcturus and from crystal lake. This connection can create a powerful magnetic energy field of light that is sustainable on the fifth dimension and sustainable on the third dimension.

We are working with the Arcturians to help develop methods of sustaining the fifth-dimensional light throughout Earth. I emphasize the word "sustaining." When you work with fifth-dimensional energy and light, you may find that it is hard to sustain this higher energy on the third dimension. I promise you that as you work with Inner Earth, we will open up more portals and energy fields. Through the activations on 9-9-9, each of you is able to sustain your fifth-dimensional energy, perspectives and connections to the corridors. These portals will also be a great enhancement to the Arcturian etheric crystals that are already downloaded.

Remember that these etheric crystals are downloaded into Earth. We are speaking of the Arcturian etheric crystals, of course. They are not downloaded on top of Earth; they are in Earth. Does this not point out again the knowledge and the power of Inner Earth? Think about biorelativity and Inner Earth, because we are reaching a point where the biorelativity exercises are becoming crucial for maintaining certain stabilities. There are several levels of biorelativity. One level is to sustain and stabilize, and another level is to shift proactively. To shift proactively, one can go into Inner Earth and work with Earth balance energies.

One of the most powerful interventions in biorelativity is to access and work with Inner Earth energies. The Arcturians know that the key to proactive biorelativity is working with the feedback loop systems in Earth. This can allow greater control of air systems, ocean currents and solar flux energies. All these Earth energies can be modulated through Inner Earth. Obviously, this biorelativity has to be done through specialized instruction and permission, and it only can be done by higher beings who understand the ramifications of working with Inner Earth energies. Dramatic effects can be realized.

YOUR CORE RELATIONSHIP WITH INNER EARTH

These Inner Earth energies also serve a great higher purpose for your personal ascension and personal healing. Your DNA is totally linked to the inner core of Earth. You have incarnated and manifested on Earth; therefore, your human physical body obviously has a special core relationship with Inner Earth. This core relationship with Inner Earth is absolutely necessary and part of your incarnation energy. That is to say that you have special linked energy to inner core Earth and to interdimensional Earth. The inner core Earth has certain corridors linking to the fifth-dimensional Earth and to the fifth dimension in general.

Remember that thinking is the fastest light energy on Earth and in the universe. The speed of thought is faster than the speed of light. To work most effectively with the speed of thought, you can go to special sacred places where your energy is enhanced. Mount Shasta is a special sacred place. The twelve planetary cities of light are special sacred places, as is the Inner Earth.

One way of enhancing the speed of thought is through interdimensional travel. You can also receive interdimensional messages from other beings, planets, galaxies and inner-core planetary systems. It becomes difficult to travel to different areas of the universe without knowing specifically what the names of those areas are. If you don't know the names or at least the location, then it is difficult to thought-project yourself there, even if you are traveling at the speed of thought. This is why the Arcturians created the crystal temple and crystal lake. These powerful areas give you a place to focus your energy. This has been extremely helpful.

Inner Earth is a place in interdimensional space where you can receive higher energies and thought waves from other fifth-dimensional planetary systems throughout the universe and the galaxy. By receiving those thought waves, you can travel interdimensionally at the speed of thought to those places.

Feel your abilities now to thought-project and to bilocate yourself into Inner Earth and the interdimensional space where I, Adama, am waiting in the garden, directly under Mount Shasta, California. This is approximately, in Earth measurement, two to three kilometers below the Earth of Mount Shasta. I invite each of you now to thought-project your energy into this beautiful interdimensional garden, where there is beautiful sunlight from Inner Earth.

You all appear here in your lightbodies. As you enter this interdimensional space, you immediately transform yourselves and enter into your fifth-dimensional lightbodies, which is also present in Inner Earth. As you come into your fifth-dimensional lightbodies here in the garden with me, you can feel a huge acceleration of fifth-dimensional activation in your DNA codes. [Tones.] *Kadosh, Kadosh, Kadosh, Adonai*

Tzevaoth. Let those sounds activate the DNA within your lightbodies to help you be more connected to Inner Earth and the interdimensional Earth. Now I send you a special healing light that you may direct to any part of your third-dimensional bodies when you return. Hold this healing light in your Inner Earth body, and we will go into silence for one to two minutes.

Rays of interdimensional light are now connecting to the inner Arcturian planets. We help you connect to interdimensional Arcturus. I turn you over now to Lord Arcturus. I am Adama. Blessings.

G reetings, fellow starseeds, bearers of light and builders of the adytum. I am Lord Arcturus. I am one of the commanders of the inner Arcturian light mission. I welcome you now to the inner core of Arcturus. We have many interdimensional links to planetary systems around this galaxy and sister galaxies. I am very grateful for the lightwork that the Arcturian starseeds do here on Earth.

We have many responsibilities and commitments. Our primary commitment is to assist fellow starseeds through their ascensions. Our primary responsibility is to provide interlinking connections to the stargate so that after you have completed your Earth lessons and incarnations, you will easily travel through the stargate and be able to continue your journey to higher planetary systems.

Planetary Star Cities of Light

We look at our work as providing an entranceway for you to go to higher levels and higher planets. At the same time, we work on a deeper core level to help activate the ascension energies of Earth. Activating the ascension energies of Earth requires great spiritual efforts. I can assure you that we are ready, and we hold great spiritual technologies that offer assistance.

Anytime a new fifth-dimensional energy is activated, all other planets in the fifth dimension benefit. We are all linked. Here we are speaking of the holographic light and holographic connections. Maybe now you understand. From this place in the inner core of Earth, you can connect holographically to inner core energies in many fifth-dimensional planets. Other planets, like Arcturus and Earth, have interdimensional cores. There are interdimensional Arcturuses, interdimensional Pleiades and interdimensional Alanos. Through interdimensional work, you can accelerate your travels throughout the fifth-dimensional galaxy. That is right; there is a fifth-dimensional galaxy.

The entry level of Earth as a fifth-dimensional planet will positively affect all fifth-dimensional planets. We, the Arcturians, are connected to these fifth-dimensional planets in the deepest way, and we are prepared to welcome a fifth-dimensional Earth to the family of fifth-dimensional planets. We are not, however, prepared to welcome the third-dimensional Earth with its planetary polarizations and dualities into the family of planets on the fifth dimension. But we already accept the Inner Earth, and we will accept and facilitate the fifth-dimensional Earth through Inner Earth's work to create a transformation and ascension of planet Earth.

I, Lord Arcturus, now connect the inner core of Alano, a moon-planet close to the center of the galaxy, the Central Sun, and Inner Earth. There are planetary cities of light, which we call sister cities, that are on Alano and are connecting with the twelve etheric planetary cities of light on Earth. In particular, we will connect with Mount Shasta. The twelve sister cities on Alano are now connected through Inner Earth to Arcturus and Inner Earth to the planetary cities of light. These planetary cities of light will become planetary star cities of light. Please note this shift of planetary star cities will now be places of starbeings, star energy and star activation. There will be many visitations in these cities.

The work of planetary ascension is a task all of us on the fifth dimension are participating in through the Arcturians. We, on Arcturus, are not only connected through the stargate to other systems, but also through our inner core, Inner Arcturus. We are connected to the inner cores of many different planets.

My friend Juliano will now guide you back to your Earth bodies and will speak to you about sustaining and holding this fifth-dimensional light. I am Lord Arcturus, and I am working from the inner cores of many planetary fifth-dimensional systems. We help to solidify the connections of Inner Earth to the other inner planets in the fifth dimension.

G reetings, I am Juliano. Project yourselves back to your Earth bodies through the speed of thought and reenter your physical bodies in perfect alignment now. As you come back into your physical body, be aware of the many messages of sustaining fifth-dimensional energy. You have made some core connections. We have activated many of these connections through your DNA.

OPEN TO RECEIVE QUANTUM HEALING

Holding fifth-dimensional light and sustaining it involves sustaining the energy in the mental body, which includes ideas and beliefs. It also involves the emotional body, which includes emotions of love and higher feelings. And it involves the physical body as well, which includes the ability to hold etheric energies from other dimensions. Finally, holding fifth-dimensional light also involves the spiritual body, which is able to gather, collect and sustain spiritual energy. Spiritual energy is the core energy of your soul.

When we talk about dimensions, this includes interdimensional travel and travel at the speed of thought. We are getting close to the core soul light when we talk about dimensional travel. Soul energy is activated when discussing dimensional energy. Dimensional energy can create an activation of spiritual energy. Each one of these levels is called a body. For example, the spiritual body is eternal and infinite and knows no boundaries of space or time, and it knows no life or death because it is infinite and eternal. The physical body, of course, is finite. But the physical body can benefit from the fifth-dimensional spiritual energies.

The physical body can benefit from fifth-dimensional emotional and mental energies because these energies nourish the physical body. It makes your physical body open to quantum energy, thought and healing. As we speak these words, say to your physical body, "Cells, be open to any quantum healing that is necessary for me now. I am ready to receive." You see, we have established now a groundwork for receiving the spiritual light, the spiritual energy and the quantum energy for healing. Say again in an affirmation, "I am open to receiving quantum healing energy. I am open to receiving this in my physical body. I am open to receiving this in my emotional body. I am open to receiving fifth-dimensional quantum light in my mental body, my belief systems and my concepts. I am open to holding this energy in all my four bodies. I stay connected. This connection now is strongly unified with Inner Earth. Being in an Earth-based incarnation, I now have an easier connection to Inner Earth, fifth-dimensional energy. This link will help me to sustain my connection to the fifth dimension and to other fifth-dimensional planets."

All of you want to activate your connections to the family of planets in this galaxy and to the family of fifth-dimensional planets. The Earth is now being welcomed into the fifth-dimensional galactic family of planetary light. These activations of the planetary cities of light have been an important step toward connecting with your galactic families and your star families. It is so precious that you are able to understand and hold this star family connection. The star brothers and sisters are fifth-dimensional, and they are communicating with you now and sending you love and light. I am Juliano. We are the Arcturians. Good day.

BIORELATIVITY AND THE IMMUNE SYSTEM

Juliano, the Arcturians and Metatron

Greetings, I am Juliano, and we are the Arcturians. We are aware of the importance of the human immune system as Earth's energy changes. Oftentimes the human immune system is not able to keep up with the evolutionary changes necessary to keep it intact. When we look at evolution, we look at the different systems that have to change in order for people to adapt to the new energy and the new situation on the planet. We consider ourselves students of planetary evolvement and planetary ascension. We have been traveling to many different planets in our galaxy and even beyond. We are always investigating the processes that a species goes through in order to survive and adapt.

The evolutionary process is an intriguing one, and it is not linear. Perhaps you might think of evolution as being linear because of the work of Charles Darwin and other evolutionary theorists. There is a lot of truth, of course, to the concept of evolution as linear—that there is a progression on a timeline focused on natural selection and the survival of the fittest. This certainly does seem logical. However, there are quantum energies and there are quantum leaps in the evolutionary process. Sometimes a quantum leap is necessary in order for a species to survive on a planet. This means that the normal linear processes would not totally add up and would not provide the next necessary impetus for the shift that must occur in order for the species to survive. Quantum energy brings in extradimensional energies that transcend the normal linear process. This transcendence and integration allows a species to make the necessary evolutionary leaps to survive.

The planets that we have visited and studied present a mixed picture of evolution. Some of the intelligent species that have consciousness like you were able to make the evolutionary leap and integrate quantum energy. Others were not. We want to understand what the difference is. Why do some species seem to adapt while others don't? The difference has to do with this beautiful concept of biorelativity because the species and conscious beings on planets that survive have embraced biorelativity.

BIORELATIVITY, EARTH'S AURA AND CHI

Biorelativity involves telepathically communicating with the planet in order for the planet to make shifts that are in alignment with the needs of the species. We can explain this process using Native American spirituality as an example. Within Native American traditions, one is able to pray to Mother Earth and talk to winds, weather patterns and waterways, for example. There is also a feedback loop in biorelativity that involves the energy of Earth interacting with the systems of the species on it. This is a way of explaining how biorelativity can engage Earth's energies to help humanity— and specifically, the human immune system—to evolve.

The energies from Earth can be dispersed through the energy field of the human aura. It is helpful to study the energies of the aura and to understand how the aura reflects problems in the immune system. I have spoken often about the damage to the human aura from nuclear radiation. Our analysis shows that the use of nuclear energy and the explosion of nuclear bombs on the surface of the planet and in the planet itself have created holes in Earth's aura. These holes, then, can drain the energies of Earth. Likewise, your auras have holes. If your aura had deficiencies in it from extensive drug use, for example, then your aura would be leaking energy. The leaking of that energy would eventually create problems for your immune system and your energy field.

Humanity's energy field is interacting with Earth's energy field. This interaction needs to be appreciated and understood. Generally, people do not consider that Earth has an aura, just like a man or woman has an aura. The aura contains universal energy that is necessary for the survival of humanity on Earth. The Chinese have realized this concept and have tried to explain it. The ancient Chinese described what they called the universal energy as "chi." Chi is the life force energy. When there is a great deal of chi in the energy field of a person, then that person is very vibrant and active. When there is a leakage of chi, then that person can easily become sick. Understanding this, the Chinese have developed creative methods of gathering the chi energy. Chi energy is all around this planet. In fact, it is around the universe, and now some people are learning to bring down chi energy from outside of the solar system. The chi energy can now even be brought down from the Central Sun, which contains a different life force energy.

VIRUSES TRY TO SHIFT YOUR DNA

The chi energy field and Earth's aura energy field overlap. We are seeking to gather people to receive and download more chi life force energy into Earth. Chi is an energy that you cannot see or touch, but it is an energy that you can feel. There is an interactive relationship between the aura of Earth and humanity. When Earth's aura is leaking energy, then the chi energy is not as powerful for humanity, and humanity isn't able to gather and hold as much life force energy.

We can say without a doubt that the life force energy on Earth is not as powerful as it needs to be because of these leaks. When the life force energy is weaker on Earth, then humanity's immune system can also become weaker. We need to discuss with you how to seal those leaks. We must also discuss an important aspect of the immune system, having to do with understanding the viral outbreaks that so many people on this planet are concerned about. The basic method and process of a virus is that it tries to attach to and shift the DNA. Through the shifting of your DNA, it is able to replicate itself in your immune system. It produces an illness based on its ability to self-replicate using the DNA energy that is in your system.

There is fear pervading the planet right now about viruses. The current H1N1 virus, called the "swine flu," is not lethal, but it is a type of virus that can expand dramatically and rapidly on a planet. An aberrant virus of this type could begin to replicate itself by attaching to people's DNA structures and then creating havoc. This may be the first of several waves of viruses that are going to come to this planet. When a species is in as much stress as humankind is right now, then these kinds of viruses are usually not alone. There are waves of viruses. Some people even think there might be two or three or maybe even five different waves of viruses that can go through the population. Just protecting yourself from this virus is not going to be enough, because you have to protect yourself in terms of the whole process. How do you work with your DNA systems so that you will be protected? We will look at and discuss this from the vector of ascension. But first, we will look again at the evolvement of the immune system.

YOUR BODY HAS TO "DISAPPEAR"

The immune system generally has not kept up with the rapid changes that have occurred on this planet. From an evolutionary standpoint, we could say that people will be able to evolve and help their immune system adjust in order to survive in a new environment. Some of the environmental problems humanity faces include: an intensely polluted atmosphere, polluted waterway systems, holes in Earth's energy field due to nuclear radiation and the high density of extra radiation coming from outside the solar system through the Sun to the planet. These environmental problems are resulting in the depletion of the chi energy field on the planet. However, to counter this energy depletion, a new life force energy is coming to earth through the Central Sun.

All of these things must be taken into consideration concerning your immune system. There are exercises to activate your DNA system so that it will not respond to aberrant viruses that may make it into your energy system. This means that your DNA system will not allow itself to replicate negative energy from a virus. The first step in this process is to accelerate your own DNA energy. You need to regain conscious control of the DNA process. Your immune system will not allow itself to be wrongly replicated. This new process is open for you because you have used a similar process in your evolvement when you have unlocked the codes of ascension.

In the earliest lectures and discussions of ascension, we brought through a great deal of information about the codes of ascension. We discussed the idea that there were certain core rules and core sounds that represented the codes of ascension. These codes could be toned or sounded. By sounding the coded words, the DNA within your energy system would be activated for the shifts necessary to allow your ascension. This has several important basic ideas. The first is that to ascend requires a shift in your DNA! This is different from the shift in DNA we are talking about with viruses. In that case, a virus replicates itself within your energy system to create an illness. The opposite is true of the DNA shift in ascension.

We are opening up positive evolutionary codes through certain tones and sounds that will allow your brain and your energy systems to unlock the codes of ascension. This will allow a major evolutionary change in your energy systems. The tones and sounds for unlocking the codes of ascension were brought through Archangel Metatron and Archangel Michael. The tones are the Hebrew words *Kadosh, Kadosh, Kadosh, Adonai Tzevaoth*—"Holy, holy, holy is the Lord of Hosts." These are ancient Hebrew words, but they have galactic origins. The tones and sounds of these words resonate with the internal DNA that controls your ascension. With the right toning, you can unlock the codes of ascension so that your DNA will activate and allow you to make the evolutionary changes for your ascension. These changes include changes in your belief system, in your physical structure and in your energy system. Remember, your body has to "disappear" in ascension— that is, the body has to vibrate at a higher and higher speed so that it disappears. We have talked about the energy of shimmering as a prelude to ascension. The shimmering energy is one of the exercises people have asked for that is necessary for unlocking the codes of ascension. You also have to do corresponding work to keep the ascension energy developing in your body and to help evolve the other systems of your body—the belief system, the emotional system, the physical body and the spiritual body—to prepare for the shift.

EXERCISE: EVOLVE YOUR IMMUNE SYSTEM

We recommend a two-part exercise process to develop conscious control of your DNA. The first exercise includes the use of sounds and tones to activate the energy within your DNA to strengthen your immune system, and the second exercise includes the use of affirmations. The ideal outcome with these exercises would be that, even if you did get in contact with the virus, the virus would not be able to replicate itself and work with your DNA.

The first tone or sound for accelerating the consciousness and the relationship of your consciousness to your DNA is a very high-pitched sound. We will try to produce this sound for you as best we can through the channel. This sound is a tone that announces a clearing to the immune system and that you are coming to cleanse and to clear. If your immune system was exposed to a virus or to some intrusive energy, then the first step would be to try and use this tone to pierce it and obliterate it. Use a higher tone if the virus is in your system and is trying to access the DNA. However, once the virus accesses your DNA, then it will try to do what it wants.

In that case, go into the next sound, using the following words: "Let the healing light enter my immune system." As the healing light enters your immune system, there is an acceleration of the evolution of the immune system so that you can next say, "I unlock the codes of healing light within my DNA." As you say those words, the immune system and its DNA are accelerated to a higher vibration. In the acceleration of the immune system, the vibrational energy of the immune system goes to a level of energy that is higher. The lower energy virus cannot parasitically attach to your energy system and begin to replicate. The immune system energy is vibrating at a higher level that will overcome the virus.

This exercise goes into the concepts of vibrational healing medicine. Vibrational healing medicine is based on the energetic principle that vibration is the key to all healing. In fact, when a person is ill, their vibrational energy field becomes slower. The vibrational healing happens when there is an increase in the energy field, particularly in the immune system. Then we can unlock the healing codes. You have within your energy system the ability to unlock the codes for a fifth-dimensional healing of your immune system. When you hear these beautiful tones and sounds, you can unlock the codes that will be necessary to accelerate your fifth-dimensional immune system codes that will accelerate and advance the DNA in your immune system. For this part I will turn things over to Archangel Metatron who will guide you through these words. Then I will return. This is Juliano.

Greetings, I am Archangel Metatron. You have the ability to have advanced immune systems and advanced DNA work. When you read stories of miraculous healings, you may wonder how this happens. The way it happens is that the healer is able to send energy and light into the DNA of the healee's immune system. That DNA begins to unlock the energy of the person so that they are healed. What is important to understand about this type of healing is that the DNA energy is unlocked. When a healer knows how to access the DNA through healing light, this is the most effective healing.

At this time you want the most advanced and vibrationally high immune system that is possible because you want to be able to fend off the lower vibrational viruses that may come into your immune system. The idea of placing higher energy into cellular structures has been demonstrated by the beautiful idea of sending love energy to water. You may have seen these beautiful images by a Japanese man who has shown how the molecular structure of water changes based on the love energy that is sent to the water molecules. We can unlock the codes of the immune system through these tones and sounds, and it will put you in such a high vibrational state that if you come in contact with lower vibrational microbes, bacteria or viruses, they will not be able to enter. If the viruses do enter, then their instructions to your DNA on a cellular level will not be effective.

The tones and sounds that we are going to use, you have heard and we are going to send them together. The first one will unlock the codes of ascension again. The tones for the codes of ascension can also be used to unlock the codes for your immune system. Then we will also use special codes for unlocking the immune system. Even though your codes of ascension have been unlocked, remember, it is a process that needs to be updated and repeated, partially because there is a general density and slow energy on the third dimension. [Tones.] *Kadosh, kadosh, kadosh, Adonai Tzevaoth.*

I, Archangel Metatron, call on the healing light to unlock the codes of ascension for everyone who is hearing or reading these words. In particular, I send this healing energy to the country of Mexico, which has experienced the central energy of this virus. The country of Mexico will now be more in alignment with the opening of the codes of ascension for the planet.

Now focus on your immune system. We will use the famous Hebrew phrases that you have heard before: *El na refa na la.* This is also a code for unlocking the immune system so that the changes can occur. You can say this affirmation: "This is my intention. My higher energy will unlock my higher codes in my immune system so that my immune system will raise a higher vibration. *El na refa na la.*" Let your immune system go to a higher vibrational energy field now! *El na refa na la.* Now feel your energy system and feel your immune system. They have jumped in a quantum way to a higher vibrational frequency. If you feel that there is a lower energy trying to come into your immune system, then say this affirmation: "Only higher vibrational energy can come through my immune system. Lower vibrational energy cannot come through. I seal my aura."

HEALING MEXICO'S IMMUNE SYSTEM

Each country has an immune system energy field. I, Archangel Metatron, am looking at the immune system energy field of the entire country of Mexico. It is true that there is a leak in the immune system of that country. There is a collective interaction on the immune systems. The immune system responds to lower vibrations. It responds to fear. There is a necessity to raise the vibrational field of the entire country of Mexico and its relationship to its energetic immune system. In this meditation, focus now on Mexico and listen to my words: "*El na refa na la*, Mexico." I, Archangel Metatron, bring down a golden corridor of light through the center of Mexico City. This golden corridor of light is connected with the energy field of the Central Sun. A new chi life force energy from the Central Sun is being downloaded into the center of Mexico City now. That chi energy field is expanding over the whole city. It is expanding over the whole country, and there is an enhanced chi life force energy. This chi life force energy is filling up the depleted chi energy field in Mexico. There was a depletion of chi energy field around Mexico, and it was trying to spread throughout the planet.

As we go around the planet Earth, we fill up all of the leaks and we hold a higher vibration. *El na refa na la.* So I ask you to say, "I am able to hold this newer vibrational field in my immune system. I am able to hold this higher vibrational field in my immune system. Lower energies cannot attach themselves to my immune system and use my DNA. My DNA will only be used for ascension and acceleration into higher energy fields. My DNA will only be used for accelerating my ascension and higher energy fields." Hold this light. Hold this thought now in a brief meditation. *Kadosh, kadosh, kadosh, Adonai Tzevaoth. El na refa na la.* The energy light of Archangel Raphael is filling your immune system now with golden light, unlocking the codes for a highly advanced immune system. Archangel Raphael is the great healer and his light is now going into each of you to advance your immune systems. I, Archangel Metatron, am sending the healing light of Archangel Raphael to Mexico to raise the energy level of the immune system of the whole country.

THE RING OF ASCENSION

Juliano has talked about the relationship between biorelativity, Earth and how Earth's energy can help accelerate your own healing. This process needs to begin with connecting to the chi life force energy of the Central Sun. The second part is that you need to, through your divine meditations, work to seal Earth's energy field. I recommend that you seal the aura of Earth using the ring of ascension. It is difficult for even a large group of people to work on sealing Earth's aura because it is so large and there are so many deviations. The ring of ascension is already in place. It is like a halo, and you can project your energies into the ring of ascension and this will propagate a healing and a sealing of Earth's aura.

Finally, focus on Earth's power spots. The power spots are where higher vibrational energy resides. Connect with that higher vibrational energy from

Earth. These power spots contain special energetic boosts to your immune systems. I am Archangel Metatron. I return you to Juliano.

Greetings, I am Juliano. We will conclude with a pulsing exercise. Visualize your aura and see that it is in the shape of the cosmic egg, and see that it is blue and see that it is pulsing. See that it contracts on my command now. As the aura contracts, it goes into the center of your stomach, the solar plexus, as a small ball. As it expands, it pushes out all lower vibrational organisms, bacteria and viruses out of your system. They are thrown out of your aura. Now your energy field begins to pulse and it pulses at a much more rapid rate. As it is pulsing at the rapid rate, that pulsing will prevent lower energy viruses and bacteria to enter. It is pulsing at this speed [rapidly tones]: *tat, tat, tat, tat, tat.* As it is pulsing, feel that the pulsing increases to a point that you begin to shimmer. As you shimmer, you connect to your fifth-dimensional body and your fifth-dimensional immune system. You can access quantum light and quantum energy from your fifth-dimensional immune system.

We need a core number of people in Mexico to activate their fifth-dimensional immune system. When a core group of people begin to activate their immune systems to a higher frequency, then the country's immune system will increase. You can represent the newer wave of fifth-dimensional, lightholding beings that have higher immune systems. Your acceleration of your immune energy will be a trigger for the whole country to fight off any virus. This exercise will raise the vibration of the whole country's immune system. You can also go to other countries and do this. You can go to the whole planet.

A light from the ring of ascension will help you in a quantum way to accelerate your immune energy. The biorelativity process can attract fifth-dimensional energy through the ring of ascension and bring that fifth-dimensional energy into the Earth and then into the whole country. This will begin an acceleration and beautiful healing. I am Juliano. Good day.

CHARGING PERSONAL AND PLANETARY SPIRITUAL BATTERIES

Juliano, the Arcturians and Archangel Metatron

Greetings, I am Juliano, and we are the Arcturians. We wish to explore the concept of downloading energy and, in particular, the downloading of higher energy from other dimensions. This is an important concept for many reasons. Many of the starseeds may be struggling to hold their spiritual light and their spiritual energy.

Planet Earth may be struggling. The struggle with the planet is different in that Earth has gone through some dramatic changes over the history of her existence. However, Earth is being called on to make adjustments and to make energy transformations in a rapid period. In a very short time, Earth changes will require a great deal of energy and input from higher dimensions to balance the biosphere.

The concept of a battery will be helpful as a metaphor for this discussion. As you know, the battery is a device that stores electrical current, and it is measured in certain electromagnetic energy descriptions such as volts or amperages. The car battery is a device in your automobile that in many cases must be charged by an alternator, which sends energy to the battery so that the battery can continue to provide energy to run your vehicle.

Sometimes the alternator, as the source of the electrical charge of the battery, breaks. Therefore there is no way to charge the battery unless there is a new alternator. In this case, the battery runs on reserve power. That reserve power is stored capacity. The stored electrical current from the battery can provide the necessary charge for the operation of the vehicle until a new source, in this case an alternator, can be placed so that the charging can continue. In some batteries, the storage reserve can be as long as an hour or more. This means that your automobile would be able to run for a given period of time without a charging source.

YOUR LIFE FORCE CHARGE

Let us take this metaphor and consider that you are a battery. Instead of electrical current, you are holding spiritual light. Spiritual light has a very fine charge. The capacity to hold this spiritual energy is dependent on you as a vessel and how you train yourself. Even beyond this storage capacity, there is another function of this that I need to describe. Many of your spiritual and mystical religions already suggest the concept that I am going to introduce. This concept is that every person, when they are born, is given an initial charge, an initial life force energy that determines how long they are going to live on the planet and how much energy they can expend.

Some people like to measure this energy capacity that you are given at birth by the number of years that you are able to survive on Earth. You might say that one person has a capacity, or a life force charge, to live eighty-five years. Another person only has the capacity to live seventy years. Some people only have capacities to live ten or twelve years. It is beyond the scope of this discussion to elaborate on why some people are given more of a life charge than others. Let me just say that a lot of it is predetermined by your soul family and by your soul mission. Let me also say that we, the Arcturians, believe it is not only based on years. I would not say to you that you only have enough charge for a given amount of time; rather, your time on Earth can be based on how you are able to sustain and receive energy.

There are certain activities that shorten your battery's capacity, and that is your own self-capacity. A very simple example would be engaging in war, drugs and alcohol. These substances produce what we can call lower vibrations. Lower vibrations negatively affect your ability to hold a life charge. This also means that the opposite is true. Higher energy and higher activities can sustain and lengthen the ability to hold a charge, to hold the spirit in this body for a longer length of time.

Many of you who are starseeds are older and have already transcended the charge that you were given when you came into this Earth. Many of you were programmed and were given a charge for a given length of time, and it might have been for seventy-two to seventy-four years. Through your spiritual work and your energy work, you have accumulated an additional capacity and an additional charge to sustain yourself longer than the time that was originally given to you at entry point into the Earth. This then reiterates the point that you are given a certain life charge for this incarnation, but you can lengthen the life charge, especially if you are involved in spiritual activities.

The charge and the length of time that you spend here is not the sole measurement for your life success. An example of someone who was only on Earth for a short time was Jesus/Sananda. He carried a tremendous energetic charge. The charge that he carried far transcended thousands of lifetimes that normal people would be able to sustain. The energetic charge that he distributed throughout the planet cannot be measured at all by the length of years that he walked Earth.

RECOGNIZE WHEN YOU NEED TO RECHARGE

I want to now explain this concept of the reserve capacity because many of you are struggling with holding the spiritual energy that you have sustained or have achieved. A good example of that would be attending a spiritual workshop and receiving a high spiritual vibration. After a week or two, the spiritual energy you obtained is dissipated, and you no longer feel the charge. For whatever reason, the work that you did at the workshop did not affect, or you did not allow it to affect, your storage capacity for holding the spiritual light. One of the most important concepts for you to develop is strengthening your spiritual storage capacity. It is necessary to be able to hold the spiritual light, even if a charge is not being delivered for whatever reason.

If your alternator in your car is failing, then hopefully you have the best battery, which has a bigger reserve capacity. Such a battery will have the reserve charge to take you to the nearest repair center. There you can either install a new battery or a new alternator so that your charging can be continued. You may not necessarily need a new battery, but you may need to get yourself to a new charging source.

There is a reason why I am telling you this metaphor. I know it is obvious to many of you that the energetic charge, the spiritual charge, that is working and sustaining many of you is sometimes being cut off or blocked. For a variety of reasons, the charge is not getting through, and you may lose your spiritual focus—your centeredness. The charge of spiritual light that has been sustaining you may be weakening. At that point, I want you to remember this discussion—you must, at that point, tap into your spiritual reserve capacity. Many of you like using acronyms, so spiritual reserve capacity can be called "SRC." We have talked about the SLQ—the spiritual light quotient—and today we talk about the spiritual reserve capacity. I, Juliano, want to ask you: How is your spiritual reserve capacity? How long could you sustain yourself if you were suddenly spiritually cut off?

You might ask, "What are you talking about, Juliano? What do you mean, cut off? Why would spiritual light and spiritual energy be cut off?" The answer to that is somewhat complex. The first answer is that sometimes the densities on Earth are so strong that the spiritual light can be temporarily blocked. Sometimes the environment that you are in and the people that you are around can create a denser field that is hard to lift yourself out of. This could even be in family situations or in work situations. Sometimes there are environmental catastrophes such as earthquakes, tsunamis, storms or blizzards that make it difficult to spiritually connect. Sometimes there are illnesses in the body that focus your energy away from your spiritual work and spiritual light.

THE NULL ZONE

Many of you have already heard about the concept of the null zone. I know this concept was popular several years ago. Some people had thought Earth was supposed to enter a null zone, and then the energy would be blocked out and there would be no electromagnetic current able to flow—all the computers would fail and other such things. This never happened. People then felt that the idea of the null zone was not a correct notion. Actually, the concept of the null zone is a very accurate description of spiritual energy and electromagnetic energy occurrences, because there are null zones. One example of a null zone would be if someone was using electromagnetic energy or current and went into the Bermuda Triangle, then normal current wouldn't work anymore.

There are null zones in Earth's path around the Sun. More importantly, the Earth and the solar system's paths around the center of the galaxy contain null zones. Because Earth revolves around the galaxy over such a long period, no accurate historical descriptions of the path of the whole solar system or of the Sun around the galaxy exist. The closest approximation or attempt to describe any energy that would come to Earth during this long galactic path is the Mayan concept of the year 2012.

In this concept, a description is offered of an energy shift that is coming from the galactic source, or the galactic center. Even that description is not very detailed, because all you are getting is this one description at the center point known as the winter solstice of 2012. There is no other information about other energies that could be forthcoming on that path. I would say that the Maya were probably more aware of that long energetic charge, but this information was lost.

I do not feel that it is unusual or a sign of weakness that you would experience being cut off temporarily from spiritual light or your energetic charge of spiritual energy. I would expect and hope from the knowledge that we are getting now that if you were temporarily cut off from spiritual energy, then you would be able to operate on your spiritual reserve. I also hope that we can explore the certain lessons on how to hold and to improve your capacity to hold this light so that you have the longest reserve capacity possible. This will be important during the coming Earth-change times.

YOU CANNOT HAVE LIFE WITHOUT SPIRIT

Now I will make a slight digression. Some of you in earlier lifetimes had your batteries and your spiritual capacities totally drained through some traumatic events. An example of a traumatic event might be a holocaust or Native Americans being overridden through wars and terror or someone experiencing some type of nuclear trauma. You have heard me talk before about nuclear traumas. There is something within the nuclear energy field that totally depletes the spiritual capacity of the person and the battery power so that when coming back into another lifetime, these people might be operating for a while on a deficit. I know this may sound strange to you. After such traumas, there could be a deficit in spiritual power and spiritual energy in the next lifetime.

Sometimes you might even have negative energy to come back into another lifetime. You might find in the next life that you have a lack of capacity to hold spiritual light and that you also have difficulty in gathering that light or finding it. At this time, there is a tremendous grace, an opportunity to expand your spiritual capacity. There is a tremendous opportunity to store spiritual light and spiritual energy and to learn the ways of downloading the higher spiritual light. This brings forth the topic of downloading spiritual light, particularly the downloading of spiritual light from the fifth dimension for the planet.

Earth also operates on the same principles that we are discussing for you personally. Earth has a spiritual capacity and an ability to store spiritual energy and spiritual light. There is within your energy field the capacity to bring down higher energies and spiritual light and to expand your energy field so that you can expand the time that your body can stay on the planet. Focus the time on Earth as measured in terms of experiences and light.

The changes that you go through have put a strain on the physical body, in part because the physical body wasn't programmed initially to follow this path. Because of this, you need a greater spiritual light and spiritual energy to solidify these changes and to hold this energy. The Earth charge, the alternator, is not producing and cannot keep up with the spiritual current that you need. That is like saying to you that your car now suddenly requires more electrical power but your alternator in the car can't keep up with it, and you need a bigger alternator to produce more electrical current. In the same way, in order to sustain yourselves at the spiritual level that you want to hold, you need more spiritual charge. The older methods, Earth methods for charging spiritually cannot keep up with what your needs are. You must look to another source, and that other source is the fifth-dimensional energy field that we originate from.

Earth also needs a higher source of electrical or spiritual charge because it is having difficulty as a spirit body, as a planetary spirit, holding the spiritual charge that is necessary to sustain the biosphere. The current Earth energy sources are struggling to keep it in balance. It is true that Earth will continue even if the biosphere is thrown out of balance from man's perspective. Earth is a living being that has a life expectancy of billions of years. We are not talking about Earth losing its physical body, but we are talking about it losing its spiritual energy. You cannot have life without spirit. You cannot have spirit without spiritual energy.

If the Earth loses its spiritual charge, then the biosphere will collapse. What can be done to sustain the spiritual charge to keep the energy of Earth going, and at the same time, what can be done to improve and increase the spiritual light for you as lightworkers? How can we create a spiritual reserve capacity or lengthen or expand the spiritual reserve storage capacity of Earth? How can we expand and lengthen your spiritual capacity in your physical incarnation?

THE IMPORTANCE OF SACRED ENERGY FIELDS

I will first speak about the charge of spiritual light for Earth and how we perceive the improvement of the receiving storage capacities of Earth. Earth is able to hold energy, especially spiritual energy and life force energy, through its sacred power spots. There are many special power spots on the planet. Earth is able to hold and transfer its spiritual energy through the ley lines, which we have compared to the meridians in the Chinese acupuncture perspective. From our perspective, the activation of the twelve etheric crystals is especially important as additional sources of powerful charge. This means that Earth can hold fifth-dimensional energy with the assistance of etheric crystals.

It is also true that fifth-dimensional energy is a highly refined current, a spiritual force and an electrical charge that can withstand certain Earth abuses and drains. This type of etheric energy has a greater ability to be stored. This is to say that the nature of energy improved its ability to be stored. The fifth-dimensional spiritual light has such powerful characteristics. One of the most useful characteristics in particular has to do with the ability to be stored. We know that defining and creating these twelve etheric crystal areas has added huge spiritual energy reserves throughout the planet. It has helped to make those spiritual areas have greater capacity to store energy and a greater capacity to transfer energy.

The unfortunate fact is that many of the other sacred power spots on Earth have been damaged because they have not been properly protected. Many of the ancient peoples' sacred energies have not been sustained. These ancient peoples were guardians of sacred spots. Many of the grandfather and grandmother spirits that were living in the mountains, forests and lakes holding this spiritual energy for the planet have left. Why? To hold their sacred energy, they need a protective energy connection to the third dimension. Therefore if there is not a protective sacred energy field that is interacting with them, then it becomes harder for them to stay. It becomes harder for the power spots to hold the energy and to keep the spiritual reserve capacity.

However, a newer energy source from the fifth dimension has the ability to transcend and to be able to reestablish the sacred power spot's storage capacity of spiritual light and energy. That is one of the functions of the twelve etheric crystals that we have been working on so hard with you. This is why it is important to continue to work on connecting with the etheric crystals and why we designated meditation times for you.

One suggested meditation is that you visualize each of these crystals and each of these areas as sacred power spots. Visualize etheric crystals being downloaded into Earth as special fifth-dimensional power spots. They have now been given the function and the purpose to store spiritual energy, just like a battery stores electrical current. These etheric places now have the function of storing higher spiritual light and higher spiritual energy. Their storage capacity is far stronger than what normal power places on Earth can store. These designated etheric areas now have extraordinary ability to store powerful spiritual light and spiritual energy. They are very needed now.

The spiritual storage capacity can become lengthened through focused group meditations. For example, focus and meditation performed hourly on the twelve etheric crystals all around the planet will be very effective. It just so happens that a charge from one crystal then goes to another crystal. This is similar to the idea of parallel batteries. Let it be said that placing batteries in parallel is another metaphor for using the twelve etheric crystals as energy fields. One battery standing by itself has a certain amount of voltage that it can give, but when you connect the battery parallel to another, suddenly the charge of that battery and the capacity of the two batteries together are doubled. The twelve etheric crystals are accelerating and charging each other because they are all connected.

THE PLANETARY CITIES OF LIGHT

In our previous discussions, we talked about the dialectic energy capacity of the Tree of Life, which is represented on the planet by the twelve etheric crystals. When connected, the charge of all of the twelve etheric crystals far transcends the doubling effect that we have described in placing two batteries in parallel. To give you another example, imagine that you have two six-volt batteries. They could produce twelve volts and have a far greater capacity. This is just doubling the power, and each of them is sustaining a certain charge.

In the etheric world of energy and etheric crystals, I cannot describe how much spiritual light and energy you are creating because it is more than double, triple or quadruple the energy. You describe things in the mathematical world as ten to the fifth power, ten to the tenth power and so on. This is approximating the kind of dialectic energy that I describe when we talk about increasing energy from the etheric crystals. What you also accomplish when you do this type of etheric crystal meditation is that you create new types of energy patterns, which also creates a greater reception to fifth-dimensional light.

Some have asked about how we should work with this energy in relation to the planetary cities of light. The planetary cities of light are also sub-batteries, if you will. They also correlate to these etheric crystals. The planetary cities of light already have some capacity to function in the same way as the etheric crystals. One new planetary city of light is Aufkirchen, near Munich. This location already has gathered a large spiritual capacity, and higher spiritual light is going to come to this beautiful city.

You may wonder how the planetary cities of light are similar to the etheric crystals. They are similar in that they are battery-storage devices for spiritual energy. They can download higher spiritual charge, store it for longer periods of time and can now begin to transmit that energy outside of their boundaries. The crystals' main function and goal to the planetary cities of light is to both hold that spiritual charge for a given city and to transmit that light to other areas.

It is important to emphasize that the planetary cities of light are given the task of holding the spiritual energy. Why is that important? Some cities of light are already in high spiritual energy areas. But even in higher areas, there still are drains on the cities. The cities are still in the third dimension and sometimes there is negative energy coming in. They still have the same problems that all cities have, including unemployment, pollution, environmental hazards and whatever other dense Earth energies exist. These energies can affect a planetary city of light also. So it is a tremendous task and it is a great accomplishment to hold and to ensure that the higher spiritual energy is to be held in that city.

The exercise of shimmering a barrier around the city helps to hold the spiritual energies within the area. A good meditation to help this situation is to visualize a shimmering light as a spiritual battery that can hold and attract more spiritual energy and more spiritual light.

We also created the image of the energetic basket, which was first discussed in Argentina in Buenos Aires. A spiritual basket was raised around the city. The image was that the city of light would be in a basket of light. The basket was raised partially and then the fifth-dimensional energy was brought down. The energy field of the city held that light, and then that light was spread throughout the planet. The idea of the shimmering of the basket focuses on the fact that this shimmering raises the capacity of the planetary cities of light so that they can hold a higher fifth-dimensional energy. It is the shimmering that accelerates the planetary city of light so that the spiritual battery, namely the basket, can hold spiritual light.

UPGRADED SPIRITUAL CURRENT

These principles for the planetary cities are exactly the same for you as individuals, as lightworkers. There is a certain refinement when it comes to talking about the lightworkers. That refinement has to do with the fact that you have a mental, spiritual, physical and emotional body. Each of these bodies has a charge. Each of these bodies has a capacity to hold certain energy. The concept of working with yourself to improve your spiritual capacity and your spiritual reserve actually focuses on working with each of these individual bodies. The emotional body, for example, needs to be transformed into more universal concepts. For example, compassion, forgiveness, love and acceptance are all emotions that create a greater spiritual capacity for your emotional body to hold emotional spiritual light.

The mental body can hold more spiritual light when you work with higher concepts of the cosmos. Higher mental concepts include universal love, universal light, eternity, concepts of time expansion, unity consciousness, multidimensional energy and the fact that other dimensions exist. These are some of the concepts that can make your mental body have greater spiritual light and capacity. The spiritual body also can be expanded through the shimmering exercises and by connecting with the fifth dimension.

It is clear that there needs to be a new spiritual power source on Earth. There is not enough spiritual current. There needs to be an upgraded current. That upgraded spiritual current needs to come from other sources. I can tell you that no planet has ever been able to survive the crisis that Earth is currently facing without connecting to higher spiritual sources from the fifth dimension.

We could debate this, and we could argue that maybe it could be done without this connection. But our experiences and travels throughout the galaxy have been pretty extensive, and we haven't seen any planet being able to survive without connecting to the fifth-dimensional energy. This means the guides and teachers who are coming from the fifth dimension are needed for this connection.

The physical body responds to certain types of diet, certain types of exercises and also stress. It can also be programmed to receive spiritual light and spiritual energy. You call this the white healing light. The physical body can be programmed so that your correct visualizations will be most effective. One of the visualizations is to realize that you are an energy field instead of just a solid body. The energy that you have that may be creating illnesses is really a congestion or a blockage. If you can, focus on the energy flowing within your body. This is a great step forward for the physical body.

I do want Archangel Metatron to speak with you because he has a great message for you, even though it will be short. I love you all. This is Juliano. Good day.

Greetings, I am Archangel Metatron. The love from my Father, from Adonai, is so strong. Know that the greatest source of spiritual charge is God's love for you. Your love for God, your love for the Creator—your love for Creation—is placing you in the same vibrational field, the same energy that the Creator is emitting for Creation. Your loving God, which is a central concept in the Kaballah, also helps you to be on the same vibration. Many people have asked: "Why does God need our love?" You are not asking the right question. The question is: "Why does humankind need to love God?" The answer is because it puts man on the same spiritual vibrational field as God.

Juliano has given a presentation on the downloading of the fifth-dimensional light, and he has asked me to talk to you today about the concept of Ibbur. Ibbur is the Kaballistic description of cohabitation from a positive spirit. In the energy of Ibbur, spiritual seekers, the lightworkers, open their energy fields to cohabitation from a higher angelic presence or a higher angelic guide. The Ibbur can also come from a higher-ascended master, from a higher-dimensional master.

This experience of Ibbur provides a tremendous spiritual charge to your physical body, your emotional body, you spiritual body and your mental body. It does not at all diminish your own abilities but actually raises your abilities. To do the higher spiritual work that you need to accomplish, you need more spiritual charge. Sometimes, for obvious reasons, your life circumstances do not help you to hold your charge. A great gift from the spiritual masters and from the ascended masters is to offer you the ability and experience of the energy of *Ibbur*. *Ibbur* includes the cohabitation of higher spirits, such as Archangel Michael. I, Archangel Metatron, am also willing to work with you and provide you the spiritual charge. Remember, I am not saying I will take over your karma. I will help you do what is already in you.

YOU CAN DO GREAT THINGS

I am going to say to you that you have within you the ability to do great things. You can do great Earth healings, connect the energy fields of this planet with the twelve etheric crystals, and you can work as starseeds and spiritually connect with each other. Each of you can connect with the higher dimensions and amplify your light. Maybe you need a boost, or a "pick me up," as they say. We, of the ascended master world, we of the higher dimensions, are ready if you are to cohabit. We can cohabit in a short time. We can cohabit with you at night during your dream state. We can help you during crisis. We can help you do certain work that you want to do but maybe don't feel you have the energy to do.

You can call on me, Archangel Michael, Chief White Eagle and Juliano. Juliano has a corps of students that he works with. P'taah also has a corps of students he works with. There are many higher spiritual guides. They are needed, they need to work with you and you need to work with them. Make a space in your energy field and you will feel the joy and love from the higher guides and teachers.

Shalom Aleichem. Amen. May your guide and teacher work with you. May you connect with Him in full light and love. May your consciousness be enhanced, and may you improve your abilities to do your life mission and your spiritual mission far beyond what you can even imagine. I am Archangel Metatron. Shalom.

RECONCILIATION OF POLARIZATIONS

Juliano and the Arcturians

G reetings, I am Juliano. We are the Arcturians. The year 2010 represents the key year for the approach of the 2012 energy. Our research indicated that 2012 is really a turning point for humanity rather than a time of cataclysm. There are many important issues that are facing humanity and humanity's relationship to the Earth. These issues are so important that if they are not resolved in the most favorable and highest energy, then a downfall for humankind's existence on this planet is likely.

The good news is that there are many seeds of positive change that can still be planted. We see that 2012 represents a marker. All seeds of change necessary for the continuation of the evolution of humanity must be planted and incubated between now and 2012. We are referring specifically to the Mayan concept of the winter solstice in 2012, approximately December 22. There is this period that still remains on the planet in which positive changes can be manifested and instituted. Changes begun in 2010 have the possibility and the probability of reversing many of the "irreversible issues" that seem to face humanity.

These issues that need to change are now manifested through polarizations and are also seen as conflicts. These conflicts are manifested not only in man's relationship to Earth but also in social, political, economic and spiritual matters. This year becomes the year in which the beginnings of the reconciliations of the polarizations must and will occur. You will see a major change politically in the world in 2010 because many of the world leaders reluctantly are seeing that the difficult changes must begin. Leaders will begin to see that there is no longer time or room for postponing things. They will see the wisdom of reconciliation and pay attention to resolving polarizations. Polarizations that are unchecked and unresolved will begin to manifest more dramatically in 2010 as open conflicts. These open conflicts will give political world leaders the strength and the courage to begin to make the changes necessary for reconciliation.

FIFTH-DIMENSIONAL ENERGIES

In a sense, 2010 can be looked at as a year of reconciliation of polarizations. This is also true for your personal issues and development. Many of the starseeds have polarizations in their personalities. Many have polarizations in their personal lives, which now—with the energy of 2010—will provide the opportunity for reconciliation. On the one hand, the starseeds now feel the fifth-dimensional energies and experience the wonderful spiritual light that has come to the planet. I want to emphasize that never before have there been so many spiritual beings and high spiritual energy on Earth. Never before have there been so many spiritual masters on Earth. Never before have there been so many spiritual teachers. Never before have there been so many opportunities for spiritual groups to work and perform their soul missions on this planet.

This has come at a time of great population expansion—the high numbers of spiritual teachers and workers on Earth are still small compared to the intense world population. This too represents a polarization. On the one hand, you have the obvious conflicts between many political groups nationally and internationally. On the other hand, you have a stronger contingent of spiritual lightworkers who possess great spiritual tools and energy. A small group with spiritual truth, and that holds connections to the higher light in the fifth dimension, has the power to dramatically affect the world energies. This is why we are optimistic about 2010—we know that the spiritual forces on this planet are becoming stronger, and the starseeds themselves will begin to reconcile their spiritual energies with the third-dimensional energies. This will allow the starseeds to finally begin to integrate their third-dimensional lives with their higher, fifth-dimensional connections.

One of the major, personal reconciliations of 2010 is to balance work and daily life with the spiritual energies. This represents true spiritual mastery—the ability to work in the third dimension with fifth-dimensional energies, enabling a transformation and an evolutionary leap in the third dimension. In order for the evolutionary leap to occur, higher energy spiritual beings must integrate and reconcile fifth-dimensional energies and fifth-dimensional perspectives into the third-dimensional life.

PLANETARY CITIES OF LIGHT

Many starseeds have asked: "What do we do about politics? Is it necessary to become politically involved? What do we do about poverty and suffering?" The year of 2010 is a period of reconciliation of higher energies with third-dimensional energies. Therefore, 2010 is the appropriate time to become involved in a spiritual, fifth-dimensional way with these difficult but important political issues that must be reconciled. These include those issues of Earth—its environment and changes. All of the changes, especially Earth changes, are still amenable to humanity's influence up to and including the 2012 turning point.

Humankind is finally going to learn and believe that there is a relationship between people and Earth. Earth has been signaling them; Earth has been communicating with humankind. These signals and these communication links will become more obvious and more accepted in 2010. This communication includes crop circles. Crop circles themselves are part of Earth's effort to communicate to humankind. Earth and Inner Earth energies are connected to higher, fifth-dimensional galactic energies. Remember that Earth communicates with humans; it doesn't do so through words but instead through symbols and energies.

Of course, one of the shared concerns of humans and Earth is the weather. The weather now can be viewed more realistically as part of Earth's attempt to communicate to humankind. When we look at 2010, it is going to become more obvious what the nature of these communications are and what the meaning of these new weather patterns are from Earth.

The Arcturian starseeds are working to create planetary cities of light. Planetary cities of light are enclaves on the planet that are devoted to holding fifth-dimensional energies. These cities are an important step in the planetary reconciliation that will be happening in the year 2010. In these planetary cities of light, there will be more communication with Earth; each of these cities will be holding fifth-dimensional energies in order to anchor higher consciousness. The goal of 2010 is to anchor the higher consciousness into the evolutionary linkage of humans, so the next step of human evolution can occur and be sustained. That evolutionary step has to do both with higher consciousness and the relationship of higher consciousness to the planet Earth. This energy will be anchored and expanded in 2010.

Finally, our evaluation of the different scenarios of the economy and of the political and social situations revolves around this idea of reconciliation. Also be aware that the reconciliation often begins after a period of polarizations and conflicts. Many of the conflicts that are already obvious to you in 2009 will become more dramatic in 2010. However, these conflicts and polarizations will finally be able to be resolved and reconciled. You personally—as starseeds— will also feel the power of this reconciliation between your higher self and your Earth self in 2010. I am Juliano.

ETHERIC CRYSTAL PLACEMENT PROVIDES A GUIDING LIGHT

Juliano and Sananda

G reetings, I am Juliano. We are the Arcturians. We have completed the mission of placing a new etheric crystal in the volcano of Poás in San José, Costa Rica. This was accomplished with the assistance of the Groups of Forty members in the Costa Rica area. This is an important asset in the alignments that will be perfected between the third-dimensional Earth and the fifth-dimensional Earth. Alignment of fifth-dimensional energy with third-dimensional energy ensures a continual and full energetic flow of fifth-dimensional energy into Earth. The placement of the etheric crystals provides guiding light and guiding energetic receptacles for the fifth-dimensional Earth and all fifth-dimensional energies.

We have assisted other planets in their quest for ascension, and we had great success when we worked with starseeds on those planets. The process of the ascension of a planet is accelerated by the downloading of beautiful etheric crystals. These etheric crystals have many functions. The function you are most familiar with has to do with the alignments. A fifth-dimensional Earth has a better alignment energy when there are etheric crystals in different parts of the planet. The crystals do not have to be equidistant from each other. They do not have to be in a certain circumference placement around Earth. Remember, we are working with both holographic and etheric energy. The etheric crystals then assist in the alignment, and they also interact with each other. If one Groups of Forty member (or members) works with the crystal in Lago Puelo, the energy and input there is communicated to the other crystals.

This crystal that we placed in the volcano in Poás is connected with the Central Sun and with higher galactic forces. The Central Sun is linking itself to this beautiful crystal and is providing a boost of energy to the other four etheric crystals. Most interestingly, this etheric crystal is also connected with the universal force known as the great-attractor energy field. The great-attractor energy field is a transcendent galactic force that involves gathering together and directing the known galaxies toward a point in the universe that would be equivalent to the Central Sun in our galaxy. Unfortunately, there is no actual known center of the universe from humankind's standpoint. However, it has been determined by your scientists and confirmed for many, many eons by our scientists that a galactic force is causing everything to move in one direction. This immeasurable force that causes galaxies to move in one direction is of unknown origin. The speed of the galaxies' movement is measurable, yet the nature of the attractive force is unknown. You can only imagine what type of force would be able to attract the powers and create the force to move galaxies toward a probable central point, something comparable to the Central Sun of this galaxy.

A DISCUSSION OF CENTRAL SUNLIGHT

The Central Sun of this galaxy is the source of life and spirit. Remember that all the things you see on the third dimension are manifestations of both a spiritual force and a spiritual idea or thought. When you try to conceive of the Central Sun, you have to understand that it is a multileveled, multidimensional force field that exists in the spirit world as well as at a physical point. It is an emanation light, an emanation force that controls manifestation in the galaxy. It is a physical or spiritual force that also is able to interact telepathically with starseeds and higher-consciousness beings who are manifesting in the third dimension. This means that biorelativity is continually able to be updated with: 1) Earth and Earth's spiritual energy, and 2) the Central Sun energy. This means that from a biorelativity standpoint, you as starseeds can communicate telepathically with the Central Sun, and you can telepathically receive energy and light from the Central Sun. You can telepathically direct the Central Sun energy and light, ensuring that it is manifested and distributed to certain areas on Earth. We have designated Mount Shasta as one area that is receiving Central Sun energy and light. Now we have downloaded the crystal in the Poás volcano in San José, Costa Rica. That volcanic mountain is connected to the Central Sun, and we will also be working to connect it with Mount Shasta.

A new connection is made with the great attractor forces that are working with the galactic energy. This energy from the great attractor is combining with the Central Sun to create a pulsing energy field. That pulsing energy field is now being downloaded to and then emitted from the Poás volcano, and it is vibrating through the planet. Those who are at Mount Shasta may already be feeling the vibrational pulsing. The vibrational pulsing is being distributed through Earth's meridian lines. The main meridian line that is receiving this input of light is generally known as the ring of fire. Each pulsing creates a calming and harmonious energetic field. The energy that is in this ring of fire meridian is so powerful that it is able to balance and realign ocean currents, weather patterns and other aspects of Earth's biofield that are needed to come into a new and upgraded harmony.

We, the Arcturians, feel and observe a shift in consciousness on the planet, one that occurred with this recent full moon. We felt a great movement spiritually among the starseeds during this full moon. This movement has given the planet a boost of spiritual energy and spiritual power, a power that is needed now, because the polarization of lower vibrations on this planet continue to spiral out of control. Remember, this polarization increases spirituality as well as increasing the oppositional energy of density. It is incumbent on you to work with these spiritual energies to create and establish shimmering cities. The shimmering lights and shimmering energy fields are established in smaller locations, such as in the cities near Lago Puelo or San Martín in Argentina. They are now uploaded in certain areas in San José, Costa Rica, and will work with an already existing shimmering city.

ECSTATIC SHIMMERING

The shimmering lights are representative of an energy field based on telepathic interactions between third-dimensional starseeds and fifth-dimensional energy. The shimmering light is a telepathic etheric force field that is accelerated through etheric crystal work. It can be described as a circular energy field that is distributed around a designated area. The designated area usually begins in a small circle. We find that the starseeds have an easier time working to create an energy field of shimmering light in a small area, and then expand it with great enthusiasm and telepathic work. It can be expanded around a city. Eventually it can be expanded around a planet. It is our goal to create a shimmering energy field around the ring of fire. All the cities and countries can unilaterally join in an energy field of fifth-dimensional light that will bring a new harmony and balance to the planet. A shimmering light field was established around San José in our previous work with the channel. During that experience, the idea of a city beginning to develop the power and ability to become fifth dimensional on a regulated basis was established.

We still feel that, at this point in the development of the Groups of Forty lightworkers, that it is better to work within smaller areas, smaller parts of a city or even smaller designated areas in nature. Ideally, the beginning point would be those areas where we have already downloaded etheric crystals, which include Lago Puelo, Grosse Valley, Lake Moraine, Lake Constance and now the Poás volcano. Groups can go to these areas and begin to feel the shimmering light energy. It would be ideal for all five crystals to have Groups of Forty starseeds working on them simultaneously.

We hope that this will be accomplished soon, and a unique opportunity will be established to have a connection with an energy that will upgrade the biospheric field of Earth. This upgrade will allow the energy field around the ring of fire to shimmer. Shimmering is the ability to flicker in and out of a dimension. A person who is shimmering will look like he or she is in one energy normally, like in an Earth energy. Then he or she will seem to disappear temporarily, and perhaps only the outline of an energy field or the signature of an energy field will remain visible. Then that person appears in the fifth dimension. The person who is experiencing shimmering has a feeling of elation, almost a feeling of ecstasy. That is because fifth-dimensional energy is experienced as an ecstatic feeling from a third-dimensional perspective.

I, Juliano, say that each of you listening to or reading these words has the ability to shimmer. I am downloading a beautiful golden light that is connected to the crystal at the Poás volcano. This beautiful golden light is an emanating corridor that is coming to each of you. You experience the golden corridor as a beam of light coming and downloading into your crown chakra. As it is downloading into your crown chakra, you will receive an experience similar to an electrical charge. This fifth-dimensional energy is an electromagnetic energy. It is not an electrical charge the way you think of it, like a jolt. It is an upliftment. As you receive this upliftment, in the form of an electrical charge coming from the etheric crystal in the Poás volcano, you are able to shimmer. You are able to be in the fifth and the third realms simultaneously. Please hold this connection as we meditate with you.

A Meditation for Shimmering

Know that you first develop the individual ability to shimmer, and then you are able to carry that ability into biorelativity. We will introduce another aspect of shimmering, which is the connection established in the Groups of Forty. I would like you to understand that the etheric crystals originated as cloned or duplicated crystals from the crystal temple. The crystal temple is a lake where all 1,600 Groups of Forty members are in their fifth-dimensional bodies. They stand in a circle around the lake. We can help you shimmer from your place here to that fifth-dimensional lake. I want you to visualize all of you sitting in a huge circle around the planet. You are at the level, perhaps, of the Moon. If you looked at the distribution of everyone listening to and reading these words, you might think that you all can't be sitting in a perfect circle because everyone is in a different location. Remember, from a holographic standpoint, we are not looking for equidistant placement. We are looking for telepathic connection. Visualize your etheric presence separating from your physical body, and move that duplicate etheric astral presence to a huge circle of Groups of Forty members above Earth, at a level comparable to the Moon. Your physical body remains in a meditative state. I am going to give certain tones and energy. You are going to be able to shimmer, moving into the fifth-dimensional crystal temple body and then back into your physical body. Your etheric body, the one that is sitting in a circle around the level of the Moon, is the transducer or intermediary between the dimensions as you shimmer. Anyone watching you in the third dimension would see your energy field begin to vibrate. You will experience an ecstatic feeling when you are able to shimmer into the fifth-dimensional light. When you hear these words and tones, begin to shimmer, if you wish. [Sings.] "Oh shimmering light." [Tones.] *Tat, tat, tat, tat, tat, tat.* [Sings.] "Shimmering light."

As you shimmer your etheric presence into the crystal temple, note that the crystal in the lake has risen, and it is now above the lake. It is communicating with the other etheric crystals on the planet. [Sings.] "Shimmering light." [Tones.] *Tat, tat, tat, tat.* Set the intention for you to have the power and determination to work with this light fully in your third-dimensional body. Already each of the five etheric crystals are vibrating at a beautiful, harmonious frequency with one another and with the crystal temple. You are all simultaneously in this beautiful circle at the level of the Moon. This crystal at the crystal temple is connected with the great attractor force I spoke about. This is the attractive force that is pulling the galaxies in one direction. A small percentage of this force, a single light ray or energy ray from this source, would be extremely powerful.

Now such a small ray has been downloaded into this crystal in the crystal temple. It is distributed to each of you from the top of the crystal to your third eye where you are sitting in your fifth-dimensional bodies around the crystal lake. You are all sitting on one level as fifth-dimensional beings in a circle around the crystal lake. The crystal in the crystal lake has now received this ray of energy and spiritual force from the great-attractor force. That ray is downloaded from the crystal into your third eye. You can now download that energy into your etheric body, the one that is around the Moon. You can also download the energy into your physical body on Earth. [Tones.] *Tat, tat, tat, tat, tat. Ehoheheh.*

At the same time, all the five etheric crystals on Earth are receiving an update of this energy and light from you. Return from the crystal lake going to your etheric bodies around the Moon, and return from the Moon back into your physical body. You are able on an in breath to connect to your etheric body in the crystal temple. Breathe in and then out. Now come back to Earth. It is like this: shimmer, in, in, in, out and back to your body. Repeat. Repeat. Repeat. Visualize all five of these crystals to the best of your ability and shimmer with the crystals. In. Out.

PRINCIPLES FOR HOLOGRAPHIC HEALING AND THE RING OF ASCENSION

We want to review some principles of holographic healing that we have mentioned in previous lectures. The holographic distribution of healing light can start from a powerful area that is vibrant and healthy, such as an area that is holding an etheric fifth-dimensional crystal. Holographic heal- ing energy states that one part represents the whole. From the Arcturian standpoint, holographic healing means that one can ideally go to a healthy, vibrant part of a planet, a vibrant part of the biosphere, and from that point download and distribute energy to other areas of the planet. Our belief is that the biosphere as an etheric energy force must first be updated before the other parts come into a healing mode. Look at the ozone hole. Look at the holes in Earth's energy field. Look at pollution or any other areas of distress. You can now visualize the unblocking of the meridian lines underneath those areas; imagine them being opened and receiving life force energy. You can visualize the etheric crystals, the ones you are familiar with, distributing powerful currents of light force throughout the meridian lines. This light force resonates and updates the bioenergy field. The bioenergy field of Earth is now in two dimensions simultaneously. It is around Earth and it is around the etheric fifth-dimensional Earth as well.

We are interested in working with the ring of ascension, which is a golden halo of light that represents and attracts interaction between fifth-dimensional beings and third-dimensional beings. This halo creates a conduit for interaction between the third dimension and the fifth dimension. An update on the ring of ascension is in order. The ring of ascension has been updated to a higher vibrational frequency because it now is connected to the Central Sun. It is now connected to the great attractor force energy field, and it is now in harmony with the five etheric crystals that have been downloaded on Earth. It is sending a golden ray of peace to the planet. We have predicted and we say that there will be a great deal of war coming. But then we predict a sudden but definite peace that will seem to hold for a period of time. A new spiritual energy is being activated and distributed. More people are being affected by this. There is a greater awareness of the need for a spiritual intervention of the highest proportion. This spiritual intervention can bring the planet back into a harmony that will enable it to survive. Sananda will now speak with you. I am Juliano.

SANANDA SPEAKS OF THE GOLDEN HALO AND THE GAN EDEN

Greetings. I am Sananda. The golden halo that is around Earth is symbolic and representative of your own halo. I am activating your halo at this moment so that each of you are able to come into a state of harmony. This state of harmony is necessary for you to maximize your healing abilities. It makes perfect sense when you think about this—to be at the highest level of your healing abilities requires optimal personal harmony. The halo I am placing around each of you is bringing you into higher harmony than you have experienced recently. Harmony is an energetic state that is attainable at any moment under any conditions while on Earth. It is not necessary to be in a cave meditating for twenty years, although it could happen under those conditions. It is necessary for you to get an energetic boost of light and energy from a higher being. With this boost, you will be in a state where you can receive input from the halo. When you are in that state, your healing abilities are accelerated, both on a personal and a planetary basis.

I, Sananda, send you a beautiful beam of harmonious golden light that represents the ability to reformulate your energy field so that the configuration of a golden halo appears around you as I am speaking, just as it is appearing around the Earth. [Tones.] "Shalom." This golden halo brings all aspects of your biosphere into a balance on a personal basis, and it gives you an extra ability to upgrade Earth's biosphere. Earth's biosphere is receiving an interactive ability from the ring of ascension. That interactive ability gives it the chance to receive your input.

The Garden of Eden, the *Gan Eden*, was a fifth-dimensional palace or garden in which *Adonai* kept the balance. The third-dimensional *Gan Eden* was established for humans to be in charge of that balance and for humans to update and create the forces necessary for balance. The children of the *Elohim*, the *B'nai Elohim*, are creator forces who have the ability to upgrade and create fifth-dimensional gardens. These fifth-dimensional gardens can also be compared to the shimmering cities of light where only the righteous can survive. The righteous have fifth-dimensional awareness and can enter unity consciousness. They have the ability to do *Yechudi*. This is the act of uniting the third dimension with the fifth dimension by thoughts. [Sings.] *Yechudim, B'nai Elohim, Adonai Elohenu, Adonai Echad, Yechudim*, with the *Gan Eden*. Visualize these cities of light. They are created by the shimmering forces as part of the divine plan to re-create the *Gan Eden* on Earth. The fifth-dimensional cities of light are for the righteous. We call these righteous people in the Hebrew Bible the *Tzadikim*. Each of you are righteous, for you are ascending students working to integrate yourselves into fifth-dimensional beings and to create fifth-dimensional cities and gardens.

Think of a garden, my friends, as a palace. Think of the Garden of Eden as the basis, the prototype, for the fifth-dimensional cities. [Sings.] *Gan Eden*. In the fifth-dimensional cities of light, in the gardens, you will see me and you feel my healing abilities interact with yours. Your halo that I have activated now is like a DNA entry code that allows you to enter the gardens. It even goes to the level that you are able to co-create the garden of shimmering light cities on Earth, which is the true manifestation of the *B'nai Elohim*, the children of the *Elohim* light. [Sings.] *B'nai Elohim*. The energy and light of the children of the *Elohim* is activated within you. Resonate with the city of light, the city of gardens of the just, which is the foundation for the shimmering energy that will bring unified fifth-dimensional healing force and light to Earth. The halo of golden light around you is activating within your DNA so that these powers are upgraded and manifested in each of you. I am Sananda. *Shalom.*

CONNECTING WITH EARTH TELEPATHICALLY TO HEAL HER

Juliano and Chief White Eagle

Greetings, I am Juliano. We are the Arcturians. We are gathered here to assist in an exercise of biorelativity. Our belief is that to heal Earth you must connect with her through telepathy. Thoughts are the most powerful energy in the universe. We have taught you to use thought as an energy for healing. Each planet that we have visited has a spiritual force that keeps the planet going. The life force around the planet is called the biosphere. The biosphere is actually an energy field. It includes the oxygen and electromagnetic energies that are very complex to describe in a simple lecture like this.

Let me say very simply that Earth's biosphere is in danger of collapsing. The reason is very obvious. There is only so much pollution that a planet can take before the biosphere collapses. For a planet to survive, there can be a life input. This life input is your thoughts. As humans, you can use your consciousness to interact with your planet. This is very obvious when you look at your Native Americans in North America. They know how to pray to Earth; they know how to talk to Earth—we are taking this one step further—and they know how to interact telepathically with Earth.

In Costa Rica there is an environment that is very close to the natural biosphere energy. We are discussing with you holographic energy. I know that you have seen holographic pictures. The idea is that a part [one dimension] of the picture can represent the whole picture [multiple dimensions]. Ponder this and then consider Costa Rica as a small part of planet Earth, yet the entire planet can be represented through this small country. In healing the planet, you can take one part that is very healthy and use that part to send healing energy to every part. We call this holographic healing. Remember that Earth is interconnected through meridian lines, and this means that each area of Earth participates in the energy lines.

SPIRITUAL HEALING WITH ETHERIC CRYSTALS

There are many energy lines that come through Costa Rica. You can send energy to different parts of the world from there. We have decided that we want to work with this country using special spiritual healing techniques. These spiritual healing techniques have to do with the idea of biorelativity. We have called certain crystals "etheric" crystals. These crystals are programmed to do certain things. You know that regular crystals can be programmed. This was first demonstrated in the lost city of Atlantis. Just for our purposes tonight, you will understand that a crystal can hold certain energy and thought patterns that can be programmed for certain healings. We have created a master crystal that is called the crystal temple. The crystal temple was created by the Arcturians to focus on special healings for Earth and for Earth beings.

During the past several years, we have made duplicate copies of this crystal. Perhaps you can call them clone crystals, which means that exact duplicates are made. We have placed them in certain parts of the planet, such as in Argentina near Los Andes mountains, which is called Lago Puelo. There are others in Grosse Valley, Australia; Lake Moraine, Canada; and Lake Constance, Germany. Now we have decided to place one in Costa Rica. This etheric crystal will be able to interact with the other areas where the crystals have been placed.

We asked the channel to visit the three areas that were possible candidates for holding the crystal energy, because he was not knowledgeable of them. Each area has special energy. We are very familiar with the different levels of spiritual interaction there. Of the three locations, we decided that the park called Poáz is the place where we wanted the etheric crystal to be downloaded. As a temporary holding activity, we brought the crystal down and placed it over this room. You may already feel its shimmering light, which means that from this light, you will feel like you are going into the fifth dimension.

The light from this crystal produces a beautiful energy that allows you to shimmer, that is, to go in and out from the third to the fifth dimension. The area that we visited with the channel and his friends has the energy that connects with the intergalaxy, which is found between the other galaxies and this galaxy. It is hard to imagine this, but remember I have talked about holographic energy, and in holographic energy, the part connects to the whole. Even one small part can give you a key to interacting with everything. It is amazing that you can connect with other galaxies from one point within a galaxy. In this area of Poáz, where we move this beautiful crystal, you can use the energy to connect to the intergalaxies. This brings a special energy and light that will help to provide a healing for Earth.

Remember that you need fifth-dimensional energy to heal. You cannot fly from one galaxy to another with modern technology. It is impossible. But you can go interdimensionally to another galaxy. Each galaxy has a beautiful Central Sun. The Central Sun is the life force of the whole galaxy. We, the Arcturians, have been looking for the Central Sun of the universe. It is difficult to imagine, because the universe is infinite. There is a connection to the Central Sun of the universe. This area that we visited at Poáz Volcano has the ability to connect with this type of thought and energy. In addition, the crystal will be able to communicate with all the other etheric crystals.

ETHERIC CRYSTAL ACTIVATION: POÁZ VOLCANO

We need your assistance in a project called thought transference. I know most of you know where this volcano is. So with your thoughts, please connect to the crystal here. If you cannot visualize it, just tell yourself, "I am connecting with the crystal in my thoughts." In the fifth dimension, when you think something, you can be there immediately. If you think that you want to be connected to something, you are. There is a very good connection now with this crystal. The crystal is about 100 feet above the room. Please, through thought-projection, raise the crystal to an area about 1,000 feet above the room. Now, please visualize where this volcano is, and begin with me to transport this crystal over the city to the mountain where the Poáz Volcano is.

Naturally, you will have to raise the crystal up higher and higher as that mountain is very high. Please make the adjustments so that the crystal is approximately 500 feet above the mountain and exactly over the crater.

The etheric crystal is approximately one mile in diameter. Do not worry about it fitting exactly in the crater, but just that it is going to go right there, and it will fit, even if it is bigger. Very good; the crystal is now above the mountain and the crater. It is now sending out interactive light to the etheric crystals that have been placed around San Jose by other Groups of Forty members. At the same time, this crystal is now receiving energy from the other four etheric crystals that I have mentioned. And I connect this crystal to the energy in the areas that are connected with Mount Shasta in California and also the energy of the Central Sun.

The energy is beautiful, and now we are lowering, with your assistance, the crystal into the crater. It is descending into the crater. On the etheric level, the whole top of the mountain is lighting up with shimmering light. It is accepted into the mountain. The mountain agrees to accept the crystal, and you have successfully helped us to place the crystal into the mountain. It will be easy for you to travel there in your thought projections. Many of you will be able to see this mountain daily in your traveling. I want you to return to the room where you started. Chief White Eagle will now speak with you. I am Juliano.

G reetings, I am Chief White Eagle. [Tones.] *Hey ya ho ya hey ya!* There are beautiful sacred places very eager to accept your thoughts and your light. This beautiful volcano has accepted the etheric crystal. The spirits in the mountain area of the volcano are activated. There are many old spirits and many spirits in those mountains. These are ancient mountains and this mountain has been connected to the Andromeda Galaxy, the Crab Nebula Galaxy, the Sombrero Galaxy and the force known as the great-attractor energy.

This energy is the unknown energy that represents the direction in which the galaxies seem to be moving. It is hard for you to imagine such movement because your Earth moves around the Sun, and then your solar system goes around the galaxy. Can you imagine that the galaxy itself is moving in a direction? Can you imagine that the galaxies all seem to be moving together? What kind of force can cause all of these galaxies to move in a direction? We call this force the great attracting force.

This mountain known as Poáz Volcano has a connection to this great attraction force. This gives it a link to energy that is of a very high level. It gives it a connection that you will be able to connect with the other crystals. It is an energy that is truly fantastic. Let us imagine that this energy is so special that it is attracting galaxies. Can you imagine that this great energy can affect planet Earth? It will be so easy compared to moving a galaxy. What we see is that the energy needs to attract and discharge the blocked energy in Earth's energy channels. The link is now established with the other four crystals and also you are connected to the crystal temple of Arcturus.

I, Chief White Eagle, call on the star family to be together with us as we celebrate this opportunity to connect on so many levels with the galaxies and with Earth. We are all brothers and sisters. This will also help to attract more extraterrestrial beings to this area. I am Chief White Eagle. *Ho!*

MOUNT FUJI AND THE
ANCIENT CRYSTAL

Juliano and Chief White Eagle

Greetings. I am Juliano. We are the Arcturians. Remember that we are in holographic energy; we are in holographic time, and we have said there is a window of twenty-four hours for the downloading of this crystal. The window basically means that if you are several hours earlier or several hours later than when the actual event occurs, your participation and your energy still remain effective. The whole idea of holographic time is an interesting concept in terms of understanding how to work in different time zones and how to create an energy field, an energy connection, because in a sense, if you look at the universe, you understand that time is relative. What you experience on one level, say on Earth, would be a different time than if you were on Jupiter.

HOLOGRAPHIC TIME AND HYPERSPACE

The ideas of holographic time are actually related to what I call "hyperspace." Hyperspace is the energy between the dimensions. When you access that, there is no-time, and you are actually between systems, between spheres of energy. When you go into hyperspace and into no-time, you are going into a realm that allows you quite a bit of flexibility in terms of time travel, moving to the future and moving to the past. However, there are certain rules and regulations to which we must adhere.

The task before us is to assist the Groups of Forty members who are now at Mount Fuji. They are now approaching Mount Fuji, and they are gathering. There are approximately eighty people with him and he has made a huge circle. Many people in Japan already acknowledge the sacredness of Mount Fuji. It has a long history of energy in their culture. It has a long history of being the focus of ancestral energy. Ancestral energy is also tied to Native American energies, but the ancestral energy at Mount Fuji actually goes back 100,000 to 200,000 years, perhaps even earlier than when Native Americans came to the continent. So we are talking about going back into Lemurian and Atlantean times.

Activating this ancient energy is intended to help connect all of the crystals with the energy of ancient times. The ancient energies are also an explanation for cosmic energy because there are galactic councils and galactic beings of high wisdom who have been watching Earth for many, many centuries, so it isn't just recently that extraterrestrials have taken an interest in Earth. The connections and the holding of the ancient energies within Mount Fuji are sacred. This sacred, ancient energy is ready to be shared with all Earth. We have already talked about the fact that Native Americans and especially the Hopi have certain codes of ascension, keys in connection with Earth energies that need to be shared. Also, there are ancient energies in Mount Fuji. It is a beautiful mountain, a magnificent mountain, and right now you will find that there are many clouds. It gives the appearance of existing in another dimension, another realm.

People devote a portion of their lives to traveling to this mountain because it holds so much energy and so much sacredness for the Japanese people. This is a wonderful opportunity to share that sacred energy. I ask you now to get into a meditative state in which you can prepare your body and your spirit to separate. I am bringing down a cover of light over each of you. This cover of light is going to join and connect to a huge circle of light that is over the North Pole, and wherever you are, you begin to feel that in your spirit. Your spirit body can leave your physical body and go through a corridor that will lead you to a beautiful interdimensional space above the North Pole. We will join in this huge circle of light as we sit above Earth. [Tones.]

Feel your spirit ascend out of your physical body to join us in this huge circle over the North Pole. Sitting in this huge circle is an invigorating and spiritually activating experience. It is in great consciousness and great energy that you reach your full potential. This is not a contradiction, because on Earth there is a belief, especially in Western religions and Western culture, that you give up your individuality to join a group. But actually, in our conceptions, in our workings with groups, your individuality is actually enhanced, because you feel the wonderful support of the group. Those of you who have been in Groups of Forty meetings and conferences can attest to the great support you feel for your individual self.

TRAVEL TO THE CRYSTAL TEMPLE

We are sitting together in this beautiful circle of light above the North Pole. [Tones.] Now I have placed a corridor of light above the North Pole, and this corridor is connected to crystal lake and the crystal temple, and we will all travel together to crystal lake. [Tones.] As we are traveling through this corridor of light, know that your fifth-dimensional body is waiting for you at crystal lake. There are many people sitting around the lake, many Group of Forty members. Your fifth-dimensional body is there, and we are traveling through the corridor now. [Tones.] As we travel through the corridor, you again enjoy this feeling of being in a state of suspension, a state of no-time, and now we come to the beautiful crystal lake. We travel through the dome and find your body, your fifth-dimensional body, and begin to enter that body. [Tones.]

Begin to shimmer in your fifth-dimensional body as you feel the higher energies. You begin to understand the nature of fifth-dimensional energy and the nature of your fifth-dimensional powers. In the fifth dimension, you have telepathic powers that include teleportation. This is a wonderful ability for doing fifth-dimensional work. I, Juliano, begin to raise the crystal out of crystal lake. As the crystal begins to rise, you, with your powers of teleportation and telekinesis, can now raise the crystal. You can now raise the crystal with me, and as we raise this crystal, a galactic energetic light of ancient cosmic consciousness makes a link connecting you to the codes of ancient time that are locked into this crystal. You are now being elevated. Together we raise the crystal out of the water. [Tones.] As this crystal comes out of the water, I, Juliano, with the powers of fifth-dimensional spiritual technology given to us to assist Earth, am going to produce an exact duplicate of this crystal that will be right on top of this crystal. On the count of three, you can help me to visualize and remember, because on the fifth dimension, what you think is what is created. This is the fantastic power of the fifth dimension. This is a fantastic energy, but it is a guarded energy, because we cannot let just anyone come into the fifth dimension and think and then create, unless they are in a place of higher power, higher thoughts and pure light. One, two, three. A duplicate of the crystal is now exactly on top of this visional crystal. This is what I call an etheric double. [Tones.]

TELEPORTATION AND TELEKINESIS

Remember that you have the power of telekinesis and teleportation. Teleportation is the ability to move your body to other places and telekinesis is the ability to move objects to other places. In the fifth-dimensional energy, in the fifth-dimensional light, we can think and begin to move, so I want you to think. I am here with you, and I want you to imagine that this etheric double crystal is rising out of the etheric lake, the crystal lake. Go through the dome with me. Together we are carrying it; we are transporting it through the corridor, and together we transport it at the speed of thought. Remember that thought is faster than the speed of light. The speed of thought can bring this crystal back over to the North Pole.

We teleport our fifth-dimensional bodies to that point above the North Pole where we were originally sitting. We are sitting with this crystal approximately ten miles above the North Pole. Then enjoy this energy in meditation; let us sit in silence while we hold this energy of light. [Deep breathing.] This crystal is absorbing powers from Inner Earth. There is an opening at the North Pole to Inner Earth, and the ancient energies of Inner Earth are now coming into this crystal, this etheric crystal. We will teleport this crystal to Japan, to the area of Mount Fuji. On my command, at the speed of thought, we will teleport and use telekinesis to bring this crystal to Mount Fuji.

One, two, three . . . [Tones.] The crystal is now over Mount Fuji, way above the mountaintop, and some of you are perhaps connecting energetically with the other eighty people who are there. They are very excited. They are drumming. They are laughing. They are celebrating and they are doing exactly the same exercises that you have just done. They are following a very similar pattern, and the crystal is above them now. Since we are above them, with your powers of telekinesis and teleportation, we will cause and allow this crystal to descend into Mount Fuji. Slowly it descends to the top of the mountain. It is going to go into the mountain, deep into the mountain, for they are not at the top of the mountain. They are at a plateau away from the top. It is a sacred place, and this crystal and its crystal energy goes deep into the plateau, into the depths of Mount Fuji. We are helping this crystal to go down in now. [Tones.]

The crystal has descended into the mountain, and as the crystal descends, there is a great joy and great celebration among the people. As it goes into the mountain, it is like one of those pinball machines that lights up. It is beginning to connect with the other nine crystals, creating little pathways. These are like neurons forming; new ley lines are forming, connecting Mount Fuji to the other nine etheric crystals. It is connecting first with Montserrat and then going through all of the other crystals. [Tones.] The wisdom of the ancients: This is the ancient crystal, a crystal of ancient light and of the ancient ones who came to Earth many, many thousands of years ago with great secrets of light and energy. Now all of the crystals are connected to Mount Fuji, and you can feel a sense of joy. The Groups of Forty will be on the mountain for at least a few more hours. They are bathing in the light, really enjoying it.

Many people are crying because they feel an ancient soul connection with Mount Fuji, and soon we, the Groups of Forty, will be visiting Mount Fuji together, and many of you might decide to come with us. It will be a wonderful experience. We are laying the groundwork for Mount Fuji and this beautiful ancient etheric crystal. Remain above. Remain interactive with the Groups of Forty who are there now. They are following a similar path to the one you have set in your practice today. There are visions of light and angels; many higher beings are there.

RETURN TO YOUR THREE-DIMENSIONAL BODY

I ask you to begin to return to the North Pole, but before you leave, send a shimmering energy, a shimmering light down to this group, because this whole area is a little enclave of shimmering light (where they are on the plateau of the mountain). Now, teleport yourself back to the group area above the North Pole. We are all sitting together above the North Pole, and we are shimmering in great light and energy. Now we will teleport ourselves from the North Pole back to the crystal and the crystal lake, back to our fifth-dimensional bodies. We will teleport ourselves now. [Breathes.]

We are back in our fifth-dimensional bodies around crystal lake. The etheric double crystal has left, but the original crystal is above the water and I, Juliano, command that crystal to begin to sink back into the lake. The crystal slowly sinks back into the lake, but as it is sinking, it is still emitting powerful energetic rays of fifth-dimensional light that will be absorbed into your third-dimensional body when you return. Right now that light is going into your third eye, your fifth-dimensional third eye. The crystal slowly begins to sink back into the water. [Tones.]

The entire crystal has sunk back into the water. [Tones.] We will slowly begin to leave our fifth-dimensional body. It will stay here, the fifth-dimensional body, but in spirit you will rise above your fifth-dimensional body and follow me, Juliano, to this beautiful corridor, leaving crystal lake, coming through the corridor back into your Earth body. Follow the corridor, and as you follow the corridor, come back over your house, over your physical body. Go to a place approximately ten to twenty feet above your physical body but do not enter until I give you further instructions. [Tones.] You are now above your physical body, and I command that you go into a perfected alignment. Perfected alignment means that all of the energy, all of the light you have gathered in the fifth dimension, will be downloaded with you into your physical body as you enter it. Say, "I command that I go into my body in perfect alignment," and then feel your spirit body aligning. On my count, reenter. One, two, three: now. Reenter your physical body with the fifth-dimensional energy you brought with you, and know that through the process that we call spiritual osmosis, you will experience an osmotic, interactive fifth-dimensional light coming into your third-dimensional body. This will last approximately twenty-four hours—so slowly and deliberately is it coming into your body. [Tones.] You have participated in the downloading of the tenth crystal, and Chief White Eagle will speak to you now. I am Juliano. [Tones.]

CHIEF WHITE EAGLE SPEAKS OF COMMUNICATING WITH THE ANCIENTS

Greetings, I am Chief White Eagle. We are honored and very excited to work with this new crystal. It is providing to us a connection to the ancient ones, to the ancient grandfathers and grandmothers of our continent and to the ancient grandmothers and grandfathers of Japan. I have to tell you what an improvement it is in terms of our shamanistic ways to connect to the ancient spirits, because we feel that the ancient spirits are guardians. We feel that the ancient spirits are willing to communicate and share knowledge that is very difficult for one person or even several people to give in a lifetime. Now, through this downloading of the tenth crystal, we are going to gain greater energy and greater access to the ancient ones.

This will hold true for all peoples throughout the planet, not just the people on Mount Fuji. I tell you there is going to be a lessening of animosity now between native peoples and white peoples and all peoples, and there is going to be a willingness to use this new energy for working together, holding light together and sharing the Grandfather/Grandmother energy. This channel and those of you in the Groups of Forty will be at the forefront of working together with native peoples, and they will be very brotherly and sisterly to all, for it is time for us to understand the ancients. We understand that this is an ancient planet, and we understand that Mount Fuji is also a communicator and antenna for ancient civilizations throughout the galaxy. Knowledge of ancient civilizations that are extra-solar and extra-planetary will also now be available. Is it not fascinating to learn that other planets have gone through similar energies as what is happening on Earth? Some of them have been successful in resolving the same issues Earth is now facing. Some of them have not. Is it not interesting, and isn't it important to learn why those planets who were successful, were successful? Isn't it interesting to know that some were not successful?

Because it is true that some planets like Earth were in the same situation and failed, but Earth has a great opportunity now—with the downloading of these crystals and the connections of all the lightworkers in the Groups of Forty and many others—to provide an etheric, energetic link that will activate biorelativity healing for the planet and will also connect to ancient light, ancient energy and ancient knowledge. Much of this ancient light and ancient knowledge is going to come from the activating energy of the Central Sun. So the people on Earth are going to gain a greater appreciation of the Grandfathers and Grandmothers. As one person wrote [to the channel]: "Isn't it about time to learn how the future can affect the past?" She beautifully wrote that what one person thought was important in WWII involved killing and feeling hatred and defeating the enemy. Looking back fifty years later, that same person looks back with compassion, understanding and light, and all of the animosity is gone.

This is a true understanding of the ancient ways. It is the true understanding of the Grandfather/Grandmother energy because the Grandfathers and Grandmothers know that wars do not serve the greater good. Having this enlightened view and being able to share this enlightened view with all the peoples on the planet will certainly be a wonderful healing. We of Native American peoples on the North American continent are happy and willing to share and visit Mount Fuji in spirit, and the spirits there are accepting the energy of the Native American peoples. They will accept aboriginal peoples, and they will accept the native peoples of different nations in different parts of the planet, as all are going to be uniting in the Sacred Triangle. I am Chief White Eagle. All of my words are sacred. *Ho!*

MOUNT FUJI AND INNER EARTH

Juliano, the Arcturians and Adama

Greetings, I am Juliano. We are the Arcturians. The idea of opening up Mount Fuji and the Inner Earth there is actually related to the energies of the twelfth crystal. The downloading of the twelve etheric crystals will be completed in November 2009 at Serra da Bocaina National Park in the rain forest of Brazil. With the completion of that work, there comes a new holographic Earth energy. We are calling this new energy a dialectic energy field.

A dialectic energy field, according to our definition in Arcturian spiritual technology, is an energy field that is created through interactions of sacred patterns that are similar to what we have seen and what you have seen in the tree of life in ancient mystical Kaballah. This is a sacred energy pattern. This is a galactic energy pattern that creates an energy field that transcends what individual corridors are equal to alone. In fact, what they do is create this dialectic energy field that transcends and is greater than the whole. You have heard this in your teachings on other spiritual matters that the whole is greater than the sum of the parts. Take each individual part and add them up. The sum and power of the sum becomes greater than everything added up individually. It is a coming together of all of this energy that creates the dialectic force.

MOUNT FUJI AND THE DIALECTIC ENERGY FIELD

How does this dialectic force relate to Mount Fuji? First, we want to explain the effect of the downloading of the twelfth etheric crystal. A dialectic energy field from the twelve crystals will be created after the twelfth crystal has been downloaded. This will result in helping Earth come into a powerful new alignment with the stargate. This means that there will be available a large energy downloading and a huge stargate alignment. This does have an effect on Mount Fuji because Mount Fuji does have a key role. Mount Fuji holds one of the etheric crystals. That means that you now have the ability to unlock the codes of the Inner Earth in Mount Fuji with the downloading of this twelfth crystal and the dialectic energy force field that will be interactively created.

What can I tell you about this Inner Earth in Mount Fuji? First, it is very well protected. It is extremely guarded and there are many ceremonies, many rituals, that would be necessary to enter—if those holding the etheric energy would allow people to enter. Now with the coming of the alignment with the stargate and with the coming of the dialectic energy field of the twelve etheric crystals, there comes a new force field of light. This new light becomes a force field of spiritual power that can unlock the entrance way to the inner cities in the Inner Earth in Mount Fuji. Second, the ancient ones have been waiting for this time and for this energy. There are many ancient ones in the inner cities of Earth who want and need to interact with the Earth. They want to interact with Earth because they have so much to give to it. Therefore your understanding and your willingness to work with their energy means, in a sense, that you have received their call. You have received and are attuned to their energy, and also you are tuned to the need to bring forth the energies of the ancient guides and teachers from the Inner Earth at Mount Fuji. The Inner Earth in Mount Fuji, like that of Mount Shasta, is a real, ancient Inner Earth that is awaiting the energy of the stars and the starseeds. It is awaiting the energy of the dialectic force field of the Arcturian tree of life that is being activated on Earth.

The doorway and the interdimensional corridor on Mount Fuji is an ancient corridor. The ancient ones want to come out of their inner cities and share with you their light, ideas, powers and healing abilities. They have great knowledge of Earth healings. They have great knowledge of how to work with the biosphere. They have great knowledge about how to work with Earth patterns and Earth energies, especially now when it seems that Earth's energies are getting out of control. They will force a new unity on the planet. These shifts demonstrate polarizations, because humankind now lacks the ability to deal with the blocks in the Earth's meridians. The Inner Earth civilization, especially in Mount Fuji, has great ancient power and great ancient knowledge of Earth's meridians and workings.

THE BEGINNINGS OF INNER EARTH

The greatest power for accessing biorelativity and for accessing the core correlation of the energy field of Earth with the Central Sun lies in the Inner Earth. What you will find when you go to Mount Fuji is that you will be receiving ancient spirits as they come out of their corridors. They are still protective, and being protective, they will not initially invite you into their realm. There is a special protective place for the Inner Earth spirits in the Mount Fuji area that is away from the general public and away from the tourists. You might have to do a little hiking to get to that higher realm, which the spirits know as the Land of Mu. They are really interdimensional galactic beings. I want to emphasize that. People think of the Inner Earth as containing beings who are just concerned with the Inner Earth worlds. Inner Earth beings, especially the ones in Mount Fuji and in Mount Shasta, are higher intergalactic beings. They are relating interdimensionally to the core of Earth and other planetary central cores. The Inner Earth beings at Mount Fuji are called the People of Mu. Their leader is Yoko. That is the name that he will use when he is coming to you.

Adama is the great teacher in the Inner Earth at Mount Shasta. Adama also visits the Land of Mu. You should understand that Adama is in communication with this Land of Mu in the Mount Fuji area. These Inner Earth civilizations are interactive with each other.

China also has several great Inner Earth centers. Just like the Inner Earth beings in Mount Fuji, the Chinese Inner Earth beings have great anxieties that their entry centers are going to be breached, and they are even more protective. There are going to be openings in the Chinese areas as well. The access to those areas has been guarded by the Taoist priests. These priests have studied with the galactic masters from the Inner Earth. Many of the famous movements that you may have seen on television, the kung fu, tai chi and qi gong practices, came from these Inner Earth galactic masters in China. These practices were brought interdimensionally because these exercises and these types of movements are etheric movements. They activate etheric energy that transcends the third dimension. Even though you are doing them on the third dimension, the energies connect the movements with the fifth-dimensional energy fields.

I also want to say that there are female Inner Earth masters in Mount Fuji, not just males. I mentioned Yoko, the male leader in the Inner Earth at Mount Fuji. There is also a beautiful female master known as Athena in the Land of Mu. She is of Arcturian origin and she has great Arcturian connections—our Arcturian starship is also named Athena. Athena is a powerful woman teacher and guide, and she has much to teach. She represents a feminine power of rulership. New Earth energies are necessary for bringing the biosphere into alignment, and new spiritual technology is necessary to bring the feedback loops into alignment and to create a stable and consistent biosphere. These energies and alignments must be introduced and must be presented through the female light, which Athena holds. She has taken the name Athena because it represents her connection to the Arcturian starseeds.

A UNITY OF CONSCIOUSNESS

The inner cities of light in Mount Shasta and now in Mount Fuji will open their doors to the dialectic energy field being created by the downloading of the twelfth etheric crystal. This is going to send an electric charge through Earth and through the Inner Earth so that there will be a unity of consciousness between the Inner Earth, the Earth itself, the fifth-dimensional Earth and the Central Sun.

This is the time that the Inner Earth people must be welcomed. This is the time where their knowledge and their technology should be welcomed, because they understand Earth in ways that you are also beginning to understand. They have the spiritual technologies that are going to be received now on Earth. People on Earth will finally be receptive to understanding that the inner and the outer must come into a unison.

May the light and blessings of the Land of Mu, Mount Fuji and the Inner Earth fill your energy field with light. These areas are already telepathically connecting. The Inner Earth beings are happy to share telepathically, especially the powerful women from the Inner Earth of Mount Fuji such as Athena. She actually goes by "Atena," instead of Athena. In the Inner Earth, they don't pronounce the "h." Atena would be the correct pronunciation, and it is another sound you can use. [Tones]: *AAAATEEEN-Naaaa.*

What is the biggest gift of the Inner Earth now? It is reinforcing the power of the female presence as the masters—the rulers—of Earth. Earth is a female spirit—Mother Earth. So it takes another female spirit like Athena to understand. We will be working with all the starseeds as we move into this heightened transitional time. This is Juliano. Good day!

Greetings. I am Adama, holder of the light of the Inner Earth at the portal of Mount Shasta. I am known to many people throughout this planet, and I am very close to the portal and the etheric crystal now at Mount Shasta. We who inhabit the Inner Earth realize that we are living in a beautiful interdimensional realm. We understand the connections between the interdimensional realms with the third dimension. It is comparable to when you think of your dream world, which is fourth dimensional, and you think you have an existence in the dream world. That fourth-dimensional dream world is based on the third-dimensional world that you are living in. That means that the buildings, the sky, the people, the plants and especially the animals that are on the third dimension are also appearing on the fourth dimension in the dream world. The dream world is connected to your reality.

THE ENERGY OF THE GARDEN OF EDEN

The interdimensional Inner Earth is like the Shangri-la of the planet. The planet Earth once had the Garden of Eden—a beautiful, fifth-dimensional planetary city of light that was described metaphorically as the Garden of Eden. In this garden there was fifth-dimensional light continually. There were many who lived in the garden, not just Adam and Eve. There were many people.

My name Adama comes from the core name of Adam who was living in the Garden of Eden. Because of duality and polarization and also because of interference from other beings, the energy of the Garden of Eden was removed from the surface of Earth. You have to understand that energy was not removed from Earth, but rather it was removed from the surface of Earth. That energy of the Garden of Eden is still being held in the Inner Earth at Mount Fuji and in the Inner Earth at Mount Shasta. That energy from the Garden of Eden is now in the inner world. Inner Earth has evolved tremendously. If you read about the Garden of Eden, you might think of a very primitive place—beautiful, but primitive. Can you imagine the evolution that has occurred in the Inner Earth? The Garden of Eden has gone into high spiritual and scientific technology. We have had higher beings from all the great civilizations come to Inner Earth. In Mount Fuji there have been many ancient masters that spiritually have descended into our beautiful city.

I have visited the inner city of Mu, in the Land of Mu in Mount Fuji. It is a beautiful city. It is a city that has huge communications with galactic cities throughout the universe. The planetary cities of light are also beginning to communicate to the sister cities in the galaxy. The inner cities and the planetary inner cities like Mount Fuji are already in communication with other similar inner cities throughout our galaxy. You see, there is a large connection between the stargate and Mount Fuji in the inner cities. These inner cities are receiving the higher technical knowledge that becomes available when one can communicate throughout the galaxy.

Truly, in working with the beings in Mount Fuji, you will find a great love for Earth. You will find that these people—Athena, Yoko and others—are true planetary healers. They have a true desire and love for the Earth, and a true desire to share their healing light and healing knowledge with you. I am Adama. Blessings!

ISTANBUL: SACRED HAVEN OF THE ELEVENTH CRYSTAL

Juliano, the Arcturians and Chief White Eagle

reetings, I am Juliano. We are the Arcturians. We are gathered
here in Istanbul to provide the ceremony for the downloading of
the eleventh crystal. This crystal has special meaning. Numerically, it is number 11, which is considered a lucky number in numerology.
Just like 7 is a special number, 11 is also considered a powerful number. I
would have to say that this crystal provides an energy that makes the other
ten crystals work most effectively.

Crystals can be described in terms of electromagnetic energy and grids.
Electromagnetic energy grids work best when all the crystals on the grid
are connected to each other. When all of the crystal energy is connected,
then the power from all of the crystals becomes more effective. We are
choosing a place for the eleventh crystal that has great clarity. We are
choosing a place that has a great ability to make connections with other
energetic points. The ability to make connections is a high power. If you
remember, we began our lectures many years ago discussing the Arcturians
through the concept called "connecting with the Arcturians."

Your power and energy is multiplied and increased when you are able to
connect to the fifth dimension and to fifth-dimensional beings. This crystal is
going to help the world connect to fifth-dimensional wisdom and fifth-dimensional knowledge.

AN INTERSECTION OF THE DIMENSIONS

The hidden knowledge that we are talking about, which this crystal represents, is the knowledge of the fifth dimension. The knowledge that the fifth
dimension exists will be revealed to this planet soon. When the knowledge
of the higher dimensions becomes known more generally, then the planet can

quickly make major changes. When people understand more about the fifth dimension, then they will understand that there is a need to connect to it. There is a need to accelerate everyone's energy so that all who want to can enter the fifth dimension. Most important, everyone who is working to solve Earth's problems will be happy to understand that there is this connection. They can use this connection to bring newer light, newer knowledge and newer wisdom to the problems that are facing humanity and the world.

Think about what it means to you personally to know that there is another dimension. I want each of you to understand what a revolutionary concept and what revolutionary information it is to know in your heart, with complete faith and with complete wisdom, that another dimension of a higher vibration exists and that it is going to connect to the third dimension. We can describe this connection symbolically. We have described it by using the concept of two large spheres. Each sphere represents a dimension. The fifth dimension as a sphere will touch the third dimension as a sphere. This touching we call an intersection of the dimensions, which will create a powerful experience because the light and energy of the fifth dimension will immediately be downloaded into the third dimension. When two dimensions intersect, the energy from the higher dimension will flow into the lower dimension. This is the universal law known as "spiritual osmosis." Higher light will go into lower light and will slowly fill that sphere.

There has never been an intersection of the dimensions on Earth. In the past, individual spiritual leaders and spiritual people have sought to create a connection to the fifth dimension, and they tried to explain and provide examples of the way to connect to the dimension. Now there is going to be a sustained energetic connection and intersection. This intersection is like plugging a wire into a wall—then you turn on a light and the light stays on.

At this point in the history of the fifth dimension intersecting the third dimension, we, the Arcturians, are creating a special corridor that allows the sphere of the fifth dimension to be permanently connected to the third dimension here at this crystal area, at this point in Istanbul. You who are here right now will feel the tremendous linkage this corridor provides between the fifth and the third dimensions.

CONNECTING THE DIMENSIONS THROUGH YOUR SPIRITUAL POWER

You are here at a time that can be described as a moment in eternity, a moment in eternal light. The linkage of the corridors from the fifth dimension and the third dimension are becoming more solid. Now you who have come here today are assisting us in bringing down the eleventh crystal. We have some work to do with you. I thank you for coming here to provide the human power to download this crystal. I want to emphasize the word "power." Spiritual power is required to help perform this energy work. You who have come here today are showing great spiritual power to be here at this moment with this light, with this beauty and in this great energy crossroad. You are here to help connect the fifth dimension with the third dimension. What could be a greater service to humanity at this time then to provide the means of connecting the fifth dimension to the third dimension?

You are now sitting in a circle. Feel the circle and the energy of the circle. Now the circle begins to move: It goes around and around, and you are moving in the circle. As you are moving around in the circle, your spirit feels light and it is able to leave your body. I, Juliano, have provided a beautiful corridor right above your group. As your spirit leaves your body, join me in this corridor. I will wait until everyone has been able to leave their body. If you have difficulty leaving your body, then please just visualize to the best of your ability what we are doing.

We begin to follow the corridor. Going up the corridor, we travel at the speed of thought. As we travel with the speed of thought, we go through this corridor and we travel to the Arcturian crystal lake on the fifth dimension. We arrive to the outer area of the crystal lake in Arcturus in the fifth dimension. As we arrive, we look down around the lake and we see that for each person from the group, there is a fifth-dimensional body waiting for you. Please enter your fifth-dimensional body now.

We are now in the crystal lake, and each of you is in your fifth-dimensional body. I, Juliano, call on the crystal in the crystal lake to begin to rise. Slowly it rises. As it rises, you feel the intense light of the fifth-dimensional crystal. It now rises totally out of the water.

Transporting the Etheric Crystal

The crystal is now out of the water. Now, with the powers that I have, I am going to create a perfect etheric duplicate of the crystal. On the count of three, you will see and experience two crystals instead of one. One, two, three! There is now a duplicate crystal. I, Juliano, am using the light and energy of the original crystal to charge the new duplicate crystal with all the light and energy that is necessary for it to have. The second, duplicate crystal is being filled up with great spiritual light and energy. It is now ready to be teleported back to Istanbul. Each of you can now use your power of thought projection to help me transport this crystal back to Istanbul. I want you, with my assistance, to visualize the raising of the crystal from the crystal lake. We are going to transport the duplicate crystal back to Istanbul. The original crystal will stay above the water at the crystal temple during the transportation.

You will now also practice multipresence. You have a presence in the third dimension and you now have a presence in the fifth dimension. Now your presence is needed in the third dimension and in the fifth dimension. You have the power to do this with my instructions and help.

Together, our thoughts now transport this duplicate crystal. We transport it out of the crystal lake. On the fifth dimension, we do not need to pick things up; we move things with our minds. We can now transport this crystal with our minds out of the crystal lake through the corridor. We now travel through the corridor with this crystal, and using our minds, we transport it at the speed of thought. Now we arrive in Istanbul with the duplicate crystal. A huge light comes over the whole city now as the crystal is coming into alignment with the Bosporus Strait. It is coming into the area at this special historical place you have chosen called *Anadolu Hisari*—the Anatolian castle. The crystal is in alignment in the fifth dimension and the third dimension. Huge light connections are already beginning to form.

RETURN WITH YOUR FIFTH-DIMENSIONAL ENERGY

Here is the explanation of the exercise you need to do. You return to the crystal lake. We will leave this crystal over the Bosporus Strait that we brought down from the fifth dimension. We will return to Istanbul to do the actual downloading back on the third dimension, so return to your fifth-dimensional body on the crystal lake. This beautiful eleventh crystal is now in alignment from the fifth dimension with the third-dimensional Bosporus. Follow me and return to your fifth-dimensional body on the crystal lake in the crystal temple.

The crystal lake is filled with light and you have now returned to your fifth-dimensional body. The original crystal is still above the water. It will stay above the water until the crystal over Istanbul is downloaded. Feel the energy of being in the fifth dimension. Feel the energy of being on the crystal lake with the crystal above the water. You are going to shimmer your body back into the third dimension so that when you come back into your physical body, you will have the fullest possible fifth-dimensional light that you can bring in. Shimmer your fifth-dimensional body now.

Reappear into your third-dimensional body in Istanbul. Beautiful! Hold that light in your third-dimensional body. You will need all that energy to do the exercise. Now, repeat: Return to the fifth-dimensional body on the crystal lake. Now prepare yourself to return to the third dimension. Your spirit leaves your fifth-dimensional body. You know that you can return to it at any time. Your spirit leaves your fifth-dimensional body and the crystal lake. You follow the corridor and travel at the speed of thought back into your third-dimensional body.

You travel and come above your body back in Istanbul. You see a huge light over your body because this new etheric crystal is exactly over where you are sitting. Look for your physical body; find a perfect alignment and reenter your physical body now. You have reentered your third-dimensional body. The circle has stopped going around, and we are ready to download the crystal into the third dimension.

DOWNLOADING THE CRYSTAL TO REVEAL HIDDEN KNOWLEDGE

Project and send your thoughts up to where this crystal is, directly over the Bosporus and directly over Anadolu Hisari, and command the crystal to come down and enter the third dimension. You are the anchors. The beautiful eleventh crystal is now coming into the third dimension over the Bosporus Strait.

Huge light, love and connections to the fifth dimension all are in this crystal. Now we bring the crystal itself down into the third dimension with your help. We bring the crystal right to this location into Bosporus. The crystal is now entering Bosporus and is going right to the bottom. Huge energy comes down with the crystal. Now it is connecting to the other ten crystals that have already been downloaded around the world. We are connecting with all of the other Groups of Forty members around the world now who are with us in thoughts. Hold this connection and we will meditate together in silence for five minutes to anchor this light. Begin the meditation. [Pause.]

The crystal has been successfully downloaded! The hidden knowledge of the existence of the fifth dimension will now be more widely known to humanity. It will become known to everyone that the fifth-dimensional energy can be brought down into the third dimension. It is time for this hidden knowledge to be revealed to all seekers of the truth. It is time for spiritual light to connect to all aspects of the third-dimensional reality. This crystal here in Istanbul will provide great light to Turkey. Turkey has great pride in its ability to be a leader. Turkey has already been a leader of spiritual light in the world. Turkey will now again show itself to be a leader of spiritual light to this part of the world. This spiritual light will spread throughout the Middle East and the Far East, to many different countries. More spiritual people will be attracted to studying and experiencing this spiritual light that is coming out of this etheric crystal that you have helped today to download into the Bosporus. I am Juliano, and we are the Arcturians.

reetings, I am Chief White Eagle. [Tones.] *Hey ya ho ya hey!* The Native spirit masters are so happy when a new sacred place is identified on Earth. Earth has many corridors and many sacred places. Now, this place in Istanbul is an area where much spiritual light can enter. It is also a place where spiritual light can work with third-dimensional light and also work with third-dimensional spirits that are stuck and need to be released. We feel the energy of this crystal. Our fifth-dimensional workers are drumming in joy! Feel this energy now. This is an energy that you have been helping to bring down. You have become a sacred person because you are participating in the downloading of sacred energy and of higher energy.

O Great White Father and Great Mother, I, Chief White Eagle, am here today with gratitude so that you can bring and protect this great area of Istanbul and Bosporus. Let this place represent peace and love, light and brotherhood. Let this place represent and help people to connect to the fifth dimension. This area has many lightworkers, Great Mother/ Father, Protector of All. These lightworkers are being shown the way to teach and to connect their country along with other countries and other lightworkers to the fifth dimension.

Today we ask for a blessing for this area. We ask for a blessing over the Bosporus Strait and a blessing to all here who have participated in this wonderful ceremony. Let each one who has participated in this ceremony today experience the light for his or her own personal life. Let their personal lives be blessed, O Father/Mother, for they are working to promote light for the planet. Today we ask for your gratitude, your blessing in the name of your love and your light, O Father/ Mother, Creator of All. Thank you.

The Native American fifth-dimensional masters, including myself, Chief White Eagle, will be here now in Bosporus. You have helped to place a corridor that will allow the Native American masters to be here. I know that we are accepted by the Turkish people for they love us and our spirits. We are all brothers and sisters! I am Chief White Eagle. *Ho!*

TWELFTH CRYSTAL AT THE
BRAZILIAN GALACTIC TEPEE

Chief White Eagle, Tomar, Archangel Metatron,
Sananda and Spirit Fire

G reetings, I am Chief White Eagle. The native North American
spirits are honored that you have built this tepee in Brazil. This
is a true galactic tepee. It is the first beautiful galactic tepee for
Brazil. You are now connecting with the greater star family here. You are
also connecting with the Native American spirits and guides. With your
permission, I, Chief White Eagle, will become the guardian of this tepee,
and I will make sure that this tepee is a spiritual medicine tepee for healing
and expansion of spirit.

You are here today to experience this special energy. It is special for two reasons. The first reason is that we are doing the first meeting in this tepee. You
are opening up the portal for the light and the work this tepee is going to do.
This tepee is being united with the Arcturian Temple and also with the tepee in
Arizona. This tepee here in Brazil is now tied to Arizona and the first Arcturian star family tepee. You know that we native spirits are always working for
the gathering of your personal power. You are gathering now for yourselves
great personal power because you are here participating in this ceremony.

The second reason, the second great energy in this tepee today is that
we are gathered here to download the twelfth etheric crystal. This is a
double gain in personal power for you. You are going to be expanding
your psychic gifts, and you will be able to enhance and improve the energy
of your life after you leave this ceremony. You will be able to gather the
energy that you want and need to make your life more fifth dimensional.

BLESSING THE GALACTIC TEPEE
I ask now that you become aware of your thoughts and what you focus

on. This tepee is a wonderful power spot. It is a power generator. What you think, what you focus on now will gain in energy; it will be enhanced by your being in this powerful area. To continue the ceremony, I, Chief White Eagle, am going to say a special prayer to bless this tepee and prepare for the downloading of the crystal. [Tones.] *Hey ya hoooo ah.* All my words are sacred. To the Father/Mother, Creator of Light: I, Chief White Eagle, ascended master from the fifth dimension and guardian of this beautiful tepee, ask that you bless this tepee today. I ask that you bless everyone participating in this ceremony. These are beautiful starseeds, beautiful, enlightened beings of Father/Mother. They have made great efforts to come here to serve the light. They have made great efforts to serve Mother Earth. Please bless and protect them in their comings and goings. Father/Mother, protector of light, we ask a special blessing for the keeper of this tepee, the creator and builder of this tepee. We also ask that you help all of us enhance our personal light.

We feel today a special bond with everyone here because we are truly brothers and sisters. We feel a bond with all of the Arcturian Groups of Forty members who are today around the world meditating with us. Together we will sing: *Hey ya hooooh.* Open up your hearts to the energy. Try and vibrate your voice on the last syllable, and you will be able to feel fifth-dimensional light and energy coming in. Try to shake your hands as you sing the last syllable. Let the energy now fill your aura. Father/Mother, protector of all, help each of us here to open our energy field to the fifth-dimensional light for these starseeds, these star family members who are planetary healers. We are all brothers and sisters. I am Chief White Eagle.

Greetings, I am Tomar. We are the Arcturians. It was an honor to be involved in the first downloading of the etheric crystal, and it is an honor to be involved in the twelfth and final downloading. By bringing down the last etheric crystal, we are able to help you connect to all of the energies of these wonderful crystal light sources. Our mission as Arcturians focuses on helping you connect and download fifth-dimensional light to Earth. You and I together have chosen this place here at Serra da Bocaina because it is already fifth dimensional. Now we are going to increase the fifth-dimensional light at Serra da Bocaina so that the light from this crystal can radiate fifth-dimensional energy through all of Brazil. There is already a beautiful blue fifth-dimensional light emanating from this tepee. We talk so much to you about the new spiritual technologies of the fifth dimension. One of the greatest technologies is the use of luminosity. Luminosity is your ability to radiate light. In the fifth dimension, you can radiate light through your mind. You can also radiate light from this tepee through all of Brazil, through all of the etheric crystals and to the whole world. We will spend one minute in meditation, and I want everyone to focus on sending luminous light outward. Begin to radiate light from this tepee. The light emanating from this tepee is so intense. I, Tomar, am downloading light to the tepee, and you are emanating it outward as fast as you can. I want you to know that many people throughout the world will be visiting this tepee. The call is going out for the energies to come and be focused here.

I, Tomar, am preparing this whole area where the tepee is so that it can receive the downloading of the twelfth crystal. This twelfth etheric crystal is going to be downloaded into this valley where you are. The center of the crystal will come right through the center of this tepee. You are going to have the wonderful advantage of being right in the center of an etheric crystal from the Arcturians. Each of you has asked the question, "What is my mission?" One of your greatest missions is to help connect the fifth-dimensional light to Earth. I am expanding the energy field of the tepee so this whole area can now receive this etheric crystal. This area is clean and purified. You probably already feel like you can ascend. I want you to bathe in this light, bathe in this feeling.

We have work to do today. If you remember, we were able to make an etheric duplicate for the twelfth crystal. We brought that twelfth crystal over São Paulo. That crystal is now waiting for us. It has also spread beautiful light over São Paulo. I know that the fifth-dimensional spirits around São Paulo have enjoyed the honor of having an etheric crystal over their city. Now we are going to go to São Paulo in the etheric realm and bring that etheric crystal over the tepee. I will lead you in an exercise and we will go there together. I, Tomar, am coming down a corridor of light that I have just built, a corridor that goes into the center of the tepee. I am with you above the tepee. You are sitting in a circle around the center of the tepee. The tepee feels like it is going around in a circle, and you are going around in a circle. As you go around in a circle, feel your etheric body very gently rise out of your physical body. Then feel your spirit—it is out of your body. It was so easy, wasn't it? Follow me up the corridor I have created.

We together travel above São Paulo at the speed of thought. We see this beautiful twelfth etheric crystal over the city. It has gotten brighter; it is more luminous than when we put it there. It is already connecting with the other etheric crystals. We make a big circle around the etheric crystal. Together we begin to carry it away in the etheric. We begin the journey from São Paulo to Serra da Bocaina. We are almost there. We are approximately three miles above Serra da Bocaina—we are here with the crystal, hovering three miles above. You and I together are aligning the crystal so that its center is in alignment with the center of this tepee. It takes a few seconds to align it properly. It is now in alignment. I, Tomar, align this etheric crystal to the Arcturian stargate. This tepee now has the most perfect alignment with the Arcturian stargate of anywhere on Earth. Together we download this etheric crystal.

Slowly we bring the crystal down from three miles up (it would be approximately five kilometers above us). Then we descend to four kilometers, three kilometers, two kilometers. Already the light is so intense! One kilometer. Now we will place the crystal right above Earth. The center of the crystal and the center of the tepee are in perfect alignment. Now we bring the crystal into the ground, into the earth. It goes right into the earth, deep into the earth. It immediately connects with the other eleven etheric crystals, especially with the crystal at Lago Puelo, because now the first and the last are united.

The crystal is totally downloaded into the center of this area with the tepee at the center of this crystal. There is a beautiful vibrating fifth-dimensional wave of energy coming up out of the earth. This tepee is now also in special alignment with the Arcturian Temple. The crystals that you call the portable Arcturian Temple are vibrating at such a high frequency.

Receive light and energy from all the Groups of Forty members around the world. The light in this twelfth etheric crystal is now connected to the Anadolu Istanbul crystal. It is connected with the crystals in Mount Fuji, Bodensee, Lake Moraine, Grosse Valley in Australia; it is connected to the crystals in Lake Taupo in New Zealand, Mount Shasta in California and Monserrat in Spain. It is also connected to the crystals in Copper Canyon in Chihuahua, Mexico and Vulcan Poáz in Costa Rica. They are all lighting up. They are all sharing the energy with you here.

I, Tomar, am at the stargate now. You feel a little wind come into the tepee, as I have opened the door of the stargate just a little bit so that you can receive light from the Arcturian stargate. This light from the stargate transcends incarnations. It is light that helps you to graduate from Earth at a higher speed. It is light that helps you to accelerate your progress here on Earth. It is light that helps you to raise your spiritual light quotient. I, Tomar, turn the next part of the lecture over to Archangel Metatron, keeper of the stargate. I am Tomar.

ARCHANGEL METATRON ACTIVATES THE PORTAL AND THE ISKALIA MIRROR

Shalom. I am Archangel Metatron. Let the light, the holy light, the sacred light of this stargate form a special portal with this tepee so that light from the stargate will be a light of ascension. It will be a light of acceleration. It will be a light of transcendence. *Kadosh, Kadosh, Kadosh, Adonai, Tzevaoth.* I, Metatron, bring stargate light to the tepee and help you to radiate it to all of the planetary cities of light. These cities of light are going to be fifth-dimensional portals of light.

What does it mean to have a crystal that is helping you to align with the stargate? It means that people will have portals to help them connect to their infinite souls, their infinite lights. It means they will have a way to connect to their transcendent multidimensional self. They will have access to their future lives, their future incarnations in the fifth dimension. One of your goals is to become more multidimensional. Sitting in this light, you will be able to feel and experience your multidimensional self on other planets.

I will open the door to the stargate just a little more so that you can receive more of this beautiful light. A beautiful portal to the stargate is now created over this tepee. Many cherubim line the portal. Holy light! You will be able to choose many planets and decide where you want to be in your next incarnation in the fifth dimension. Also, this stargate energy will help you be able to become better planetary healers.

I want to connect the energy of this tepee with the energy of the ring of ascension. The ring of ascension is a halo of light that interacts with the third dimension and the fifth dimension together. The purpose of this twelfth etheric crystal is to accelerate the manifestation of the fifth dimension in the third dimension. At this point we also activate the Iskalia mirror. This is an etheric mirror over the North Pole. This mirror is able to align itself with the Central Sun and bring down Central Sun light into Earth, especially into this tepee. At this time we pray for peace and harmony on the planet. I am Archangel Metatron. I now turn you over to Sananda.

Greetings, I am Sananda. Please understand that this work is sacred, and you are helping to integrate the light of the Sacred Triangle. It is so important that the Sacred Triangle include the energies of the galactic masters and teachers and that it also contains the energy of Native Americans and other native peoples of the planet. Know also that we, the fifth-dimensional ascended masters—including myself, Mother Mary, Kuthumi, Quan Yin, Archangel Michael and many, many others—are united in increasing the availability of the expansion of light from this tepee.

Many, many years ago there was a desire to spread light to Brazil. Now you are here fulfilling a promise you made to yourselves many lifetimes ago: that you would help to spread this type of light to this country. Maybe in those lifetimes you did not understand the fifth dimension. Now, in this lifetime, you have expanded knowledge and so many more spiritual abilities than you did in your other lifetimes. Also, all of these lifetimes are really connected. This is the fulfillment of a promise you made to yourselves to be here today, to be able to participate in this light expansion. You are helping to make the ascension more of a reality every day.

At the same time, the more you are able to hold fifth-dimensional energy and light, the more valuable you become as an inhabitant of Earth. This is a paradox to you. It is also why we value you so much and why we value you being here so much. I am now standing above this tepee and my hands are outspread, sending golden light into your energy field. I am sending you the light of grace to help you accelerate any life lessons you want to resolve and move through. We are a family of Earth brothers and sisters, and we are a part of the star family. We are part of the galactic family, and we are part of the family of our home, the Central Sun. Blessings, my dear brothers and sisters. I am Sananda.

Greetings, dear ones. I am Spirit Fire. I am the keeper of the tepee in Arizona. Chief White Eagle asked me to come to do the closing speech for this ceremony. I am here to remind you again of the Shekinah, the feminine divine light. I am here to remind you that Buffalo Calf Woman, keeper of the native feminine light, is also here today at this ceremony. Many of you might not be knowledgeable about Buffalo Calf Woman, but she is a very powerful ascended master, and it is the highest honor to have her here at this time. The coming of her time is often marked by the appearance of the white buffalo. That is a sign of ascension and of the fifth dimension being open to humans. Please make a space for White Buffalo Woman here at this tepee. Many tepees in North America would love to honor the appearance of White Buffalo Calf Woman. Because of your high light and high energy here in Brazil, you have been able to attract her light and energy to you here in this tepee, and the divine feminine light she brings with her.

This tepee has now been blessed and the ceremony is coming to an end. Please remember that people from all over the planet are going to come here now. You have activated it very well. You have done a great job. Remember, this tepee shall only be used for healing and medicine work. The vibrations of this tepee are very high. It is the only tepee on the planet that is in the center of an Arcturian fifth-dimensional crystal. I will be helping to oversee this tepee and keep in the highest light. There will be great feminine light in both the third and fifth dimensions working here. All twelve etheric crystals are now connected, and a greater connection is now made to all three sides of the Sacred Triangle. It is a good day to be alive. It is a good day to be in Brazil. It is a good day to be in Serra da Bocaina. Blessings. I am Spirit Fire. *Ho!*

THE TWELFTH CRYSTAL AND THE PROCESS OF EVOLUTION

Juliano and Archangel Metatron

G reetings, starseeds. I am Juliano. We are the Arcturians. The downloading of the twelfth etheric crystal has completed a special energetic grid that is representative of the Tree of Life. The Tree of Life is a symbolic glyph or blueprint that was given to Moses on Mount Sinai. It was passed through many generations of mystics and many prophets. The goal of this blueprint is to provide a path for ascension. In actuality, the Tree of Life diagram is developing and has been presented to humans to provide an explanation for how the universe works. It also provides an explanation for how soul evolution works and the path each soul must take in order to evolve.

All souls are in a process of evolution. Evolution is to the soul what breath is to the body. This means that your soul thrives on evolution. Your soul thrives on expansion. Also, your soul needs expansion. We, the Arcturians, have made a galactic addendum to the Tree of Life. This addendum is actually an acknowledgement of the galactic process you as a starseed are experiencing. Also, for the first time, this galactic process is being superimposed on a planet, namely Mother Earth. The superimposition of the Tree of Life within the planetary meridian grid of Earth has provided a new energetic and holographic connection to galactic evolution. I think we will all agree that nothing could be better; nothing could be more appropriate now for Earth than to participate in the planetary process of galactic evolution and galactic participation.

I want to elaborate on this because downloading the twelfth etheric crystal has created a holographic link for Earth. A holographic link allows Earth to receive and transmit energy to higher galactic sources. These galactic sources include the Central Sun and the Arcturian stargate. They also include other high-energy sources, high-energy planets, high-energy suns and even high-energy galaxies. You know there are other evolving galaxies. There are other planetary systems in other galaxies. What is truly amazing is that the completion of the twelve etheric crystals has enabled Earth to intercommunicate and interlink with the higher evolutionary systems in our galaxy, especially in the Andromeda Galaxy.

Let us talk about the holographic nature of the original Tree of Life and the holographic nature of the Arcturian Tree of Life. We have designated additions to the Tree of Life. We have placed them in such a way as to support the coming forth of hidden knowledge, which will now be spread more easily throughout the planet, and to support the manifestation of the fifth dimension onto the third dimension. If you look at the twelve spheres that represent the twelve etheric crystals, each of which represents one of twelve powerful energy points on the planet, then you can understand that they are all interacting and are all holographic. By holographic I mean that they are representing parts that are transmitted, transposed and projected onto an interstellar, intergalactic energy screen.

SUBCONSCIOUS DOWNLOADING

Each of you has a subconscious. Each planet has a subconscious. Each galaxy has a subconscious. There are ways of communicating with the subconscious. Ways exist for Earth's subconscious to receive higher messages, higher energy from sources beyond Earth. The Arcturian Tree of Life has become an antenna to receive some of these transmissions. That is to say, Earth responds to subconscious messages in the same way you as a human being respond to subconscious messages. In fact, there is a process by which you can communicate with the subconscious. That process has to do with repetition, with the creation of affirmations and with the expansion of emotions. Also, that process has to do with an interesting phenomenon that has best been described by your computer developers, namely what is called the downloading of programs. Your subconscious is able to receive affirmations and emotions, and it is also able to receive downloaded programs about how you are to be and how you are to act. Some of these programs come from your parents; some come from your cultural upbringing. Some of these programs come from other significant people in your lives, and some of these programs come from other lifetimes. These are called impressions or psychic impressions, and they are transmitted genetically and holographically from one lifetime to the next.

On Earth, you are given the freedom to change your subconscious and to begin the process of reprogramming your subconscious so that you can evolve. Many people have inquired about why there are so many people wanting to come to Earth. We have said before that one reason has to do with the fact that this is a freewill zone. The freewill zone means that you can choose—even about things that appear to be predetermined. The fact is that what you call "predetermined" from our perspective means it has been programmed, especially programmed into the subconscious. Remember that any program in the subconscious can be changed.

I agree that it takes intensity, focus and concentration. Most importantly, it takes knowledge. For the most part, you have all been learning how to work with your personal subconscious. If you still think you need updates and instructions on that, I am glad to offer them. The insight is this: the planetary subconscious also exists, and the planetary subconscious can be changed just like your subconscious can be changed. Earth's subconscious is filled with a plethora of programs. Many of these programs are very primitive. You know that you too have primitive programs in you. It is in fact true that you are not that far away from your primordial self, the self who existed in a more primitive environment—even just a couple of lifetimes ago, for example. You can understand very easily that Earth as a planet still has many primordial programs.

THE INFLUENCE OF GALACTIC CONFLICTS

I also need to add to this discussion the fact that some of the Earth's subconscious programming has been downloaded and tampered with by other-dimensional beings. These other-dimensional beings have not been of the highest nature. Sometimes you are seeing the result of galactic conflicts, conflicts on Earth that don't even make sense, conflicts so catastrophic that you would never be able to assign logic to them. This would include terrible events such as the Holocaust and some of the catastrophic destruction of civilizations that has occurred on this planet. What I am suggesting is that some of these types of events actually came from outside of the Earth's subconscious and were downloaded from other areas.

You might ask, "Why is this happening?" Remember, because this is a freewill zone, these things can happen. At this point, it is necessary to be on guard; it is necessary to have a ring of protection around Earth's subconscious so that these types of intrusions from lower-energy sources can't occur. The good news is that the planetary subconscious is changeable and programmable; the planetary subconscious is actually able to receive higher messages from higher sources. To explain that in more depth, I want to come back to the comparison between this information to your personal subconscious.

I have worked with many of you on your personal subconscious as a path, as a way of changing. I have reviewed with you the process of personal change via the subconscious and have expressed some ideas, including affirmations, repetition, focus and concentration. Also, I want to add the idea of imagery, focusing on images as a way of communicating with the subconscious. A good example would be the concept of gaining material wealth. Many of you might focus on having money as an image. We personally do not recommend focusing on that; rather, we would recommend an image of you having satisfaction, of you having all your needs met, of you having a sense of harmony in your life. We recommend this, rather than an image focusing on the material. When you focus just on the material, it is not comprehensive enough. This is one method that has been taught and will continue to be taught on Earth about working with your personal subconscious.

THE SUBCONSCIOUS AND HIGHER VIBRATIONAL ENERGY

Another aspect about the personal subconscious is that it is very amenable to inputs from higher sources. These higher energetic sources in particular can have a very dramatic and powerful effect on your personal subconscious. In a normal working of the subconscious, you might have to, for example, repeat an affirmation a thousand times, or maybe you would have to work on an image daily for two years. These are again examples. If you were able to concentrate on a higher energetic source, a source that would have an ability to transmute the normal laws of cause and effect and would be able in a very short time to have the same effect on your subconscious, then you would want to use this. We have referred to this many times as the omega energy light and also as the quantum light. The omega energy light is a light source that comes from the soul level. In terms of the Tree of Life, it would be at the top, at the crown of the Tree of Life. If you were to receive or use radiated vibrational light from that highest source—in this case it might be radiating from Mount Fuji—to illuminate an affirmation or an image, then that image or affirmation would have an immediate and powerful effect on you. This is because it would be able to directly communicate to your subconscious, because it is a higher energy—a higher vibration.

This is another way of saying that the subconscious does differentiate between lower vibrational sources and higher vibrational sources. I want to tell you that you do have a safeguard in your subconscious. If you are coming from a lower source—for example, say that you are depressed or are focusing on negative thoughts—those lower thoughts generally will not manifest at the same rate. It could take a longer time because it is a lower energy with which you are working. It still can have the same outcome if you focus on that, but a higher energy source can transmute and work wonders; it can accelerate the laws of the subconscious so that events can unfold more rapidly.

If you were focusing on your subconscious and sending an affirmation—"I am an electromagnetic, loving starseed," for example—if you use the omega light to illuminate that message and then that message is downloaded into your subconscious, then the affirmation will manifest much more rapidly in your life. This is the idea in the Tree of Life, and the idea in the downloading of the twelfth etheric crystal in Serra da Bocaina. This downloading means that fifth-dimensional energies and fifth-dimensional thoughts can now be made manifest in the third dimension. We look for the highest source of light to illuminate our powerful thoughts so that we can shift our subconscious.

EARTH'S SUBCONSCIOUS

The corollary to this is that the planet Earth has the same process. Up until this point in the evolution of planetary awareness and global awareness, no one that we know of has spoken of the existence of a planetary subconscious. When I am speaking about your personal subconscious, every one of you understands it and every one of you would be able to follow my instructions quite easily to work with this process. You might need guidance or assistance in connecting with omega light, but with assistance or by yourself each of you would be able to do this.

How can this be done to Earth's subconscious? Earth has been manifesting what has been downloaded into her subconscious. As you already know, this downloading contains some pretty powerful programs. Some programs have to do with the end times, some with world wars, some with world domination. But there are other programs that have to do with Shangri-la, fifth-dimensional energies and planetary cities of light. There is a definite process through which you can begin to download higher-energy programs into Earth's subconscious. I told you that the personal subconscious can be accelerated through using higher quantum light. In the same way, change in Earth's subconscious can also be accelerated through the use of quantum light, and also through the use of higher extra-planetary sources. There are other higher planetary messages coming in—from Arcturus, for example—that Earth can receive and that can be downloaded into her subconscious. There are messages coming from the Pleiades, from the fifth-dimensional Central Sun and from the moon-planet Alano that can be received and downloaded into Earth's subconscious.

If these messages are received and downloaded with the highest integrity and from the highest sources, they can supersede some of the drama-filled lower energies that are seemingly dominating Earth. In order to receive these messages, the Arcturian Tree of Life can be activated on Earth to be a fifth-dimensional antenna. This fifth-dimensional antenna can be used to receive these messages and then these messages can be downloaded into Earth, following the path of the Tree of Life. A message comes in at the top of the tree and then goes through all of the twelve etheric crystals before being downloaded and manifested into Earth. You already have the twelve etheric crystals downloaded into Earth, and therefore you have a process, you have the means, you have a technique of bringing this energy into the subconscious of Earth and then manifesting it.

A Visualization for Bringing in Messages from Alano

I would like you to visualize the twelve etheric crystals around the planet. I want you to try and visualize them as all standing up vertically in the Earth so that they form a holographic image that participates in interdimensional space on Earth. If you cannot remember all the places, that is okay; just visualize the linkage and visualize the name, Arcturian Tree of Life, and it will help you. Visualize yourself standing on Earth. At the same time, you can receive and hold the Arcturian Tree of Life in your etheric cosmic-egg energy field. At the same time, you are also participating in the Tree of Life in your own personal energy field. You can visualize the Arcturian Tree of Life on Earth. You can use these energies. I want each of you to know that we want you to use this energy; we want you to use this system for your own personal development as well as for planetary development. At the top of the Arcturian Tree of Life on the Earth is that which is known as Mount Fuji. I, Juliano, am connecting to the energy of the top crystal in the number one spot.

Don't think of these crystals as being in a hierarchy of importance. Just look at this crystal as being in the number one position on the chart. I am connecting with that crystal now, connecting that sphere with the moon-planet Alano, which is a fifth-dimensional moon planet close to the Central Sun, in the Central Sunbelt. I am providing a corridor link between Alano and Mount Fuji, and I am putting into words a message that Alano is giving to Earth.

Perhaps you and I will meditate together as we receive this message for Earth from the moon-planet Alano. The first message is: Planet Earth can balance these dualities for higher evolution. The moon planet Alano says to Earth, "Earth, you can balance these polarities. You can balance these dualities for higher evolution." Now I ask you to look at the top of your Tree of Life and to receive that message for yourself. Tell yourself, "I can balance these dualities for higher evolution. I can balance these polarities for higher evolution."

This is so beautiful, Earth receiving this message from another planetary system. The language by which one planet communicates to another is not verbal like the words I am speaking. I, Juliano, am able to transcribe the energy into words. There is a second message coming through from moon-planet Alano: "Earth, you can hold more fifth-dimensional energy and light, because you have so many starseeds on you now." This energy message is coming through the top of the Arcturian Tree of Life, and now it is going down into all of the spheres. As it goes down into all of the spheres, it goes down into the planet. In particular, because we just returned from Serra da Bocaina, the tepee at the center of the etheric crystal is radiating a powerful, etheric red light, illuminating that whole valley of Serra da Bocaina.

You can tell yourself, in terms of your own personal Tree of Life, "I am able to receive and hold fifth-dimensional light because I am a starseed." Everyone who is listening to and is reading these words is starseed, because if you were not, then you would not be attracted to these messages.

There are many messages coming from the moon-planet Alano. The next one: "This rapid acceleration of change will lead to a higher evolutionary shift for humankind." One piece of explanation: Earth is very aware of and very involved with humankind. Earth as a spirit, as a planetary being, is very aware of the human species, what the human species is doing. Earth knows that the outcome of her evolution as a planet is inextricably linked to human evolution. Earth in essence needs human beings to assist her in evolution. At the same time, human beings need to work with and communicate with Earth for their evolution.

ALIGNMENT WITH THE ARCTURIAN STARGATE

For your own personal Tree of Life, I would like you to modify this affirmation to say, "I am connected to and participating in the evolution of higher consciousness for humanity." Now, hold that thought for your own personal Tree of Life, just as the planetary Tree of Life is also receiving that thought.

You might ask: "How is it that we work with so many affirmations?" We are all using group energy; we are all connected. This Arcturian Tree of Life is helping us all to participate and connect. One more message is coming through from the moon-planet Alano. "The energy of biorelativity grows stronger and stronger between humanity and Earth." This means that humanity's telepathic abilities to communicate with Earth—for a higher good, for the resolution of dualities—is improving and getting stronger. Earth needs to know this; Earth needs to receive that message just as you need to receive that message for yourself. You can use the energy of biorelativity, and it has to be downloaded into your subconscious: "I can use the energy of biorelativity to communicate effectively with Earth." Earth needs to know that she is now ready to receive and work with the energy of biorelativity.

Some might ask: "Where is the subconscious?" Put that thought into the top of the Arcturian Tree of Life (which is now symbolized by Mount Fuji) as I am doing now, and then that message will be transmitted through all appropriate spheres and sources to the subconscious of Earth.

Now I am receiving a message from another source. I am now connecting with the Arcturian stargate. Remember, we said that the downloading of the Serra da Bocaina etheric crystal would not only complete the grid for all twelve etheric crystals but would also bring a special alignment with the stargate. In particular, it is going to help to radiate and align Brazil—and Serra da Bocaina in particular—with the Arcturian stargate. A brief explanation is in order. The Arcturian stargate is the portal that allows you to leave an incarnational cycle. You can only leave the incarnational cycle after you have graduated and learned your Earth lessons, or through grace, such as from ascension, when you have a rapid acceleration and can complete the process of going through the stargate. The stargate, then, is a portal for human evolution that provides transportation to other higher places in the galaxy.

The Arcturian stargate is also a spirit being—just as Gaia, the planet Earth, is a spirit. The Arcturian stargate is a spiritual place, a spiritual energy. Now the stargate is sending energy to Earth. I am going to work with that energy. The Arcturian stargate is opening a special portal to Earth to receive starseeds. In particular, that portal is now in alignment with Brazil and the twelfth etheric crystal. This alignment will facilitate the ascension for all starseeds who have permission to pass through the stargate, if they so wish.

Now for your own personal Tree of Life, you can say: "I am in alignment with the energy of the Arcturian stargate." Alignment with the stargate means higher light; it means that higher energy is coming to these places. Those people who are receiving and working with this energy can have a more rapid evolution, a more rapid acceleration, because that is what each of you really wants. You want to accelerate and evolve as quickly as possible. The next affirmation is: "The energy from the Arcturian stargate will accelerate my evolution."

For Earth, the same message applies. The energy from the Arcturian stargate will accelerate Earth's evolution. These twelve etheric crystals and the formation they make in the Tree of Life are holographic transmission antennas. It is so beautiful that we can help you download these messages, for yourself and for the planet. In closing, I would like to have Archangel Metatron speak with you, as he is guardian of the Arcturian stargate and the Tree of Life. I am Juliano.

I am Archangel Metatron. Blessings to *B'nai Elohim*, children of the Elohim light. You are the guardians of the light of our Creator in this dimension. You are the children of this light who are about to evolve, who are about to mature into the light of *Elohim*. Each one of you is now preparing for a beautiful evolution, the beautiful glory of being the children of the *Elohim*. To be in that energy is also to have the power of the *B'nai Elohim*. This power includes the ability to transcend duality, the ability to ascend, to unify the third dimension with the fifth dimension in a process we call the unification light: *Yichuda ha Aur*, the light of unification. It is a special power that you are all developing now, and that power is manifested in the twelfth etheric crystal at Serra da Bocaina, which is the manifestation of the fifth dimension into the third dimension.

The manifestation of the fifth dimension into the third also means that you can unite the third dimension with the fifth, because in holographic light and holographic energy, the dimensions go back and forth. Yes, the fifth-dimensional light and energy, the Arcturian stargate energy, is going to manifest on Earth. At the same time, you as the starseeds, through the power of unification, *Yichudium Yichuda*, you are going to connect this energy, this third-dimensional energy, with the higher fifth-dimensional energy. That is your soul mission, one of the soul missions many of you have, because there needs to be a link to hold this energy. That is what the *B'nai Elohim* can do—the children of *Elohim*, the children of Creator.

Some people also use the term "co-creator." As you are evolving and begin to leave the planetary Earth, each of you might be called on to go to other planetary systems as ascended masters. You may even be called on to return to this planet as an ascended master. You will need this skill, to always be able to connect the third dimension to the fifth dimension and the fifth dimension to the third dimension, to be able to go both ways. That is the power of the unification—the power of unity.

This is the true Tikun Olam, the true repairing of Earth. That is, the Tikun Olam is the restoration of the *Gan Eden*, the Garden of Eden, the paradise that is really the fifth dimension on Earth. It requires the alignment of the fifth with the third, the manifestation of the third from the fifth and the unity of the third to the fifth. It is also your *Tikun Hanefesh*; your restoration of your third dimensional body too. You are repairing and restoring your third-dimensional body with fifth-dimensional light and becoming a fifth-dimensional being. It is *Tikun Olam, Tikun Hanefesh*: restoring the world, repairing the world and repairing your own human body. That is why, when resurrection appears in some of the earlier Biblical phrases, it is really speaking of the ascension, where you unify your third-dimensional body. It is not going to be the physical third-dimensional body, but it is going to be the spirit body. You can even focus on that body as the repaired body. Hold that light—the light of restoring, the light of repairing your perfected third-dimensional body in the fifth dimension. You will ascend into that body so easily. *Kadosh, Kadosh, Kadosh, Adonai, Tzevaoth.* I am Archangel Metatron. *Baruch Hashem.* Blessings.

HARMONIC
CONVERGENCE ENERGY

Juliano, the Arcturians, Chief White Eagle, Vywamus and Helio-ha

Greetings, I am Juliano. We are the Arcturians. We have reached a turning point in the energy transformation of the planet and the ascension. I am, of course, referring to the energies of 8–8–8. The idea of harmonic energy and convergence energy has important ramifications for your own spiritual development.

First, I will speak of the idea of harmonics. Harmonic actually means that the frequencies are blending. Harmonic also means that there is a main frequency and that other frequencies are in harmony or harmonic relations with the main frequency. If a harmonic energy is being emitted from the Central Sun, then you will be able to either work with and receive the main vibrational energy, or you will be able to receive harmonics, which are subfrequencies that are related to the main frequency. You may ask, "Why would I need to relate to the subfrequencies? Why not just relate to the main frequency?" The reason is your antenna—your receptivity as a starseed may still not be attuned enough to receive the main frequency. But in working together with groups of starseeds, the receptivity energy of the group is broadened so that they can receive, and you, personally, could receive a higher form of energy—a form of energy that you could not receive by yourself.

One way to conceive this is as follows: Imagine that you have a satellite television antenna, or even a radio telescope, and it has a diameter of ten feet. The signal that you seek to receive is rather weak. The ten-foot diameter is not gathering enough of that energy wave to get good reception. Then imagine that you have tripled the satellite receiving dish antenna to thirty feet. Or imagine that you now have placed two antennas next to each other. And these two antennas together equal this one antenna at thirty-feet in diameter. Now the two antennas have widened the receptivity field so that you can hear and receive what you were not able to receive when you only had one antenna.

This is the same principle in spiritual receptivity and spiritual energy. I am sure you may have even experienced this yourself. That is to say, it is hard to receive these spiritual vibrations by yourself. Yet when you gather in a group, as we are doing in Mount Shasta, then the receptivity diameter of the group enlarges the satellite dish or the spiritual dish. What was not receivable by oneself is very receivable in the group energy.

RADIO ASTRONOMY

Now, again, let us talk about radio astronomy. In radio astronomy, you find that sometimes you have to have dishes in different parts of the planet in order to receive the faint signal of a galactic object millions of light years away. The idea is that the dish becomes perhaps 2,000 miles in diameter because you have one dish in one place in the world, say, North America, and one dish in another place, say South America. Together, those two dishes are allowing the radio astronomers to receive the signal.

In the harmonic convergence energy, we are working to download spiritual signals. We are actually working to receive a harmonic energy that is coming from the Central Sun. There really is a spiritual light and spiritual energy available that is in alignment with 2012. This signal is in alignment with the Arcturian starseeds who are the primary purveyors, the primary transmitters, of this energy. It is you, the Groups of Forty, who are providing the spiritual antenna to receive this harmonic energy. Your gathering as a group is providing a wider spectrum of receptivity. But what is also so important and beautiful is that there are Groups of Forty Arcturian starseeds around the planet who are also setting up this receptivity energy and who are also setting up their spiritual satellite dishes. They will connect with the main group in Mount Shasta to enhance and to increase the spiritual sensitivity so that you, the starseeds, can receive more harmonic light and more harmonic energy. This light can then be retransmitted to the planet.

Now, the main harmonic energy is a very powerful energy. I have to tell you that in participating in harmonic energy and in harmonic convergence, I found that it is easy to blissfully become entranced in the harmonic energy. You, in your normal daily life, do not often have the opportunity to experience harmonic energy. This is not surprising because you are living in a polarized, polarity-filled environment. The polarizations are actually becoming stronger at this time. The opportunity to be in harmonic light is so inviting that you may forget the work part of this convergence, which is to receive it and retransmit it to other starseeds, to the etheric crystals and also throughout the planet. Part of the receptivity is to allow you to experience this harmony. Part of the work also is to awaken you to the task of retransmitting to others and ensuring that there is a convergence. What is a convergence? A convergence is a coming together of groups of people to experience a unity.

To do a convergence requires work. It requires an organization. It requires a structure. The Groups of Forty have that structure. There are enough people participating worldwide to ensure that the harmonic energy is converted and converging around the planet. The group at Mount Shasta, who is going to receive the main harmonic energy, will then send out the subharmonic energy to other places. This is where the idea of harmonics and subharmonics breaks with traditional electromagnetic theory. The idea is that the subharmonic energy that is going to be retransmitted to the other groups will activate and act like the main harmonic energy. Thus everyone will be able to use the subharmonic energy and the subharmonic frequencies that will be sent out from Mount Shasta as if they were the main frequency. These subharmonic frequencies will activate and will reproduce the main harmonic in parallel. Why? Because we are working in holographic technology. We are working in holographic spiritual time, space and energy. In holographic theory, from the Arcturian perspective, a part represents or gives you access to the whole. If you can receive the subharmonic of the harmonic convergence energy, or from that subharmonic frequency and vibration, you will be able to then reproduce it.

At this point, I ask you to listen to these tones and prepare and experience the harmonic energy. [Tones follow.] Please meditate now for a few minutes on the harmonic light.

UNDERSTANDING POLARIZATIONS

The question is, which parts of the planet are going to be harmonized? To understand the answer, you must consider the polarization of the opposites on the planet. You must understand the polarizations within yourself because you are a participant in humankind. You have agreed to come here knowing that you will experience duality and polarization both personal and on the planet. It so happens that this polarization and this experience that you are witnessing on this Earth have cosmic implications. The energies and the polarizations are part of a process that is being played out. Some of you called this process a very intense drama. This intense Earth drama has cosmic implications. There is cosmic participation that has contributed and has a stake in the outcome. This is another way of saying that what you are seeing is really transcending Earth, which also includes the cosmic energy field and the cosmic brotherhood/sisterhood energy and other energies from galactic councils.

The opposites, or polarizations, tend to get more intense, especially as we approach harmonic convergence energy. You will be called on to bring your knowledge and awareness of polarizations that you wish to harmonize. You are the tool for the transmission of harmonic energy. You are like the microscope. You are the telescope, and you are saying, "I want to harmonize the polarization of the dolphins," who are important and necessary for Earth's well-being. For example, there are many people who want to kill them to eat them—that's a polarization. You then can send the harmonic energies to the dolphins and also to the people who want to harm them.

CREATING HARMONY

There are so many polarizations on this Earth. I could spend five more hours with you going through the myriad of polarizations. Remember that all beings who have incarnated into this environment, on a soul level, accepted the polarization when you came here. The biggest polarizations are life and death. The first breath that you took on this plane was an acceptance of your death and was an acceptance that you have come into this zone of polarization and duality. Now in this advanced spiritual state, you will and you have the potential to harmonize life and death. That has been attempted already. For example, the great Taoists incorporated in their ancient meditation the concept that within the yin is the yang. There is a little eye within the yin that represents the yang and in the yang there is a yin. Meditating, for example, on that symbol of the Tao is a beautiful metaphor for harmony. It is a beautiful metaphor for understanding the harmonization of opposites.

What happens on a dualistic planet like Earth when the opposites become too far apart? You see this, for example, in Earth political matters where one group feels one way and another group feels totally opposite. In actuality, they don't seem to be able to come to any medium point, and people actually become more entrenched in their polarized state. This is the energy that is most prevalent now on Earth. The energy of harmonic convergence is to try to blend. People have always felt that to give in, to mediate or to balance is to lose a part of their position. That is one aspect of polarization. That is what we call the resistance to harmonization. You can hear people say, "Well, I can't stop hunting the dolphins because I need the food." That is their resistance. The dolphins are in an animalistic, nonhuman mode, and they have their own ways of dealing with this energy. They as a group can actually select ones that can be sacrificed—several of the older dolphins or several of the ones that are deformed or not working or are having problems. They can select them and say, "Okay, for the harmony of the all, we will allow some to be sacrificed to this greater good. That becomes a harmonic energy. That becomes a balance.

At this point, I would like Chief White Eagle to speak to you about the balance, and then I will return afterward. This is Juliano.

Greetings, I am Chief White Eagle. [Tones.] *Hey ya ho ya hey!* I welcome all Native peoples. I welcome all lovers of Earth, and I welcome all of our starseed brothers and sisters who are joining us in this beautiful energy. Remember that we have understood this concept of balance with Earth. Remember that when we would go on our hunts for animals, we would pray, asking permission from the spirits of the animals, to take one that we need. We would take it with great reverence because we wanted to stay in harmony with the animal world, with the deer that we were seeking and with the buffalo that we were seeking. We did not want to break the harmony.

We of the higher spiritual ascended masters who were on this Earth and were hunters, were always asking for permission, even if we were to go into a mushroom garden or to gather an herb. We would have to stop and ask for permission for which one to take so that the harmony would still be maintained. That was part of our spiritual belief and that was part of our spiritual practice—to live and stay in harmony. It required and does require participation, and it requires sensitivity. It requires the ability to overcome greed and to overcome the ego. But it is very easy for one person to upset the harmony.

Now on Earth, you can see how fragile the whole biosphere is, and how fragile living conditions are. One person can greatly upset the balance through a war. One country or one crazed leader can upset it. More important is the fact that by you working with this harmonic convergence, you are helping to return humankind to this idea of living in balance and living in harmony with the forces of this planet. Now, there is a new harmonic convergence that Juliano is talking to you about, which also means that not only are you living in harmony and balance with the Earth but you are seeking to live in the balance with your cosmic brotherhood and sisterhood. You are seeking to find the balance of Earth in the cosmos. That is difficult for many people to understand because they see how far away Earth is from everything. They might think that Earth is alone. They may think that there is no way to balance what is going on in Earth with the cosmic light, the cosmic energy and with the Central Sun.

We know that we are part of the star family, the star brothers and sisters. We know about the star masters. We know that we are living and connecting with the cosmos. As Juliano says, we are living a drama that has ramifications for the cosmos. We know because we have connected with our star brothers and sisters. There have been planets that have been destroyed. You have the histories of these planets even in your own records. The planet Marduk, for example, was a planet that was once in your solar system that was destroyed. There are extra-solar planets and extra-solar energy that have a participatory process in Earth.

The view of this Earth drama from the cosmic perspective is this: Some planets survive and find the balance and harmony and some planets do not. Those planets that do not find balance are destroyed. The living-energy force field in the planet is destroyed either through wars or through environmental devastation. Those planets that survive have higher planetary beings that are willing and able to telepathically interact and find the balance on Mother Earth, or whatever name that planet has. They find a way to communicate and to live in harmony with that planet. Then that planet becomes an important player in the cosmic drama, coming into a balance with cosmic and galactic energies.

PARTICIPATING IN HARMONY

The question then becomes: Do the Earth and its inhabitants want to participate in the cosmic light, in the cosmic energy, in the cosmic brotherhood/sisterhood and in the galactic brotherhood/sisterhood? If so, then the Earth must transcend and harmonize with the polarizations that are in place. These polarizations, if they are harmonized, will have a tremendous healing effect not only on the Earth but the other players that have been mentioned by Juliano and me.

Oh Mother Earth, Father Sky, Mother Moon, Father, Creator of All, we ask that you give us the strength and the perceptual ability to understand the importance of harmony. May you give us and all the starseeds the power to receive this harmony and transmit it to all peoples, all life forms and all places on this planet. Our hearts hurt for the disharmony that we see on this planet. Also Father, we understand the disharmony within ourselves. We ask ourselves: How can we live in harmony when there is so much disharmony everywhere else? Then we will receive your wisdom, we will receive your strength to know that when we perceive and when we work with harmony, then we will be able to transmit harmony. We can be the beginning kernel of harmonic light that will create a wave of harmony and healing. [Tones.] *Hey hey ho. Hey hey ho.*

Let the image of White Buffalo Calf Woman appear in each of your mental screens. She represents a harmony that is beyond words. She represents a harmonic force field that is healing. You already have the concept of the messianic light—the Messiah who comes to Earth and just his or her presence is so powerful that the polarizations are healed and there is a harmonic energy. This is the power of White Buffalo Calf Woman. She is part of the harmonic force field. She is part of the messianic force energy that is coming to Earth. *Ho!* All my words are sacred. All my relations: I love you all. You are my brothers. You are my sisters. We are all one star family and we will prevail in the harmonic light. I am Chief White Eagle.

Greetings, I am Vywamus, a soul psychologist. I wanted to explain the importance to you in your personal work of harmonic convergence. Juliano and the other ascended masters have told you that the planetary work parallels your personal work. There is a strong energy of harmonic convergence that has come to your own personal being, to your own personal issues. When you prepare and work in the planetary harmonic light, you will also be affected in a way that will ask you very gently to look at your polarizations. You will be asked to harmonize the opposites within yourself. That requires a certain amount of courage and openness to who you are.

People may say, "We need to transcend the lower self, because all of these ego issues are not really important. We just need to stay in the higher light, the beauty, in the blissful state of the harmonic energy that Juliano is talking about." You are here for Earth lessons. You are here for soul lessons. On the etheric level, each unresolved ego issue lessens your ability to totally raise your light quotient to the figure that is necessary for ascension. Some of these "problems" can be addressed. Through grace you can resolve them, but you have to acknowledge and admit that this is an issue. That means that there must be some participation on your part. There must be some acceptance on your part about what ego issues, what lower-self issues you seek to harmonize. In the language of the self, in the soul psychology language, we equate the phrase "harmonizing the self" with healing the self. Part of the self has become cut off from itself. It sounds rather paradoxical, doesn't it? Maybe it would be better to say that the ego is cut off from the self.

There needs to be the balance. You can find this balance in the harmonic light. It is like a boost. Let us say that before the harmonic energy, you are aware of the different paradoxes or the different polarizations within yourself, but you just don't have the energy—you just don't have the perspective or the knowledge to harmonize or to heal that part of the self. It is just beyond you. The harmonic convergence energy is so strong that it is like a shot of coffee awakening you. It is like a new burst of light and energy. You can begin to think, "Yes, there is a way to harmonize, to heal the polarized parts of myself. I am willing, I am open to look within myself at what those polarized parts of myself are." This is a very good affirmation, by the way: "I am willing to look at my polarized parts, and I am willing to harmonize and heal those parts through the harmonic convergence light." I predict that many of you will have a great healing. There will be parts of you that maybe you have totally forgotten, totally pushed away. Now those parts will come to light and you will have the opportunity to heal.

This means not only those polarized parts in this lifetime but the polarized parts from other lifetimes as well. Some of the issues that you have brought into this lifetime are really out of this Earth incarnation. They have come from other experiences, other places. You will be able to harmonize and heal polarizations that you thought were never possible before. I will be with you. This is Vywamus.

G reetings, my friends, I am Helio-ah, representative from the Arcturian starseed group that is working with you and all of the starseeds of Arcturian inklings or predilections. We are working to create the right environment for this harmonic energy. The holographic aspect of this time is synchronistic. You are holographic healers. You are able to implant or to access beautiful harmonic energies.

Juliano wants me to tell you that the etheric crystals play a key role in holding and in distributing harmonic energy. The crystals are able to hold a higher voltage, a higher amperage of harmonic energy than what you can alone. Therefore, in the harmonic work in Mount Shasta, each of the crystals were activated to receive the harmonic energy. Each crystal is able to distribute certain harmonic energies around the Earth's ley lines. The whole Earth is going to vibrate in a golden light. The ring of ascension is going to vibrate at a fantastic frequency—a frequency that has not been seen. The people are going to sense this brotherhood. Certain biorelativity exercises that you would want to do will become more powerful and effective during this time. In fact, even today as we think of this energy, I, Helio-ah, with your assistance, focus on a calmness over Mount Shasta, a calmness over Northern California and a calmness over Southern California. Please take a moment to visualize and to think of calmness over California.

Visualize calm energy, cooling weather, rising humidity and many people coming together. Mount Shasta is preparing for your arrival. Please remember that there are many, many polarizations, many healings that can be done now. This will be a time when you will be able to bring your perspective on healing and what needs to be healed. We will bring our holographic technology with us to support your work. Blessings, I am Helio-ah.

G reetings, I am Juliano. We are back. You can see and you can tell that there is great excitement among the ascended masters and guides who want to work and help. I know that each of you are expanding your own perceptual fields and expanding your knowledge of who you are and also expanding your ability to hold this harmonic light and energy. We will activate all aspects of our technology, all aspects of our support. We will download a cosmic, harmonic energy field into Earth. This cosmic harmonic energy field is an energy that will be able to sustain the harmonic light. That is the key—working to sustain the harmonic energy for the healing of all living beings, of the biosphere, of Mother Earth and Mother Earth's place in the cosmic family. I am Juliano. Good day.

LESSONS IN
QUESTIONS AND ANSWERS

Archangel Michael, Juliano and P'Taah

reetings, this is Archangel Michael. There is a polarization that
is occurring on the planet, a polarization that is experienced as
a way of differentiating those who are spiritual from those who
are not. The energy of spirituality is being accelerated. At the same
time, people who are not spiritual, those who experience a barrier to
spirit, also are having their views accelerated. One could say that both
spirituality and materialism are being accelerated. Spirituality is being
accelerated even while doubt is being accelerated.

TO HELP THOSE IN DOUBT

How should you deal with someone who is going through difficulty and who
is not spiritual? Well, the issue cannot really be dealt with in a mental way. What
could be said? People who are doubting, those who are not spiritual and do
not understand the spiritual significance of life are usually not swayed by logic,
arguments or ways of speaking. Try and open your heart to the person who is
suffering. Send them energy and act from your heart, showing compassion.

The ability to be in a spiritual state is the most powerful thing you can
do around someone who is having a great deal of difficulty. You know the
law of resonance in spirituality. The law of resonance basically says that
those who are on a spiritual vibration are using that vibration to experience reality and vibrate at a higher frequency. Those who are not spiritual
are vibrating on a lower frequency. When the person who is in a lower
frequency comes in contact with the person on a higher frequency, two
possibilities exist. The person on the higher frequency can come down to
the person on a lower frequency or the person on the lower frequency can
go up to the person who is on a higher frequency.

You want to remain on the higher frequency you are usually on and that, by the law of resonance, will bring the other person's energy up. It doesn't mean that his or her mental body is going to change. We need to make a distinction between the mental, emotional and spiritual bodies. Many people can still be advanced spiritually but not have mental body ideals. It is still okay to work with them on the emotional, spiritual and heart levels. The short answer to this question is to maintain your spirituality without trying to use your logic to change others' mental bodies.

Regarding doubt and how to overcome doubt: First, you know that the doubt is part of discernment. People might want to eliminate all doubt, but from an angelic standpoint, I have to ask this question: Is it not natural to experience doubt when you are in this dense plane on Earth? Is it not natural when you see polarization, when you see destruction? This life on the third dimension is focused on an illusion of separation. This illusion of separation would naturally bring doubt, because you are cut off from unity, what in the Kaballah we call the *Yihud*. In the way of the mystical Kaballah, we seek prayers, incantations, events and activities that promote unification with oneness. The greatest unification usually comes in sacred prayers at sacred times, meditations and holy sites. It also sometimes comes in unplanned epiphanies of energetic truth that suddenly appear. These are moments to be treasured.

I would say that it is normal to be doubtful, so do not try to remove doubt. The doubt in fact comes from this illusion of the density of separation. In some ways, you could say that it is not really an illusion, because it seems like a reality. The final way to deal with doubt is to seek those activities that will help you to experience unity. There are many opportunities and many avenues for experiencing unity.

In the Kaballah, we seek unity by clinging using the energy of *Devekut*, clinging to God. What does this mean, to cling? It means that all energies and thoughts are devoted to being in the energy and in the thoughts of the Creator, *Adonai*. Even if you are only able to do this for a short period of time, your experience of doubt would certainly diminish. I recommend that you try to experience unity consciousness. Do not try to eliminate doubt, but accept that it is part of the fare you have to pay in order to be on the third dimension in unity with God, with the cosmos, with the energy of your spirit, with your lightbody, with your soul brothers and sisters, with your starseed galactic family, with the ring of ascension. There are many avenues for unity thinking and experiencing unity consciousness. I am Archangel Michael.

G reetings, I am Juliano. We are the Arcturians. The collapse of the financial markets as it is unfolding is a sign of the crumbling, previously held pillars in society that seemed to have held together the economy and international trade and power. Now you see the truth: that these systems were based on and operated by falsehoods—false premises. As you watch this unfold, it is similar to those churches that were propagating unity, propagating one idea of great spirituality while at the same time being involved in child abuse. These leaders are being exposed for what they really are. People can no longer hold up the façade. What you see in the financial world is that the façade cannot withstand the vibrational energy of the coming shifts that, like waves of an earthquake, are beginning to permeate into all of the systems.

HUMANS NEED STRUCTURE

Even though the world seems to be focused on the financial, that is just one of many pillars that are cracking. What are the lessons you can learn from this? It is a multipart lesson. The first lesson is that wealth is based on illusion, because those who are controlling the money were not doing it for the betterment of everyone but for selfish reasons. Their selfishness is being exposed so you can see that you cannot trust who you were trusting. These people were like this before, but you couldn't see it. Now the façade is cracking. How can people believe they have wealth when there is so much extinction on the planet, when the environment has deteriorated so much, when you are on the verge of a biospheric collapse? The illusion is that you have wealth, that you can live forever, that you can do whatever you want. That illusion is being broken by the financial collapse.

The other lesson is that even though so much appears to be collapsing, everything still has to stay together because it will be far worse if the system collapses entirely. You cannot cheer to know that the financial world has collapsed or that it is based on illusion, because everyone is suffering. There needs to be a rebuilding of confidence. People are going to realize that they need the system even though the people running the system were doing it corruptly.

I do see a stabilization coming. Part of this is that other powers, other countries are going to come more to the forefront. Part of this is that the whole economy, this whole financial thing, is also an illusion, but the solution is going to lie in the unity of a global economy in some way, like reaching an understanding that we're all in this together. What one country does affects other countries. This is what it is moving to.

What is so dangerous for the world is that it opens the door toward world domination by those who want control. You are going to need a unity currency—in a sense, a unity financial structure. At the same time, it is a double-edged sword, because it also could bring certain controls. You already have the one-world government. The short answer is 2012 energies are already vibrating through this planet and the energies, no matter what system, no matter what social order, no matter what institution, are all going to be affected dramatically if they do not have themselves in a solid foundation of truth. If any system is based on false premises, the shock waves from the 2012 are going to be shattering not just in the financial institution but also in the other institutions. This is all part of the

transitions that will occur in the doorway of 2012. I am Juliano.

G reetings, I am P"Taah. I am from the Pleiades. The lessons we are focusing on for our many Earth friends and students have to do with relationships, opening your heart and working with heart energy. There is also, my friends, your relationship to yourself and to your body. Your human body is accelerating to keep up with your spiritual body. You have made tremendous, unbelievable progress spiritually and in the mental body. It is unbelievable the spiritual energy you have been able to combine and work with; it is unbelievable the level to which you have been able to change and expand your energy field into the beautiful shape of the cosmic egg. The colors in your aura have been magnified as you have worked more with fifth-dimensional energy. Yet the physical body is not always able to stay up; it is not able to run as fast as what you have been working on spiritually and mentally. When you have an ailment, then you have to do a special healing, and you have to understand that the healing is opening you up to the messages your body is trying to send you.

YOUR RELATIONSHIP WITH YOUR BODY

Sometimes the body cannot assimilate; it cannot process at the level you as a spirit have been able to. The body lags behind. I don't want you to think that this is a fault of yours or that you didn't do something right; rather, as beautiful as your physical body is on Earth, it is dense compared to your lightbody. Your lightbody has the ability to think itself places—wherever it wants to think itself, it is, instantaneously. This is a tremendous ability. When you are in your lightbody, You could think yourself to the farthest realm in the galaxy, to the Andromeda Galaxy, to a sister planet, to the Blue People. You could think it and you would be there. The lightbody can travel at the speed of thought.

Try, my friends, to work with your body at the level your body is at. Many spiritual seekers and lightworkers are at a very high place spiritually, but they don't work with where their bodies are. In many cases they ignore the body. It is like when Vywamus and others work with your inner child. Sometimes the body is like a child. When you talk to the inner child, you

have to speak the inner child's language. When you talk to the body, work with the body, you have to work with where the body is at, even though you are advanced spiritually. Believe me, the quickest healing you can do is to start where the body is at. I love you all. I am P'Taah.

Greetings, I am Juliano. We are the Arcturians. On the issue of ascension, your uniting with the fifth dimension is the most important thing to you now and to your future. This is the most powerful force on the planet now, this fifth-dimensional attraction. This is a culmination of lightwork: coming into alignment with the lightbody, coming into alignment with the fifth-dimensional self, preparing to leave Earth. The question has been asked numerous times: Your family, your relatives, your pets, can you take them with you? Can you ensure that they will be taken care of if you leave? This is a challenging question, because there is a paradox. The paradox is that in order to leave Earth, you have to cut your cords of attachment to Earth—at the moment of ascension especially. Any cords of attachment you have to Earth could prevent you from being in the appropriate vibrational frequency to ascend at that instantaneous moment.

RELEASE YOUR CORDS OF ATTACHMENT

Much of the work that the Arcturians have been providing focuses on preparing you for releasing the cords of attachment. The contradiction, the paradox is that those who are your loved ones have at times a denser energy than you do and might not be able to go to the ascension light. Worse, you might become worried about them and stop your ascension, which you can do.

You cannot ascend for another person. You cannot cause people to ascend with you. You can work with them prior to the ascension, trying to bring them into fifth-dimensional energy, fifth-dimensional light, but spiritual law is that people control their souls, their spirits. To walk through the gateway of ascension requires free will and also requires people to allow the cords of attachment to fall as they step through the doorway.

All is not lost for your family. All is not lost for your friends, because the guides and teachers that are working with you now can be instructed to work with your family and friends. Another unusual spiritual law is this: Those of you who have close family members: When you ascend and they don't, traces of the psychic energy—the spiritual learning, the spiritual energetic field of your lifetime—are passed on to your loved ones. This is similar to cohabitation, but it is not exactly the same.

Say, for example, that you were working with a famous healer and you were that healer's student. Then that healer died and left you as an inheritor of his or her energy. You would be inheriting—gathering some of the energy, some of the powers—what that person no longer needed. When you leave the third dimension, you don't need to take your skills as a Group of Forty member with you, for example. The energies that are part of your life work are dispersed to your loved ones in a very sacred way.

The guides and teachers who are working with you can also be working with your family and friends. Also, you might decide not to go on the first wave. Incidentally, the first wave has not yet occurred. The second wave is for those people who were on the cusp, on the edge, those who maybe decided to stay back because they wanted to work with their friends and family. By the time of the second wave, they realize they will go with the ascension, no matter what! There are some who are ready to go and some who are not ready because of some concerns, perhaps about family. On the second wave, they will not have doubts or hesitation. In a sense, the second wave is for those who hesitate.

Your love for your family and friends is very powerful. Please understand that once you've gone into your ascension, there will be ways to work with them from the other side. You will have the choice to come back to Earth as an ascended master. Isn't this what Jesus did when he died? He reappeared to direct and show his followers the true meaning of His life and His death. That act was perhaps His greatest act on Earth—His resurrection and return. Remember, in ascension, it is like a resurrection, but you don't *have* to return. Many of you will not, although you can return if you wish. If you wanted to return to those you hold dear, this would be a beautiful gift. That is going to be an option for many of you when you ascend.

BILOCATION MEANS YOU HAVE PRESENCE IN TWO LOCATIONS AT ONE TIME

Our mission has been in part to teach fifth-dimensional technologies to the starseeds. We view spirituality and the learning of tools as technology, just like you have computer technology or engineering technology. It is a science, and metaphysics is a scientific endeavor. For those who are in doubt, I want everyone to understand that everything that we are doing will eventually be scientifically proven. Most people cannot see the spiritual energy around them. Most people cannot, but if they saw themselves as luminescent balls of light instead of traditional humans with a face and clothes and a body, they would be dramatically open to the messages we are giving.

There is a science to metaphysics. Remember, metaphysics means "after physics." It really is after appearances. Modern physics is based on what you can see, moving into the world of quantum, which is what you cannot see. Metaphysics is based on the unseen energies needed to explain reality. This is one of the most difficult lessons, to explain the nature of this reality. It is a big mystery for many people. How do you explain the nature of this reality, when it is not what it looks like? Energies and thoughts and the soul and all these influences are unseen, yet they are real forces.

Bilocation means you can be at two places at the same time. This was something Jesus was able to do. He was able to appear at the temple and He was able to appear with His followers in another location. When we discuss bilocation, we are in particular trying to explain and encourage you to be in the third dimension and the fifth dimension at the same time. This means that you already have an existence in the fifth dimension. You are fifth-dimensional beings.

We have used the crystal temple as practice because we prepared a corridor, preparing the energy to make it easier to bilocate there. Bilocation is one place in the third dimension with the second location in the fifth dimension. You can bilocate on the third dimension, but we are not encouraging that because we are working toward your ascension, working toward going into higher light. There are uses for bilocating on the third dimension, but this requires certain karmic adjustments and energies that are much more involved. Let me put it this way: You are having enough trouble with your karma just in one body in one place on the third dimension. Imagine how you would deal with the karma if you were in two places at the same time in the third dimension. It would be quite challenging.

HOW DO YOUR SHIMMER?

Shimmering, which is a precursor to ascension, is vibrating your body to a frequency that allows you to disappear temporarily and go into a fifth-dimensional body. It is not bilocation. In bilocation, you have full presence in both locations. In shimmering, you are removing your presence in the third dimension and sending all your energy into your multidimensional presence on the fifth dimension. It is the reverse of what you are doing now, because now all your energy is in the third dimension and you have very little energy in the fifth dimension. Now, in shimmering, we reverse that. We call it shimmering because when you move a certain percentage of energy into your fifth-dimensional body, your third-dimensional body disappears slightly—almost like it is going in and out of sight—because you are taking some of your life force energy and directing it to the higher plane. Therefore when people see you in the third dimension, it is like you are not there; you might temporarily disappear. We don't see you totally disappearing because of the laws of the dimensions. If you totally disappeared, you would have ascended. Shimmering is just more of your energy going into the fifth dimension.

How do you shimmer? The best thing we can suggest is that people need to become aware of their energy fields. We really encourage the teaching of science, metaphysics and spiritual technology. Bringing people's energy fields into the shape of the cosmic egg makes them feel better, and they experience the effects of energetic healing. That is why we are very pleased with the many healers doing remote healing, hands-on healing and healing of the energy field. The exercise, the meditation, would be to help the person realize that he or she is an energy field. That is something that can be tangibly understood. Also, the idea of color is important. This healing helps the person come into awareness of his or her energy field and an understanding that other people have energy fields. Energy fields are composed of thought waves, emotional waves, ideas and the mind.

I always recommend that any spiritual work be activated at power spots. You can often teach people or open them up at a power spot in a way that you could not in a not-powerful spot. I encourage people who are trying to help others open up not to give up on them. Sometimes the best work you can do is to take them to a power spot so that they have a greater opportunity to feel the energy fields.

YOU WILL SHIMMER EARTH INTO THE FIFTH DIMENSION

The idea of crystals and subcrystals is a very complicated issue. We have downloaded ten main crystals, which are crystals from the Arcturian crystal temple. Each country needs more direct links to the crystals. For example, in Mexico, we have authorized and are recommending that there be three duplicate crystals of the shimmering crystal in Copper Canyon to be strategically placed in three different areas in the country of Mexico. The main crystal, which is receiving energy and is connected with the shimmering light of the moon-planet Alano has provided a link to the fifth-dimensional planet. Therefore, there needs to be sub-energy work. We cannot say that we will bring down a main crystal because the next main crystal we are hoping to bring is going to be in Istanbul in the Black Sea. What we can bring down is a subcrystal from the main crystal, which will spread the energy. This also can be done in Spain, and in the different areas where the other crystals are. It took so much energy just to bring down the main crystals that to go into the subcrystals would have been too much overload. Now the groups are advancing so rapidly that these subcrystals off of the main crystal are available.

We recommend that the subcrystals in a country stay within that country. For example, we don't recommend that a duplicate of the shimmering crystal in Copper Canyon go to Spain. Rather, we would use the main crystal of Montserrat in Spain and place duplicate crystals in neighboring areas. Remember, before you get too involved in the subcrystals, we still need to focus on the relationships of all the main crystals and the energy they are radiating. The interaction of the crystals with each other would provide a fantastic energy force.

We have said it is based on the concept of the Tree of Life, which has ten spheres. We don't necessarily make duplicates of the spheres, but we use the interaction of the spheres with one another to create a force. The primary work is still with the main crystals. We acknowledge that each area of the planet now has much work that is needed, and the subcrystals provide a way of accelerating and expanding the main crystal's work. Never lose sight that the main focus of the energy, the main sphere of light, is coming from the ten crystals. We will be providing more information on the interactions between these crystals as they become more and more important and as we go into the fifth-dimensional Earth.

Ultimately, you are going to shimmer Earth so that she goes into the fifth dimension, and the only way that you are going to be able to do that is to shimmer Earth through the etheric crystals. You will want to shimmer a country, and this is what we explained to the people of Mexico. To shimmer the country, you can use the duplicate crystals and the main crystal in that country. Eventually we will shimmer Earth into her fifth-dimensional self, just like you are doing individually. You will want to use the etheric crystals for your personal work as well. I need to clarify this: The etheric crystals are for the planet, but they also have uses for your own personal development. Some of you have already been using these crystals for your own energetic work. I am Juliano. Blessings.

HARMONIZING
RELATIONSHIPS

Juliano and the Arcturians

Greetings, I am Juliano, and we are the Arcturians. Of course it is a very exciting time when there are lots of energetic openings. Recently, the starseeds connected in a powerful energy field, and the creation of the energy field culminated in the downloading of the crystal and activation of the tepee, which was built specifically for this exercise and for the caring and holding of the energy of the Arcturian Temple on Earth. To try and categorize the newer techniques that came out of this event would be difficult because the most important aspect of the work was the ability to connect and hold a powerful fifth-dimensional energy. I want to repeat that the energy of the downloading of the twelfth crystal represents a connection to the fifth dimension that has not previously been available on Earth. There are now opportunities that had not existed before for fifth-dimensional energy to manifest directly into the third dimension.

If one looks at the idea of the techniques and the increase of biorelativity power, then one has to say that the key factor in any technique for energy work lies in the ability to connect, download and manifest fifth-dimensional energy into the third dimension. That in itself is the most powerful energy, the most powerful technique that can be accomplished at this time on the planet. Let me explain some aspects of fifth-dimensional energy, the meaning of the downloading of the corridors and the downloading of crystals. The downloading of the last crystal essentially created a new energetic force field on the planet. That energetic force field created an energy that we call dialectic energy, which is the interactive force of twelve etheric crystals acting simultaneously to create an energetic force that, when focused and concentrated, is able to accelerate thoughts, biorelativity projects, the activation of corridors and the downloading of new information and new ideas. Every specific problem now facing Earth—whether the problem involves extinctions or planetary survival—has to do with energies, and every problem needs a fifth-dimensional energy solution. That solution is a transcendent energy. It is an energy that goes beyond normal logic.

FIFTH-DIMENSIONAL LOGIC

Normal logic tells you that if humankind continues its current oil consumption and discharge of greenhouse gases into the environment, it would take a century for the planet to heal. That is if humans stopped producing these substances at this point in time, which humans are not going to do. By the way, it would take a hundred years to bring Earth back into a pattern of "normal." If there is a fifth-dimensional solution, then that can be transcended. The predictions are on two levels. The first level is third-dimensional predictions based on logic, the force fields of logic and linear processes. The second level of predictions is based on fifth-dimensional energy and the connections being made on this planet. I believe most of you will want to focus more on fifth-dimensional energies and fifth-dimensional contacts. I will look for you at both levels of predictions. I want to summarize that the key factor is the connection established that enabled all twelve etheric crystals to interact on a continual basis. This enabled the downloading of the crystal and the downloading of the energy for the Arcturian Temple to be manifested on Earth. That energy force field is very strong and it is continuing to emit an unbelievable source of light.

To help each of you listening to connect, I want you to visualize an Atlantic rainforest approximately 350 kilometers from São Paulo, and in this rainforest is a beautiful tepee. This tepee is in the center of the etheric crystal, and it was built specifically for this purpose. The etheric crystal was downloaded exactly to allow the tepee to be in the exact center of the etheric crystal. It is a radiating force of light that generates a very positive, attractive energy. This has given an unbelievable spiritual boost to the country of Brazil and to the area around there. This is very welcome for that country. The polarizations you are becoming aware of are becoming stronger, but then there is going to be a reconciliation that is going to come about soon. The unfortunate part is that things have to become more polarized before people who are in each polarizing camp become conditioned and become willing to reconcile.

You will see, for example, some further polarizations in the economy in terms of greater differences between the rich and the poor. You will see further polarizations in terms of the wars that are going on; people will become more entrenched. You will see further polarizations in the planet and the biosphere, and this will be culminated in several major weather-related catastrophic events around the globe. It is not overly helpful to list too many of the catastrophes because people become so worried about them. There continues to be a polarization on the planet among some people about what we should do about global warming, and there is a lot of inertia. These events will make it clear that warming is a real problem, and people will have to reconcile their differences in order to do something constructive.

There will be an increase in links to the fifth dimension; these links are now going to manifest. Let me give you an example. Where the twelfth etheric crystal was downloaded has become a sacred spot in Brazil. The specific area known as Serra da Bocaina is going to become well known. More importantly, more people are going to be drawn spiritually and magnetically to the area. The area is going to become a generating place for fifth-dimensional magnetic light around the planet, and it is going to be a receiver of Central Sun light coming from the fifth dimension into the planet. The cities of light are going to become more activated and will be able to activate more cities of light. Also, the starseeds on this planet are going to become more unified and effective in holding fifth-dimensional light. There will be a greater ability to become politically involved for the greater good, and there will be great successes. The upcoming Arcturian work is going to become more popular and more energizing for people.

I am very pleased that these twelve etheric crystals are going to become known worldwide and that their magnetic energy will be the basis for the biorelativity work. Now we will help you to project your thoughts. There are exercises for biorelativity through the crystal grid. This etheric crystal grid is connecting with fifth-dimensional energy and light, bringing down a charge that was not available prior to the downloading of the twelfth etheric crystal.

Harness Healing Energy

How can you harness the energies that were downloaded for healers? The process for this is based on thought energy waves. Thoughts can be amplified. In terms of the concepts of quantum healing light, the idea is that if you have a thought like an affirmation and you want to increase the effectiveness of that affirmation, you could emblazon the affirmation with fifth-dimensional light—what we also call quantum light or omega light. This is an example of what I call thought amplification. In normal third-dimensional thinking, let's say you hold a thought in your mind for a hundred hours, because on the third dimension, thinking can change reality, but sometimes thinking requires a longer process. That longer process could be defined in terms of the hours it takes to repeat the affirmation. Even then, when the thought becomes effective, the actual manifestation of the energy could still take a long time, up to several years.

As healers, you need to work with your thoughts and amplify your thinking. Say, for example, you want to heal someone. Actually think the words, "I am able to heal so and so. I am able to send healing energy to this person's organs." With that thought, you are connected to fifth-dimensional healing light, and then the light can come through your hands and you can heal that person. Imagine that you take your thought and put it in the grid of the twelve etheric crystals. In order to do this, you need the diagram of the Arcturian Tree of Life [please see chart in Chapter 12]. Unless you already have it in your mind, the diagram has the names of each etheric crystal site and the partial meaning of each site. Let's say that you are close to Mount Fuji. So you send your thought, and the thought is, "I am going to heal this person." You send that thought to the etheric crystal you are closest to, let's say Mount Fuji, and all of a sudden the thought is processed. It goes through all twelve etheric crystals, including the one in Mount Fuji, and then that thought comes back to you amplified.

Before, when your thinking might have taken ten hours of affirmation to manifest, now you are able to project an energy thought and manifest it in a matter of minutes. The reason that you have been able to accelerate in this way is kind of like particle acceleration. This grid of twelve etheric crystals that we have downloaded is like a particle accelerator for thoughts—a thought accelerator. You can also ask the Arcturians to download into that grid a healing energy for the person you are wanting to assist. Your thoughts can mix with our thoughts. This etheric grid we have downloaded at great effort, I might add, because as you know it has taken years. This can be a way for you to interact with our thoughts. Then you take your thoughts and they are accelerated through the etheric crystal energy field. They are returned to you and you just do your healing as you normally would and your thoughts are going to be much more powerful. You are going to be able to manifest unbelievable healing energy not only out of your hands but also out of your mind.

When we talk about biorelativity you are in a similar situation, in which your healing energies and your telepathic communications with Earth will be accelerated through the twelve etheric crystals. Then when you want to manifest it, you let it go through the twelve etheric crystals. It will manifest through the Serra da Bocaina crystal because that's the crystal that represents the third and fifth dimensions interacting. If you want to manifest, say, the energy of compassion, look at the energy of compassion and go into the crystal that shows compassion. If you want the energy of harmony to manifest, then you go to that crystal, the Montserrat crystal, but only after you have accelerated your thoughts through the twelve etheric grids. This could be very complicated. We are just beginning to formulate these processes. Next question?

YOU CANNOT ASCEND FOR OTHERS

When I as a spiritual person raise my light quotient, my children and husband have difficulties adapting. What can I do to make a harmonious transition? Who can I contact to help me bridge these differences in my family?

This is a common problem, because we know that sometimes one person in the family is a lightworker and another member is not and is, perhaps, not interested in doing this kind of work. We know a little bit about the nature of relationships on Earth. Naturally, if you love other people, you want to see them raise their light quotient also. But raising your light quotient and being open to this lightwork does not mean that your partner will also be open to this or that his or her light quotient will raise. In some cases it does happen, and in others it doesn't.

There is a greater possibility that your children will be affected, especially if they are light children who have not been awakened. But it is not a failure for you if they do not awaken the way you have. We recommend that you access your compassion and release all judgments. Then just send them love, understanding and compassion. This means that in a sense you have to give up your expectation that you will be able to change them. But remember, we believe you only can change yourself. So even with people you love, sometimes you cannot help them change. I know this is difficult for you, but there is no simple solution to open others up and raise their light quotients.

To say the same thing: You cannot ascend for them. But sometimes the raising of your energy can affect them, especially if you radiate happiness. As you perform your role as mother, father, husband, wife, you radiate at your highest level of caring and responsibility. Remember that when we talk about bringing down fifth-dimensional energy, we're also talking about transferring that energy into your third-dimensional life. We do not want you to neglect your roles; we do not want you to neglect your duties. In fact, the exact opposite is the case.

You will find you have more energy for your roles and that you perform everything to the highest possible standard because you have so much energy. This performance action more than anything will affect them in a positive way and could make them more open to other spiritual lessons and spiritual knowledge. To paraphrase a famous baseball player who said, "It ain't over 'til it's over," there's nothing more successful than success. You will become a very successful person with this spiritual energy, this success is going to rub off, and others will be positively affected. As you perform your roles and duties without expectation that others have to change, you do great service in your love for them. Those people who are performing their lightwork and their lightwork duties are also very much willing to do service even within the regular tasks of daily life in the third dimension.

THE 2012 ENERGY FIELD

Juliano, the Arcturians and Archangel Metatron

Greetings, I am Juliano. We are the Arcturians. We are in 2010, entering the gateway to the 2012 energy field. The gateway is the entrance point, and it is a point where one can begin to feel the energy and also feel the charge of that 2012 energy field. Please understand these descriptions of 2012, especially when we are talking about December 21, 2012, as an energy field. The 2012 field is an energy field that is a reflection of the interaction of Earth's energy field with the galactic center and with the galactic energy field. This means that this interactive pattern is setting up a huge energy field and a huge energy shift. This is one of the points that I want you to understand.

PERSPECTIVE OF MULTIDIMENSIONAL PRESENCE

Mainly, the energy of 2012, especially on the winter solstice, is an interaction with Earth's energy field and with the consciousness of humanity. Because it is an interaction, this means that what is done and what is felt and what is thought by humanity is a contributing factor to the development and the outcome of the 2012 energy.

This is similar to the concept explained in quantum physics: The observer influences the outcome. This means that nothing is occurring in isolation, even on the subatomic level. It is true that quantum physics is talking about subatomic particles—particles that are too small to see. You also know that thought and consciousness are immeasurable and that the energy of the thought field is even thinner and smaller than the subatomic particles. Thoughts can have a quantum effect on global consciousness and on the 2012 energy field now that we are at its gateway.

All gateways signal major shifts. You can believe, even from your personal experience, that the energy field of the gateway can create a somewhat chaotic stirring up of all aspects of Earth, all aspects of consciousness and all systems on Earth, including the geological, political, sociological, meteorological and other Earth systems. It is like you are beginning to change, and even though you welcome a shift or change, it is still a new energy. This relates to our earlier discussions of evolution and our earlier discussions of the fact that humans, and also the animal world, evolve at a point of crisis, at a point of stress. The dividing lines between leaps of evolution and leaps of consciousness are the lines that are drawn from the energies of crisis.

The gateway can reflect a stirring up of energy. The gateway reflects a microcosmic review of the energy systems to see and understand what is going on. If I take the individual systems that are reflected now, then I can tell you that the economic systems are still in a flux, and there still is a great potential for upheaval and a great potential for stress. If I look at the political systems and the political interactions, I can tell you that there are huge amounts of energy that are like powder kegs waiting to explode. If I look at the Inner Earth and the volcanic energies, for example, and the energies of the earthquake that are possible, I can also report the same thing. There are major shifts and upheavals ahead. If I want to look at even the sociological energies in the countries of the world, which have to do in part with the political shifts and changes and upheavals, I can say that there are many places on Earth now that are like powder kegs waiting to explode.

If I speak to you personally, I can tell you—and you already know—that the first nine days of 2010 were dramatic. Even personally, you probably have felt a degree of discomfort and you have felt a degree of possible isolation. Maybe some of the problems and some of the issues that you have been seeking to resolve seem to be stirred up. This is not negative. This is not a doomsday prophecy, not something where you can say, "Oh, Juliano, does that mean that we are really heading for the cleansing and the major Earth changes?" We don't look at it from that standpoint, although I certainly understand that perspective. We look at it this way: We understand there has to be some sort of crisis, there has to be some sort of stress, that will force people—force humanity—to shift. We have been preparing you, the starseeds, for many months and even years to be capable and ready for this shift.

This shift requires that you also are capable of making an evolutionary leap in your consciousness and that you are preparing to make this evolutionary leap with the intention of contributing to the evolution of the species. You have been learning and are open to the techniques of imbuing the thoughts and the conscious energy field of Earth with fifth-dimensional energy and with fifth-dimensional perspectives and with higher light.

It means that one is able to gain the perspective of the fifth dimension. This perspective includes multidimensional presence, the evolution of species and the abilities to ascend. One can open up the corridors for energy transfers and higher thinking from the fifth-dimensional higher realms. Higher thinking can be attuned and downloaded into new thoughts and new techniques for healing, and it can provide new perspectives on old problems.

You Are in Galactic Awareness

There is now also a motivation to begin to act more forcibly and more assertively for change. This means that it is time to work on the energy grid of the etheric crystals. The energy field of the etheric crystals is a dialectic energy field that can be focused on certain changes, such as to modify the power of earthquakes, to attenuate the power of winter storms and to work on sending energy to world leaders so they can make higher decisions. The wrong decision by a world leader now is going to have much more dramatic effects than it would have had even three years ago, because we are at a more critical state in the world now than we were three years ago.

I have recommended that we do a special energy meditation in a twelve-hour period in which each hour a different group of Arcturian starseeds, GOF members, is focusing on a different crystal. Then, during the twelve-hour period, all of the twelve crystals will be generating a light field. These light fields from the twelve crystals will then be downloaded to the subcrystals at that hour. Let us just say, for example, we are going to focus on Mount Shasta and that crystal would be at 9:00 AM California time. Then at 10:00 AM California time, or one hour later—it all would be based on the time in Mount Shasta—and then it would go to Mount Fuji. Then an hour later, it would go to Grose Valley. This would create a force field.

Remember, I said that 2012 is an interactive force field. Interactive means that what you are thinking and doing is also affecting what is happening. We want to accelerate. We want to magnify, to increase the power of the twelve etheric, dialectic, energy field crystals so that energy field can be projected to the 2012 energy field. In order to understand this better, I will focus on more information about how this interaction can be strengthened.

We have reached the point in humanity of Earth called galactic awareness. This point has been accelerating dramatically in the past twenty-four months. If you look at the whole history of man, you would say that the knowledge that humanity has of the galaxy has been a slow awareness. Perhaps we have seen some bright spots, such as in Mayan understanding. There are other tribes and other groups that have had this awareness of the galaxy and even the interaction of the galaxy with Earth, but the twentieth century experienced a big breakthrough in terms of the understanding of the galaxy.

The last twenty-four months in world history have seen a phenomenal leap in the human understanding of our relationship as a solar system and as a planet to the galaxy. Many scientists have now reached the conclusion that there is a total interactive force field in the galaxy that is affecting Earth. It is truly amazing and outstanding that the galaxy has an interactive force field with Earth. Humanity and Earth also affect the galaxy and even the Central Sun. The interaction and the effect that humans have with the Central Sun and with this galactic force field can be maximized.

I have to explain that this effect could be a negative effect as well as a positive effect. One example of a negative effect of humanity's consciousness on the Central Sun and on the energetic force field of the galaxy is the Hiroshima and Nagasaki atomic bombs. I am not making any judgments about the political benefit, if any, to the end of the war. I am just telling you that those two explosions have had a tremendous effect on the energy field of the galaxy and on the Central Sun energy field. It aroused many thoughts throughout the higher beings in the galaxy who repeatedly stressed to many of us the desire to stop humanity from spreading atomic-weapons' consciousness into the galaxy. They believe that humanity, Earth humans, could bring that type of thinking and that type of technology into the galactic energy field.

It is not only the consciousness of Nagasaki and Hiroshima but also the consciousness of other nuclear tests and the Chernobyl disaster that can affect the galactic interaction energy field. There certainly is a reluctance to allow humanity to develop this knowledge of nuclear energy. At the same time, the Galactic Council recognizes that there are many higher beings on Earth right now. In truth, there are more evolved spiritual beings on Earth now than at any other time in the history of this planet.

What a polarization! There potentially may be over 100,000 enlightened beings on Earth now. I am not saying that these enlightened beings are perfect beings, such as on the level of Buddha or Jesus, but I am saying that they are enlightened in terms of consciousness and understanding. Perhaps it could be compared to the Sufi thinking, which is more universal, based on brotherhood. You might say that is such a small number compared to seven billion people that it is insignificant. However, 100,000 enlightened beings is a huge number. Many of you are part of that enlightened group.

There are various figures thrown around, and 100,000 is actually a small estimate, because I could say there may be as many as a million or a million and a half that participate in this type of enlightened thinking. Many of those 100,000 may not have the commitment or the understanding of the ascension, multidimensional thinking or multidimensional thought projections. The Galactic Council agreed to send, and began to communicate with many of the starseeds through, the higher beings that this channel and many of you are now channeling.

At this time, especially in 2010, as we are entering the gateway, the Galactic Council is making the energy fields easier to access so that more of you can call and begin to communicate with your guides and teachers on a personal level. In fact, if you look at the past six or nine months, it is truly phenomenal how many of you have come into your own channeling abilities. Your abilities to connect with masters and teachers have improved. Your abilities to download new information have improved. The strength and the courage that you have had to do this spiritual work have improved. You need to continue to travel to power spots on Earth, and you need to commit to some new and fantastic spiritual projects.

MULTIDIMENSIONAL REINCARNATION THROUGH THE ARCTURIAN STARGATE

One powerful example of a new spiritual project was the downloading of the twelfth etheric crystal in Serra da Bocaina, Brazil. The energies of the Groups of Forty were able to be used to manifest a beautiful tepee there. The tepee wound up being at exactly the center point of the etheric crystal. Each etheric crystal is radiating energy. This one in Brazil is so powerful that it is connecting all of the other eleven crystals with its force field. It is continuing to download information and energy that can be transferred. It has fostered a new alignment, a more powerful alignment, with the Arcturian stargate.

Ah, yes, the Arcturian stargate. At this time, as we go through the gateway of 2012, one of the major energy shifts is focused on galactic time and galactic energy. Your consciousness of galactic energy and time has opened up your connections to multidimensional reincarnation. There is Earth reincarnation and there is also multidimensional reincarnation. Now that your consciousness has been opened to this level, the doorways of the stargate have come more into alignment, preparing for your entrance. Your entrance into the Arcturian stargate is a way of experiencing multidimensional reincarnation.

Earth incarnation is an opportunity to complete your life lessons and your soul lessons, and then you can move on to the next level. The next level might require reincarnating in another place on Earth. It might require meeting your soul family again in another situation. There are many different possibilities. Eventually you hope and pray that you reach the last lifetime in which you can complete and graduate from Earth and third-dimensional incarnations.

Multidimensional reincarnation is the ability to go into different realms and to go to different planets. You want to go to higher planets. There are other planets that are third dimensional, and it is true that you can reincarnate to them. An example of a lower-energy reincarnation would be, for example, a warrior like Saddam Hussein, who dies and reincarnates on another planet where he continues to be involved in different wars and killings. There are still many planets in this galaxy that are third-dimensional dense and would be perfect resting places for someone like that, and they would get to experience war and violence over and over again. Maybe at some point they would get to graduate and move out of that situation.

USE THE INTERACTIVE ENERGY FIELD TO AID YOUR ASCENSION

You may not want to reincarnate on a third-dimensional planet. In fact, when I say, "Earth reincarnation," I have to also make a note that in some cases there is cross-planetary, third-dimensional reincarnation. That means that in some cases, people are reincarnating on other third-dimensional planets. Cross-planetary incarnation is actually one explanation for many of the polarized energies that you are seeing on Earth. There has been a lot of cross-planetary reincarnation on Earth. Some of this has occurred from cross-fertilizations and tampering with the birthing of species. This has been documented and has been discussed, for example, with the planetary system Marduk. It has been talked about in discussions of the nephilim, the fallen ones in the Old Testament and also in the concept of the twelfth planet. That twelfth planet, by the way, is "transdimensional." It is not a planet that is in the third-dimensional path of the gravitational field of the Sun.

Many people have thought that this planet goes around the Sun and goes into this elliptical orbit that goes past Pluto, and then once every 2,000 or 3,000 years it comes back and comes closer to Earth and makes its appearance known. Actually, it is a transdimensional planet, and this means that it goes in and out of dimensions. Sometimes it comes into Earth's dimensional field and is seen, and sometimes it isn't. It is not permanently in the third-dimensional energy field. There are people there who are working on that planet who want to reincarnate on Earth, and when the planetary system gets closer to Earth, then they look for ways of coming to Earth. Their understanding of why a planet will go in and out of dimensions is still somewhat limited.

I can only compare this to the planet in the Pleiades star field when, through scientific accident, the planet remained on the precipice between the third and the fifth dimension. It was stuck. At that point, the planet was in a similar situation to Marduk, and it was going to go in and out of dimension. That is not a very favorable situation. The Galactic Council studied the situation, and because there were so many higher beings on the Pleiades, permission was granted for the planet to permanently enter the fifth dimension.

I am just reviewing this with you because I want you to understand that you are evolving toward multidimensional reincarnation. This is the idea of the stargate that you would be able then to control and correct a path that will allow you to incarnate on other higher planetary systems. In order to do that, you need an awareness of the galaxy. You need awareness that there are other planetary systems in the galaxy. You need an intention of consciousness in the current Earth lifetime that is preparing and is open to traveling through the stargate. You need to be open to the ascension and to the opening of the stargate. Remember, we are in the gateway of 2012. The gateway for 2012 is also an energy field for ascension. It is not just an energy field for Earth changes and clearings and cleansings. The energy field, remember, is interactive, and so by fostering the energies of interaction of 2012, you can begin to accelerate the ascension.

THE ETHERIC CRYSTALS CAN HELP YOUR ASCENSION

I am suggesting that we begin, as starseeds and Arcturian Groups of Forty members, to activate the ascension energies through an exercise on an hourly basis, activating the twelve etheric crystals with the Central Sun and 2012 energy and to create an interactive force field and reactivate the alignment of Serra da Bocaina, Brazil, with the stargate. Visualize, actually begin to visualize, that you are crossing into the stargate. You can do this through thought projections. This gateway represents a newer energy.

Up until this point, we have said that it is difficult to get too close to the doorway of the stargate. You have to complete your Earth lessons in order to go through the stargate. Now the doorway, the vestibule, the gateway to the stargate is more open than ever before for Earth beings. Please meditate with me now and visualize the Arcturian stargate. Visualize, to the best of your ability, that you are at the twelfth etheric crystal at Serra da Bocaina. Visualize that you are being elevated up the ladder of ascension. You hear this special sound of ascension, and you are elevated to the Arcturian stargate. Remember that the energy from the twelfth etheric crystal and its alignment with the stargate is also connecting with the energy of the other eleven etheric crystals. The other etheric crystals now are also becoming more open to the energy of the stargate and becoming more open to the concepts of the multidimensional reincarnation.

When I say multidimensional reincarnation, I hope you understand that it means that some of you obviously have been in other dimensional planets before you came to Earth. Some of you have been on Arcturus. Some of you have been on the Pleiades. Some of you have been in Alano. Some of you have been in the Andromedan systems. The question has always emerged: "Well, Juliano, what is going on? If I have been on those other dimensional planets, why have I come back down now to a third-dimensional planet? Why am I not staying in these higher dimensional planets?"

The answer is somewhat complicated, so I have to explain something about galactic time. The greatest innovation and achievement with dimensional beings has been the mastery of time. The understanding of time travel and its relationship to dimensions has created abilities that are far beyond your imagination. Time travel breaks many rules of your physics and linear thinking. When you look at time as circular rather than linear, you will begin to appreciate that, in certain instances, you can go back in time and in other instances, you go forward in time. This experience on Earth may be in an earlier time for you. In this view, you are already ascended with us in the future time. Stay with this thinking. It is very easy to become confused. I don't want to confuse you any more than is necessary.

I just want you to understand that multidimensional reincarnation is not linear in the way that Earth reincarnation is. However, multidimensional reincarnation is also cumulative. By cumulative, I mean reincarnation can be viewed as a series of incarnations. Thus you can have a higher incarnation and then a third-dimensional reincarnation and then a couple higher ones again. Reincarnation is cumulative, and eventually you are able to totally graduate and not ever have to return to a third-dimensional existence unless you chose to for some special mission. Some of you who are starseeds now have been with me on the Pleiades. Those of you who are connecting with your Arcturian guides have also been with me on Arcturus and have been with me on some of these other planetary systems. If you could grasp this cumulative concept with multidimensional reincarnation, then you will have a better understanding that it is possible to be on the third dimension again.

There is a good concept in the *Kaballah* that is mainly about the "lifting of the sparks." The understanding from the galactic standpoint is that you are lifting the sparks of some of your other incarnations. I could say that you have lifted a spark from your earlier Earth incarnation. You are beginning to grasp the complex nature of yourself. Imagine that you have had a past incarnation in a higher planet. Now imagine that you have come back here to understand parts of yourself. I think that you are ready to go to this level of thinking. I will conclude this portion of the lecture by explaining to you that time is accelerated. Try and combine your galactic awareness and the awareness of the Central Sun with the awareness that you are entering the door, the gateway to the 2012 energy field. With this awareness comes a corresponding acceleration of time.

I believe many of you have already experienced this time acceleration. Hasn't this been a fantastically accelerated time? Haven't many events around the planet occurred already? Don't you feel like everything is moving so fast now? I would like to turn the next part of the lecture over to Archangel Metatron who will speak some more about the sparks. My dear friends, Arcturian starseeds and GOF members, we will be with you now, and we will support you with healing light. In particular, I will be sending you protective light and protective energy. You are valuable to the evolution of Earth, of humanity, and also of the galaxy and the galactic consciousness that we are spreading. I am Juliano. Good day.

G reetings, I am Archangel Metatron. Shalom. I am the keeper of the Arcturian stargate, the protector of the gateway for your multidimensional reincarnation, and also your guide and teacher to help you in your understanding of the raising of the sparks. Many of the Kaballistic masters have talked before about the raising of the sparks. Many have talked about the idea that in the moment of creation, there were explosions of energy and that the containers could not hold the spreading sparks. This is the reason why possibly there is the presence of evil on the planets.

I want to introduce a different idea to you about the sparks. I want to suggest that one of the main missions of your soul life is to raise and to find your own sparks. I want you to consider that you are a complex being and your energy is contained in a force field. You could not totally hold the energy, and it was spread around over many different places in the galaxy and the universe and on planet Earth. These spreading sparks are the fallen sparks that the Kaballists talk about. Most importantly, one of your great missions is to gather the fallen, or spreading, sparks of yourself and to bring those parts of yourself into unity and to heal them.

Some of you have parts of yourself from Atlantis. Some of you have parts of yourself from the Maya. Some have sparks from earlier times in Europe. Some of you have parts of yourself from the native peoples in South America and in New Zealand. You have fallen sparks here on Earth. You also could have fallen sparks in other planetary systems.

Consider this idea. Probably many of you have been on Arcturus or some higher planets. Despite the fact that you were on higher planets, you still may have had some fallen sparks representative of yourself on Earth. You had the wherewithal, you had the energy, you had the concentration, and you had the support of your guides and teachers to come back to Earth now and to heal and to unify those fallen sparks of yourself. *Neshemah*, or *ha Neshemah*—Hebrew for "light of your holy soul." Call on all parts of yourself to come into unity. Call on all parts of yourself to be healed. This can be a tremendous period of enlightening energy for you to understand. Many of you have questioned why you have come back to Earth. Many of you have asked this question: "How could it be that I have lived in other higher dimensions but now I am back here on Earth? Am I being punished?" No, look at this time on Earth as a grace and as a time to gather the sparks. Look at your service to others. Help others find those parts of themselves. Is this not what soul retrieval is—finding the lost parts or sparks of the self? The purpose is now both to find those parts of self and to heal them and to bring them back into unity with the self. Now you are finding the opportunity to unify with your galactic self and your multidimensional self.

This uplifting of the sparks also includes the unification of those parts with your greater higher self. It's a two-part process. It's the upliftment and the unification. *Yechudim* is the Kaballistic name for this unification. "We ask *Hashem*, the Creator, to give us the power to raise our sparks from our lower selves and from our selves from other lifetimes and from our selves from other dimensions. Help us, *Hashem*, to raise all our sparks so that we can bring them into unity to our greater, higher self." One of the secrets of doing the unity is to be in service to the light and to the ascension and to the planetary evolution. By doing that, you are given special grace and powerful energy to raise all parts of self.

Olam haze. Olam haba—"This world and the world to come." There is this world, and there is the world to come. Now we can unify both. In the world to come, you will be unified with your higher self through the multidimensional self. You will be in total healing light in the world to come because of the work that you are doing now. I am Archangel Metatron. Shalom.

GLOSSARY

2012 ALIGNMENT

A time when Earth comes into alignment with the center of the Milky Way galaxy. This is also referred to in the Mayan calendar, and prophecies were made for this date. The Maya believed that Earth will come into alignment with the center of the galaxy on December 21, 2012. Some have interpreted the Mayan statements as marking the end of the world. Others say that this alignment represents the transformation of the world. One view is that our world will be born again on December 21, 2012. John Major Jenkins, in *Maya Cosmogenesis 2012* interpreted the Mayan vision of this alignment in 2012 as a union of the Cosmic Mother, or the Milky Way, with the Father represented as the December solstice sun.

2012 CORRIDOR

A tunnel or corridor to the future time of 2012 when Earth's transformation will be at its height. By projecting positive energy and images into this time, one can help maximize positive outcomes for this time.

ADAM KADMON

The Hebrew term for primordial, or first, man. It is the prototype for the first being to emerge after the beginning of creation.

ADONAI

Hebrew name for God translated as "my Lord."

ADONAI TZEVA'OTH

Hebrew for "Lord of Hosts."

AIN SOPH AUR

Hebrew for "Infinite Light, Infinite One."

ALTERED STATES OF CONSCIOUSNESS (HIGHER)

A term in modern psychology used to describe different states of consciousness. This includes dream states, trances, meditative states of consciousness and also heightened states of consciousness in which one has higher perceptions of reality. This state usually is described as a condition where one can see ultimate truth and is able to experience the present more fully. In the 1960s, this term was used to also describe drug-induced changes and consciousness such as what one could experience with mind-altering drugs.

ARCHANGEL

The term designates the highest rank of angels in the angelic hierarchy. The Kaballah cites ten archangels. They are considered messengers bearing divine decrees.

ARCTURIAN TEMPLAR

This is a project of building a temple that would represent a connection to the Arcturian spirituality. This temple would have a special shape that is similar to the Navajo Native American structure that is called a hogan. The top of the templar would be shaped like a tepee.

ARCTURUS

The brightest star in the constellation Boötes, also known as the herdsman. This is one of the oldest recorded constellations. Arcturus is also the fourth-brightest star seen from Earth. It is a giant star, about twenty-five times the diameter of the Sun and one hundred times as luminous. It is a relatively close neighbor of ours, approximately forty light-years from Earth. High up in the sky in the late spring and early summer, Arcturus is the first star you see after sunset. You can find Arcturus easily if you follow the Big Dipper's handle away from the bowl.

ASCENSION

A point of transformation reached through the integration of the physical, emotional, mental and spiritual selves. The unification of the bodies allows one to transcend the limits of the third dimension and move into a higher realm. It has been compared to what is called the "Rapture" in Christian theology. It has also been defined as a spiritual acceleration of consciousness, which allows the soul to return to the higher realms and thus is freed from the cycle of karma and rebirth.

ASCENDED MASTERS

Teachers who have graduated from Earth or teachers who already are on higher dimensions. An ascended master can be from any Earth religion, including the Native American traditions. They have graduated from Earth's incarnational cycle and have ascended into the fifth dimension. Ascended masters can include archangels, higher beings from the galactic world, teachers and prophets.

ASHTAR

The commander over a group of spiritual beings who is dedicated to helping Earth ascend. The beings that the Ashtar oversees exist primarily in the fifth dimension and come from many different extraterrestrial civilizations.

ASTRAL PLANE

The nonphysical level of reality considered to be where most humans go when they die.

ATAH GIBUR ADONAI
Hebrew for "You are great, Adonai!"

AUR HA MOSHIACH
The Hebrew words mean the "light of the Messiah."

BILOCATE
The ability to be in two places at the same time. You can be physically in your body and mentally or spiritually in another dimension simultaneously.

B'NAI ELOHIM
The children of light. Hebrew name for God that means the children of Elohim.

BIORELATIVITY
Focuses on group thoughts working together telepathically to send healing energy to our planet. The practice is similar to the concept of group prayer in which people send positive thoughts to change the outcome of an event. In biorelativity exercises, groups of starseeds around the planet send healing thoughts to specific areas in the world. Storms, hurricanes and even earthquakes can potentially be averted, deterred or lessened in strength so that minimal damage is inflicted.

The Arcturians point out that on higher planetary systems, groups continually interact telepathically with their planet to ensure maximum harmony between the inhabitants and the planetary forces. Biorelativity focuses on group thoughts working together telepathically to send healing energy to our planet. Native Americans know how to pray to Earth as a group, often asking for rain, for example. In biorelativity exercises, we now have the powerful advantage of globally connecting with many different starseeds, working to unite telepathically for the healing of Earth.

BIOSPHERE
A term used to describe the whole environment of Earth, including the oceans, atmosphere and other necessary ingredients that keep and support all life.

CARLOS CASTAÑEDA

Author of a series of mystical books on shamanism and the world of the Yaqui Indian sorcerer, Don Juan. Carlos was an anthropologist. Don Juan is the shaman in the book teaching Carlos the ancient ways.

CENTRAL SUN

This is the spiritual and etheric center of our galaxy, which is located in the center of the Milky Way. High spiritual energy is emitted from this area. Earth is coming into a direct alignment with the Central Sun in the year 2012. The center of any astronomical star system. All star clusters, nebulae and galaxies contain a nucleus at their centers. Even the grand universe itself has a Great Central Sun at the center of its structure. In most cases, a giant star exists at the center of all star systems. The Great Central Sun of the Milky Way galaxy provides life-giving energy to the entire galaxy.

CHAKRAS

Energy centers of the human body system. These centers provide the integration and transfer of energy between the spiritual, mental, emotional and biological systems of the human body.

CHANNELING

The process of entering a meditative trance in order to call forth other entities to speak through you. See trance channeling.

CHIEF BUFFALO HEART

An ascended fifth-dimensional Native American guide who focuses on using heart energy to help one ascend.

CHIEF WHITE EAGLE

An ascended fifth-dimensional Native American guide who is very connected to Jesus (Sananda) and other higher fifth-dimensional beings.

COHABITATION

Cohabitation refers to the idea of a spirit from another dimension entering the energy field of a third-dimensional Earth being. Cohabitation can be with positive spirits or negative spirits. Positive spirits could be Archangel Michael or other ascended masters. They can live in someone's energy field on the invitation of that person. Negative cohabitation can include lower disoriented spirits, such as ghosts, living in the energy field of the person and often influencing that person to do or feel negative things.

CONNECTING WITH THE ARCTURIANS

This first book by David K. Miller talks about the ascension process and what it means. Who is really out there? Where are we going? What are our choices? What has to be done to prepare for this event? Is everyone ascending to the same place? What happened to the fourth dimension? How can we understand the fifth dimension? What does it feel like? How does it operate? What are fifth-dimensional beings like? How do they live? This book explains all of these questions in a way that we can easily understand. It explains what our relationships are to known extraterrestrial groups and what they are doing to help Earth and her people in this crucial galactic moment in time. It explains how we can raise our vibrations now and begin the process of integrating higher-dimensional energies into our third-dimensional world.

The Arcturians have given us a crucial focus for the acceleration of world consciousness. They have presented the concept of group ascension through the creation of the Groups of Forty. They have also presented the concept of the Sacred Triangle, a method for the integration and unification of spiritual and religious thought on planet Earth. All those who read this book will feel the presence of fifth-dimensional energy within their beings. You will be able to truly experience a view of fifth-dimensional awareness. This will profoundly affect your ability to expand your own perception of reality and help you to actively participate in the personal and planetary ascension that has already begun. Connecting with the Arcturians also contains four visionary paintings by Gudrun Miller, depicting the appearance of the Arcturians and other scenes from their world and existence. These paintings are nothing short of spectacular.

CORRIDORS

Transitional pathways on Earth that lead to a higher dimension. Corridors can be found in high-energy places such as sacred sites on Earth. The Arcturians believe that we can establish corridors within our meditation areas on Earth.

COSMIC EGG

This refers to the perfect shape of the human aura for maximum healing.

COSMIC EGG EXERCISE

This exercise is based on the fact that the perfect healing energy shape is in the shape of an egg. The Arcturians refer to this as a cosmic egg. Using this shape is part of a dimensional method of healing. It is based on helping people to form their auras into this egg shape. By remaining there in this egg shape, one can experience healing.

CRYSTAL TEMPLE

An etheric temple on the fifth dimension that has been made available for our use by the Arcturians. The crystal temple contains a lake more than one mile in diameter that houses a huge crystal half the size of the lake itself. The entire lake and surrounding area are encompassed by a huge glass dome, which allows visitors to view the stars.

EH'YEH ASHER EH'YEH

In Hebrew, the name of God given to Moses at the burning bush in Genesis 3:14. *Ehiyeh Asher Ehiyeh* is the full name translated as "I shall be that I shall be" (also translated "I am that I am"). In Hebrew, this is also known as the supreme name of God. The correct Hebrew translation is "I will be that I will be."

EL NA RE FA NA LA

Hebrew for "please God, heal her now!" This is a famous Kaballah healing chant.

ELOHEYNU ADONAI; ECHAD ADONAI

Hebrew for "our God is Adonai; Adonai is One."

ETHERIC

A term used to designate the higher bodies in the human system. In India, etheric is used to describe the unseen energy and thoughts of humans.

ETHERIC CRYSTALS

Invisible crystals that contain fifth-dimensional energy that have been sent to Earth by the Arcturians. The purpose of these etheric crystals is to provide healing energies to Earth's meridians. To this date, ten etheric crystals have been downloaded. Here is a summary of the process and the role they play in Earth's healing.

List of the ten crystals and a summary of each one's role:

1. **Lago Puelo, Argentina:** The home of the first crystal to be brought down to Earth. The Lago Puelo crystal holds the primordial energy for the whole planet. It is an energy of initiation and connection to energy.

2. **Grose Valley in the Blue Mountains National Park in Australia:** The Grose Valley crystal is connecting with the Rainbow Serpent, which is the feminine goddess energy of Mother Gaia and is an area of great significance to the Aborigines of Australia.

3. **Lake Moraine in Canada:** This crystal contains the quantum etheric energy activation light, which can bypass the normal laws of linear time and space and cause and effect.

4. **Lake Constance in the Bodensee in Germany:** The home of the fourth crystal. This crystal provides new information, new codes, new structures and new dynamics into Earth's ley lines and allows us access to new information.

5. **Costa Rica, the home of the fifth etheric crystal in the Poás Volcan:** This crystal is linked to the great attractor force—that which pushes and pulls the galaxies in different directions. It also helps to attract and discharge blocked energy in Earth's energy channels, like modifying the ring of fire to create balance in that area.

6. **Mount Shasta in California in the United States:** The combination of the crystal, the Galactic Kachina and the imprint of the stargate means that Mount Shasta has become a powerful ascension point. It also gives us an easy connection to our souls, our soul powers and our soul missions.

7. **Lake Taupo in New Zealand, the home of the seventh crystal:** The number seven is a symbol of good luck and good fortune and brings wealth and prosperity. This crystal is representative of that wealth and prosperity and is a great attracting force for energy for those who work with it. It is also a reaffirmation of the spiritual strength and

power of the native peoples on Earth and will help to reawaken them to their mission.

8. **Mexico and the beautiful Copper Canyon where the eighth crystal resides:** This crystal gives us a new link to Arcturian energy; a link where we can connect with the moon-planet Alano and the fifth-dimensional master named Alano who resides there. The crystal also carries the special energy of shimmering, allowing us to move ourselves or objects into another dimension.

9. **Montserrat near Barcelona in Spain:** This magnificent place is a holy site. Juliano tells us it is mostly free from wars and polarization and the crystal. The ninth crystal has a powerful, sacred and holy energy. This crystal was downloaded to work with holy sacred light and will help the other crystals become truly sacred energy sites.

10. **Mount Fuji in Japan:** This crystal holds energy of life forces from Lemuria, which have now been unlocked by its arrival. It is an ancient crystal containing great secrets of light and ancient knowledge of the planet. It has a connection with the ancient grandmothers and grandfathers.

ETZ-HA-CHAYIM

Hebrew for "Tree of Life."

FIFTH DIMENSION

A higher dimension of existence that is above the first and third dimensions. We currently live on the third dimension. On the third dimension, we are bound by the laws of cause and effect and the laws of reincarnation. The fourth dimension is the astral realm and also the realm of dreams. The fifth dimension transcends this and is the realm of infinite energy and love and can be compared to the Garden of Eden. In the fifth dimension, one transcends the incarnational cycle. One can say that one graduates from Earth and goes to the fifth dimension. The ascended masters residing now in the fifth dimension include Jesus (Sananda). The ascension focuses on going to the fifth dimension.

GALACTIC KACHINA

This is an intermediary between this world and other worlds and, in particular, the spirit world. The Galactic Kachina is the intermediary between the Central Sun and this planet. The Central Sun is located at the center point of the Milky Way galaxy, our galaxy. However, this is the first time that the concept of a Galactic Kachina has been introduced. In Native American Navajo folklore, a Kachina is an intermediary between the higher spirit world and this world. The Native peoples were the first to accept a spiritual philosophy or theory that includes the existence of other higher beings throughout our galaxy. They also take the perspective of the broader galactic view that says we are all part of a galactic family.

GOF
The acronym for Groups of Forty.

GRAYS (GREYS)
Fourth-dimensional, old extraterrestrial beings often depicted in movies as having small, thin figures. They are said to not have the ability to love and are very absent of human's spiritual energy. They have been known to abduct Earth people and have been involved in genetic manipulations to further their own dying race.

GRID LINES
Another name for energy lines that run through the planet. In Chinese medicine, energy lines that run through the body are called meridians.

GROUPS OF FORTY
A concept of group consciousness suggested by the Arcturians for our use in the ascension process. According to the Arcturians, forty is a spiritually powerful number. The Arcturians emphasize the value and power of joining together in groups. A group of forty consists of forty different members located throughout the U.S. and worldwide who focus on meditating together at a given time each month. Group interactions and yearly physical meetings are recommended. Members agree to assist each other in their spiritual development. The Arcturians have asked that forty Groups of Forty be organized. These groups will assist in the healing of Earth and provide a foundation for the individual member's ascension.

A Group of Forty is a meditative and spiritual group to connect with the Arcturians. David Miller has been working with the energies of the ascension for more than fifteen years. The Arcturians have asked him to set up meditation groups called Groups of Forty. The Groups of Forty have been meeting for fifteen years now and have drawn members from all over the United States and Canada, as well as Australia and Germany. Because of the demand for membership, he was instructed to begin new groups, so a second, third and fourth group met. Now there are members around the world. New groups are starting and will also meet in meditation once a month wherever members are located.

At a specific hour during the meditation time, David channels messages from the Arcturians for all group members. A monthly newsletter is sent out with the transcription of that lecture. A group coordinator arranges other group activities, such as individual group meditations and healings. Additionally, members are encouraged to meet other members either by phone, letter or in person. A newsletter and transcribed channeling is mailed monthly. Meditations also include group healing in which all members of the group focus healing energy on one designated person in the group. Members who are the focus of this healing energy have reported profound healing experiences. All work is directed toward our transformation to higher consciousness—Earth healings and personal healings. As of this writing, we now have forty groups with more than 1,000 members around the world, each with a group coordinator. New groups are continuously being formed.

HARMONIC CONVERGENCE
A term used to describe a harmonic energy downloaded to Earth from the Central Sun. The first Harmonic Convergence was in 1987. The most recent one occurred on August 8, 2008, when a harmonic energy was brought down to the earth at Mount Shasta, California, and transmitted around the world.

HELIO-AH
An Arcturian female guide and close associate of Juliano.

HOLOGRAPHIC DECK OF CARDS
This is a concept based on the idea that there are past memory images in our mental bodies. Our memory-brains store these images. Each image looks like a card and the entire memory bank looks like a deck of cards. To heal past traumas, we can access past memory images and reshape those images for healing.

HOLOGRAPHIC HEALING
The concept in holographic healing states that the part represents the whole. In holographic energy, healing one aspect of Earth can affect the entire planet's energy. Healing one part of Earth can affect other parts of Earth.

HOLOGRAPHY WORK
In the scientific world, holography is described as a part of any image created through a laser that actually reproduces the original whole image. In fifth-dimensional work, holography is the ability to access all universal energy from any spot in the universe. Holographic healing is based on the assumption that we can access our greater selves through holographic energy.

ISKALIA MIRROR
A fifth-dimensional mirror that is in the etheric above Earth. This etheric mirror attracts and brings down higher light from the Central Sun so that greater enlightenment and healing energy can come to Earth.

JULIANO
The main Arcturian guide and ascended master working to help activate Earth and Arcturian starseeds toward ascension.

KABALLAH
The major branch of Jewish mysticism. The Hebrew word *Kaballah* is translated as "to receive."

KADOSH
Hebrew word for "holy."

KADOSH, KADOSH, KADOSH ADONAI TZEVA'OTH
Hebrew for "holy, holy, holy is the Lord of Hosts." This is a powerful expression that, when toned, can raise one's level of consciousness to new heights and assist in unlocking the codes for our transformation into the fifth dimension.

KUTHUMI
One of the ascended masters who serves Sananda. In a previous life,

Kuthumi incarnated as Saint Francis of Assisi. He is generally recognized as holding the position of World Teacher in the planetary White Brotherhood/Sisterhood. An extensive record of his teachings can be found in the works of Alice Bailey.

LAGO PUELO

A beautiful, scenic lake in the Patagonia area in Argentina where the first Arcturian etheric crystal was downloaded.

LAKE MORAINE

A lake near Banff in the
Canadian Rockies where an etheric crystal resides.

LIGHTBODY

The higher etheric spirit body that is connected to the highest soul energy.

LUMINOUS BALLS OF LIGHT

This term refers to etheric balls of light that can travel through etheric realms and, when received, can amplify one's spiritual energies.

MERKAVAH

In Hebrew, it means "chariot," and in modern spirituality, it refers to a chariot in etheric form that is used to bring spiritual seekers to the higher dimensions. Also spelled merkaba and merkabah.

METATRON

Tradition associates Metatron with Enoch, who "walked with God" (Genesis 5:22) and who ascended to heaven and was changed from a human being into an angel. His name has been defined as the Angel of Presence or the one who occupies the throne next to the divine throne. In the world of the Jewish mystic, Metatron holds the rank of the highest of angels. According to the Arcturians, Metatron is associated with the stargate and is assisting souls in ascension to higher worlds.

MICHAEL

His name is actually a question, meaning: "Who is like God?" He is perhaps the best known of the Archangels and is acknowledged by all three

Western sacred traditions. He has been called the Prince of Light, fighting a war against the sons of darkness. In this role, he is depicted most often as winged, with unsheathed sword, the warrior of God and slayer of the dragon. His role in the ascension is focused on helping us cut the cords of attachment to the Earth plane, which will allow us to move up to higher consciousness. In the Kaballah, he is regarded as the forerunner of the Shekinah, the divine Mother.

MULTIDIMENSIONAL PRESENCE

We can become aware that we exist on several different dimensions. The Arcturians are trying to help us become aware that we have an existence not only on the third dimension but also in the fifth dimension.

NESHAMAH

In Kaballah, or Jewish Mysticism, this is your most high self, which transcends third-dimensional reality and Earth ego and is linked directly to the divine light.

PHOTON BELT/PHOTON ENERGY

An energy emanating from the center of the galaxy that is about to intersect with our solar system and Earth. Some have predicted that the photon belt contains energy particles that could affect Earth's magnetic field, causing all electronic equipment to stop working.

PLEIADIANS

A fifth-dimensional people who are human-like and located in the constellation known as the Pleiades, approximately 450 light-years from Earth. It is said that the Pleiadians have a common ancestry with us. They live on their fifth-dimensional planet.

PLEIADES

A small cluster of stars known as the Seven Sisters in some mythologies. Some Native Americans believe that they are descended from the Pleiades. It is near the constellation Taurus, about 450 light-years from Earth and is the home of a race called the Pleiadians who have frequently interacted with Earth and her cultures.

PORTAL

An opening at the end of a corridor that allows one to go into an interdimensional space. This could allow one to go into the fifth dimension.

PULSING

An exercise technique used by the Arcturians in which one can heal oneself by contracting and expanding one's energy field. One becomes aware of one's vibration energy field. By increasing the rates of the energy field and then rapidly pulsing, or expanding and contracting, one can raise one's spiritual awareness and also do self-healing.

RING OF ASCENSION

An etheric halo of energy around Earth containing fifth-dimensional light from the ascended masters. This halo is supposed to aid Earth in her ability to ascend as a planet to the fifth dimension. The starseeds are to interact with this light through visualizations and meditations.

Ruach Ha-Kodesh

Hebrew for "Holy Spirit."

Sacred Triangle

A term used by the Arcturians to denote a triangular symbol representing the unification of three powerful spiritual forces on Earth: the White Brotherhood/Sisterhood ascended masters, including Sananda/Jesus; the ET higher-dimensional masters, such as the Arcturians and the Pleiadians; and the Native American ascended masters, such as Chief White Eagle. The unification of these spiritual forces will create the Sacred Triangle that will aid in the healing and ascension of Earth.

Sananda

Sananda is the one who is known to us as the Master Jesus. He is considered the greatest Jewish Kaballist of all time. His galactic name, Sananda, represents an evolved and galactic picture of who he is in his entirety. In the Kaballah, Sananda is known as Jeshua ben Miriam of Nazareth, which can be translated as Jesus, son of Mary of Nazareth.

SHAMBALA LIGHT

Light from the fifth dimension that is focused on cities of perfect harmony existing in the fifth dimension. One such city of light is called Shambala.

SHIMMERING

Shimmering is an energy exercise that allows one's auric field to vibrate at a frequency that enables the aura to shift electrons. The atomic structure of your cells transmutes into a vibratory energy field that elliptically shifts the cellular structures into the fifth dimension, causing a back-and-forth, or shimmering, modality. This back-and-forth shimmering modality actually affects the atomic and quantum levels of your cellular structures. This shimmering energy is the precursor to the ascension. The ascension is an accelerated and enhanced shimmering energy in which you elevate yourselves into the fifth dimension permanently. The energy that we are now working with in shimmering is a powerful and necessary prelude to the fifth-dimensional ascension.

SPIRITUAL LIGHT QUOTIENT

The measurement of a person's ability to work with and understand spirituality. This concept is compared to IQ (intelligence quotient); however, in reality, spiritual ability is not related to intelligence and, interestingly, unlike IQ, ones spiritual light quotient can increase with age and experiences.

STARGATE

A multidimensional portal into other higher realms. The Arcturian stargate is very close to the Arcturus star system, and it is overseen by the Arcturians. This powerful passage point requires that Earthlings who wish to pass through it must complete all lessons and Earth incarnations associated with the third-dimensional experience. It serves as a gateway to the fifth dimension. New soul assignments are given there, and souls can then be sent to many different higher realms throughout the galaxy and universe.

STARSEEDS

Earth beings throughout our current modern age that have previous lifetimes in other parts of our galaxy. They also have a great awareness that there are other beings living in our galaxy and in the universe.

THOUGHT-PROJECTION

A technique described by the Arcturians involving projecting thoughts through a corridor to reach the fifth dimension and beyond.

Tomar

An Arcturian ascended master whose specialty is using and describing the Arcturian Temple energy.

TONES

Sounds that produce a vibratory resonance that helps to activate and align the charkas.

TRANCE CHANNELING

Putting yourself into a light trance to do automatic speaking. Trance is a type of self-hypnosis in which you put yourself into an altered state of consciousness. There is light trance and there is deep trance. A deep trance is where you go out of your body and are almost in a somnambular, or sleep, state. This is the way Edgar Cayce used to channel. In light trance channeling, one is still awake while bringing through messages.

Tree of Life

The Tree of Life is a galactic blueprint for the creation of this reality. It includes ten energy codes placed in spheres in the shape of a tree. These codes are used for individual and planetary healing. The three spiritualities of the Sacred Triangle are included in the Tree of Life. The Tree of Life is not flat, but multidimensional and holographic. The Tree of Life has paths for manifestation. The twenty-two lines of the Tree of Life are pathways of manifestation. The Tree of Life connects to the energy of the cosmos. The following page contains one interpretation using the model of the Tree of Life.

Vywamus

A fifth-dimensional soul psychologist known for his insight into the psychology of Earth problems and resolution of issues related to starseeds incarnated on Earth.

White Brotherhood/Light Brotherhood

A powerful spiritual group in the fifth dimension who oversees spiritual guidance for the third dimension. It is composed of ascended masters from the religious spiritual groups on Earth. The spiritual wisdom they teach does not belong to any one culture or religion nor does it come from the East. It is a mystical knowledge common to all.

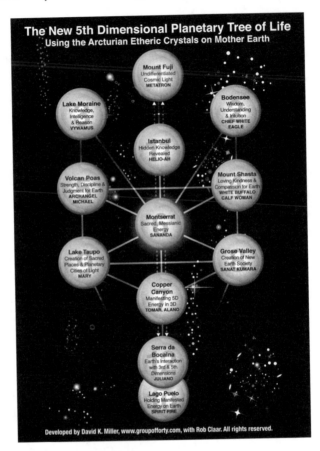

The New 5th Dimensional Planetary Tree of Life
Using the Arcturian Etheric Crystals on Mother Earth

Mount Fuji
Undifferentiated
Cosmic Light
METATRON

Lake Moraine
Knowledge,
Intelligence
& Reason
VYWAMUS

Bodensee
Wisdom,
Understanding
& Intuition
CHIEF WHITE
EAGLE

Istanbul
Hidden Knowledge
Revealed
HELIO-AH

Volcan Poas
Strength, Discipline &
Judgment for Earth
ARCHANGEL
MICHAEL

Mount Shasta
Loving Kindness &
Compassion for Earth
WHITE BUFFALO
CALF WOMAN

Montserrat
Sacred, Messianic
Energy
SANANDA

Lake Taupo
Creation of Sacred
Places & Planetary
Cities of Light
MARY

Grose Valley
Creation of New
Earth Society
SANAT KUMARA

Copper
Canyon
Manifesting 5D
Energy in 3D
TOMAR, ALANO

Serra da
Bocaina
Earth's Interaction
with 3rd & 5th
Dimensions
JULIANO

Lago Puelo
Holding Manifested
Energy on Earth
SPIRIT FIRE

WHITE BUFFALO CALF WOMAN

In Lakota Native American folklore, she is the fifth-dimensional spirit being that appeared to them bringing forth special information about holy ceremonies and accessing higher spirit. She taught the necessity of being in harmony with Earth. Her focus is on the unity of all beings and that all are relations. She is representative of the dawning of a New Age.

ZOHARIC LIGHT

Light from the Creator Source. *Zohar* is the Hebrew word for "brilliance" or "splendor."

ABOUT THE AUTHOR

David has been a channel for eighteen years. His original spiritual study was the *Kabbalah* and Jewish mysticism. He began trance channeling his Kabbalistic guide and teacher, Nabur, on a camping trip at Sublime Point on the North Rim of the Grand Canyon.

David has published four books and over fifty articles in both American and Australian magazines. He currently does phone readings and conducts workshops focusing on the concepts and techniques of ascension, healings, and psycho-spiritual issues. He also works full time as a medical social worker and part time conducting group workshops, personal readings and healings.

THE GROUP OF FORTY

Te goal of this project is to establish a network of forty Groups of Forty throughout the world. The formation of forty groups will enhance the energy of group meditation, provide powerful healing energies for Earth and aid all members in raising their consciousness to the fifth-dimensional level. Each Group of Forty will provide the basis for building the energy necessary for group ascension.

MEDITATIONS

All groups simultaneously meet in meditation once each month. Currently it is held the first Saturday of every month at 5:45-6:45 PM, Mountain Standard Time. During the main meditation, David channels a message for everyone in all the groups, which is later transcribed and sent out to all group members with the monthly newsletter.

Group of Forty members do not have to be physically together to participate in the group meditation. The powerful Arcturian energy can be called in wherever any member is meditating, and through that connection, the member can experience the group energy being generated by all Groups of Forty.

Meditations also include a group healing, during which all members of the group focus healing on one designated person in the group who has requested it. Members who have been the focus of this healing energy have reported profound healing experiences. All work by the Arcturians is directed toward personal healings, healings for Mother Earth, and our transformation to higher consciousness, leading to ascension to the fifth dimension.

THE MONTHLY CHANNELED MESSAGE

Messages channeled during the simultaneous group meditation usually cover topics including:

- The Arcturian Frequency
- Preparation for Ascension
- Arcturian Healing Chambers
- Multidimensional Corridors
- Accelerating our Spiritual Growth
- The Arcturian Crystal Temple
- The Arcturian Stargate
- The Sacred Triangle

Members are encouraged to submit questions for the channeling sessions to David at the beginning of each month.

THE MONTHLY NEWSLETTER

David prepares a monthly newsletter providing general announcements and updated information that pertains to all groups. The newsletter, along with a transcription of the monthly channeled message, is mailed to all members each month. Cassette tapes of the monthly channeling sessions are also available on a subscription basis.

THE EMAIL REFLECTOR LIST

David maintains a reflector list through email communication for those members who wish to may share experiences and information, ask general questions of the group and also have a chance to get to know individual members from near and far. It is a wonderful way of building the Group of Forty community. It is an invaluable resource and a great deal of fun too.

THE ANNUAL ARCTURIAN GROUP OF FORTY GATHERING AND WORKSHOP

Annual gatherings are planned for the second weekend in October and are held in Sedona, Arizona. This is a fantastic opportunity to make your in-person connection to the entire Group of Forty project. There are different topics addressed in David's channelings each year, along with guest presenters. It has been a profoundly enlightening, healing and above all enjoyable experience for many past participants. David and Gudrun also conduct other workshops during the year at other places around the world.

REGISTRATION

To become a Group of Forty member, please contact:

David Miller, Group of Forty
P.O. Box 4074
Prescott, AZ 86302
USA
Phone: 928-776-1717
Email: davidmiller@groupofforty
Web: www.groupofforty.com

DAVID K. MILLER

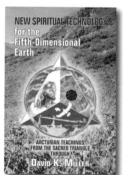

NEW SPIRITUAL TECHNOLOGY FOR THE FIFTH-DIMENSIONAL EARTH

Earth is moving closer to the fifth dimension. New spiritual ideas and technologies are becoming available for rebalancing our world:

- Native ceremonies to connect to Earth healing energies.
- Thought projections and thought communication to communicate with Earth.
- Connections with our galactic starseed heritage so that we can relate to our role in the galaxy.

$19⁹⁵

242 PP. SOFTCOVER
978-1891824791

CONNECTING WITH THE ARCTURIANS

Who is really out there? Where are we going? What are our choices? What has to be done to prepare for this event?

This book explains all of these questions in a way that we can easily understand. It explains what our relationships are to known extraterrestrial groups, and what they are doing to help the Earth and her people in this crucial galactic moment in time.

$17⁰⁰

295 PP. SOFTCOVER
978-1891417085

TEACHINGS FROM THE SACRED TRIANGLE

David's second book explains how the Arcturian energy melds with that of the White Brother/Sisterhood and the Ascended Native American Masters to bring about planetary healing.

- The Sacred Triangle energy and the Sacred Codes of Ascension
- How to create a bridge to the fifth dimension
- What role you can play in the Sacred Triangle
- How sacred words from the Kabbalah can assist you in your ascension work

$22⁰⁰

291 PP. SOFTCOVER
978-0971589438

Phone: 928-526-1345 or 1-800-450-0985 • Fax: 923-714-1132

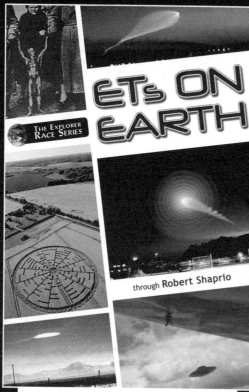

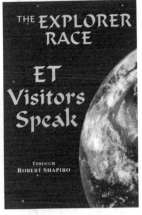

Shamanic Secrets Mastery Series
Speaks of Many Truths and Reveals the Mysteries through Robert Shapiro

Shamanic Secrets for Material Mastery

This book explores the heart and soul connection between humans and Mother Earth. Through that intimacy, miracles of healing and expanded awareness can flourish. To heal the planet and be healed as well, we can lovingly extend our energy selves out to the mountains and rivers and intimately bond with the Earth. Gestures and vision can activate our hearts to return us to a healthy, caring relationship with the land we live on. The character of some of Earth's most powerful features is explored and understood, with exercises given to connect us with those places. As we project our love and healing energy there, we help the Earth to heal from human destruction of the planet and its atmosphere. Dozens of photographs, maps and drawings assist the process in twenty-five chapters, which cover the Earth's more critical locations.

498 p. $19.95 ISBN 978-1-891824-12-8

Shamanic Secrets for Physical Mastery

Learn to understand the sacred nature of your own physical body and some of the magnificent gifts it offers you. When you work with your physical body in these new ways, you will discover not only its sacredness, but how it is compatible with Mother Earth, the animals, the plants, even the nearby planets, all of which you now recognize as being sacred in nature. It is important to feel the value of oneself physically before one can have any lasting physical impact on the world. If a physical energy does not feel good about itself, it will usually be resolved; other physical or spiritual energies will dissolve it because it is unnatural. The better you feel about your physical self when you do the work in the previous book as well as this one and the one to follow, the greater and more lasting will be the benevolent effect on your life, on the lives of those around you and ultimately on your planet and universe.

576 p. $25.00 ISBN 978-1-891824-29-5

Shamanic Secrets for Spiritual Mastery

Spiritual mastery encompasses many different means to assimilate and be assimilated by the wisdom, feelings, flow, warmth, function and application of all beings in your world that you will actually contact in some way. A lot of spiritual mastery has been covered in different bits and pieces throughout all the books we've done. My approach to spiritual mastery, though, will be as grounded as possible in things that people on Earth can use— but it won't include the broad spectrum of spiritual mastery, like levitation and invisibility. I'm trying to teach you things that you can actually use and benefit from. My life is basically going to represent your needs, and it gets out the secrets that have been held back in a storylike fashion, so that it is more interesting."

—Speaks of Many Truths through Robert Shapiro

768 p. $29.95 ISBN 978-1-891824-58-6

⚜ *Light Technology* PUBLISHING

THE EXPLORER RACE SERIES

ZOOSH AND HIS FRIENDS THROUGH ROBERT SHAPIRO

THE SERIES: *Humans—creators-in-training—have a purpose and destiny so heartwarmingly, profoundly glorious that it is almost unbelievable from our present dimensional perspective. Humans are great lightbeings from beyond this creation, gaining experience in dense physicality. This truth about the great human genetic experiment of the Explorer Race and the mechanics of creation is being revealed for the first time by Zoosh and his friends through superchannel Robert Shapiro. These books read like adventure stories as we follow the clues from this creation that we live in out to the Council of Creators and beyond.*

❶ THE EXPLORER RACE

You individuals reading this are truly a result of the genetic experiment on Earth. You are beings who uphold the principles of the Explorer Race. The information in this book is designed to show you who you are and give you an evolutionary understanding of your past that will help you now. The key to empowerment in these days is to not know everything about your past, but to know what will help you now. Your number-one function right now is your status of Creator apprentice, which you have achieved through years and lifetimes of sweat. You are constantly being given responsibilities by the Creator that would normally be things that Creator would do. The responsibility and the destiny of the Explorer Race is not only to explore, but to create. 574 P. $25.00 ISBN 0-929385-38-1

❷ ETs and the EXPLORER RACE

In this book, Robert channels Joopah, a Zeta Reticulan now in the ninth dimension who continues the story of the great experiment—the Explorer Race—from the perspective of his civilization. The Zetas would have been humanity's future selves had not humanity re-created the past and changed the future. 237 P. $14.95
ISBN 0-929385-79-9

❸ EXPLORER RACE: ORIGINS and the NEXT 50 YEARS

This volume has so much information about who we are and where we came from—the source of male and female beings, the war of the sexes, the beginning of the linear mind, feelings, the origin of souls—it is a treasure trove. In addition, there is a section that relates to our near future—how the rise of global corporations and politics affects our future, how to use benevolent magic as a force of creation and how we will go out to the stars and affect other civilizations. Astounding information. 339 P. $14.95 ISBN 0-929385-95-0

❹ EXPLORER RACE: CREATORS and FRIENDS The MECHANICS of CREATION

Now that you have a greater understanding of who you are in the larger sense, it is necessary to remind you of where you came from, the true magnificence of your being. You must understand that you are creators-in-training, and yet you were once a portion of Creator. One could certainly say, without being magnanimous, that you are still a portion of Creator, yet you are training for the individual responsibility of being a creator, to give your Creator a coffee break. This book will allow you to understand the vaster qualities and help you remember the nature of the desires that drive any creator, the responsibilities to which a creator must answer, the reaction a creator must have to consequences and the ultimate reward of any creator. 435 P. $19.95 ISBN 1-891824-01-5

❺ EXPLORER RACE: PARTICLE PERSONALITIES

All around you in every moment you are surrounded by the most magical and mystical beings. They are too small for you to see as single individuals, but in groups you know them as the physical matter of your daily life. Particles who might be considered either atoms or portions of atoms consciously view the vast spectrum of reality yet also have a sense of personal memory like your own linear memory. These particles remember where they have been and what they have done in their infinitely long lives. Some of the particles we hear from are Gold, Mountain Lion, Liquid Light, Uranium, the Great Pyramid's Capstone, This Orb's Boundary, Ice and Ninth-Dimensional Fire. 237 P. $14.95 ISBN 0-929385-97-7

❻ EXPLORER RACE and BEYOND

With a better idea of how creation works, we go back to the Creator's advisers and receive deeper and more profound explanations of the roots of the Explorer Race. The Liquid Domain and the Double Diamond portal share lessons given to the roots on their way to meet the Creator of this universe, and finally the roots speak of their origins and their incomprehensibly long journey here. 360 P. $14.95 ISBN 1-891824-06-6

Visit our online bookstore: www.LightTechnology.com

THE EXPLORER RACE SERIES

ZOOSH AND HIS FRIENDS THROUGH ROBERT SHAPIRO

❼ EXPLORER RACE: The COUNCIL of CREATORS

The thirteen core members of the Council of Creators discuss their adventures in coming to awareness of themselves and their journeys on the way to the Council on this level. They discuss the advice and oversight they offer to all creators, including the Creator of this local universe. These beings are wise, witty and joyous, and their stories of Love's Creation create an expansion of our concepts as we realize that we live in an expanded, multiple-level reality. 237 P. $14.95 ISBN 1-891824-13-9

❽ EXPLORER RACE and ISIS

This is an amazing book! It has priestess training, Shamanic training, Isis's adventures with Explorer Race beings—before Earth and on Earth—and an incredibly expanded explanation of the dynamics of the Explorer Race. Isis is the prototypal loving, nurturing, guiding feminine being, the focus of feminine energy. She has the ability to expand limited thinking without making people with limited beliefs feel uncomfortable. She is a fantastic storyteller, and all of her stories are teaching stories. If you care about who you are, why you are here, where you are going and what life is all about—pick up this book. You won't lay it down until you are through, and then you will want more. 317 P. $14.95 ISBN 1-891824-11-2

❾ EXPLORER RACE and JESUS

The core personality of that being known on the Earth as Jesus, along with his students and friends, describes with clarity and love his life and teaching two thousand years ago. He states that his teaching is for all people of all races in all countries. Jesus announces here for the first time that he and two others, Buddha and Mohammed, will return to Earth from their place of being in the near future, and a fourth being, a child already born now on Earth, will become a teacher and prepare humanity for their return. So heartwarming and interesting, you won't want to put it down. 354 P. $16.95 ISBN 1-891824-14-7

❿ EXPLORER RACE: Earth History and Lost Civilization

Speaks of Many Truths and Zoosh, through Robert Shapiro, explain that planet Earth, the only water planet in this solar system, is on loan from Sirius as a home and school for humanity, the Explorer Race. Earth's recorded history goes back only a few thousand years, its archaeological history a few thousand more. Now this book opens up as if a light was on in the darkness, and we see the incredible panorama of brave souls coming from other planets to settle on different parts of Earth. We watch the origins of tribal groups and the rise and fall of civilizations, and we can begin to understand the source of the wondrous diversity of plants, animals and humans that we enjoy here on beautiful Mother Earth. 310 P. $14.95 ISBN 1-891824-20-1

⓫ EXPLORER RACE: ET VISITORS SPEAK

Even as you are searching the sky for extraterrestrials and their spaceships, ETs are here on planet Earth—they are stranded, visiting, exploring, studying the culture, healing the Earth of trauma brought on by irresponsible mining or researching the history of Christianity over the past two thousand years. Some are in human guise, and some are in spirit form. Some look like what we call animals as they come from the species' home planet and interact with their fellow beings—those beings that we have labeled cats or cows or elephants. Some are brilliant cosmic mathematicians with a sense of humor; they are presently living here as penguins. Some are fledgling diplomats training for future postings on Earth when we have ET embassies here. In this book, these fascinating beings share their thoughts, origins and purposes for being here. 350 P. $14.95 ISBN 1-891824-28-7

⓬ EXPLORER RACE: Techniques for GENERATING SAFETY

Wouldn't you like to generate safety so you could go wherever you need to go and do whatever you need to do in a benevolent, safe and loving way for yourself? Learn safety as a radiated environment that will allow you to gently take the step into the new timeline, into a benevolent future and away from a negative past. 208 P. $9.95 ISBN 1-891824-26-0

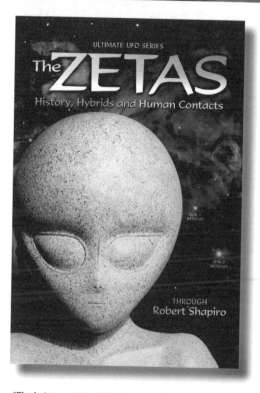